# Global Comparative Media

# Global Comparative Media

Vivek Tyagi

RANDOM

RANDOM PUBLICATIONS

NEW DELHI (INDIA)

**Global Comparative Media**

---

ISBN 978-93-5111-632-5


Published in 2015 in India by

**RANDOM PUBLICATIONS**

4376-A/4B, Gali Murari Lal, Ansari Road
New Delhi-110 002
Phone : +9111-43580356, 011-23289044, 011-43142548
e-mail: sales@randompublications.com,
info@randompublications.com, randomexports@gmail.com

*Type Setting by* : Friends Media, Delhi-110089
*Printed at* : Thomson Press (India) Ltd

# Preface

The conceptual framework developed in this study turned out to be an important contribution to the field of the comparative media systems research because it provides a systematic and applicable approach to analyze differences and similarities of the relationships between media and politics.

Comparative media system research has been subject to several changes since its establishment. The number of categories to describe media systems grew and approaches got more complex. Another trend is that researchers factor in political systems more intensively to explain and compare media systems. A more fundamental development is the shift from normative to empirically based approaches.

Journalism, at its best, is one of the arts of democracy. Journalists provide the news and analysis by which a society communicates with itself, allowing some measure of self-government. The public absorbs a daily barrage of news images that, over time, help to define one's sense of place in society and within a global community. News stories parade our injustices, vanities, power struggles, disasters, accomplishments and peculiar interests. Citizens, following the major issues in the press, become aware of their shared and competing values. Through journalism, a society debates how to reform its institutions and face the future.

The structure of the mass media will therefore have fundamental implications for the political and cultural orientation of the public. Hence, an understanding of the mass media will throw considerable light on the structure of Western society, the relationship between the public and those who possess power, as well as the ideologies produced by the media and their impact on the public. All scholars generally agree that the media do have the capacity to set the agenda of public discourse about political affairs, and it is widely recognised that the media has a significant role in actualising the diffusion of Western ideology and culture throughout the world. However, they differ over the degree to which the media limits the public's understanding of current affairs and the overall consequences of this.

The study of the effects and techniques of advertising forms a cornerstone of media studies.

I would like to thank my team for standing beside me throughout my career and writing this book. My special thanks go to "Random Publications" who have published the book.

– *Vivek Tyagi*

# Contents

# 1

# Global Media Structure

## STRUCTURE OF THE MEDIA

A healthy media environment should be plural and diverse, able to carry the wider range of views, information and opinion that exists in any society. For example it may be that the media environment is fragmented, or politically partisan. The history of dictatorship, repression or conflict may mean there is little tradition of independent professional journalism. Each set of circumstances will require a different approach. In most societies there is some kind of state broadcaster, however discredited. Alongside the stimulation of a healthy and vibrant private media it is important not to neglect the state broadcaster. New and restored democracies should begin the process of transforming it into a genuine public service broadcaster. The requirements of the print media and the broadcast media are quite different in this respect. Within the general confines of the law, the print media can be left alone to develop in so far as the market permits.

But to achieve the right plural mix of broadcast media – the balance between public service broadcasting and straightforward commercial interests-requires state intervention. The first, basic task is for any administration to ensure that people can access the means of communication – including the reception of broadcasts, provision of electricity supplies, access to telephones and Internet. There is a need to ensure the infrastructure exists to develop a broadcast industry.

### INDEPENDENT REGULATOR

Another early task should be the creation of an independent regulator to allocate wavelengths and undertake the necessary licensing procedures. This body should be established by law and be independent of any government interference, either directly by appointing its membership, or indirectly by controlling its funding. Its members should be chosen through an open and public process and it should be accountable to the wider public through the legislative arm of the state. (For a more detailed elaboration of these principle see *Access to the Airwaves* published by Article 19 ). The regulatory authority should rapidly produce a frequency plan showing how the airwaves will be shared between the public and private broadcasters and community broadcasters. In addition – where relevant-it should specify the regional and local allocations and how the status of minorities will be guaranteed.

## PUBLIC SERVICE BROADCASTING

It is sometimes assumed that the policy objective in a new or restored democracy is simply to allow the maximum private ownership of the media, on the grounds that this will produce the widest and most diverse range of voices. Some caution should be exercised however. In a bitterly divided society, the profusion of media, with no overall "national voice" capable of helping foster an imagined community can exacerbate rather than heal divisions. In these circumstances a high priority should be given to establishing a national public service broadcaster whose composition and programming can reflect the diverse strands of the society in question. Experience shows that the production of programmes, which are informative, educative or demonstrate distinct cultural or linguistic strands, which are crucial to the development of national identity – are most easily achieved by the creation of an effective public service broadcaster.

This is not an easy task however. A public service broadcaster requires a clearly articulated vision, some kind of national consensus on its objectives, complete freedom from political interference and a conscious attempt to engage viewers and listeners. The goals of public service broadcasting should be defined in law.

These will include the provision of comprehensive and balanced news coverage, the promotion of local programme production – including through the use of quotas – guaranteed universal access and a commitment to serve all regions, cultures and linguistic groups. The first stage is to establish the PSB overseen by a fully independent governing body whose autonomy and independence is guaranteed by law–as with the regulatory authority.

Specific guarantees should be given on editorial independence and on funding arrangements. The governing body should be accountable to a multi-party body of some kind – the legislative assembly if one exists-and its primary role will be to appoint the managers to run the PSB and to ensure subsequently that the public service mandate is being fulfilled. The governing body should not interfere in the day to day running of the broadcaster; appointments processes should be open and transparent and staff be protected from unfair dismissal. Another option is to establish a framework where all media have a public service function. In this case, public service obligations will be placed upon all broadcasters, probably through the regulatory authority that issues licenses. This approach needs to be considered very carefully. It may well be appropriate in a very divided society where all the media has been affected by conflicts in the transition to democracy, or in circumstances where state revenues are so scarce that there is no realistic possibility of providing any state funding for a single PSB (as is the case where fiscal revenues are very low).

Whichever approach is adopted, independent civil society has a role to play as a watchdog, ensuring that the public service remit is fulfilled. Consideration should therefore be given to the creation of media forums which involve civil society and which can consider the performance of the public broadcaster and the policies of the governing body. There needs to be a consistent commitment to consultation with the public, through civil society organisations and through the political parties and other forums. In new or restored democracies establishing the legitimacy of a single national voice is vital. There needs to be – for example – news bulletins and programmes which everyone in the society can watch, regardless of their position on issues of the day, confident that they are receiving balanced and authoritative coverage.

## THE CORPORATE STRUCTURE OF THE MASS MEDIA

It was Walter Lippman who coined the phrase "the manufacture of consent", enjoining it as a means of population control. Lippman's concept may indeed be in effect today. In this regard, the status of the mass media and its faithful propagation of the established opinion that Western policy is fundamentally benevolent in intention, is an issue of paramount importance. What role has the media played in clarifying the real principles and motives of Western policy to the public, and what does this entail for the nature of Western democracy and the role of the population in the formulation of policy? The mass media is clearly one of the most powerful institutions in society; it is, for most of the public, the ultimate source of all their information.

The structure of the mass media will therefore have fundamental implications for the political and cultural orientation of the public. Hence, an understanding of the mass media will throw considerable light on the structure of Western society, the relationship between the public and those who possess power, as well as the ideologies produced by the media and their impact on the public.

All scholars generally agree that the media do have the capacity to set the agenda of public discourse about political affairs, and it is widely recognised that the media has a significant role in actualising the diffusion of Western ideology and culture throughout the world. However, they differ over the degree to which the media limits the public's understanding of current affairs and the overall consequences of this.

Nevertheless, the vast extent of the manipulation of the media under the sway of business interests has been harshly revealed in the statement of John Swainton, Chief of Staff of the *New York Times*. "There is not one of you who would dare to write his honest opinion," he reprimanded his colleagues at his retirement party in September. "The business of a journalist now is to destroy the truth, to lie outright, to pervert, to vilify, fall at the feet of Mammon and sell himself for his daily bread. We are tools, vessels of rich men behind the scenes, we are jumping jacks. They pull the strings; we dance. Our talents, our possibilities and our lives are the properties of these men. We are intellectual prostitutes."

**The Independent Media: A Myth**

It is generally clear that the media has failed to generate genuine public awareness of the actual nature of Western policy. Majid Tehranian, for example, who is Professor of International Communication at the University of Hawaii and Director of the Toda Institute for Global Peace and Policy Research, points out that:

"In their scholarship, William Appleton Williams, Noam Chomsky, Richard Falk, Ramsey Clark, Ali Mazrui, and other critics of US foreign policies have provided an abundance of evidence to support the charges on the counter-democratic role of the United States in much of Asia, Africa, and Latin America."

British historian Mark Curtis, former Research Fellow at the Royal Institute for International Affairs in London, similarly confirms:

"Mutual Anglo-American support in ordering the affairs of key nations and regions, often with violence, to their design has been a consistent feature of the era that followed the Second World War... Policy in, for example, Malaya, Kenya, British Guiana and Iran was geared towards organising Third World economies along guidelines in which British, and Western, interests would be paramount, and those of the often malnourished populations would be ignored or further undermined. Similarly, US interventions overseas-in Vietnam, Nicaragua, the Dominican Republic, Cuba, Chile, etcetera-were designed to counter threats to the Western practice of assigning the Third World to mere client status to Western business interests. British and US forces have acted as mercenary-and often extremely violent-mobs intended to restore 'order' in their domains and to preserve the existing privileges of elites within their own societies."

Development specialist Dr. J. W. Smith, who is Director of Research for the California-based Institute for Economic Democracy, is even more explicit: "No society will tolerate it if they knew that they (as a country) were responsible for violently killing 12 to 15 million people since WW II and causing the death of hundreds of millions more their economies were destroyed or those countries were denied the right to restructure to care for their people. Unknown as it is, and recognizing that this has been standard practice throughout colonialism, that is the record of the Western imperial centres of capital from 1945 to 1990... While mouthing peace, freedom, justice, rights, and majority rule, all over the world state-sponsored terrorists were overthrowing democratic governments, installing and protecting dictators, and preventing peace, freedom, justice, rights, and majority rule. Twelve to fifteen million mostly innocent people were slaughtered in that successful 45 year effort to suppress those breaks for economic freedom which were bursting out all over the world... All intelligence agencies have been, and are still in, the business of destabilizing undeveloped countries to maintain their dependency and the flow of the world's natural wealth to powerful nations' industries at a low price and to provide markets for those industries at a high price."

That the media has failed to accurately portray the real nature of Western foreign policy to the public, playing instead the subservient role of a propaganda machine for elite interests, is therefore quite obvious. The question that then remains is, why does the media – conventionally believed to be critical of the establishment-behave in a way that conforms to the false picture presented by the government and corporate elite of their own policies? The anwer is simple: in a nutshell, the mass media *is* the establishment.

To begin our analysis then, we will discuss a propaganda model of the mass media. It is thus useful to begin with what is arguably the most thorough model of the media-that proposed by Edward Herman (Professor Emeritus of Finance at Wharton School in the University of Pennsylvania) and Noam Chomsky (Institute Professor of Linguistics and Philosophy at MIT), both of whom are leading critics of US foreign policy.

There are particularly pertinent reasons to begin with their model-the primary one being that it is arguably the most thoroughly researched and empirically verified model available. Herman and Chomsky's landmark study, *Manufacturing Consent: The Political Economy of the Mass Media*, comes under the recommendation of America's leading national media watchdog and research group, Fairness and Accuracy In Reporting (FAIR). It is also recommended as an essential resource for media literacy by the Grand Rapids Institute for Information Democracy (GRIID), affiliated with the US-based Community Media Centre (CMC). The Oxford-based research and publishing group Corporate Watch (not to be confused with the US-based organisation of the same name), which works in cooperation with a variety of other human rights and environmentalist organisations, describes the study as "one of the most incisive critiques of the media's role in society". The respected journal *Publisher's Weekly* gives the following review of *Manufacturing Consent*:

"Herman of Wharton and Chomsky of MIT lucidly document their argument that America's government and its corporate giants exercise control over what we read, see and hear. The authors identify the forces that they contend make the national media propagandistic-the major three being the motivation for profit through ad revenue, the media's close links to and often ownership by corporations, and their acceptance of information from biased sources. In five case studies, the writers show how TV, newspapers and radio distort world events... Extensive evidence is calmly presented, and in the end an indictment against the guardians of our freedom is substantiated. A disturbing picture emerges of a news system that panders to the interest of America's privileged and neglects its duties when the concerns of minority groups and the underclass are at stake." Indeed, according to the leading American media scholar Robert W. McChesney, Professor of Journalism and Mass Communication at the University of Illinois, any significant attempt to comprehend the structure and operation of the mass media must begin with Herman and Chomsky's study. He further observes that:

"This book promises to be a seminal work in critical media analysis and to open a door through which future media analysis will follow... Edward Herman and Noam Chomsky are certainly well qualified to provide a simple yet powerful model that explains how the media function to serve the large propaganda requirements of the elite. Together and individually, they have written numerous articles and books which have chronicled the ways in which the US media have actively promoted the agenda of the elite, particularly in regard to US activities in the Third World. Manufacturing Consent is a work of tremendous importance for scholars and activists alike... Each chapter is meticulously researched and most draw heavily on the authors' earlier works in these areas."

All this provides us with ample reason to begin with Herman and Chomsky's model. Contrary to the claims of the mainstream critique of radical media analysis, a propaganda model does not entail a grandiose conspiracy theory. Rather, this model is based on analysing the politico-economic influences on the mass media, and considering the extent to which those influences both have the potential to condition the media's reporting tendencies in accord with the interests of those who possess power. In other words, the model constitutes a 'guided free market' model, advocating that the media's reporting is influenced by the same factors that dominate corporate activities-the maximisation of profit and therefore the market. The next step is to document the occurrences where this potential is actualised. In this sense, according to the propaganda model the media is conditioned by the profit-orientated considerations of corporate elites. As Professor McChesney observes:

"Herman and Chomsky quickly dismiss the standard mainstream critique of radical media analysis that accuses it of offering some sort of 'conspiracy' theory for media Behaviour; rather, they argue, media bias arises from 'the preselection of right-thinking people, internalized preconceptions, and the adaptation of personnel to the constraints' of a series of objective filters they present in their propaganda model. Hence the bias occurs largely through self-censorship, which explains the superiority of the US mass media as a propaganda system: it is far more credible than a system which relies on official state censorship."

## PRIVATE BROADCASTING

A crucial role for the governing authority and the regulator is providing the ground rules that enable fair competition between the public broadcaster and the private broadcasters. The government's main responsibility is to ensure a level playing field economically. In particular there should no attempt to use the tax system to favour one broadcaster over another. The allocation of government advertising must be strictly monitored to ensure fair access by all media. License fees should not be set so high as to favour the wealthiest and most powerful corporations – the ideal is to create relatively low entry costs. In general, while it is impossible to be prescriptive in the abstract, any economic measures that affect the media should be fair, transparent and non-discriminatory.

The regulator has an important role to play in overseeing more complex issues that involve the fostering of a dual broadcasting system (public and private). It is unrealistic to think that modern PSBs can be created solely on the basis of public funds – they will nearly all require a degree of advertising. There is a role for a competition regulator in this field as well as the broad cast regulator – the mix of powers being dependent upon the general capacity of the state to support such institutions.

## ECONOMIC SUPPORT

In many societies the market for the media is very weak. In these circumstances the media, particularly newspapers are funded by powerful groups – parties, factions, businesses – to act as mouthpieces for their own interests. A good public service broadcaster is one possible antidote to this. Creating a climate where a genuine media market can develop is another. International support can be crucial in providing support with start up costs, professional expertise, even equipment and materials. What new and restored democracies should be wary of however is allowing the international community's funding to act as a substitute for the development of a domestic market.

One possible model is to establish a Media Development Fund, administered by respected local media professionals from across all communities, which can provide low cost loans to help new media get established. Models for this exist in different parts of the world. Loans are preferable to grants as they encourage serious business plans and moves towards genuine economic independence.

While financial support should not be made conditional upon a particular editorial approach, which would compromise the independence of the media, it is reasonable to impose some conditions that will help produce professional balanced journalism. For example, financial support could be made conditional upon non-discriminatory employment practices, or on an insistence that jobs are not the exclusive preserve of one ethnic group. Another approach would be to establish a not-for-profit holding company that has a major stake in leading media companies, which guarantees editorial independence and uses its profits to promote the objectives of free expression through grants and activities.

## CULTURE AND JOURNALISM

Laws are the foundations of a democratic society and economic structures and reality determine the broad shape of the media. Neither however is any guarantee of independent, balanced, professional journalism. They can provide the conditions for independent professional journalism to flourish but no more than that. New and restored democracies should consider how to help build a culture of professional journalism. There are a number of international organisations of journalists and employers that support this activity and the programmes may be of value.

In some areas media centres have been established to provide a professional base for journalists to work, receive training and support. It seems sensible for new and restored democracies to encourage media organisations to cooperate in establishing such a centre – in the past competing proposals or even competing centres have complicated the media environment.

Journalism training should be given a high priority. Past experience suggests that such training concentrates on the following areas:-

- Building a general awareness of democracy and human rights
- Encouraging independent analysis and thought
- The techniques of investigative journalism.

Most professionals are influenced by their peers – in fact peer pressure is the most likely means of improving skills and ethics. For this reason the establishment of an independent journalist association should be given a high priority, linked to a respected international association like the International Federation of Journalists. Such an association can provide a direct advocacy on behalf of the profession, particularly on pay and conditions issues and on questions such as unfair dismissal cases between local staff and employers, in which it would be unwise for the international community to intervene.

In parallel to this, steps should be taken to foster – through civil society initiatives – the development of employers associations, linked in turn to the World Association of Newspapers or the Association of Independent Broadcasters.

The most important role for these associations is in creating a climate of self-regulation. Self regulation is always better than imposed regulation because it is likely to be more effective (people are always more committed to freely chosen values than to those forced upon them) and, of course, it respects the independence of the media. Such associations provide useful means of disseminating good practice, and can help create peer pressure to respect editorial independence, human rights norms and democratic values.

## CIVIL SOCIETY

Trade unions and employers associations are one manifestation of civil society but there are many others which play an important role in helping foster the conditions for media development. One weakness that may have to be overcome in a new or restored democracy is the absence of a stable civil society and of a culture in which the values of freedom of expression are assumed. While regulation can play and important role in creating the climate for this culture, it cannot guarantee it. A whole range of civil society groups will have an interest and a stake in the media coverage of their society. They can monitor the media regularly and can play an important role during elections checking for evidence of bias. They can also play a significant role in helping shape media policy providing an interface between the practitioners, public officials, the international community and the general public.

Providing the structural stability for the media in new and restored democracies requires the right blend of a mix of approaches. It will almost certainly need a legal and policy strand, some kind of economic support, careful thought given to establishing the right mix of media structures. It will require fostering an active climate of professional journalism and civil society intervention. In these circumstances there will be a need for on-going research, monitoring and evaluation of the approach adopted. Local organisations and media professionals can work with international organisations and experts but primacy should be given to local control and direction of policies. New and restored democracies should be aware that the media environment of a country is not just shaped by domestic forces. Local communities will have access to international media outside of the country's context – the World Service, Voice of America and a range of European alternatives will provide coverage that does not derive from local experiences. The internet and VoIP protocols permit a new kind of citizen journalism that transcends traditional media boundaries. The priority for a new or restored democracy is to create a domestic media that can help support democracy and human rights in the country concerned. This in turn will require sustained and serious commitment by the country and by any international donors that are involved in reconstruction. It will also require the ability to learn from past mistakes– a process that is assisted enormously if new and restored democracies can share information and expertise.

## ANGLOPHONE BIAS IN THE WORLD MEDIA

It has been observed that the world's principal suppliers of news, the news agencies, and the main buyers of news are Anglophone corporations and this gives an Anglophone bias to the selection and depiction of events. Anglophone definitions of what constitutes news are paramount; the news provided originates in Anglophone capitals and responds first to their own rich domestic markets. Despite the plethora of news services, most news printed and broadcast throughout the world each day comes from only a few major agencies, the three largest of which are the Associated Press, Reuters and Agence France-Presse.Although these agencies are 'global' in the sense of their activities, they each retain significant associations with particular nations, namely France (AFP), the United States (AP) and the United Kingdom (Reuters). Chambers and Tinckell suggest that the so-called global media are agents of Anglophone values which privilege norms of 'competitive individualism, laissez faire capitalism, parliamentary democracy and consumerism.' They see the presentation of the English language as international as a further feature of Anglophone dominance.

## VIS-A-VIS RELIGIOUS ISSUES

Media bias towards religion is most obvious in countries where the media are controlled by the state, which is in turn dominated by a particular religion. In these instances, bias against other faiths can be explicit and virulent. But even in countries with freedom of religion and a free press, the dominant religion exerts some amount of influence on the media. In nations where Christianity is the majority faith, reporters tend to focus on the activities of the Christian community, to the exclusion of other faiths. But the opposite may also occur, with media self-consciously avoiding reporting on any religious matters at all in order to avoid the appearance of favoring one faith over another, or presenting religious faith and phenomenon in a negative light.

This type of bias is often seen with reporting on new religious movements. It is often the case that the only view the public gets of a new religious movement, controversial group or purported cult is a negative and sensationalized report by the media. For example, most new or minority religious movements only receive media coverage when something sensational occurs, *e.g.* the mass suicide of a cult or illegal activities of a leader in the religious movement. According to the Encyclopaedia of Social Work (19th edition), the news media play an influential role in the general public's perception of cults.As reported in several studies, the media have depicted cults as problematic, controversial, and threatening from the beginning, tending to favour sensationalistic stories over balanced public debates. It furthers the analysis that media reports on cults rely heavily on police officials and cult "experts" who portray cult activity as dangerous and destructive, and when divergent views are presented, they are often overshadowed by horrific stories of ritualistic torture, sexual abuse, mind control, etc. Furthermore, unfounded allegations, when proved untrue, receive little or no media attention.

## OTHER INFLUENCES

The apparent bias of media is not always specifically political in nature. The news media tend to appeal to a specific audience, which means that stories that affect a large number of people on a global scale often receive less coverage in some markets than local stories, such as a public school shooting, a celebrity wedding, a plane crash, or similarly glamorous or shocking stories. For example, the deaths of millions of people in an ethnic conflict in Africa might be afforded scant mention in American media, while the shooting of five people in a high school is analyzed in depth. The reason for this type of bias is a function of what the public wants to watch and/or what producers and publishers believe the public wants to watch.

Bias has also been claimed in instances referred to as conflict of interest, whereby the owners of media outlets have vested interests in other commercial enterprises or political parties. In such cases in the United States, the media outlet is required to disclose the conflict of interest. However, the decisions of the editorial department of a newspaper and the corporate parent frequently are not connected, as the editorial staff retains freedom to decide what is covered as well as what isn't. Biases, real or implied, frequently arise when it comes to deciding what stories will be covered and who will be called for those stories.

Accusations that a source is biased, if accepted, may cause media consumers to distrust certain kinds of statements, and place added confidence on others. For example, if readers believe that a particular newspaper is conservatively biased, they may feel that a pro-liberal article in that paper *must* be true. Conversely, they may assume that a pro-conservative article in that paper is suspect. Because of the possibility of influencing the public in this way, accusations about which media outlets are biased, and how, have become a very common occurrence. Media ethics is the subdivision of applied ethics dealing with the specific ethical principles and standards of media, including broadcast media, film, theatre, the arts, print media and the internet. The field covers many varied and highly controversial topics, ranging from war journalism to Benetton advertising.

## UNILINEAR WORLD-VIEW OF DEVELOPMENT

We shall discuss, briefly, the important features of the theories of development under each paradigm and their implications for the strategy of development in the Third World countries. We shall discuss the main features of each and every paradigm of the unilinear world-view of development. Let us start with the mainstream paradigm.

*Mainstream Paradigm:* Of those paradigms, which project development as becoming more like the West and developing countries as latecomers to the process, with certain initial conditions, which should be overcome to experience the transition to development, the more familiar is what could be described as the 'Mainstream paradigm'. It includes most of the familiar development theories like the "big-push' ' or "balanced growth" theory of Rosenstun Rodan, the "vicious circle" theory of Ragnar Nurks, the "unbalanced growth theory of Alber Hirsheman, the "dulasim" theory of Arthur Lewis, the "stage theory" of

W.W. Rostow and the "neo-Malthusian" theory of Harvey Leibenstin. In spite of differences in the framework, point of emphasis etc., There are certain aspects, which are common in these theories, the most important resource for development is a savings or accumulation of capital. The transition from underdevelopment to development is essentially a process of moving from a low savings ratio of about 5% of the GNP to a high savings ratio of about 12% or more. "Development is a process of transforming an economy, which is predominantly agriculture-based and other related primary activities, towards predominance of industry and non-primary activities." Therefore, these theories describe the initial conditions or barriers responsible for the low savings, and suggest strategies to overcome those hurdles, which would put the underdeveloped countries on the path of development like the West. The persistence of the low savings is due to the vicious circle of poverty: low investment, low productivity, low income. There is also the vicious circle on the demand side like the low inducement to invest because of the low level of productivity due to low level of investment. Once this low savings syndrome is overcome, then aid or foreign investments help on a sustained development, either through balanced investment or investment in the unbalanced sectors, that would set up inducements and pressures. In the process of mobilizing savings and channelling the same for development, the mainstream theories consider state intervention, either through the governmental planning or state programmes, as essential. Most of the newly independent countries have embarked upon the development strategies, which were inspired by the theories of the mainstream paradigm.

*Counter-revolution Paradigm:* In contrast, the Counter-revolution paradigm considers the state intervention as the cause of inefficiency and distortions in the resource use. According to this paradigm, the state intervention through licensing and regulation leads to 'directly unproductive profit seeking', corruption, and red tape. Minimizing the state's role, and allowing the market to play the role in allocation of resources, would improve efficiency, competitiveness, and rapid growth. This paradigm has gained some popularity only in the 1980s, by which time there was widespread disenchantment with the interventionist policies. In recent years, this paradigm is at the basis of the package of liberalization that is recommended by the World Bank and the International Monetary Fund.

*Structural Paradigm:* The origins of the structuralist paradigm could be traced to the writings based on the Latin American experience. There are two variants of the structuralist paradigm, one referring to the distortions in internal structure, and the other pointing to the global or international structure, It is the 'international structuralism' of the Rural Prebisch that is more familiar. According to the paradigm, the world is divided into the developed capitalist countries forming the core of 'the Centre', and the underdeveloped countries forming 'the perihery' over the years, there emerged a division of labour with the Centre producing and exporting manufactured goods and the Periphery depending on the production and export of the primary products. While the income elasticity of demand for high technology and high productivity-based manufactures is high, it is low for the primary products. As a result, while the demand for the manufactured goods increased faster, ensuring higher prices for their exports, the demand for the primary products increased slowly, and the export prices did not keep pace with the rise in the prices of imported manufactured goods. There was, in the long-run, deterioration in the terms of trade of the primary exports from the less-developed countries. All the benefits, technical progress and productivity flowed to the developed countries, keeping the periphery in a continued state of underdevelopment. To break this structural distortion and to initiate the development process in the periphery, it is necessary to pursue a policy of protection for the manufacturing sector from the developed countries. The strategy directly flowing from the structuralist paradigm is Import Substitution Industrialization (ISI). Though it has caused sufficient problems later, the ISI was a very popular strategy of development, particularly in Latin America.

*Orthodox Marxist Paradigm:* The familiar Marxist concept of development is associated with the five epochs or stages:

- Primitive Communism,
- Ancient Slave State,
- Feudalism,
- Capitalism, and
- Socialism.

Each of these epochs is marked by a corresponding mode of production. Development, in this framework, may be viewed as one of the transitions from feudalism to capitalism. The Orthodox Marxist theory also visualized the future of the underdeveloped countries, entirely in terms of the developed capitalist countries. Karl Marx wrote that "the country that is more developed, industrialized, only shows to the less developed the image of its own future." It is such an image of development that led Marx and Engels to believe that the capitalist colonial expansion would result in the spread of development of capitalism in the countries. Contrary to such expectations, as capitalism spread all over the world, a greater part of the world has experienced only its disintegrating effects, without benefiting from its creative side. Moreover, the united industrialization of the West was possible only at the expense of the so-called underdeveloped world, which was doomed to stagnation and regression. The classical Marxist writings, by concentrating on the European experience, anticipated the spread of development and not underdevelopment. They did not have much to say in the process of underdevelopment. There appears to be not much analysis of the historical experience of the colonial countries in

Asia and Africa. Hence the criticism that Marx's writings were Europe-centric, denying all the history and experience of the colonial countries.

## NON-UNILINEAR WORLD-VIEW OF DEVELOPMENT

So far, we have discussed how the developing countries could attain the status of the developed countries. We have said that the process adopted by many Third World countries is unilinear moving from one step to another logically. Now, here, we shall discuss some paradigms which are not one-liner. Their nature is not that systematic. So, let us move ahead.

*Populist Paradigm:* The term "populist" is used here in the absence of any other term that is adequate to describe this approach. Tine theories under the "Populist" approach question either the need or possibility of the less-developed countries developing on the lines of the already developed capitalist countries. The Gandhian thinking on the appropriate development for countries like India, and some contributions from anyone like E.F. Schumacher, who wrote Small is Beautiful, may be considered as part of the "populist" paradigm. Gandhi thought that the Western type of development had nothing to commend to societies like India. His contention was that the Western industrialisation had brought along with it immorality, crime, and cultural degeneration. "Development in a country like India should make the village as the centre, and provide employment and livelihood through a network of cottage and village industries. 'Gram Swaraj' or 'village united development' would not only ensure against the evils of industrialization and urbanization, but also absorb millions of people without uprooting them from their appropriate village industries. The contribution of Schumacher is also inspired by the Gandhian thinking. It is well-known through his book, Small is Beautiful. The two severe problems of the less developed countries, according to him, were mass unemployment and mass migration to the urban areas. Much of the

Western type of industrialization initiated in the less developed countries helped only a fraction of the population living in the urban areas, while the mass of the population living in rural areas was bypassed. Thus, in the less developed countries, there emerged in what is known as "dual economics" of urban and rural areas, each within different patterns of living, widely separated from each other, living as two different worlds. That the rural masses would be absorbed by the Western type of industrialization is utterly unrealistic. What is needed is the creation of appropriate technology that would promote employment opportunities through a network of small production units, a primary condition for such a development involves education, organization, and development. Populist paradigm is discussed as an alternative strategy by not housed by any less-developed country. This is partly because of the dominance of the mainstream paradigm in the initial stages of independence, and the creation of an impression among the people that development means becoming like the West. After raising such false hopes, any attempt to adopt a Gandhian or "populist" alternative strategy, it is feared, would hot be liked by the people, Most of the less developed countries hold on to the "mainstream" paradigm, its failures notwithstanding.

*Neo-Marxist Paradigm:* A serious challenge to the unilinear world-view of development did not arise until the emergence of the neo-Marxist paradigm. There are quite a few economists who can be called neo-Marxist, but here, we are concerned with the writings of Paul Baran, A.G. Frank, and the related "dependency theory". An attempt is made here to capture the neo-Marxist paradigm, as far as possible, in terms of the original writings. The essence of the paradigm lies in the fact that, at present, the less developed countries cannot develop like the West.

It stresses the interconnectedness of development and underdevelopment, of traditional and modem, and indeed many other social, political and economic factors. It seems many conflicts and clashes of interest in the development process occur, both between nations and between social classes within the underdeveloped countries. It emphasizes the historical factors, especially, the active process of how underdevelopment has come into being in the various Third World countries. Paul Baran declared that underdevelopment of most of the world was a direct result of the dynamics of monopoly capitalism, which had Mocked the primary accumulation of capital in the underdeveloped regions, and smothered their novice industries. He sums up his thesis as follows: 'thus the people, who came into the orbit of Western capitalist expansion, found themselves, in the light of feudalism and capitalism, enduring the worst features of both worlds. Their exploitation was multiplied, yet its fruits were not to increase their productive wealth; they went abroad or served to support a parasitic bourgeoisie at home. They lived in abysmal misery, yet they will have no prospect of a better tomorrow. They existed under capitalism, yet there was no accumulation of capital. They lost their time-honoured means of livelihood, their arts and crafts, yet there was no modern industry to provide new ones in their place. They were thrust into extensive contact with the advanced science of the West, yet remained in a state of the darkest backwardness." Referring to India as a case in point, Baran observes, "India, if left to herself, might have found in the course of time a shorter and surely less tortuous mid towards a better and richer society. It would have been, however, an entirely different India, had she been allowed as some more fortunate countries were, to realize her destiny in her own way, to employ her resources for her own benefit, and to harness her energies and abilities for the advancement of her own people." The most forceful presentation of the neo-Marxist thesis is found in Andre Gunder Frank:

"Underdevelopment is not just the lack of development. Before there was developed, there was no underdevelopment. This relation between development and underdevelopment is not just a comparative one, in the sense that some places are more developed) and yet there is underdevelopment". A.G. Frank contents that underdevelopment as we know it today, and economic development as well, or the simultaneous and related products of development on a worldwide scale, and over a history of more than four centuries, at least, of a single integrated economic system: Capitalism. Though integrated in the sense that its far-flung parts are interrelated, and in the sense that it internally generates its own transformation, the capitalist system is also wrought by contradiction. One part exploits another; though it also diffuses back some of the fruits of the economic and cultural development based on that exploitation.

## DEVELOPMENT EXPERIENCE: THE THIRD WORLD

After the Second world war, many colonies got independence, and started re-building their nation. The leaders of these newly independent countries were desperate to bring their nations out of the vicious circle of poverty, un-educated, disease, hunger, etc. Thus, 'development' became a key word in most of their speeches. And the meaning of development was as varied as the countries. We shall discuss the experience of these countries, known as the Third World countries, in the field of development. About three quarters of all humanity, numbering three and a half billion people, living in the developing countries in Asia, Africa and Latin America, spanning two thirds of the earth's land surface, constitute the Third World. A Third World because it belongs neither to the group of industrialized capitalist countries nor the socialist countries, wherever such countries still exist. These Third World countries vary greatly in size, natural resource endowments, in the structure of their economics, in the level of economic, social, and technological development. The diversities are fairly marked, making even the Third World less homogeneous. But the unifying aspect is that, in these countries, the need to overcome poverty and secure a—better life for their people is primary. Yet, it is ironic, by the end of the 1980s, it could be seen that the achievements of the Third World during the post-World War II decades had not fundamentally changed the status of these countries in relation to the world economic system. "They remained poor, subordinate, and powerless. In general, their national self-reliance had not increased, in some country's dependence intensified as they tried to modernize". Poverty persisted and the income gap between the developed countries and Third World widened. The growth in the Third World rarely removed the structural inequalities and cleavages. On the contrary, the income gap between the rich and poor became wider. As a result, the economic growth brought along with it the problem of growing disparities, tendencies towards disintegration and instability. The social and economic status of women leaves much to be desired. And there was growing dependence of these countries on the developed ones. In spite of the fact that any of the developing countries are dependent on international trade, their share of the world trade has dropped from over 30 per cent in the 1950s to about 15 per cent by the end of 1980s. A considerable part of the declining share has been due to the deteriorating terms of trade. These countries are becoming increasingly dependent on aid and borrowings from abroad, resulting in a growing foreign debt. There has been an increase in the participation of the multinational corporations in these countries, and their influence on economic policies has been growing. The Third World accounts for hardly two percent of investment on research and development, thus leaving these countries technologically dependent. Most often the imported technologies are inappropriate, leaving little scope for expansion of much needed employment opportunities. Faced with the growing international inequalities in economic power and influence in the existing world economic order, the Third World countries lobbied for a better deal, which resulted in the U.N. Resolution popularly referred to as the New International Economic Order (NIEO), which sought a programme of action towards an equitable world. Some of the important aspects of NIEO were

- Renegotiating the debts of the developing countries;
- Redefining the terms of trade, and assuring greater access to the developed country markets;
- Reforming the IMF and its decision making process; and
- Attainment the UN official development assistance targets.

Except for some attempts to negotiate debt repayment in a few cases and some discussion in UNCTAD an access to trade, not much progress has been made. In fact, the tendency has been towards disparities between the rich and poor countries by subordinating their interests to those of the former.

## NEW PERSPECTIVE OF MEDIA PLANNING

In India, we are experiencing an economic slow down. Consumer buying is on the decline. Ad spends are curtailed Agencies are becoming learner. Clients are becoming more discerning about media usage. Though they are cutting and budgets, they want more effectiveness. In common parlance, this is called 'more bang for the buck.' Clients have become extremely vigilant on how agencies spend their money on media. Intuitive media decisions and exploratory tactics are out. Everything has to be substantiated. It is necessary to stretch every media rupee more and more. Though the broader media mix is planned annually, media planners are continuously shuffling the actual vehicles they choose channels or programmes in case of TV and publications in case of print. Clients want to know how involved their target audience is with a particular programming. Even though demographics cover the reach objectives, the target audience may be a passive viewer. Research on the involvement of the target groups is getting more attention. Agencies are making use of proprietary consumer involvement tools that help them measure media preferences of target audiences.

There is a shift from planning based merely on reach to planning based on awareness/involvement. The client wants to know whether his target audience has actually seen the campaign. He wants to know whether the client was at home when the commercial was telecast. Media planning goes beyond media buying. It has to focus more sharply on consumer decision-making process and the importance of media in that process. Media has to make accountable. Media planners have started using more efficient media evaluation matrices. Audience involvement scores are now weighted while arriving at ROI on media spends.

**MEDIA PLAN**

1. The first step in media planning is the collection of useful information about the people or the market to be reached through advertising. The more detailed and specific the target market data available on geography, age group, sex, income, attitudes, interests, etc., the more appropriate the media selection would be. However, it is well understood that the available advertising budget is an important guide to the media selection. The task is to select a medium most suited to the target market at a given budget cost. This concept of "what-can-you-afford?" in media planning is equally relevant to small as well as large companies, for they do have something like a budget or an appropriation of fund for promotion. Irrespective of the size of the company, it finally settles for how much money it can afford to put in for a particular market for advertising and/or for promotion.
2. The second significant step in media planning is to decide upon the nature of the message to be conveyed to the target market. However, this decision necessarily follows a thorough understanding of the consumer profile. The message or the copy, by which name it is more accurately called, is decided in the light of the aspect of consumer Behaviour or motivation which is intended to be influenced.
3. Having gathered this significant information, the next logical step is to search for an ideal match of the audience characteristics of media with the target market profile and, at the same time, check for the perfect adaptability of the message (copy) requirement with the media. Following the media planning decision process, we have to take into account the other media concepts explained in the following paragraphs.
4. Reach is expressed in terms of the number of households or individuals reached by a given medium over a period of time. This is usually expressed in terms of percent of total households or individuals in the target market. Sometimes, there is a possibility of duplication, *i.e.*, two media may reach the target audience. National magazines have a different reach from that of the regional' ones or other media, such as TV, radio, etc. National readership surveys

provide information about published materials, whereas several other conducted studies may provide the reach percent of other media. One can buy reach with print in a specific geographical market by taking a combination of newspapers or magazines.

Frequency refers to the average number of times different households or individuals are reached by a medium in a given period of time. The frequency of advertisement exposure of the target market depends upon the amount of reinforcement of the image required or the amount of reminding required having sustaining patronage from the target customers. The greater the frequency, the greater the probability of the advertisement message making a deep and lasting impression.

To understand these concepts dearly consider the following illustration. A sample of viewers represents 10 TV Households (HHs)-Q to Z who watch a programme A over a four week period.

## THE CORPORATE STRUCTURE OF THE MASS MEDIA

It was Walter Lippman who coined the phrase "the manufacture of consent", enjoining it as a means of population control. Lippman's concept may indeed be in effect today. In this regard, the status of the mass media and its faithful propagation of the established opinion that Western policy is fundamentally benevolent in intention, is an issue of paramount importance. What role has the media played in clarifying the real principles and motives of Western policy to the public, and what does this entail for the nature of Western democracy and the role of the population in the formulation of policy? The mass media is clearly one of the most powerful institutions in society; it is, for most of the public, the ultimate source of all their information.

The structure of the mass media will therefore have fundamental implications for the political and cultural orientation of the public. Hence, an understanding of the mass media will throw considerable light on the structure of Western society, the relationship between the public and those who possess power, as well as the ideologies produced by the media and their impact on the public.

All scholars generally agree that the media do have the capacity to set the agenda of public discourse about political affairs, and it is widely recognised that the media has a significant role in actualising the diffusion of Western ideology and culture throughout the world. However, they differ over the degree to which the media limits the public's understanding of current affairs and the overall consequences of this.

Nevertheless, the vast extent of the manipulation of the media under the sway of business interests has been harshly revealed in the statement of John Swainton, Chief of Staff of the *New York Times*. "There is not one of you who would dare to write his honest opinion," he reprimanded his colleagues at his retirement party in September.

"The business of a journalist now is to destroy the truth, to lie outright, to pervert, to vilify, fall at the feet of Mammon and sell himself for his daily bread. We are tools, vessels of rich men behind the scenes, we are jumping jacks. They pull the strings; we dance. Our talents, our possibilities and our lives are the properties of these men. We are intellectual prostitutes."

**The Independent Media: A Myth**

It is generally clear that the media has failed to generate genuine public awareness of the actual nature of Western policy. Majid Tehranian, for example, who is Professor of International Communication at the University of Hawaii and Director of the Toda Institute for Global Peace and Policy Research, points out that:

"In their scholarship, William Appleton Williams, Noam Chomsky, Richard Falk, Ramsey Clark, Ali Mazrui, and other critics of US foreign policies have provided an abundance of evidence to support the charges on the counter-democratic role of the United States in much of Asia, Africa, and Latin America."

British historian Mark Curtis, former Research Fellow at the Royal Institute for International Affairs in London, similarly confirms:

"Mutual Anglo-American support in ordering the affairs of key nations and regions, often with violence, to their design has been a consistent feature of the era that followed the Second World War... Policy in, for example, Malaya, Kenya, British Guiana and Iran was geared towards organising Third World economies along guidelines in which British, and Western, interests would be paramount, and those of the often malnourished populations would be ignored or further undermined. Similarly, US interventions overseas-in Vietnam, Nicaragua, the Dominican Republic, Cuba, Chile, etcetera-were designed to counter threats to the Western practice of assigning the Third World to mere client status to Western business interests. British and US forces have acted as mercenary-and often extremely violent-mobs intended to restore 'order' in their domains and to preserve the existing privileges of elites within their own societies."

Development specialist Dr. J. W. Smith, who is Director of Research for the California-based Institute for Economic Democracy, is even more explicit: "No society will tolerate it if they knew that they (as a country) were responsible for violently killing 12 to 15 million people since WW II and causing the death of hundreds of millions more their economies were destroyed or those countries were denied the right to restructure to care for their people. Unknown as it is, and recognizing that this has been standard practice throughout colonialism, that is the record of the Western imperial centres of capital from 1945 to 1990... While mouthing peace, freedom, justice, rights, and majority rule, all over the world state-sponsored terrorists were overthrowing democratic governments, installing and protecting dictators, and preventing peace, freedom, justice, rights, and majority rule. Twelve to fifteen million mostly innocent people were slaughtered in that successful 45 year effort to suppress those breaks for economic freedom which were bursting out all over the world... All intelligence agencies have been, and are still in, the business of destabilizing undeveloped countries to maintain their dependency and the flow of the world's natural wealth to powerful nations' industries at a low price and to provide markets for those industries at a high price."

That the media has failed to accurately portray the real nature of Western foreign policy to the public, playing instead the subservient role of a propaganda machine for elite interests, is therefore quite obvious. The question that then remains is, why does the media – conventionally believed to be critical of the establishment-behave in a way that conforms to the false picture presented by the government and corporate elite of their own policies? The anwer is simple: in a nutshell, the mass media *is* the establishment.

To begin our analysis then, we will discuss a propaganda model of the mass media. It is thus useful to begin with what is arguably the most thorough model of the media-that proposed by Edward Herman (Professor Emeritus of Finance at Wharton School in the University of Pennsylvania) and Noam Chomsky (Institute Professor of Linguistics and Philosophy at MIT), both of whom are leading critics of US foreign policy.

There are particularly pertinent reasons to begin with their model-the primary one being that it is arguably the most thoroughly researched and empirically verified model available. Herman and Chomsky's landmark study, *Manufacturing Consent: The Political Economy of the Mass Media*, comes under the recommendation of America's leading national media watchdog and research group, Fairness and Accuracy In Reporting (FAIR). It is also recommended as an essential resource for media literacy by the Grand Rapids Institute for Information Democracy (GRIID), affiliated with the US-based Community Media Centre (CMC). The Oxford-based research and publishing group Corporate Watch (not to be confused with the US-based organisation of the same name), which works in cooperation with a variety of other human rights and environmentalist organisations, describes the study as "one of the most incisive critiques of the media's role in society". The respected journal *Publisher's Weekly* gives the following review of *Manufacturing Consent*:

"Herman of Wharton and Chomsky of MIT lucidly document their argument that America's government and its corporate giants exercise control over what we read, see and hear. The authors identify the forces that they contend make the national media propagandistic-the major three being the motivation for profit through ad revenue, the media's close links to and often ownership by corporations, and their acceptance of information from biased sources. In five case studies, the writers show how TV, newspapers and radio distort world events... Extensive evidence is calmly presented, and in the end an indictment against the guardians of our freedom is substantiated. A disturbing picture emerges of a news system that panders to the interest of America's privileged and neglects its duties when the concerns of minority groups and the underclass are at stake." Indeed, according to the leading American media scholar Robert W. McChesney, Professor of Journalism and Mass Communication at the University of Illinois, any significant attempt to comprehend the structure and operation of the mass media must begin with Herman and Chomsky's study. He further observes that:"This book promises to be a seminal work in critical media analysis and to open a door through which future media analysis will follow... Edward Herman and Noam Chomsky are certainly well qualified to provide a simple yet powerful model that explains how the media function to serve the large propaganda requirements of the elite. Together and individually, they have written numerous articles and books which have chronicled the ways in which the US media have actively promoted the agenda of the elite, particularly in regard to US activities in the Third World. Manufacturing Consent is a work of tremendous importance for scholars and activists alike... Each chapter is meticulously researched and most draw heavily on the authors' earlier works in these areas."

All this provides us with ample reason to begin with Herman and Chomsky's model. Contrary to the claims of the mainstream critique of radical media analysis, a propaganda model does not entail a grandiose conspiracy theory. Rather, this model is based on analysing the politico-economic influences on the mass media, and considering the extent to which those influences both have the potential to condition the media's reporting tendencies in accord with the interests of those who possess power. In other words, the model constitutes a 'guided free market' model, advocating that the media's reporting is influenced by the same factors that dominate corporate activities-the maximisation of profit and therefore the market. The next step is to document the occurrences where this potential is actualised. In this sense, according to the propaganda model the media is conditioned by the profit-orientated considerations of corporate elites. As Professor McChesney observes:

"Herman and Chomsky quickly dismiss the standard mainstream critique of radical media analysis that accuses it of offering some sort of 'conspiracy' theory for media Behaviour; rather, they argue, media bias arises from 'the preselection of right-thinking people, internalized preconceptions, and the adaptation of personnel to the constraints' of a series of objective filters they present in their propaganda model. Hence the bias occurs largely through self-censorship, which explains the superiority of the US mass media as a propaganda system: it is far more credible than a system which relies on official state censorship."

## QUALIFYING MEDIA RIGHTS

Both Canada and the United States have landmark decisions issued earlier in this century expressing a strong commitment to the principle of a free press, even though "freedom of the press" was not formally part of any constitutional document in Canada prior to the Charter of Rights and Freedoms in 1982. This section, however, looks at cases in three areas that would come under Justice Brennan's "structural" model requiring the court to balance individual concerns about free press against the broader rights of the community. The three areas are libel, journalist's privilege, and covering the courts.

The Supreme Court of the United States has constitutionalized a major part of defamation law. Before 1964 and the Court's decision in New York Times v Sullivan, the Supreme Court had considered defamatory publication to be outside protection of the First Amendment. With that decision, however, the Court ruled that the principle of "strict liability" would not apply to elected public officials seeking to recover damages for civil libel.

Instead, they would have to meet a new national, uniform standard of fault by having to prove "actual malice", which Justice Brennan, writing for the Court, defined as publication "with knowledge that it was false or with reckless disregard of whether it was false or not."

Canadian courts have not adopted this approach to the civil defamation. In a recent case, Hill v Church of Scientology, the Supreme Court of Canada was asked in arguments by the appellants to adopt the actual malice rule from the United States, but the Court declined.

Justice Cory, writing for the majority, reviewed the development of this standard in the United States, including critiques of the actual malice rule, and explained how the courts in England and Australia had refused to adopt it. He concluded that "None of the factors which prompted the United States Supreme Court to rewrite the law of defamation in America are present in the case at bar."

His conclusion was that "the common law of defamation complies with the underlying values of the Charter and there is no need to amend or alter it." Earlier in his opinion, he refused to separate an individual's public and private rights to recover damage to reputation.

"The fact that persons are employed by the government does not mean that their reputation is automatically divided into two parts, one related to their personal life and the other to their employment status. To accept the appellants' position would mean that identical defamatory comments would be subject to two different laws, one applicable to government employees, the other to the rest of society.

Government employment cannot be a basis for such a distinction. Reputation is an integral and fundamentally important aspect of every individual. It exists for everyone quite apart from employment." In the end, by continuing intact the English common law tradition in civil defamation, the Canadian Supreme Court keeps Canada more in line with other Western democracies, which set themselves apart from the American tradition that grants considerable protection to the news media to comment on government and criticize public officials and public figures with less fear of being successfully challenged under libel law.When the Canadian Court specifically rejected the American approach in its decision in Scientology, it did so out of respect for the tradition of common law, the proper role of the legislature in these matters, and the fundamental right to reputation over freedom of expression.

## JOURNALIST'S PRIVILEGE

Neither Canadian nor American courts have been willing to grant journalists the same common law privilege from having to testify as is provided for doctor-patient, lawyer-client, and priest-penitent communications. In both countries, the general rule is that journalists will not be offered absolute protection from having to disclose the identity of a source or confidential information if it is considered relevant and necessary.

The U.S. Supreme Court's 1972 decision in Branzburg v Hayes dealt specifically with the application of a First Amendment protection for journalists from having to testify when confidential sources or information is involved. Most significant was the dissenting opinion by Justice Stewart who offered a three-part test that is used in state and federal courts in applying federal or state common law protection or statutory protection under a state "shield" law.

The test requires: first, there is probable cause to believe the journalist has relevant information; second, that the information sought cannot be obtained in another way less injurious of the First Amendment; and, third, that there is a compelling and overriding interest in the information.

In Canada, the issue of journalist's privilege had not been dealt with by the Supreme Court until 1989, when it decided a case similar in many ways to Branzburg v Hayes. In Moysa v Alberta a reporter for the Edmonton Journal refused to identify her sources of information, claiming confidential privilege protection under common law and the Canadian Charter.

The Court affirmed the decision of the two lower courts that the reporter in this case had no special privilege to refuse to testify before the labour board. While the Court did not feel compelled by the facts of the case to address the "broad and important constitutional questions" before it, Justice Sopinka in his opinion for the majority did refer to an earlier pre-Charter decision when the Court acknowledged the four criteria cited by Wigmore for when a motion for confidential privilege should be granted.It is likely that the Wigmore test will play an important role when and if the Court is presented with the right case requiring a consideration of the constitutional questions not addressed in Moysa. However, from Justice Sopinka's opinion, news media appellants can expect to have to establish with evidence that a direct link exists "between testimonial compulsion and a `drying-up' of news sources."

## THE CONCEPT OF DEVELOPMENT IN MASS MEDIA

Here, we shall have the occasion to see the difficulties involved in defining and measuring development. Also we can see the changing perceptions of development as it evolved over a period of time. Since much of the writing on development are by economists, the definitions often start with economic development. It is not that there is a general agreement on the definition of economic development, but it will serve as a simplified starting point. We shall define economic development as "the process of increasing the real per capita income of a country over a long period of time accompanied by changes in its structure and institutions. For example the Indian government is inviting the foreign business companies to invest in India. This invitation, if accepted by several foreign companies, might create a large number of jobs. This means that the employed people will have a steady income, probably an increased one. I am sure you know that per capita income is calculated by dividing the yearly total income of all the citizens of a country by the number of its population. Therefore, less unemployment means higher per capita income. Once the people have money at hand, they will definitely satisfy their immediate requirements such as food, clothing and shelter. The real development is not in the figure of the per capita income.

It must be seen and felt—take, for example, the opening up of the Indian economy to the outside world. If we have less unemployment in India, it will make for more livable houses, which means lesser number of people sleeping on the footpaths of the cities like Calcutta or Bombay; more transport facilities, which means less crowded buses and trains; lesser beggars in the streets of metropolises; a less number of illiterates, etc. These are the signs of development—real development.

"The process involves not only changes in the economic structure, but is interlinked with the entire social, political and cultural fabric of society." It is necessary to note that development does not mean a mere increase in the per capita income or mere industrialization, but "a process involving a number of qualitative changes", nothing less than the "upward movement of the entire social system." Some may interpret development as "attainment of a number of modernization ideals, such as a rise in productivity, social and economic equalization, modem knowledge, and improved institutions and attitudes..." Hopper and adequate development are not done by dislodging people from their roots, culture or environments. Proper development always helps people to be self-sufficient and self-reliant.

*Measurement of Development :* Having noticed the difficulties in defining development, we can easily see the problems that would arise in the measurement of development. As in the case of the definition, we may begin with the measurement of economic development. Economists have, traditionally, measured economic development by the level of per capita Gross National Product (GNP), which, in simple terms, means the total national income divided by the population. This measure was adopted by the United Nations, in

1950, when it classified all countries with a per capita income of less than $ 200 as less developed countries (LM3). This was a rough but convenient measure for the UN to identify the less-developed countries for the purpose of providing economic aid. However, the limitations of the per capita GNP as a measure of development are well known. We can mention at least four such limitations here.

- First, it is based on national income statistics, which does not include major portions of real income, like the contribution of work done in the household. This will seriously undermine the value of the real per capita income of countries like India, where the household work provides a substantial proportion of goods and services.
- Second, it is an average and does not say much about the structure of production or distribution of the national income. For example, Kuwait's per capita income, in 1990, was $32,680, the highest in the world, and that of the United Arab Emirates was $ 19,860. It does not mean that these countries are developed, and that is why the UN has categorized them as developing countries.
- Third, progress in a narrow sector, like natural resource—exports, oil, minerals, timber might show high per capita income as in Kuwait and the U.A.E., Trinidad and Tobago, ($3,610), Gabon ($3,330). But, by no stretch of imagination, can these countries be considered ten times more developed than India with a per capita income of $350 in 1990. Also the purchasing power of local currency is higher than the dollar in the U.S. or other countries. You can easily perceive that Kuwait, Brunei, the U.A.E., etc. are rich in non-renewable resources. Once these resources are consumed, the development process in these countries might cease. Therefore, this kind of development is hollow and temporary.
- Fourth, the per capita income may increase even in the face of increasing unemployment. For instance, today we see that the gross national income of the USA has increased. The normal process and the assumption is that with the growth of per capita income unemployment diminishes. However, in societies which use high technologies, *i.e.*, Labour-displacing or capital-intensive societies, the per capita income may rise with the rise of unemployment. For example, computerization or the use of robots might cause a rise in the unemployment rate.

In spite of these well-known limitations of the measurement of 'economic development' in terms of per capita income, it is still used widely because of the lack of a more satisfactory measure. The World Bank continues to classify countries on the basis of per capita income. In 1990, the UN classified the countries as

- Low income economies: those with a GNP per capita of $610 or less,

- Middle Income economies: $61 1-7,6 19, and
- High income economies: $7,620 or more.

You should note that there has been growing criticism of this per capita income based concept. One such criticism is that it leads to the misconception of the tasks of development. The growing disenchantment with a GNP per capita has resulted in a number of alternative ways of measurement of development. One such proposition is that "development means reducing unemployment, mitigation of inequality and eradication of poverty," According to this concept, a country may not be called developed, if it has poverty and high degree of unemployment and inequality. Yet another concept of development has suggested an index of physical quality of the life index (PQLI), which emphasizes quality of life as evidenced by the state of literacy, life expectancy, infant mortality, etc. Yet another notion of development emphasizes freedoms, capabilities, and entitlements for a better life, which could be expressed in terms of a scale, similar to those considered under quality of life. One of the recent entries in the alternative development perspective is sustainable development. It draws attention to the need to conserve resources so that the process of development would be sustainable without endangering the resources for the future generations." Thus, it is clear that the concept of development has advanced far ahead of the income confines of per capita income.

*Characteristics of Developing Countries vis-à-vis Development:* Faced with these complexities in conceptualizing development, there are many textbooks which try to present underdevelopment in terms of certain common characteristics of the developing countries. These include:

- Low levels of living,
- Low levels of productivity,
- High rates of population growth,
- High and rising levels of unemployment,
- Underemployment, and
- High dependence on agriculture and other primary production.

*Development, in contrast, is associated with some of the characteristics of the developed capitalist countries. These include, the opposite of the characteristics mentioned above, and include:*

- High levels of living,
- High levels of productivity,
- Low or no population growth, and
- The predominance of industrial or non-agricultural activities.

Such characterization, at best, provides a description of the development, and underdevelopment, but it does not offer any basis for an explanation as to why and how countries are underdeveloped or what are the ways in which countries can develop. These are questions, which are the central concern of the development theories.

# 2

# Global Journalism Ethics

## INTRODUCTION

What global journalism ethics entails for journalism and democratic oversight is yet to be determined. However, we gain some insight by examining three topics: new forms of communication, pluralism and patriotism.

## NEW FORMS OF PUBLIC COMMUNICATION

The future of oversight of the security sector must take into account two large-scale changes in the media environment. One change is that journalists now report upon pluralistic societies in a pluralistic world. Another is the evolution of new forms of communication and public dialogue through what is called the "new media" – the Internet and other communication technologies. Initiatives to support democratic oversight that ignore these new forms of communication will miss important opportunities for deliberation, monitoring and self-governance. A significant portion of the mainstream news media and media-savvy elites tends to think of oversight according to a traditional model of journalistic communication. According to this model, oversight happens as a result of the public receiving information, analysis and argumentation contained in major newspapers and television broadcasts. Armed with the facts, members of the public form their own judgments on the issues before them and judge the performance of their politicians, institutions and government agencies. Oversight is the product of the formation of rational public opinion that, at least in democracies, restrains governments and militaries.

This model is a modern formulation of the 19th century liberal theory of the press, which preceded the 20th century notion of public self-governance through objective reporting. On the liberal view, the journalist acts like a tutor of the public, creating and shaping public views through weighty opinion pieces and strong political coverage. The journalist acts as a watchdog of government abuse of its powers on behalf of the public. With the rise of the doctrine of objectivity in the early 1900s, an additional idea was added to the doctrine of self-governance. The objective journalist laid the facts before the public in an impartial manner. Citizens made their own judgments, based on the facts. The objective journalist attempted to be an independent voice amid the cacophony of partisan voices in the public sphere. This model of oversight continues to operate as a background assumption in many articles on the news media, despite the fact that the liberal theory of the press has been subjected to withering criticism. Much of the criticism is based on Stephen J. Ward draft – please do not quote February 8, 2003 the belief that the free marketplace of ideas and the formation of public opinion are neither rational, nor open, nor fair.

The development of global technologies signals the arrival of new forms of public communication and new means of oversight. Citizens with common interests have new ways to seek out information for themselves and to debate issues. Citizens consult weblogs, interactive Web sites, Web forums, and alternative on-line journalism for diverse perspectives. They use the Internet to "drill down" into the deep background and history of a topic, or use hyperlinks to access the original documents that prompted yesterday's news reports. Citizens can see for themselves much of the material that reporters used, making perspicuous any "spin" in the news article.

Moreover, the informal nature and inter activity of on-line communication is creating a web of participants who expect to have an opportunity to engage in 'real-time' debate among their list serve colleagues and experts from around the world. All of this means a decreasing role for the old forms of mediation practiced by the journalistic gatekeeper in mainstream newsrooms. New forms of public discourse are emerging and with them, new habits and expectations among information-hungry audiences. On-line public discourse displays a distinctive and far-reaching feature: it addresses people as participants in an interactive process. It is not content with the old Transmission Model of journalism, where the journalist is active and the audience is relatively passive. In the old model, the journalist is one who writes with 'authority.' The journalist, not the audience, gathers the sources, does the research, and verifies the facts. Journalism is not a dialogue. It is, rather, the transmission of results structured according to the various genres of journalism.

The emphasis is on the final product, not the process. Communication in the Transmission Model is one-to-many and non-interactive. In new on-line communication, the journalist is more an initiator of conversation than a transmitter of pre-digested facts or settled opinion. On-line communication is multi-media and non-linear. Stories on the Internet combine text, audio and video, supplemented by hyperlinks and chat forums, to put forward certain perspectives and debate public issues. The audiences expect to be given the opportunity to engage in debate, to pursue their own research on the Net, and to respond immediately by e-mail to what the journalist writes. This new environment changes how journalists see themselves and how they regard public deliberation. Instead of claiming to write the last word, many on-line journalists acknowledge that their articles are perspectives on complex topics.

A commentary is a fallible stab at a defensible point of view. Readers are expected to use a plurality of perspectives to come closer to the truth. John Pavlik, a new-media expert at Columbia University, thinks that the Internet's ability to Stephen J. Ward draft – please do not quote February 8, 2003 provide layers of information should result in a more "contextualized" journalism for a pluralistic public sphere. Jon Katz, the American columnist, has described how writing commentary on-line contrasts with writing editorials for a newspaper. Within minutes of posting his articles on the Internet, a host of experts from around the world use e-mail to provide Katz with counter-evidence, counter-argument, original documents, graphics and new studies. Katz often finds himself writing not one article on a topic, but a series of articles with updated facts and alternate perspectives. Katz says inter activity can be a humbling experience: "The only thing I can compare it to is being tied to the back of a car and dragged through the street." These evolving modes of communication have implications for ethics and democratic oversight.

The first implication is that if NGOs, international organizations and other groups wish to strengthen public discourse and oversight in the years ahead, they should consider how public deliberation could be fostered through new media. On-line communication could be used to help members of the public inform each other on security issues. In mainstream news media, the transmission of facts, expert analysis and the results of investigations will carry on. The mainstream news media will continue to be important to oversight, given their central role in the media system. But a good deal of the conversation in the future will occur outside traditional forms of journalism. To participate in and facilitate this conversation, journalists need to design coverage of issues in ways that encourage active engagement by citizens, both in their newspapers and on their Web sites. The nature of media oversight is changing.

It is no longer the specialty of the "beat" or investigative journalist, who digs up information, checks sources, places facts in context and sends it off to readers. Democratic oversight is becoming a multi-media dialogue among journalists, experts, freelancers, Web site providers, video journalists, human rights groups and ordinary citizens. Journalists will have to act more like Sherpas, leading people to other sites and perspectives. One benefit of the new media may be the swift distribution of information that governments and militaries would rather keep hidden from view. In an age of portable cameras, powerful communications satellites and the ability to send video over the Internet, more people will be able to participate in the exchange of information on the activities of para militaries, armies and security forces on the ground in previously remote areas of the world. The new media also present problems for oversight and accurate information exchange.

With all new forms of communications come new ways to spread rumour, lies, hatred and manipulated images. The challenge of media oversight in the future will go beyond finding ways to access and distribute information globally;

it will include finding ways to confirm information as reliable. Another challenge will be to make sure that the interaction of participants does not fragment into a plethora of parochial discussions. Effective oversight will require that there are forms of media and communication used by a substantial cross-section of citizens from around the world. Deliberation on politics or social issues will lack impact if the global public sphere becomes a universe of many small 'publics' engaging in arcane discussions that are intelligible only to relatively small groups of enthusiasts or experts. Another challenge will be to use the global public sphere to enlarge perspectives through provocative and critical exchanges of informed views. The new media will not foster public understanding and oversight if on-line communication is dominated by Web sites that only reinforce existing beliefs and prejudices.

Nor will democratic oversight improve if on-line communication is used to rant, rather than rationally exchange views and information. At least some portion of the new public sphere will have to embody a culture of critical, but tolerant, communication where journalists and non-journalists subject their claims global public scrutiny. Achieving this goal in a time of acute cultural tensions will not be easy.

**Writing for a Pluralistic World**

A primary rationale for global journalism ethics is political and cultural pluralism. Pluralism represents one of the greatest challenges of our age. The world is not a cozy McLuhan village where the media act as electronic extensions of humankind's nervous system, bringing us all closer together in a benign manner. Our world *is* connected electronically like never before, but this grid of connections co-exists with a collision of cultures, values, customs, religions, social structures and philosophies. The assertion of universal rights and the transmission of a global commercial culture co-exist with a resurgence of particular traditions, religions, languages and ethnic politics. Cosmopolitan attitudes run up against communal perspectives. To compound matters, this pluralism is refracted through the prism of a news media of striking images of angry, conflicting voices and of powerful, manipulative agents. It remains to be seen whether we, as a species, have the ability to evolve mentally and ethically to live in this pluralistic world.

Will we blow ourselves off the planet, degrade the environment and continue to live in a world of grave inequities and the threat of terrorism? Will humankind's penchant to divide people into "us" and "them" remain dominant?

One of the important roles for Global Journalism in the future will be assisting groups who have radically different ideas of what is 'good' in life to negotiate a way to live together.

A pluralistic society cannot hope to achieve consensus on what the 'goods' of life are among religious, ethnic and other groups. But it can hope to achieve an "overlapping" consensus among groups on fair procedures for resolving disputes. In one sense, global journalism ethics is an extrapolation of this viewpoint to journalism, and to the international scene. The global journalist belongs to one of the institutions that can help groups negotiate and agree on ways to live together and resolve disputes, short of war or terrorism. To act as an international "go-between," the journalist must become a sort of anthropologist, sensitive to nuances in cultural differences, knowledgeable in the history and ideas behind movements, and able to convey the meaning of puzzling Behaviour to people outside that culture. Journalists must be careful about how they "frame" stories. Special efforts need to be made to find viewpoints and experts from all countries involved in internationals issue, rather than relying heavily on local officials.

The model of "public journalism" developed in the United States in the 1990s offers some ideas for how to approach Global Journalism, if we think of public journalism on the international stage. Public journalism has its critics, but what is of value is the idea of journalists as active and inventive facilitators of public discussion. Public journalism seeks to overcome the alienation of citizens from the political process by using all forms of media to invite citizens to participate in the solution of community problems. Public journalists seek out different voices in their communities, hold town hall meetings and avoid the 'conflict' model of reporting that portrays each issue as an uncompromising struggle between two camps for power. Public journalists reject the image of the journalist as a disengaged, cynical observer looking down on society as it screws up. Instead, the journalist is a fair, well-researched catalyst of public deliberation. I suggest that this image of the journalist is part of the identity of the global journalist.

Writing for a pluralistic world has implications for journalism education. The issues that face journalism education in the West are not primarily issues of technological training but issues of liberal education. We need journalists with critical thinking skills, cultural awareness, expertise in crucial topics, and knowledge – about science and technology, and national and international institutions. Journalism education should shift from industrial training, linked to an apprenticeship model, to the education of journalists as critically aware world citizens. In the long run, better skills and education will have an impact on journalism and, eventually, media oversight.

They will perpetuate the prejudices of their times and their local environments. One of the greatest obstacles to Global Journalism is narrow patriotism and excessive parochialism. In every crisis, in every war, journalists come under pressure to be patriotic. Journalism history is redolent with examples of how journalists discarded any pretense to objectivity for jingoism, ethnocentrism and even xenophobia, especially when their country was in trouble, or their leaders sounded a call to arms. Patriotism, in this context, is not just a love of one's country; it is an extreme, emotion-driven patriotism that demands that all citizens "get on side" and support uncritically the government's actions. The social pressure that such patriotism can exert on both the public and the news media has never been clearer than since September 11th. Patriotism puts pressure on journalists to suspend or water down the standards of journalism: to root for the home team, to minimize dissent, to censor the "enemy" and to maintain morale. Supporting the home effort becomes a primary aim, overriding other journalistic functions such as acting as a watchdog and providing a forum for diverse views. Journalists, caught up in such mass emotions, ignore or forgot that government will use fear and uncertainty to push for major restrictions on civil liberties, including press freedom, and that a nervous public will be less inclined to object voraciously.

The idea that special times call for special measures is fraught with danger. The primary ethical duty of journalism, even in times of crisis, is *not* a patriotism of blind allegiance, or even a journalism of muted, careful criticism. The primary duty of journalists is *not* to the state, but to the public. That public duty calls for hard-edged news, investigations, analysis and multiple perspectives on the most important issues. We need a journalism that, more than ever, assumes some responsibility to "prepare" the public for difficult decisions ahead. Journalists serve the citizens of their country and the world by being critical, independent journalists. Canadian journalists, for example, need to ask whether their government will follow the lead of the United States in its War on Terrorism, and where that path leads. Journalists need to help citizens to unearth the historical roots of their troubles and deepen their understanding of other religions, other cultures. News organizations need to help the public debate the difficult decisions ahead. Journalists should maintain skepticism Towards all sources, test facts, detect hoaxes, reject rumors, and report controversial opinions. They must protect their independence in dealings with governments and military leaders. All avenues of influence, all forms of inducement will be used to shape the war coverage. Most of all, journalists must avoid the temptation to write stories that portray the military and defence options as reducible to a Stephen J. Ward draft – please do not quote February 8, 2003 medieval engagement of the forces of light against the forces of "pure evil." Journalists must deal with the stubborn complexity of the world, not shrink it down to digestible sound bites. Journalists are not indifferent to acts of terrorism or to the fate of their country. But, knowing that they, like all people, have such feelings is all the more reason to be vigilant that no one manipulates these honest emotions. In the fog of war, truth is the first casualty. Appeals to patriotism, if not challenged, only thicken the fog.

**Concrete Steps**

Journalists, media scholars, foundations and other groups can foster a fledgling Global Journalism by taking a number of concrete steps. They should consider forming new international alliances and organizations to promote journalism from a global perspective. Some international groups exist, such as Reporters Without Frontiers and the International Communications Forum. Often, these groups are focused on only one issue, such as reporters killed or thrown in jail. Other groups lack strong links to major journalism organizations. We need alliances between scholars, institutes, journalism organizations and unions, schools of journalism that take a broad interest in professional standards from a global perspective. These coalitions could provide resources and educational Programmes for journalists writing on specific issues. They could sponsor international journalism fellowships, journalism sabbaticals and study opportunities abroad.

They could monitor the news media for good and bad coverage, speak out against clamp downs on the press and expose attempts to manipulate the facts. International alliances could publish an annual report on the state of Global Journalism and the free press. Global Journalism organizations could provide moral, financial and legal assistance to journalists and news organizations struggling to be an independent voice in certain countries. Such organizations could liaise between journalists and the growing list of international agencies whose activities may impinge on the work of journalists, such as International Criminal Tribunal for the former Yugoslavia in The Hague. More news organizations, NGOs, and other agencies could support attempts to develop a free and responsible news media in developing and war-torn societies. 9 Ethically, journalists and other media professionals could begin to draw up statements of journalism principles that begin to articulate the common values that news media around the world should be embracing – or at least discussing and debating.

We need a debate on the 9 A Global Journalism perspective will be crucial to the development of such Programmes. Western journalism Programmes should be sensitive to cultural differences. Journalism development should not be an unreflective exporting of Western media values to a foreign country, or a "top-down" process where elite journalists 'talk down' to local Stephen J. Ward Draft – Please do not Quote February 8, 2003 principles of global journalism ethics. An example of an international statement of principles is The Sarajevo Commitment adopted in September 2000 by participants to a World Media Assembly in Sarajevo. The commitment commits the participants to independent, fair and factual informing and to opposing "hypocrisy, oppression, exploitation." The commitment states: "We shall not cease to strive until every gun is silent, every injustice righted and every human being enabled to live a life of satisfaction and purpose." The commitment is idealistic, to be sure. But it points Towards an increased ethical commitment of the media Towards a safer and more humane world. Declarations could be bolstered by UN conferences on media and information rights, and the protection of journalists.

Scholars should also show leadership. Interdisciplinary studies and journals by ethicists, communication scholars and experts on international affairs could explore the economic, political and ethical implications of a global media. Ethicists can contribute by showing how the concepts of current codes of ethics are too parochial and need to be changed to reflect the global media environment. Perhaps the best place to start is to hold workshops, round tables and conferences where participants develop ideas for ethical handbooks and manuals. The process will involve a fundamental re-thinking of our basic journalism concepts. We will have to face tough questions such as how journalists can be independent and objective yet also act as global agents. A media that has taken on global proportions is still constructing stories according to the standards and practices of a pre-global media of the 20th century. Most discussions of ethics refer to the duties of the individual journalist, an individual news organization or the ethics of a country's media system. Many ethical codes are the codes of specific organizations or a particular medium like photography. The codes speak of impartiality but in times of conflict, the patriotic impulse soon reveals that the journalist's impartiality exists within a larger zone of partiality.

There is a need for more international journalism forums on the Web that stimulate multi perspective discussions. My editorship of *Global Journalism Ethics,* an interactive forum on the Web site of the World Press Institute in St. Paul's, Minn., is a small step in that direction. Ethical analyses of media issues are posted on the site, and journalists and ethicists from around the world respond with comments and criticisms. I can foresee the day when there will be many more forums like this, linking major journalism organizations on every continent. journalists. Development Programmes should be flexible enough to allow local journalists to interpret and apply the principles of journalism in ways that speak to their situation and cultural values.

In the West, the 18th century saw journalists of the daily press begin to address citizens in the new public sphere. Nineteenth century journalists became standard-bearers for an ascendant liberalism – as partisan essayists, as news-writers, as reformers, and as revolutionaries. The 20th century journalist became an employee of the business of news, an informer and entertainer for a mass society of consumers.

As the 20th century progressed, chains of newspapers developed into multi-media, global media empires. With each revolution in journalism, the ethics of the press evolved to articulate the new relationship between journalist and reader. The ethic of a fourth estate arose by the late 1700s, liberalism gave birth to the idea of a maximally free press that directed public opinion. A mass commercial press encouraged the doctrine of news objectivity.

Given the new media environment at the start of the 21st century, I expect another evolution in journalism ethics. This evolution must walk between the extremes of native idealism and despondent cynicism. Native idealism underestimates the economic and political forces that would debase journalism. Cynicism despairs at those forces. In the aftermath of the First World War, Walter Lippmann, the influential American columnist, began to doubt the liberal theory of the press. He questioned whether public opinion was formed in a rational manner in the public sphere. He pointed to the unreliable practices of the press and their lack of professionalism. He noted with alarm the growing legion of press agents manipulating public consent. Lippmann called public opinion a "phantom" and doubted the ordinary person's ability to understand complex policy options.

Lippmann was, in effect, questioning two major assumptions of the liberal theory of the press:

(a) A press freed from government control would be a serious informer of citizens and advocateb of progressive causes, not a superficial provider of 'content' for consumers.

(b) The public sphere was a democratic sphere, an open marketplace of ideas.

He warned that if liberty depended on factual news from the media and a truly informed citizen, then liberty and democracy were truly in trouble. Today, Lippmann's warnings are still worth pondering. But we should not despair and we should not lose faith in ordinary citizens. Instead, we should take up the challenge to create a more reliable, truly informative news media. As citizens of the world, must do what we can to construct communication systems that provide some degree of genuine oversight over governments. As scholars, we need to study the nature of new forms of communication and articulate the values that should guide such powerful Stephen J. Ward draft – please do not quote February 8, 2003 technology.

As journalists, we should strive to act as engaged, public informers and intellectuals, not aim to be media stars or 'personalities.' Only if these new values and ideals are embraced will globalization in journalism mean something more than the development of satellites, broadband connections, smarter computers, converging media and global media companies. Only if journalists re-examine their ethical role amid these changes, will they survive as critical informers and not become mere "content providers." Journalism must strive to be one of the arts of democracy in a global context, a force for humanity, for toleration, for peace and for cross-cultural understanding.

Established in 2000 on the initiative of the Swiss government, the Geneva Centre for the Democratic Control of Armed Forces (DCAF), encourages and supports States and non- State governed institutions in their efforts to strengthen democratic and civilian control of armed and security forces, and promotes international cooperation within this field, initially targeting the Euro-Atlantic regions. The Centre collects information, undertakes research and engages in networking activities in order to identify problems, to establish lessons learned and to propose the best practices in the field of democratic control of armed forces and civil-military relations.

## DEFINING DEVELOPMENT JOURNALISM

This, however is not what some are calling "development journalism." Development journalism is an oxymoron. Developing countries need good journalism and good journalists, period. And they need journalists industrious enough to look beyond the polished news releases and briefings put out by well endowed foreign organizations, curious enough to find local sources of expertise, brave enough to present home-grown solutions to pressing development problems.

The task is not easy. Ironically, information about local research is often more difficult to obtain than the work of experts in Northern institutes of higher learning and international organizations. Developing-country scientists and researchers may also be more reluctant to talk to media, for a host of reasons political and otherwise. And they may be less skilled at presenting their message.

### Lack of Training

Journalists themselves often lack the training needed to understand both the content and language of research, and its importance to national development efforts. Limited press freedom must sometimes also be factored in. Overcoming these hurdles requires training both researchers and journalists. Efforts need to be made to strengthen the capacity of developing-world journalists to cover local research to ensure that their societies benefit from the contributions of their best minds.

### Developing-Country Research

A number of organizations are now doing so. Canada's International Development Research Centre (IDRC) and London-based SciDev.Net, for instance, are collaborating in making the results of developing-country research better known around the world.

They are also supporting the World Conference of Science Journalists to be held next October. The conference will provide a unique opportunity for journalists to share expertise and exchange experiences in covering development, not as a separate beat but as the very fabric of national social, political, and economic life.

## JOURNALISM AND DEVELOPMENT

The approach to journalism called development journalism emerged in the 1960 out of dissatisfaction with the dominance of Western news and communication ideals in development countries. Supporters of development journalism believe that the Western approach to media was not appropriate in developing countries where cultural and economic circumstances radically differs from the West. The world was thus in need of an entirely new type of journalism specifically designed to function in the cultural and political structures of developing countries. This approach to journalism is called development journalism. The term development journalism was first introduced by Allan Chalkley in 1968 during a conference for finance journalist arranged by the Press Foundation of Asia in the Philippines.

Supporters of development journalism believes that news structured according to Western news criteria such as *conflict, actuality, and sensation* will lead to a news coverage focusing on political decisions in larger cities, technological progress or activities in the public sphere. However, the majority of the population in developing countries lives in rural areas and faces entirely different problems. According to the Bangladeshi media researcher Golam Rahman this is a considerable problem in Bangladesh. Local newspapers in Bangladesh are often published from town areas and do not cover news that are relevant to people in rural areas where conditions are remarkably different (Rahman, 1999). This is why MMC has put up two local grassroots newspapers, which are published from rural areas and focusing on rural peoples needs and problems.

"The grassroots journalist are wiring about domestic violence, improvement of schools, corruption or articles which spreads information about health or peoples right," says the chairman of MMC, Kamrul Hasan Monju. "They are putting focus on social and cultural problems which are rarely given importance by mainstream media. Often they are writing about problems they have experiences themselves or identified in their local areas," he explains.

## INFORMATION FOR SOCIAL CHANGE

The female grassroots journalist Roni is for example trying to change men's attitude towards domestic violence, by describing the problem from the eyes of the women. Her articles on a small village called Lal Nagur were followed up by a local seminar and started a campaign for women's right on a national level. In several cases the grassroots journalist are in this way able to involve other civil society organisations and local or national politicians and in this way put focus on a specific area. By following up her articles with a seminar, Roni emphasises the importance of involving the population of the village and create a public debate. This is a specific characteristic of development journalism. According to Allan Chalkley the task of development journalists is way more than just to pass on fact, but to open the readers eyes for the reasons for various problems and make the reader identify possible solutions (Romano, 1999). This approach to development journalism is inspired by the paradigm within development theories known as the participatory approach. The participatory approach is based on the philosophy that the beneficiaries of development projects must be involved in the planning and shaping of the projects. This approach to development is especially focused on strengthening civil society and hereby media.

When applying this paradigm to communication the aim is to involve people in the journalistic process on a local level. The focus of development journalists should therefore be on what their readers find important for the media to cover. In dialogue with the readers journalists must thus identify the readers' problems and find appropriate solutions. Journalists are in this way given an active role as a catalyst for social change. Readers are no longer seen as passive recipients or targets of communication. On the contrary the readers must take an active part in the communication process. This approach to communication in called *participatory communication*.

## RIGHTS AND INFORMATION

The purpose of involving people is to create empowerment. Empowerment can be defined as a process by which people gain more control over their lives and become aware of their rights and opportunities (Waisbord, 2005). Thought their articles the grassroots journalists are successful in informing people about their rights. Jahan was for example writing an article about people who charged money on medicine, which is supposed to be free. After Jahan wrote published the story in the local newspaper the blackmailing stopped. "The blackmailers got scared because they know that people and the local authorities know that the medicine is free. And now they know that there is a journalist in this area who is keeping an eye on them" she says, when I meet her in the Information centre in Feni. The Information centres are constructed by MMC and is part of the organisations attempt to give rural people access to media and information.

MMC has put up information centres in most villages in the districts where they work. In the centres people meet to listen to the radio and read the national and local newspapers as well as the two grassroots newspapers Lok Sangbad (The people's newspaper) and Metho Bharta (News from the field).

The few people who are able to read are reading allowed for those who cannot. About 53 percent of the population is illiterate. Most of them live in rural areas. "Previously only two ore three families in the village had newspapers. Now I feel that something in my day is missing if I have not red the newspaper in the information centre," says one of the men in the village. A study by the Bangladesh Enterprise Institute from 2005 shows that more than percent of the population neither have access to newspapers, radio or television. Most of them belong to marginalized groups and are thus both economically and socially disadvantaged. They often live in areas that are cut off from the country's economic centre (Hansen, Hansen and Quist, 2002). This is one of the major challenges for development journalism and democracy in Bangladesh. Furthermore the grassroots journalist faces the challenge of lack of freedom of speech as well as all other journalist in Bangladesh. In 2007 Reporters Without Borders reported of at least 40 cases where journalists had been arrested, prosecuted or subjected to violence in Bangladesh. One of the journalists behind this statistic is the Jharna.

When Jharna was 19 year old she write a number of articles about cases of rape, drug dealing, trafficking and violence in the area where she lives. "I knew who the criminals were because they used to hand around near my house," she explains. But after the article was published, the criminals were not only hanging out. On day when Jharna came home she discovered that a gang of criminals had broken into her house and attacked her mother and grandmother and damaged a lot of Jharnas personal papers. She reported the incident to the police but the Police refused to take any action. She thinks it is because the police and the politicians are making money on drug dealing. "The government controls the police, so the police will never do anything in cases like this," she explains.

## NEW STAGE IN JOURNALISM ETHICS

Since the birth of modern journalism in the 17th century, journalism has gradually broaden the scope of the people that it claims to serve — from factions to specific social classes to the public of nations. The journalistic principle of "serving the public interest" has been understood, tacitly or explicitly, as serving one's own public, social class or nation.

The other principles of objectivity, impartiality and editorial independence were limited by this parochial understanding of who journalism serves. For example, "impartiality" meant being impartial in one's coverage of rival groups within one's society, but not necessarily being impartial to groups outside one's national boundaries.

Global journalism ethics, then, can be seen as an extension of journalism ethics — to regard journalism's "public" as the citizens of the world, and to interpret the ethical principles of objectivity, balance and independence in an international manner.

Journalism ethics becomes more "cosmopolitan" in tone and perspective.

Components of global journalism ethics

The development of global journalism ethics has the following tasks.

### CONCEPTUAL TASKS

New philosophical foundations for a global ethics, which include:

- Global re-interpretation of the ethical role and aims of journalism
- Global re-interpretation of existing journalism principles and standards, such as objectivity, balance and independence

- Construction of new norms and "best practices" as guides for the practice of global journalism.

**Research Tasks**

More research into the state of journalism, amid globalization:

- Studies of news media in various regions of world
- Studies on the evolution and impact of globalization in news media, with a focus on ownership, technology and practice
- studies on the ethical standards of new media in different countries
- studies on news coverage of international problems and issues.

**Practical Tasks**

Actions to implement and support global standards:

- Application of this global perspective to re-define the coverage of international events and issues
- Coalition-building among journalists and interested parties with the aim of writing a global code of ethics that has wide-spread acceptance
- Initiatives to defend and enhance free and responsible news media, especially in areas where problems are the greatest.

How would a global ethics be different?

Philosophically, the distinct conceptual element of a global ethics can be summarized by three imperatives:

**Act as Global Agents**

Journalists should see themselves as agents of a global public sphere. The goal of their collective actions is a well-informed, diverse and tolerant global "info-sphere" that challenges the distortions of tyrants, the abuse of human rights and the manipulation of information by special interests.

**Serve the Citizens of the World**

The global journalist's primary loyalty is to the information needs of world citizens. Journalists should refuse to define themselves as attached primarily to factions, regions or even countries. Serving the public means serving more than one's local readership or audience, or even the public of one's country.

**Promote Non-Parochial Understandings**

The global journalist frames issues broadly and uses a diversity of sources and perspectives to promote a nuanced understanding of issues from an international perspective. Journalism should work against a narrow ethnocentrism or patriotism. What do these three imperatives imply for specific standards of journalism, such as objectivity? Under global journalism ethics, objectivity becomes the ideal of informing impartially from an international stance. Objectivity in journalism has usually been understood as the duty to avoid bias Towards groups within one's own country. Global objectivity takes on the additional responsibility of allowing bias towards one's country or culture as a whole to distort reports, especially reports on international issues. Objective reports, to be accurate and balanced, must contain all relevant international sources and cross-cultural perspectives. In addition, global journalism asks journalists to be more conscious of how they frame the global public's perspective on major stories, and how they set the international news agenda. The aim of global journalism should be more than helping the public sphere "go well" at home, as civic journalists say. The aim should be to facilitate rational deliberation in a global public sphere.

Global journalism ethics implies a firm journalistic response to inward-looking attitudes, such as extreme patriotism. It was disturbing to see how some news organizations during the Iraq War of 2003 so quickly shucked their peacetime commitments to independent, impartial reporting as soon as the drums of war started beating. Cosmopolitanism means that the primary ethical duty of a global journalism in times of conflict and uncertainty is not a patriotism of blind allegiance, or muted criticism. Public duty calls for independent, hard-edged news, along with investigations and analysis.

## PROBLEMS AND OBSTACLES

### Universal Values?

Among advocates of global ethics, there is disagreement over whether ethicists need to identify "universal values" among all journalists, or humans. Do such universal values exist? What might they be? Recently, a growing group of ethicists have attempted to identify a common core of values in various places: in codes of journalism ethics, in international treaties on human rights, in anthropological studies of culture.

One view is that neither universal values nor universal consent is required for a plausible, global code. This view sometimes stems from a contractual or 'constructionist" view of ethics. The constructionist does not believe that ethics depends on "finding" or "discovering", through empirical means, a set of universal values that all rational people acknowledge. Rather, the correct method of global ethics is to see whether all or most interested parties are able to "construct" and agree upon a set of principles through a fair process of deliberation. On this view, it is also not clear that a set of values must gain universal consensus — a demand that seems unduly strong, given the variety of new media in the world. A weaker requirement would aim at the construction of a set of principles agreed to by most major journalism associations and news organizations.

### Getting Specific

Global journalism ethics will have to amount to more than a dreamy spiritualism about the brotherhood of man and universal benevolence. Conceptually, there is work to be done. Global journalism ethics must show, in detail, how its ideas imply changes to norms and practices. What exactly do journalists "owe" citizens in a distant land? How can global journalists integrate their partial and impartial perspectives? How can journalists support global values while remaining impartial communicators?

### Reforming Media Practices

The slow, complex, practical task of developing better media practices is no less imposing. Exhorting individual journalists to be ethical will be futile unless supported by an institutional climate that encourages global values in the newsroom. Aware of such difficulties, some journalists may accuse global journalism ethicists of being unrealistic in thinking that news organizations will provide the education, expertise and extra resources needed to achieve a high-quality cosmopolitan journalism.

## PRINCIPLES OF GLOBAL JOURNALISM ETHICS

Journalism, at its best, is one of the arts of democracy. Journalists provide the news and analysis by which a society communicates with itself, allowing some measure of self-government. The public absorbs a daily barrage of news images that, over time, help to define one's sense of place in society and within a global community. News stories parade our injustices, vanities, power struggles, disasters, accomplishments and peculiar interests. Citizens, following the major issues in the press, become aware of their shared and competing values. Through journalism, a society debates how to reform its institutions and face the future. Vigorous journalism is the lifeblood of a deliberative democracy.

Journalism, at its worst, is an art of the demagogue and the despot. It is the propaganda tool of powerful interests who subvert popular self-governance by manipulating the channels of information. Journalism is debased if it falls into the hands of unethical media owners and journalists, or when editorial resources are squandered on entertaining stories. Journalism falters when it fails to question the powers that be, and when budget cuts strangle investigative journalism. Journalism degenerates when the business of journalism overwhelms its democratic functions, seeking profit through every cheap trick in the history of popular printing – jingoism, sensationalism and fear mongering. Journalism is an anti-democratic art when news organizations wield power without responsibility and journalists forsake their public responsibilities for fame and money. Five centuries after the first periodic papers were introduced, journalism still struggles to avoid debasement, let alone to live up to its democratic duty. In today's climate of fear, terrorism and regional conflict, the democratic function of journalism is sorely needed. The news media bear a substantial responsibility in helping citizens control their armed forces and shape security policy. In theory, the media should contribute to democratic oversight through revealing information, sharp analysis, thoughtful commentary and in-depth investigation. In reality, the news media provide adequate oversight only if many conditions are satisfied. A self-governing society requires an aggressive press led by major news organizations willing to spend time and resources on testing official positions and offering alternative views. Journalists Stephen J. Ward Draft – Please do not quote February 8, 2003 2 must have sufficient education and skill to pursue the issues and make them intelligible to others.

Reporters and editors must be able to act independently of commercial and ideological pressures inside and outside the newsroom. Self-governance needs a supportive legal and political climate. There must be mechanisms that guarantee access to government records and mechanisms that force bureaucracies to be open and accountable. In addition, the general public must support a critical and watchdog press, not only in times of peace but also in times of uncertainty. A sufficient cross-section of the population must not be alienated from public life, but willing to play a part in policy deliberation and political action. Often, these conditions are not satisfied. In Canada, we have witnessed a worrisome pattern over the past year and a half. The ability of government to monitor the daily Behaviour of its citizens has increased while the ability of citizens to oversee its government has decreased. Under the banner of "anti-terrorism," the Canadian government has introduced laws that allow officials to compile dossiers on every citizen, and to monitor e-mail and other communications. More laws may follow. These initiatives buttress an already entrenched attitude of secrecy in government. The freedom-of-information commissioner of Canada has called this attitude a "culture of secrecy" while the privacy commissioner of Canada has accused the government's new security initiatives as risking a "permanent loss" of basic civil rights and freedoms.

The privacy commissioner's warning caused only a ripple of interest in Parliament and in the news media. The federal bureaucracy is so protective of its public records that the Canadian Association of Journalists hands out an annual "Code of Silence" award to the most secretive government department in Canada. Last year, the 'award' went to the federal Department of Justice for giving itself the power, under new anti-terrorism legislation, to override the Access to Information Act and withhold information relating to international affairs, national security and defence that it deems sensitive. Two year's ago, the winner was the Ontario Ministry of the Environment for withholding information about the Walkerton water tragedy, in which a town's contaminated water supply claimed seven lives and sickened hundreds more.

The Canadian legal environment works against a vigorous investigative journalism. Canadian reporters do not have American-styled "shield laws" that protect them from being forced to hand over video, audio tapes, pictures and notebooks to state prosecutors. Canadian reporters do not work under a First Amendment. Reference to a free press in the Canadian Constitution is briefly mentioned in Section 2(b) of the document. It is preceded by Section 1, which notes that such 1 George Radwanski, Privacy Commissioner of Canada, interview on "The House," CBC Radio One, Feb. 1, 2003. Stephen J. Ward draft – please do not quote February 8, 2003 fundamental freedoms can be abridged under certain broad conditions. Canada does not have "whistleblower" legislation that protects officials who make important information public. Canadian libel laws are much tougher on journalists than in the United States.

Moreover, the public has reason to be skeptical about whether today's news media can play a serious role in democratic self-governance. Skeptics can point to the prevalence of soft, superficial or sensational news. For at least a decade, intense commercial and technological pressures have prompted editors to ignore or "dumb down" complex issues, or to treat issues as a conflict between hostile camps. The process of public policy is portrayed as a cynical power game, of interest only to insiders and elites. As a result, the public credibility of the news media spirals downward, making it more difficult for journalists to claim that the news media are a legitimate watchdog. A depressing number of citizens fail to see a clear distinction between a journalist and a media personality, or between journalism and 'media' in general. After years of cost-cutting, staff reductions and closing down of foreign bureaus, how many newsrooms have the knowledge, the sources and the resources to cover complex international stories?

Nevertheless, the terrorist attacks of September 11th rudely awakened journalism from its superficial slumbers. The serious, unavoidable, implications of living in a connected world stared us in the face. Both citizens and journalists have been put in a difficult position, torn between the need for security and the need for liberty. Recent polls indicate that Canadians share this ambiguity about their world. Polls show that Canadians feel that the world is a more dangerous place, and therefore there is a need for increased security. Yet the polls also indicate that some Canadians fear limitations on free speech. They fear that police and security personnel will abuse the increased powers. Equally interesting is polling that shows that Canadians believe that understanding the world beyond their borders is a necessary condition for coping with this new environment. The hypothesis of this chapter is that journalists and news organizations, to carry out their democratic role, need to adopt a different ethic to guide their practice.

Radical changes in news media and in society call for a radical reformulation of journalism ethics, its standards and goals. I argue that journalists, media scholars and others should work Towards what I call *global journalism ethics* for a global media environment. Journalism should transcend its centuries-old parochialism and seek a more cosmopolitan attitude. Once we start to adopt the perspective of global journalism ethics, however, common principles of journalism ethics, such as objectivity and serving the public, become unclear. I suspect that nothing short of a wholesale conceptual Stephen J. Ward draft – please do not quote February 8, 2003 revolution will do. By itself, the adoption of a new ethic won't create a better news media; but it is a step in that direction.

By global journalism ethics, I mean an approach that defines the primary responsibilities of the news media from a global perspective. The essential features of this approach are as follows: Acting as global agents: Journalists should see themselves as agents of a global public sphere, with new and increased responsibilities. The goal of their collective actions is a well-informed, diverse and tolerant global 'infosphere' that provokes citizens to become engaged in issues and provides a counter-balance to the lies of tyrants and the manipulation of information by special interests.

Serving citizens of the world: The journalist's primary loyalty is to citizens of the world. Journalists should not define themselves as attached primarily to factions, specific causes, or even to the public of their countries. Serving the public means more than serving one's local readership or paying audience. Journalists are answerable, ethically, to the information needs of world citizens. Non-parochial understanding: The journalistic duty to inform takes on the demanding task of framing issues broadly, using a diversity of sources and providing multiple, critical perspectives. The aim is help citizens gain a nuanced, in-depth understanding of issues.

This form of journalism opposes all attempts to define issues according to narrow ethnocentrism or patriotism. Global Journalism helps to reduce the power of slanted information and simplistic claims to spread xenophobic ideas and spark conflict. New international initiatives: Journalists should promote a global ethic by developing new international organizations, by initiating 'media training' Programmes and by taking advantage of new interactive forms of communication to strengthen the media system and encourage rational deliberation in the global public sphere.

Why should journalists contemplate an ambitious and still vaguely defined, global ethic? Because journalists work increasingly in a global news environment. Their reports, via satellite or the Internet, reach people around the world and influence the actions of governments, militaries, humanitarian agencies and warring ethnic groups. Their reports help to shape the way that See polling on Canadian attitudes Towards military and security matters by Ipsos-Reid Corp. from September 2001 to Stephen J. Ward draft – please do not quote February 8, 2003 citizens see the world and their place in it. Journalists now report for a large virtual community spread around the globe. The impact of writing or broadcasting or posting a story transcends borders. From an ethical point of view, the distinction between local and non-local stories begins to crumble when news Web sites are accessible from anywhere and everywhere in the world. With this increase in reach and impact come new and more onerous responsibilities. Journalism ethics changes and expands. Journalists now must consider the potential impact of their work on an electronic diaspora of readers and Internet users. If quality global media can inform the global community, irresponsible and parochial journalism can help to wreak havoc. Unless reported accurately and with diversity, North American readers may fail to understand the causes of violence in Middle East, or a drought in Africa. Jingoistic reports can portray the denizens of other regions of the world as possible combatants, bloodthirsty lunatics or part of a shadowy, undefined threat. In times of insecurity, the news media can amplify the views of fear-mongering officials who want to stampede populations into joining a call to arms, or to supporting the swift removal of the civil rights for minorities. Not all newsrooms will bear the same responsibility for widening the journalistic ethical viewpoint.

A small newspaper in rural British Columbia will bear less responsibility than major news organizations such as CNN, the BBC, the Canadian Broadcasting Corporation, the major news agencies, leading newspapers and widely accessed Web sites. Moreover, no one can expect realistically that news organizations will completely transcend the perspectives of the country in which the majority of their journalists live. There are strong economic, psychological and cultural forces that keep new organizations focused on specific demographical and geographical audiences. Nevertheless, journalists cannot evade the potential or actual global influence of their work. They should not ignore their contribution to a less tolerant and less enlightened global public sphere. Global journalism ethics requires that such organizations do everything possible to enlarge the perspectives of their newsrooms, their stories and their audiences. In journalism, the term "globalization" does not refer only to the development of global communications and global corporations. The term has an ethical sense, referring to the professional standards that should guide this expanding news media. January 2003.

# 3

# The "Development Media"in Asia

## INTRODUCTION

Neglected by the authors of the four press theories were media in the poorer countries of the world-development media. The press in South Asia may best be described by the concept of development journalism, a concept developed later to supplement the four theories, as the development of communities and giving voice to the underprivileged are major goals of many of the local media in the region.

The development press is popular in the region perhaps because South Asia is the least economically developed region on the continent. More than half of the world's underweight children lived in India, Bangladesh, and Pakistan, said a recent UNICEF report on the global progress on children's issues.

In India, approximately 47% of the under-five population was underweight. The report found that South Asia was the only region that showed a gender bias with regard to child nourishment, with girls more likely to be underweight than boys. The issue of undernourishment points to the problems of poverty, lack of education, and inequality in the region.

In India, communication not only means the transfer of information, but also includes the participation in the society and in the community. The Indian brand of development journalism "focuses on the needs of the poor, the deprived, and the marginalized and emphasizes their effective participation in developmental planning". It motivates the participation of the people and advocates for their interests instead of the views of the policy makers and the planners. And it promotes social justice for all. Journalists in the country believe that the media should not only carry stories about health campaigns like the one against AIDS but also discuss issues that are important for a civil society because only the mass media can reach the vast rural population and give them a voice in debates affecting their lives.

The mass media can also play a crucial role in social progress, as any transitional society will encounter new attitudes, a new mindset, and a new value system. Development journalism enthusiasts in India conducted workshops for social activists to train them to write stories about development issues and workshops for local editors and journalists to familiarize them with realities and issues in local communities. Commercial newspapers also play a role in development journalism.

The Jharkhand-based Prabhat Khabar had been doing development journalism by giving people information on science, information technology, economics, and the comparative financial progress of different states. The paper also conducted "readers'courts,"where readers could interact with journalists and discuss ways of improving the quality of the paper, much like the role of the focus groups in civic or public journalism in the United States.

Radio plays a special role in development journalism in South Asia because of its easy and wide reach in the vast rural areas, where literacy rate is still relatively low. The Indian communications NGO (non-government organization) had been highlighting the importance of community radio in India for over half a decade and called for the extension of community broadcasting.

In India, awards are given to mentors of development journalism for encouraging and nurturing journalists to investigate and write on development issues and for supporting journalism initiatives towards "a common social good". Journalists and media researchers in India and Pakistan criticized some of the mainstream media for their elitist approach, focusing on the prominent while ignoring the plight of the underprivileged in rural communities by following Western news values.

The degree of press freedom in South Asia, however, varies considerably from country to country. Once the largest colony in the world, India is the largest democracy in the world today. Only under Prime Minister Indira Gandhi was an attempt made to curtail press freedom by declaring a political emergency to suspend civil rights.

The government of Narasimha Rao tried to prevent exposés of government corruption under the pretext of protection of privacy. Despite such government attempts at control, the press in India has largely remained private, free, and vibrant. Cushrow R. Irani, editor-in-chief and managing director of The Statesman, said that India's press today is as free as it chooses to be. N. P. Chekkutty, editor of Media Focus, wrote, "The Indian media works in an atmosphere of freedom. We are the purveyors of free thoughts and opinions. We do reflect the freedom of expression the Constitution guarantees to our citizens, and we, therefore, are the epitome of a free, liberal society".

With the freedom it enjoys, the press in India often plays its watchdog role seriously. "Newspapers in India are completely free, as free as the newspapers in the United States, as they are privately owned and free of censorship". It is the newspapers that have exposed corruption in India, though some journalists are attacked for their investigative reporting. The Indian press has always been vigilant about protecting its freedom and aggressive in reporting. Free as it may be as the press in the United States, the Indian press clearly differs from the Western libertarian press system in the perception of its mission. For its social role, the Indian press may be closer to the civic or public journalism in America, which also prescribes an advocacy role for the press. However, in India development journalism represents the aspirations of many journalists, while in America the ethical implications of civic and public journalism are still being debated.

In India, press freedom is guaranteed by the Constitution and the independent court system, which is very similar to the situation in neighboring Pakistan, formerly a part of India before its independence. Behind India, which has a relatively low literacy rate of 65%, Pakistan's literacy rate is even lower at 38%, which limits the growth of its press industry.

There are about 1,330 newspapers in print in Pakistan, but only 1% of the population buys a newspaper. The press in Pakistan is independent of the government and mostly privately owned.

Major public issues are debated in the press, which has become an instrument for change. In Pakistan no law governs the registration of publications. In recent years, Pakistan has been moving Towards greater press freedom, and its press is among the most outspoken in South Asia. In both India and Pakistan when the government tries to crack down on critical press coverage of the government, the courts often strike down government charges in support of press freedom.

There are exceptions to the constitutional guarantees of the freedom of speech and of the press in Pakistan, the most important of which is the "reasonable restrictions imposed by law in the interest of the glory of Islam". The Constitution prohibits the ridicule of Islam, of the armed forces, or of the judiciary.Development journalism is perhaps less developed in Pakistan than in India. Circulation of newspapers in the rural areas of the country is one of the lowest in the world because of the urban orientation of the papers and the cost of subscription in addition to a low literacy rate. The rural market is largely untapped.

The dramatic increase in the number of publications in recent years is not supported with trained staff. Many journalists, especially rural ones, lack the basic skills to cover the complex issues important to their communities. However, electoral politics has increased the importance of rural centres in the emerging democracy of Pakistan. Supporting development journalism, the Pakistan Press Foundation (PPF) was established to help raise the standards of journalism, particularly of the vernacular and regional press, and to promote greater awareness of social and development issues through the media. In 1999, PPF restarted the rural journalists'skills development project.

By 2002 hundreds of Pakistani rural journalists have attended the workshops. The emphasis of the workshops is on improving basic skills of newsgathering and news writing, as participants are given exercises using actual issues, such as violence against women, environmental issues, child labour, bonded labour, and crime rates. The end of monopoly of the electronic media in Pakistan provides new hopes of reaching a rural audience as radio is acknowledged to be a more suitable and affordable means of providing local communities with a voice of their own. It is more interactive and more suitable for community development. In less than six years, between 2000 and 2006, the broadcast sector completely changed the monolithic landscape that existed for about fifty-three years.

But the proliferation of radio stations has created the co-existence of robust liberty and open lawlessness, and commercial interests dominate the airwaves while development journalism still needs time to take hold. Research on the topic, however, is several steps ahead of the media industry.

Development journalism is regarded as an Asian model of journalism, stemming from the dissatisfaction with the Western news values that do not serve the cause of national development. Western news values of timeliness, prominence, proximity, conflict, and the bizarre exclude the ordinary people in the news unless they are involved in accidents, violence, or catastrophes.

Development journalism, on the other hand, should focus on the educational function of the news, stories about social needs, self-help projects, and obstacles to development. In the exploration of the development journalism model by Asian media researchers, the watchdog role of the media was emphasized, and the media were urged to remain vigilant against government involvement.

In Sri Lanka, three newspaper groups dominate the island's newspaper scene - the ANCL, the Upali Newspapers Ltd. and the Wijeya Newspapers Ltd. The ANCL has been under government control since 1973, while the other two are privately owned but have close family connections to political parties. In the broadcasting sector, Sri Lanka was perhaps the first British colony to introduce radio broadcasting a few years after its inauguration in Europe in 1920s. The country liberalized its radio and TV sectors ahead of the rest of Asia.

It permitted the establishment of more commercial radio stations than any other country in the region and put the state-controlled Sri Lanka Broadcasting Corporation under considerable competitive pressure. It also allowed private radio stations to broadcast news and current affairs, unlike some of its neighboring countries.

Efforts at setting up community radio have never stopped in Sri Lanka. Universities in Sri Lanka and UNESCO played host to regional workshops on community radio for participants from South Asian countries. The goal of such workshops was to make community radio a reality in South Asia and encourage-cooperation among community radio advocates in the region. Radio still is a popular medium in South Asia, particularly in rural areas. In Sri Lanka telephone boxes, where a radio station button is installed, allow listeners to contact a station without paying a fee. The system makes it easier for listeners to participate in the Programmes and solve problems in the communities.

The mass media in Sri Lanka also play a role in environmental education. Most people in both urban and rural areas use different media outlets as their primary source of environmental education, especially the print media. Television is the next major source of information for the urban population, while radio for the rural population. The media cover environmental issues in the form of news, editorials, investigative stories, entertainment, and educational Programmes.

Development journalism in the country can have a bigger potential if the government allows even greater participation by the public in media discussions, which is often limited when there is an increase in guerrilla warfare in the country.

It is evident from the above discussions that the degree of press freedom under the development concept varies from country to country, and that is where the controversy with the concept lies. While one scholar describes it as "the pursuit of cultural and informational autonomy"and "support for democracy"among other goals, another scholar criticizes it as "a rationale for autocratic press control"and "guided press".

Where do all the discussions about the press systems in Asia leave us theoretically? When theories encounter major difficulties in serving as a guide to the understanding of the realities they are supposed to describe, new paradigms are needed. So are the criteria of the Freedom House for assessing global press freedom and civil liberties when their rankings fail to reflect changing realities. Obviously, more factors should be taken into consideration than the current criteria.

The Last Rights concluded that the four theories were a "durable"but now "questionable"map and that a "more adequate"map is needed. The book presented inspiring criticism of the four press theories but stopped short of proposing a new paradigm.

## MEDIA DEVELOPMENT ORGANIZATIONS

There exist several organizations that use journalism as a form of media development. Such organizations include Search for Common Ground, BBC World Service Trust, and Journalists for Human Rights.

### CURRENT STATE

In 2008, journalism came under heavy fire. The decline of print newspapers has led to a sharp increase in job cuts for journalists. In 2008 alone, approximately 16,000 journalists were terminated – a budgetary response to declining subscription dollars and the inability to adapt to a free-news-driven society. With advertising revenues taking a harsh rapping from the transitional shift of a subscription-based/advertising model to online ad placements, the discrepancy in advertising revenue is making it difficult for traditional newspapers to survive.

Newspapers are forced to maximize their current staff in a response to declining advertising and circulation revenue. As formerly relied upon revenues shore-up, newspapers are exploring radically new ways of reaching readers. *The New York Times* has partnered with Amazon's Kindle DX to bring current subscribers and Kindle users NYT content. This, along with other social media properties, are ways in which traditional media are fighting to stay relevant in the digital age.

Journalism is a fiercely competitive career area, with many more attracted to the occupation than there are jobs. It is not hard to see why journalism is such an attractive career choice: journalism is a fast-paced, ever-changing sector with constant variety. There are, however, some less attractive features to consider. Journalism is not highly paid when compared to many other graduate careers, working hours can be unsocial, and often vacancies are for a fixed term rather than being permanent posts. An important recent development within the media industry has been the rise of multi-media groups with print, broadcasting and internet interests, and there is consequently a closer relationship between them, with growing opportunities for journalists to move between media.

Over the past year there have been very significant job losses in journalism. Newspapers are employing fewer journalists, many local and regional papers have merged or moved from daily to weekly editions, and there is increasing collaboration between journalists working on different publications within the same group-a recent example is MEN media (part of the Guardian group) who now produce all their local newspapers from one shared newsroom, rather than each paper having its own journalists. These developments have been accentuated by a sharp decline in advertising revenue, on which most newspapers and magazines depend.

**Range of Job in Insector**

Journalists can work in a number of settings, with the most popular being print journalism (newspapers and magazines) and broadcast journalism (radio and television). Journalists also work for internet-based publications, within organisations producing in-house publications, for press agencies, in public relations and in media liaison. skills attributes

Apart from some relevant experience, and evidence of your ability to write, employers will want to see that you are curious, intelligent, passionate, aware, self-reliant, persistent and accurate in what you record. A recent survey of working journalists showed that 90% singled out curiosity as the one indispensable quality, while 98% stressed urgency about delivering information to the public. You would do well to have evidence that these are factors which motivate you. Entrffi Points

**Print Journalism Newspapers**

Many would-be journalists aspire to work on a national paper, although it is common to begin on a local or regional paper before moving to a national. In recent years nationals that have offered trainee positions include The Financial Times, The Daily Telegraph, The Evening Standard, The Times, Trinity Mirror (owners of the Daily Mirror) and the Daily Mail. The Guardian sponsors two students to take a one-year postgraduate course, and also has occasional one-year trainee posts, while The News of the World runs a two-year scholarship scheme, which includes work placements both in the UK and overseas. Some national newspapers may neither recruit annually nor publicise their schemes, so your investigative skills will be required to track the openings down.

Given the cutbacks currently taking place in all nationals, it is likely that fewer such schemes will run in 2009/2010, and any that run will be exceptionally competitive. Regional newspaper groups have also frequently run trainee schemes (examples include the Express and Star group and Newsquest), although such schemes often require candidates to already hold a pre-entry NCTJ (National Council for the Training of Journalists) qualification.

**Print Journalism Magazine Journalism**

Consumer magazines occasionally advertise for trainee journalists, but you can expect few, if any, such opportunities to appear on our online vacancy database, with most publishers advertising in their own publications or on their own websites, advertising in The Guardian (Mondays) and/or Press Gazette, or just recruiting people who have undertaken (usually unpaid) work experience with them first.

The specialist business and trade press recruit actively, and our vacancy database has had several such vacancies in the past year. Some magazines and journals also look for writers with specialist knowledge, for example New Scientist has recruited trainees for six-month internships. Specialist postgraduate courses exist in periodicals journalism.

**Broadcasting Journalism TV and Radio**

The BBC recruits journalists for local and network Radio, as well as TV, although increasingly their journalists are multi-skilled and work in both media. It offers a small number of training positions each year for which competition is intense, with most successful candidates already having significant journalism experience. ITV Regional News and Sky News also run news trainee schemes, and offer work placements to students genuinely committed to news.

### Press Agencies: Journalism Openings

Reuters advertises each year a training scheme for applicants with a demonstrable interest in business and finance, as well as a foreign language. Other Press Agencies usually only recruit experienced journalists or those who have already completed a recognised journalism course.

### Online Journalism

While online journalism is no longer enjoying the phenomenal growth of recent years, it does provide some opportunities. Some post-graduate courses specialising in online journalism are also available, although increasingly more general post-graduate journalism courses include on on-line element. But generally, paid opportunities in this sector are for experienced professionals, or those with a relevant postgraduate qualification and suitable work experience.
eflPerien¢e and Hofi to Get it

Get involved in student media at Oxford. Student publications, including Cherwell and Oxford Student, and the student radio station Oxide provide excellent opportunities to gain relevant experience. Also seek out experience on newspapers, magazines, websites or in the broadcast media during vacations. Getting vacation experience is not easy, and while occasionally opportunities are advertised by us, you should also apply speculatively to the media that interest you.

Above all, most editors look for evidence of sustained interest in and commitment to journalism. The generalisation applies less to those offering required specialist knowledge but will apply almost invariably to the arts graduate looking for a training position, who will particularly need to build up such evidence and experience. Offering articles to local or free newspapers is one way in which you can build up your cuttings file-any employer is going to want to see what you have already had published. Think of ideas for new stories or new angles on familiar stories. Test them out by submitting copy.

### The Biggest Mistake of Journalism Professionalism

Efforts to professionalize journalism began early in the twentieth century as a response to the hyper commercialization of newspapers and the "anything goes" approach to news that emerged in the late nineteenth century as a means of increasing street sales through sensationalism, twisting the truth, and outright lies.

The impetus for journalistic professionalism originated among publishers who wish to counter the trend and it gained support of journalists who saw it as a means of improving their working conditions and social standing. Journalism training and higher education Programmes, professional societies for journalists and editors, and codes of ethics and conduct emerged as part of professionalism. These promoted the core values of accuracy, fairness, completeness, and the pursuit of truth.

These efforts improved industry practices, pushed out the worst journalists and publishers, and creating some trust in the content of news. They also created environments in which advertisers were willing to promote their wares in newspapers and made news organizations more financially sustainable.

It did so in two ways. First, professional journalists were taught and accepted the idea that they should worry about the journalism and leave the business to itself. Second, journalists, along with other employees, decided to seek improvement to their compensation and working conditions through unionization—thus becoming adversaries of management rather than partners in the management of news organizations. Both developments clearly improved journalism and lives of journalists; however, they also separated journalists from business decisions and removed them from any responsibility for the organization's actions and sustainability.

Although some protests over editorial interference, owner avarice, and the corporatization of the news industry were heard in the 20th century, few efforts to alter the situation developed because the enterprises were willing to share a sufficient portion of the riches generated with journalists and because companies employed more journalists, improved newsrooms, built networks of bureaus, and provided resources to undertake interesting reporting activities.

That has all changed. The reporting resources are gone, the networks of bureaus are being dismantled, many enterprises can't afford their own facilities, and journalists are being widely laid off. All of this is being done with little input and influence from journalists and editors precisely because they spent nearly a century denying responsibility and involvement in business decisions.

Today, many journalists are arguing for the creation of new types of news organizations—primarily not-for-profit enterprises—and they are repeating the same mistake. Most are suggesting, or already setting up, organizations in which journalists still have little say on strategy and business matters. Many are content merely with the idea that the new enterprises won't be profit driven. That, however, is not enough.

Journalists need to be equally responsible in ensuring they produce news and information that has value. They need to be responsible for ensuring their new organizations create the revenues and organizational strength needed to carry out high quality journalism. They need to ensure that organizational decisions make the organizations and the journalism offered viable. If journalists continue to deny responsibility for the operation and survival of their news enterprises, it will be impossible to create sustainable news organizations for the future.

## CONSTRUCTING ALTERNATIVE PRESS THEORIES AND MODELS

Both Eastern and Western media researchers have tried to redress the deficiencies of the four-theory model by creating their own models. Three more theoretical concepts-development journalism, democratic-participant media, and the revolutionary media-were developed to accommodate the progress and changes in press systems and to supplement the dominant paradigm's four press categories.

Of the new theoretical concepts, development journalism has caused more controversies because the degree of press freedom varies greatly from society to society, and the very concept may imply a role for the government. The controversy also seems to stem from the fact that the deciding factor in creating the four press theories was the presence or absence of press freedom, which was defined mainly in terms of government control.

Based on such a criterion, how can one type of press system allow vastly different degrees of press freedom in different societies? When a new concept cannot be fit into the established paradigm, it becomes "controversial."Progressive, insightful, and creative as these new theories are, they are mostly supplementary to the established four press theories.

More ambitious efforts were made by Ralph Lowenstein, J. Henry Altschull, John C. Merrill, and Shelton A. Gunaratne, who constructed alternative models reclassifying press systems. Ralph Lowenstein developed a "progressive typology,"according to which, "press systems evolved from authoritarian to libertarian, to social libertarian or social centralist, and then to a big futuristic question mark".

This typology seems to have the same tendency as the established four theories of basing its discussions mainly on the development paths of Western press systems, which makes it less relevant to the evolution of press systems elsewhere in the world. J. Henry Altschull proposed three basic media models - market, Marxist, and developing. To make the concepts value free, Altschull described them as market, communitarian, and advancing. In trying to reclassify media systems, Altschull brought in the element of culture and belief systems.

He explained that the market system emphasized the "individual"while the communitarian system focused on the "communal life"or the "collective."Altschull also analysed the role of the media - preserving status quo under both market and communitarian models and advocating change under the advancing model. He explained that there were variations within each model, giving the classification much flexibility.

With the exception of the advancing model describing press systems in the South, Altschull's models were also based mainly on the analysis of Western media systems even though he classified his models also as East, West, and South, where East refers to Marxism and the former Soviet communist bloc in Eastern Europe rather than to Asia.

The only Eastern society mentioned in the analysis was Japan. Altschull explained that despite the variations within the market model, the basic belief systems - hostility to a communitarian belief system - remain intact. "Discord notwithstanding, the broad sweep of the first movement of the symphony is heard throughout the industrialized capitalist world, in Japan as in Denmark and Canada".

Despite Western influence, the Japanese society, steeped in Asian culture and Confucian traditions, has no such hostility.

As discussed earlier in this chapter, the press club system in Japan dictates communal Behaviour within the industry by discouraging competition and scoops and encouraging collective reporting. A mixture of the East and the West, Japan proves to be a difficult case to be classified.

John C. Merrill's circular model shows that individualistic press systems gravitate Towards libertarianism and more collectivistic systems are at the authoritarian end. Merrill said, "... the basic model is a simple spectrum, with authoritarianism at one end and libertarianism at the other. All press systems fall somewhere along this continuum".

Merrill's model resembles Altschull's models without the "advancing"or "South"element. Men-ill's model has the merit of built-in flexibility. The classification of a press system depends on in which direction the system gravitates. But it is still difficult to place Japan on Merrill's model. The Japanese press is mostly free from government control, but it is not individualistic. The press club system emphasizes collective action, but it cannot be described as authoritarian.

The models proposed by Altschull and Merrill represented major improvements over the four-theory model - AltschulPs model moved away from the exclusive emphasis on government control, and Men-ill's model had the merit of built-in flexibility to accommodate different types of press systems and changes within those systems.

Despite Men-ill's inclusion of the communitarian factor, the two models still seem to largely rely on Western philosophies, scholarship, and examples of Western media performances. Jiafei Yin (2003) called for the construction of a new model, which would be based on a broader foundation of both Western and Eastern philosophies and cultural influences, but did not produce an actual model.

Shelton A. Gunaratne brought in both Eastern and Western philosophical, religious, and cultural traditions in building his model-The Dao of the Press. There are two parts to Gunaratne's model: one part is the libertarian-authoritarian (L-A) continuum with varying shades of social responsibility across the continuum, and the other part is a centre-semiperiphery-periphery world system with individuals and groups, nation-states, and the world system at different levels.

And all the three levels "autopoietically adjust the degree of free expression"along the L-A continuum. Gunaratne's model emphasizes both

Eastern and Western cultural values in the definitions and interpretations of the term "social responsibility,"giving the model much needed flexibility in accommodating different shades of social responsibility found in world cultures.

Merrill also addressed the relativity of the concept of responsibility among societies and even within a society. Similar to many of the previous press theories and models, Gunaratne's L-A continuum also focuses on the libertarian-authoritarian dichotomy, reflecting Western emphasis on freedom and liberty.

With the rich heritage of Asian philosophies and cultures, can a new model reflect diverse global cultural values and describe and explain press systems around the world without bias either from the West or the East?

After all, different cultures prioritize values differently. Therefore, press theories that are supposed to address global press systems should have a wider base to reflect a broader, more balanced global view. With adequate attention to factors such as world history, global cultures, and economic pressure, the problems inherent in the four established theories because of the authors'Western bias and their sole focus on governmental influences can be addressed.For a new paradigm of press theories, the optimal balance between specificity and universality should also be considered. The four theories of the press have the beauty and elegance of a very simple but clear structure - four categories under a dichotomy, which aimed to describe and explain press systems in the whole world.

Conveniently general as they are, the four or five theories have difficulties in providing a reliable guide to the global press systems. The universality of the theories is limited. However, if categories are too specific and accurate in describing particular press systems, there may be too many categories for the model to be an effective guide.

One other important factor that needs to be paid attention to in building a more reliable press model is that the model should be dynamic so that it can accommodate the changes in the press systems around the world. Obviously, press systems in the new democracies in Eastern Europe are very different from the press systems in the West even though they all operate under democratic systems now.

The press systems in the new democracies in Asia, such as Indonesia, Cambodia, the Philippines, Taiwan, and South Korea, vary from those in Eastern Europe despite the fact that they are all new democracies and share some similarities. And the press system in China today cannot be compared with the Chinese press system two decades ago, or the press system in North Korea. It would defeat the purpose of having models if every time any changes occur, new models have to be created.

## A DICHOTOMY OF VALUES, EAST AND WEST

A new paradigm of press theories requires new ways of thinking in order to broaden the foundation. In this section, an examination is conducted of the dominant Eastern and Western cultural values, which are by no means exclusive to either the East or the West but rather reflect the quintessence of each.

To summarize Asian, or more particularly the Confucian, culture, leading Confucian scholar Tu Wei-ming said: "Industrial East Asia, under the influence of Confucian culture, seems to have developed a different kind of modern civilization, less adversarial, less individualistic, and less self-interested. One sees there the coexistence of market economy and government leadership, democratic parity with meritocracy and individual initiatives with group orientation."

## THE INDIVIDUAL VERSUS THE STATE AND FAMILY (THE GROUP)

Western libertarian philosophy values the independence and rights of each individual. John Stuart Mill's On Liberty spelled out classic liberal individualism-it "set out the limits to the legitimate interference of collective opinion with individual independence". Mill wrote that the only warranted interference with the liberty of an individual is for mankind's self-protection, that is, to prevent harm to others, and that no power should be exercised over an individual for his own good. "Over himself, over his own body and mind, the individual is sovereign."

The Confucian thought, however, focuses on the state and the family. Confucius believed that only when the state and families are strong can the well-being of individuals be guaranteed. In the equation of the state, family, and individuals in Confucian societies, individuals are often encouraged and expected to sacrifice their own rights and interests for the sake of the state and family if contradictions should arise, which is in sharp contrast to Mill's belief that the individual is sovereign.

In Confucian societies, the state is sovereign. In Western culture, individualism is extolled, but in Eastern culture, people are taught to think about "us." In the West, ideal societies are composed of free individuals while in Confucian societies the individual "is not viewed as an isolated individual but as a centre of relationships".

The Chinese tradition has largely been influenced by a Confucian-based relational and social definition of person instead of by any concept of discrete individuality. "Under the sway of this relational understanding of human being, the mutuality and interdependence of personal, familial, societal, and political realization in the classical Chinese model can and has been generally conceded."

## FREEDOM AND RIGHTS VERSUS RESPONSIBILITY

John Locke, an early libertarian, believes that freedom is essential to the full development of a human being. Merrill summarized Locke's philosophy as

"Each person has a natural right to be free and not to be subjected to the will of another." Freedom, for Locke, is a "natural" right. "Besides being bound by natural law, humans possess natural rights, in particular the right to life, self-defence, and freedom. They have also duties; in particular, the duty not to give away their rights". The Enlightenment in eighteenth century Europe led to the rise of classical liberalism and capitalism. It also led to the French and American revolutions, which uprooted the power of religion and the aristocracy in France and heavily influenced the most distinguished leaders of the American Revolution-Jefferson, Washington, Franklin, and Paine.

"The language of natural law, of inherent freedoms, of self-determination, which seeped so deeply into the American grain, was the language of the Enlightenment..". "Give me liberty or give me death." Patrick Henry's rallying call meant that there was no compromise over liberty-to be free is the precondition to live.

In the East, the emphasis is on being responsible and loyal rather than on being free. Western libertarian philosophers' focus of attention falls on the welfare of the individual, so it is only logical that these philosophers advocate that these individuals should be equal and free to pursue what they want. Confucian thought lays emphasis on the group; hence, there is the concern of being responsible and loyal to the group. In his research, Tu pointed out the Asian focus on the ethic of service and obligation.

## THE "COMMUNIST PRESS" IN ASIA

Today's Asia hosts the majority of the world's remaining communist countries - China, Vietnam, Laos, and North Korea. Trying to understand the press systems in these countries using the Soviet communist press theory as a guide would be misleading. The communist press theory was based on the model of the Soviet press system, which can't satisfactorily describe the varied press systems in these remaining communist countries today, especially the Chinese press system after more than twenty years of sweeping economic liberalization and opening to the outside world.

The Freedom House rated China 7 for political rights and 7 for civil liberties, not free for 1997-98 (on a scale of one to seven with one being most free and 5.5+ being not free), the same ratings for 1972-73, which meant that for the twenty-five years in between, political rights and civil liberties in the Chinese society remained the same. For its 2005 survey on press freedom, it ranked China the 177th out of a total of 197 countries studied. The Freedom House rating was in sharp contrast to the 1998 U.S. State Department report, which stated that Chinese citizens benefited from "(h)igher disposable income, looser economic control, greater freedom of movement, increased access to outside sources of information, greater room for individual choice, and more diversity in cultural life". Emmons wrote that, "There are those who believe that the media and freedom of speech, in general, never have been as uninhibited as they are today...". Emmons cited in his paper, "Surprisingly, the average Chinese citizen enjoys significantly more personal freedom today than ever before".

When China is undergoing economic reforms, what exactly does "media reform"mean? It meant the public's right to know according to late premier Zhao Ziyang; it meant commercializing Chinese media and building a stronger media industry according to late reform architect Deng Xiaoping; and it means the relevance of the media to the people according to current Chinese leader Hu Jintao. Reforms bring choices, and freedom means having choices. Since the reform started, China's media outlets proliferated. Today China has around 2,000 newspapers, more than 9,000 magazines, 1,000 radio stations, and 200 TV stations broadcasting 2,900 channels. The choices and competition on the media market today stand in sharp contrast to the one voice on the media scene in the past when every city had only one Party paper. Choices, instead of one voice, symbolize the major changes Chinese media consumers have experienced.

Introducing the profit motive, which is absent from the Soviet press model, into the media sector was another reform measure that caused sweeping changes to the industry-it changed the nature of the media in China. Economic reform of the media in China began almost as early as the overall economic reform. And media commercialization becomes an important part of the development of the market economy as the government has adopted a policy of gradually cutting subsidies and encouraging commercialized financing. Advertising, the capitalist genie, has returned to the world of communist media. To meet the new challenge, the press, including the ones directly under the control of the Party, is becoming increasingly commercialized. Even the official Xinhua news agency and the Party paper, People's Daily, are diversifying their product line to increase profits.

To be competitive on a booming media market, where the number of journalists has doubled in twenty years, media in China have to appeal to the readers, some of them by resorting to sensationalism. To speed up the reform, the government announced in June 2003 that it would end subsidies to all the newspapers in China except three papers and one journal, and all the publications in China had to sever their ties to government departments and stop mandatory subscriptions. Those titles earning less than 50% of their revenues through voluntarily paid subscriptions had to be shut down. By November that year, a total of 1,452 Party and government newspapers had been affected, 673 of which had been suspended from publication.

The overhaul of the Chinese press system has substantially changed the economic and administrative relationships between the government and the press. From then on, the press has been financially independent of the government, even though the state remains the owner of the press. The biggest challenge facing Chinese editors today is to strike the right balance between being politically correct and economically viable.

In fact, one of the major problems hampering the development of the Chinese press today is the low ethical standards held by some local and commercial papers. Hunan TV, a challenging rival of China Central TV (CCTV), developed a huge following with a series on an orphaned woman looking for her biological parents. In its reporting, the network turned an old rape case into a love story, resulting in being sued. Some media outlets were given warnings and reporters detained for extorting large sums of money from people allegedly involved in wrongdoing.

It is no longer rare in China today that newspapers are exposed for their sensationalism, fabrications, or staged news, which are commonplace in a free press environment but seldom occur under a tightly controlled communist media system. Orthodox communist papers are serious and "clean."

The Soviet press model mostly prescribes a promotional role for the press - the press should be an agitator, an organizer, and propagandist for the socialist cause, but never a watchdog. In the Chinese press today, there is no lack of exposés or negative news, which is a taboo in the rigid communist media model, as bad news is perceived as demoralizing.

Given the rampant corruption among government officials in China, some high-level government officials encouraged the press to play the watchdog role by engaging in more investigations. Zhang Baoming, head of the State Administration for Production Safety, called on the media for more active participation in the investigation of major industrial accidents, almost every one of which, he said, was connected with corruption.

Caijing, a financial magazine, made a name for itself for its investigative reporting of the financial sector. Who would have imagined that the communist press would engage in investigative reporting? Former Chinese Premier Zhu Rongji tried to promote the watchdog role of the media.

Commenting on a popular talk show on China Central Television, "Focal Point"(Jiaodian Fangtan), which routinely exposes official corruption and mismanagement, Zhu praised the programme as "a mirror and watchdog of the government and a supervisor of the government through public opinion". Wu Guanzheng, secretary of the Central Commission for Disciplinary Inspection, also urged the media to play the watchdog role in the national campaign against corruption. He said media publicity was vital to the campaign, and the authorities should listen to "the voice of the media."

The Zhejiang provincial government encouraged the news media to provide tips directly to its inspection department as the government found it effective to follow and prosecute corruption cases exposed in the media. The government even offered rewards of up to 20,000 yuan ($2,500) if the tips were verified and led to prosecution. In contrast, the municipal government of Nanjing was widely criticized for stipulating that all corruption exposés be signed off by the person exposed in the story.

In Qijiang County, Chongqing municipality, hidden cameras were installed to monitor the performance of government officials. The Southern Metropolis Daily and the Beijing News both carried editorials, arguing that the watchdog role of the media would be much more powerful and effective than the hidden cameras, as it is a bottom-up rather than a top-down approach. In many cases, the news media are playing such a vigorous watchdog role that a "Witness Protection Law"is being proposed as investigative reporting invites reprisals. Some news sources were detained, jailed, or sent to labour camps. In one case, an editor was beaten to death by Taizhou city police for an embarrassing exposé.

Attacks against journalists have increased in China in recent years as reporters have become more aggressive in reporting sensitive social issues. At least 100 journalists were physically attacked in 2003. In 2002, the central government was investigating provincial government officials in Jiangxi and Zhejiang provinces for punishing journalists who exposed problems in their jurisdictions. The Soviet communist media did not carry exposés. In China, exposés of high-ranking officials, though allowed, still have to be approved by the government however. One other important feature of the communist press system is the state ownership of the media. The majority of the media outlets in China today are still owned by the state.

However, foreign investment is entering the Chinese media sector, and such investment as mandated by the rules of the World Trade Organization is increasing with the deepening of press reforms. Interest in China among international media groups surged in 2005 after the Chinese government issued rules allowing foreign investment in joint-venture television, radio, and film production companies. News Corporation, Viacom, and Sony Pictures were among the big names involved in joint ventures with Chinese media companies. The current policy stipulates that investors are denied decision-making power in the media outlets'editorial content. But in practice, the situation is getting murky. The editorial staff of the China International Business, a monthly economic review, gets its salaries from Ringier AG of Switzerland. Such business arrangements are not rare. Many foreign publishers sign deals in media advertising or consulting but actually help produce content.

Under the Soviet press system, there was tight control of information and very limited access to government information, resulting in more propaganda than information in the news media. In China today despite government control, access to information has gained substantial progress in recent years.

In 2000, the government of Anhui Province took the unprecedented step of issuing a regulation banning its officials from refusing interviews to the press. Other provinces and cities followed suit. Such regulations were unimaginable before the reforms or under the Soviet media model. The central government now has also installed a spokesman system to meet the needs of the press, both national and international.

In Shanghai, a reporter, based on a city ordinance mandating the disclosure of public information, sued the city planning department for repeatedly declining interviews. This was the first such case in China where a reporter sued a government department for violating his rights to reporting.

The reporter complained that city government departments often denied interviews to him. The city ordinance required city departments to disclose information concerning the economy, city management, and public services. Such ordinance was listed as top priority in the legislative plan of the State Council.

It would make disclosure as the principle and non-disclosure as the exception rather than the other way around as in the past. China is opening up. It has opened up its market to the world, including the media market, even though it is only the entertainment media for now. It is not difficult today to find popular foreign consumer magazines on the newsstands in China. International Data Group, a Boston publisher, alone has invested $20 million in China, publishing twenty-eight titles and planning another four. These operations are either in the form of joint ventures or through licensing the titles and content for publication in China.

China is also working on an international media centre with a total floor space of 130,000 square meters, which will serve as an office building for more than 100 foreign media organizations in Beijing. And in 2001, Reuters's Qing Niao Web site, a site for trade information and e-business, made a low-key entry into China. The Soviet communist media model was a closed system. But China has opened up, and it wants to reintegrate itself into the world community. The one medium that provides a public forum for the ordinary Chinese and connects the Chinese people directly with the rest of the world is the Internet, which claims about 137 million users in China by the end of 2006, the second largest in the world after the United States.

China has witnessed the fastest growth of Internet use among countries whose annual per-capita is less than $2,000, and the number of net users is expected to increase by at least 15% annually before 2010. The Internet is breaking through the silence of traditional media by posting stories rejected by official newspapers. With its power of reaching millions of people at the same time, the Internet has directly helped in effecting legislative changes in the country by exposing police brutality, which brought about public outrage on an unprecedented scale and caught the attention of legislators and the government.

The Internet, with its public forums where people can discuss topics shunned by the traditional media, is producing a better informed, more vocal public and a more open society. Inadvertently, it has ushered in a public discourse that has been absent for almost half a century. It also enabled direct communication between ordinary citizens and government officials. The acceptance of the Internet in China itself is one important indicator of the passing of the rigid communist media system in China, as Internet, a revolutionary medium, defies total control. Some media researchers argue that as long as there is government control, the media in China should be categorized as communist media.

It is true that there is still government control of the media in China - there are news topics on which diversity of opinion is not allowed, there are websites that are blocked, and there are newspaper editors that have been fired. However, since the start of the reforms, the changes that are occurring in China have substantially reduced government controls. These changes are happening because of the intention of the government to open up, the new financial independence of the press, the proliferation of media outlets, and the availability of the Internet. Sometimes the sheer size of the country poses a challenge to effective control. For example, when the government could not effectively implement a ban on satellite dishes in 1994, it changed its policy by licensing them instead.

A year later the government also specified permissible Programmes and viewing hours. Foreign affairs used to be an area off limits for public discussions in the media. The advent of the Internet with its convenient online forums has made it a hot topic for public debate. Government control of the press is a universal phenomenon. The issue is the degree of control. In the age of the Internet, total control is out of the question. And in the case of China, that control is being relaxed and challenged from all sides. More recent examples include the suspension and the return of the supplement of a major newspaper in Beijing and the debate over a section of a draft law on managing disasters and accidents.

The weekly "Freezing Point"published by the popular China Youth Daily, which stands out from other newspapers in China for its aggressive reporting and biting commentary, was shut down in late January 2006, and its editors removed to its research department because some government officials were not happy with one article.

The case was widely publicized by the media worldwide. The supplement resumed publication one month later following public outcry against such heavy-handedness against the press, including staff letters protesting the actions and an open letter to top Party officials signed by thirteen prominent scholars and former officials who were contributors to the supplement.

The writers of the open letter included Zhu Houze, a former Central Propaganda Department official; Hu Jiwei, a former editor-in-chief of the People's Daily, and He Weifang, a law professor from Peking University, who said, "The purpose (of the letter) is to change the current incorrect policies on freedom of speech"(f 3), The letter said although not all signatories approved of the article, they all supported Freezing Point's right to publish it.

They quoted Chinese leader Hu Jintao as saying no organization in China has special legal privileges. The letter said that the newspaper suspension was neither legal nor sensible and it violated citizens 'basic rights to speech and freedom of information, which are their constitutional rights.

Another controversy arose over a draft law on emergency management, which included industrial accidents, natural disasters, and health and public security crises. Part of the draft law addressed the news coverage of emergency situations by the media, stipulating that media outlets could face fines between 50,000 yuan (U.S.$6,250) and 100,000 yuan (U.S.$12,500) if they reported the emergency situations without authorization or released fraudulent reports and if such reports led to serious consequences.

The law was drafted following the aftermath of the outbreak of SARS, when health department officials hid the facts from the public, resulting in rampant rumors in the press and in the streets. Government officials said the purpose of the law was to ensure timely release of accurate information by local officials.Opposition to the draft law was loud and clear. A legislator, He Keng, said journalism had its own rules and argued that the watchdog role of the media was not strong enough in China. The New Express, a commercial newspaper published by the Yangcheng Evening News, carried an editorial arguing that the law would diminish the watchdog role of the media, that there was no guarantee that the information released by government departments was accurate and that some "natural disasters"were man-made.

In a column in the outspoken Southern Metropolis Daily, Changping pointed out that in the case of coal mine disasters, often local officials and mine owners colluded with each other in covering up the facts of accidents as both profited from the mines. In such situations, how could the media wait for the local government to release accurate information? Changping argued. One often ignored issue is the self-censorship in the newsrooms in China, which sometimes applies tighter control than the government does for the interests of the media organization or the management. For a lack of laws and regulations, the new media are trying to police themselves.

Nineteen websites jointly issued a set of self-disciplinary rules against bloggers'personal attacks, fabricated stories, plagiarism, and pornographic and violent content. Hosts of the sites said they were ready to delete such materials once they appear on their sites. Min Dahong, a journalism professor said that many big websites in the world have explicit written rules on deleting or editing users'messages that they regard as abusive, defamatory, offensive, obscene, or in violation of a specific law.

Ultimately how much freedom or control the Chinese media will experience is not only up to the government; it is also up to the editors and reporters of the media, especially those leading media organizations in Beijing, as to how far they will push. So far the most vigorous push comes mainly from local media outside of Beijing.

Following China's example, Vietnam started its own economic reforms in 1986 and "remains wedded to the Chinese model of reform". Its press system is also undergoing similar changes. The liberal economic reforms eroded the pervasive authority of the Party. As a result, "Vietnam is no longer as tightly controlled as it used to be although it does remain an authoritarian one-party system". Facing a rise in corruption like China, the government encouraged the press to expose corruption, made new laws to facilitate news gathering, and warned against officials trying to obstruct journalists.

Even though strict censorship still exists in Vietnam today, meaningful independent journalism is possible on certain occasions. There are instances where journalists successfully challenged the police and the court in violating reporters'rights in newsgathering and forced the police and the court to back down.

"In terms of freedom, the press here in Vietnam has been getting better and more aggressive". One editor at Lao Dong (Labour), Nguyen Due Tuan, said, "There is no question we have more freedom today.... Now, reporters like to see how far they can push and still get their stories published".

Similar to the situation in China, editors in Vietnam now have more discretion in deciding the content of their publications. The press in Vietnam is surprisingly lively in terms of the types of newspapers and magazines. Since the reforms, both the quantity and quality of the press have improved.

The press today is becoming more information oriented than ideology dependent, as the importance of information is generally recognized in a more market-oriented economy. The Internet entered Vietnam in 1997. By the end of 2006, the number of Internet users had reached 14.5 million.

Despite government announcement that access to the Internet would be unrestricted, the Freedom House reported that in 2004 the Vietnamese government suppressed dissent on the Internet with new guidelines of government control and censorship, including a permanent monitoring system aimed at the country's privately run Internet cafes.

Despite the reforms, the majority of the media outlets in Vietnam are still state-owned. But the government has permitted some form of private ownership of periodicals, a bolder step than China's. The condition for ownership is that the publication should be a joint undertaking between the owners and the relevant state agency. An example is the Vietnam Investment Review, the first foreign-owned, Western-style periodical in the country. The government also abolished direct subsidies to the press even though some form of state funding is still continuing. As a result, the press is forced to become more commercialized, and the survival of the press is subject to market forces, which seems to dictate a success formula of tabloid journalism. Some papers publish uncommon crime stories gathered from police records, all in the name of exposing social problems. In the pursuit of profits, newspapers in Vietnam start to face criticisms about their low ethical standards. Some journalists in Vietnam now claim that they are having more debates on "responsibilities and morals of journalists"than on press freedom.

Early in the reform, the sensationalism and the increasingly aggressive investigative reporting alarmed the Party leaders, who worried that the state was losing control of information flow and wanted to rein in this threatening trend. The government began clamping down on the press in 1989 and tightened control of the media by establishing a new press department aimed at monitoring and controlling press coverage about security matters, issuing new rules regarding passing information to foreign news organizations, amending the 1990 press law, requiring compensation if news coverage leads to losses to the business interests of organizations or individuals.

The government also reminded the press to champion the fight against corruption and other social evils instead of seeking profits alone, but questioning Party rule remains expressly prohibited. The Vietnamese leaders are still ambivalent about the degree of control and the liberal reforms, which help with the country's economic development but threaten the power and control of the Party. North Korea may be the only communist country in Asia left with a press that could still fit the Soviet media model. There has been very little change in the country despite the fact that other remaining communist countries in Asia are undergoing major reforms to open up and revive their economies. Perhaps because of the poor performance of its economy, the widespread and chronic famine, and tremendous external pressure to change, the government is exercising strict control of information flow across its borders.

As a result, information about the country is scarce even with CNN's 2006 documentary, which was shot inside the country with a hidden cell-phone camera. North Korea is the most censored country in the world. Its people experience the world's deepest information void, and the country has no independent journalists.

The main role ascribed to the press is that of spreading the viewpoint of the government. All newspapers and broadcasting stations are under direct government control, and all news is positive. According to the 2003 annual report by Reporters Without Borders, all the news media in the country focused on the personality cult of Kim Jong Il.

The report said three subjects dominated the coverage in the print media: the personality of Kim Jong II, praise of the army, and criticism of the country's foes, especially South Korea, the United States, and Japan. In a story, the official Korean Central News Agency reported that Kim Jong Il was so beloved that after a deadly munitions train explosion in a populated area, people ran into buildings to save the ubiquitous portraits of the "Dear Leader" before they rescued their own family members. Nothing was mentioned in the news media about the malnutrition among children and urban populations or the failure of the government's "self-reliance"policy. In the leading Party paper, the Rodong Shinmun, commentaries carry greater weight than news stories, and reporters do not compete for scoops among themselves, who are given instructions from the Central Party Committee's propaganda and agitation department on what to cover and in how many pages.

Anyone disobeying the instructions is severely punished. Reporters may be jailed for a commentary that deviates from the Party line. Harassment, psychological pressure, intimidation, and round-the-clock surveillance are routine. The North Korean newspapers do not carry any advertisements except a handful of government notices. For the mass media in North Korea, there is neither private ownership nor market competition. North Korea's revised 1998 constitution guarantees citizens'rights of freedom of speech, of the press, of assembly, demonstration, and association.

But the government prohibits the exercise of these rights in practice. There are strict controls to prevent access to any kind of news coming from abroad. Radios sold in North Korea can receive only domestic programming. Radios obtained from abroad must be altered to work in a similar manner. The national news agency has Internet sites hosted in Japan. Direct access to the web is limited to the privileged few ("North Korea,"2003). And to prevent Western influence, very few journalists in North Korea receive training in the West.

It is also hard for the foreign media to do reporting inside the country as they are all portrayed by the regime as liars seeking to destabilize the government. Foreign journalists visiting North Korea have to be on guided tours. However, in 2006, the Associated Press became the first Western news organization to have a permanent bureau in the country. AP Television News's full-time office in Pyongyang operates in association with the country's state-run broadcaster and is staffed mainly by local reporters. With the increase in international trade, even North Koreans have started to have greater contact with foreigners, which might result in greater access to information from the outside world.

The press in North Korea seems to be the prototype of the communist press, but it does not represent the trend where the press in other communist countries is heading. It is misleading to put the press systems in China, Vietnam, and North Korea in the same category. To do so, media researchers have to disregard the sweeping changes in the Chinese and Vietnamese press.

## INDIVIDUAL FREEDOM AND HAPPINESS VERSUS PUBLIC GOOD AND RESPONSIBILITY

Mill, a defender of personal and political liberty, said in his On Liberty:

"The only freedom which deserves the name, is that of pursuing our own good in our own way, so long as we do not attempt to deprive others of theirs, or impede their efforts to obtain it".

Mill's "sovereign self" echoed the U.S. Bill of Rights and the Declaration of Independence in upholding individual freedom and rights and the pursuit of happiness, not individual or collective responsibility.

So when President Kennedy demanded, "Ask not what your country can do for you; ask what you can do for your country," it was refreshing to the American youth as their civic education focused mostly on the value of equality, freedom, and rights embedded in the Constitution when they grew up. Confucius teachings emphasize a strong commitment to the world and encourage sacrifice of self-interest to be ethical. The Confucian concept of the ethical links up directly with the public good. And Confucius believes "self-realization is fundamentally a social undertaking, therefore, 'selfish' concerns are to be rejected as an impediment to one's own growth and self-realization".

## THE ROLE OF THE MASS MEDIA IN NATIONAL DEVELOPMENT

Herman and Chomsky (1988) attribute to the mass media the role of inculcating individuals 'with values, beliefs and codes of conduct that will integrate them into the institutional structures of the large society.' They postulate that in societies which are characterized by major social conflicts and concentration of wealth, the mass media can fulfil this role only by systematic propaganda.

They continue: 'In countries where the levers of power are in the hands of a state bureaucracy, the monopolistic control over the media, often supplemented by official censorship, makes it clear that the media serve the ends of the dominant elite'. Herman and Chomsky's propaganda model focuses on inequality of wealth and power and its effects on mass media interests and choices, and how these 'are able to filter out the news fit to print, marginalize dissent, and allow the government and dominant private interests to get their message across to the public'.

Riegel (1977) cautions that 'the objective of governments in communications is not to promote 'world-mindedness' or education in the sense of increased understanding and appreciations of the ideas and cultures of other nations and peoples in a world community, but rather to preserve and strengthen the sense of nationality and the national status quo.' Expropriation of the media of mass communication was a major feature of the newly-independent countries in Africa, even though these countries had neither a sense of nationhood to preserve, nor national institutional structures to which the mass media could integrate citizens. The disparate peoples in former European colonies that gained independence as African nations with full status at the United Nations had no consensual values in culture, politics, or economics, nor was there agreement on the mode of political leadership and how those leaders were to be chosen and changed. As Riegel (supra) says, 'Bringing emerging nations into the twentieth century in communications usually translated into providing governments with tools to combat differences and tribal and other fragmenting loyalties for the purpose of promoting national unity and discipline.

Bluntly stated, this translates into turning nomadic Africans into soldiers'. Discounting Riegel's sarcasm and overstatement, he aptly captures the essence of the problem. Most African countries explicitly stated that it was the role of the mass media to create national unity and foster development. In fact this was deemed so important that many governments became the mass media through nationalization.

Journalists suddenly became civil servants and government spokespeople. Most journalists did not object to this development and actively supported government nationalization in the belief that this was being done for patriotic reasons, and that politicians would play their traditional role of leadership and leave journalist to play theirs of watchdog and sentinel. Some were effusive in their support.

For instance, Tanzanian journalist Ng' wanakilala (1981) argued that what was crucial was whether the media were used for liberation or oppression of the popular masses. He enthused: 'where a government is committed to the development of all the people, media takeover by the government is an act of liberation and emancipation.'

Others such as Kenyan editor and publisher Hilary Ng'weno (1969) were willing to accept a certain amount of limitation of press freedoms associated with democratic societies. He suggested that the media should impose limitations upon themselves rather than have the government impose censorship, and that such action was justified because: 'The challenge to the press in young countries is the challenge of laying down the foundations upon which future freedoms will thrive...

Under some of the conditions (of poverty, illiteracy and disease) in which vast numbers of Asians, Africans and Latin Americans live, it would be sacrilegious to talk about press freedom, for freedom loses marring when human survival is the operative principle upon which a people live... In such countries, the first duty of the press, as indeed fany other institutions or individual, is to encourage greater national unity.'

Some politicians like the late president of Ghana, Kwarne Nkrumah, a former journalist who used his paper to whip up support for his political party 'during the struggle for Ghana's independence, rejected the idea of an independent press. He argued that 'Within the competitive system of capitalism the press cannot function in according with strict regard to facts' (Nkrumah, 1965). Nkrumah believed in activist journalism, insisting that journalistic practice involves choice of topics and arrangements of facts in a way that fits in with the preferences of the owners. He argued that, in privately-owned media, the journalist often 'finds himself rejecting or distorting facts that do not coincide with the outlook and interest of his employer or the medium's advertisers. Under the pressure of competition for advertising revenue, trivialities are blown up, the vulgar emphasized, ethics forgotten, the important trimmed to the class outlook.

Enmities are fanned and peace is perverted.' Nkrumah believed that a journalist should have high ideals, be a political act visit and party member, and 'His newspaper a collect be organizer, a collective instrument of mobilization and a collective educator, a weapon first and foremost for the overthrow of colonialism and imperialism and to assist total African independence and unity.

The true African journalist often works for the organ of the political party to which he himself belongs and in whose purpose he believes. He works to serve a society moving in the direction of his aspirations. ' Ng'weno and Nkrumah's arguments remain the two most powerful inspirations and justifications for African's mass media policy. They also provide the utilitarian underpinnings of development journalism as an occupational self-perception and a theory of the press.

In the decade of the 1960s, arguments such as these provided the rationality for government action. Radio and television stations were nationalized where they existed because, after all, they had been mouthpieces of colonial authorities.

The broadcast facilities were required, so the argument went, for the education of the masses, creation of a sense of national identity, and to unify the new nations. In some countries such as Tanzania, for instance, not only was the broadcast system put under the powerful ministry of information, but newspapers were also nationalized and turned over to the ruling party. In others, such as Kenya, only the broadcast networks were nationalized and made a part of government bureaucracy; some independent (foreign-owned) newspapers remained.

But many governments or the political parties in power established their own newspapers as well. Kenya's first Minister for Information and Broadcasting, Rarnogi Achieng Oneko, justified government involvement in newspaper publication on egalitarian grounds. He said the government would establish rural newspapers because 'commercial newspapers aim primarily at making profits, so they are not likely to undertake the publication of newspapers for small linguistic groups' (quoted in Mytton, 1983).

Oneko's reasoning makes sound social policy and business sense. But it should also be borne in mind that the political strengths of a vast majority of African politicians are in their rural homes where they return every election time for votes, not in the cities where they live. More importantly, the other thing Oneko did not say was that the government aimed to fill the vacuum left by private investors with newspapers through which government officials could talk down to the small linguistic groups. Through UNESCO support, the Kenya government has established a network of rural newspapers which, by and large, have become just another voice of the government whose information officers publish them.

It is hard to argue against the principles behind government participation and control of the mass media in Africa given the fact that in some of these countries the only newspapers present were those established by government, there being no able individuals or private sector interests that could invest in newspapers, leave alone broadcast systems. There were no models for cooperative ownership of mass media, and this has not been encouraged to-date.

As Ng'weno (1969) put it, the need for self-restraint by the mass media in fragile democracies will always be there given the forces at play in their politico-economic arenas. But such arguments ring hollow in an environment of flagrant neglect of responsibility by the people in power.

It is a truism that a cowed and subservient press has served African dictators superbly and no politician or soldier in power would wish to change the status quo. It can no longer be legitimate to urge restraint by journalists who daily witness wanton profligacy from government officials and politicians some of whose only qualification to leadership is that they bombed their way into power. And neither is it legitimate to ask the media to look the other way when some elected leaders betray their vows to defend the constitution and instead tinker with it constantly.

Bagdikian (1983) says that there are moments in history when all established power becomes uneasy. He says such are usually 'times of social change when those in control are operating with an obsolete picture of the world and are alanned at suggestions of flaws in the system they govern. (But) their hostility at such times may be directed at what they most need to recognize.'

Most of the established powers in Africa today are operating with obsolete pictures of the world. Here's the most salient picture they see: constant threats to their governments from armed bandits lurking to seize power on behalf of some hostile foreign government; for this they blame everyone else but their own policies and actions. The rest of the world, on the other hand, sees this: Sudan = hunger, war; Liberia = mass murder, breakdown of civil society; Mozambique and Angola = civil war, communist threat; Kenya = corruption, tribalism; Tanzania = benign neglect of economy, communism; Nigeria = military dictatorship, tribalism; Zaire = corruption, political thuggery, tribalism; and just outright medieval societies in many parts of Africa.

These pictures may be distorted. But consider these other pictures that are not seen: the linkage between the endemic political instability in Third World nations and their poverty; the linkage between poverty and the integration of the global economy; and the linkage between an integrated global economy and the history and perpetuation of empire. By some inexplicable conjuncture of bad luck and sheer circumstance, we are often told, the private interests of local and international political economic elites so merged that Africa's development must now be negotiated with endogenous multilateral and bilateral agencies. This is hardly surprising given the fact that colonial structures in government and the economy remained largely intact at independence 'for stability and continuity.' But where 'revolutionary' governments undertook measures to alter Neo-colonial superstructures, the result was often military take-over of government, drying up of economic aid coupled with a blitz of negative foreign media propaganda and, invariably, very well financed and armed 'liberation' wars. Against this backdrop is a vast majority of African people who feel that the trust which they placed on their politicians had been betrayed.

Thus, lacking popular support, many African governments have fallen; others have resorted to increasingly authoritarian methods to contain all stripes of criticism, often interpreted as dissent Even patriotic journalists like Ng'weno (1969:4) began to grumble that the trouble with most African countries is that 'governments tend to treat themselves as the sole judges of what constitutes the national interest.' Many independent journalists have been hounded out of town, arrested, tortured, or jailed to reveal 'their foreign paymasters.' Many of the remaining journalists have been cowed through the calculus of survival and economic necessity.

Another conjecture of local and international opinion in the 1980s held that there was need for change in Africa. The international media had just 'differed' that millions of people were dying in Ethiopia and Sudan as a result of drought and civil war. Suddenly philanthropists in the west were at hand to marshall aid for the victims. Pressmes for structural changes of African economies were also stepped up and the international media began to report atrocities of African governments and guerrillas engaged in bush combat as though these were new. Yet most African civil wars have been fought since the early 1970s! 'The root process of peaceful change begins with the right of the aggrieved to be heard. Thus presenting the best evidence of the need for change,' says Bagdikian (supra). 'And the voice of the aggrieved, being heard by the general citizenry can create consensus for a remedy. The media are crucial to this process.

It may be argued that in an integrated world such as we have today. The role of the mass media in social change is an international cooperative effort, and that reporting Africa's developmental problems requires resources which its media institutions cannot afford. Moreover, as we have seen, governments are the mass media in many African countries and this does not allow for the necessary criterion that governments require for the development of democratic institutions. Regrettably however, the narrow ideologises of international media would seem to make them unlikely supporters of popular structural and democratic change in Africa. In addition, there is little likelihood that they will shed in a hurry their cold-war approach to news gathering so well documented by Herman and Chomsky (1988) and Aronson (1990).

Moreover, Bagdikian (1990) tells of 'private ministries of information and culture' in western industrial democracies. He says these private ministries are media monopolies, endless mass media chains which manufacture public information as industrial by-products for sale worldwide. We are told that money from such sales finance the purchase of oil, mineral and agricultural concessions throughout the world; the media chains also have interests in the armaments industry and reap hefty profits from fratricidal wars in Africa and the Middle East We are also told by Aronson (1990) that these private ministries of information played a leading role in fuelling the hysteria that came to be known as the cold war through disinformation and propaganda that same cold war which has transfixed Africa in a dance of hunger unto death, and in a macabre ritual of fratricide.

We see many such 'objective' reports about African hunger, African inhumanity to fellow Africans, and African corruption. What we don't see are the causes of such miseries and the linkages between these things and the events that have shaped the destiny of Africa throughout the nineteenth and twentieth centuries. Africa played no active role in the events of this century. It might all together become invisible at 'the end of history' as the rest of the world simply becomes too ashamed to acknowledge its existence. The capitulation of African journalism to local bullying and international calumny is the more regrettable because there is no one that will be sentinel and watchdog of this unhappy continent; no one to amplify 'the voice of the aggrieved:) Hence there are reduced chances for peaceful social change in the continent.

## THE ROLE AND INFLUENCE OF MASS MEDIA

Mass media is communication—whether written, broadcast, or spoken—that reaches a large audience. This includes television, radio, advertising, movies, the Internet, newspapers, magazines, and so forth.

Mass media is a significant force in modern culture, particularly in America. Sociologists refer to this as a mediated culture where media reflects and creates the culture. Communities and individuals are bombarded constantly with messages from a multitude of sources including TV, billboards, and magazines, to name a few. These messages promote not only products, but moods, attitudes, and a sense of what is and is not important. Mass media makes possible the concept of celebrity: without the ability of movies, magazines, and news media to reach across thousands of miles, people could not become famous. In fact, only political and business leaders, as well as the few notorious outlaws, were famous in the past. Only in recent times have actors, singers, and other social elites become celebrities or "stars."The current level of media saturation has not always existed. As recently as the 1960s and 1970s, television, for example, consisted of primarily three networks, public broadcasting, and a few local independent stations. These channels aimed their programming primarily at two-parent, middle-class families. Even so, some middle-class households did not even own a television.

Today, one can find a television in the poorest of homes, and multiple TVs in most middle-class homes. Not only has availability increased, but programming is increasingly diverse with shows aimed to please all ages, incomes, backgrounds, and attitudes. This widespread availability and exposure makes television the primary focus of most mass-media discussions. More recently, the Internet has increased its role exponentially as more businesses and households "sign on." Although TV and the Internet have dominated the mass media, movies and magazines—particularly those lining the aisles at grocery checkout stands—also play a powerful role in culture, as do other forms of media.

What role does mass media play? Legislatures, media executives, local school officials, and sociologists have all debated this controversial question. While opinions vary as to the extent and type of influence the mass media wields, all sides agree that mass media is a permanent part of modern culture. Three main sociological perspectives on the role of media exist: the limited-effects theory, the class-dominant theory, and the culturalist theory.

# 4

# Rise of New Media Communication

## INTRODUCTION

The rise of new media has increased communication between people all over the world and the Internet. It has allowed people to express themselves through blogs, websites, pictures, and other user-generated media.

Flew (2002) stated that as a result of the evolution of new media technologies, globalisation occurs. Globalisation is generally stated as "more than expansion of activities beyond the boundaries of particular nation states". Globalisation shortens the distance between people all over the world by the electronic communication and Cairncross (1998) expresses this great development as the "death of distance". New media "radically break the connection between physical place and social place, making physical location much less significant for our social relationships".

However, the changes in the new media environment create a series of tensions in the concept of "public sphere". According to Ingrid Volkmer, "public sphere" is defined as a process through which public communication becomes restructured and partly disembedded from national political and cultural institutions. This trend of the globalized public sphere is not only as a geographical expansion form a nation to worldwide, but also changes the relationship between the public, the media and state.

"Virtual communities" are being established online and transcend geographical boundaries, eliminating social restrictions. Howard Rheingold (2000) describes these globalised societies as self-defined networks, which resemble what we do in real life. "People in virtual communities use words on screens to exchange pleasantries and argue, engage in intellectual discourse, conduct commerce, make plans, brainstorm, gossip, feud, fall in love, create a little high art and a lot of idle talk". For Sherry Turkle "making the computer into a second self, finding a soul in the machine, can substitute for human relationships". New media has the ability to connect like-minded others worldwide. While this perspective suggests that the technology drives – and therefore is a determining factor – in the process of globalisation, arguments involving technological determinism are generally frowned upon by mainstream media studies. Instead academics focus on the multiplicity of processes by which technology is funded, researched and produced, forming a feedback loop when the technologies are used and often transformed by their users, which then feeds into the process of guiding their future development.

While commentators such as Castells espouse a 'soft determinism' whereby they contend that 'Technology does not determine society. Nor does society script the course of technological change, since many factors, including individual inventiveness and entrpreneurialism, intervene in the process of scientific discovery, technical innovation and social applications, so the final outcome depends on a complex pattern of interaction. Indeed the dilemma of technological determinism is probably a false problem, since technology is society and society cannot be understood without its technological tools.' This however is still distinct from stating that societal changes are instigated by technological development, which recalls the theses of Marshall McLuhan

Manovich and Castells have argued that whereas mass media 'corresponded to the logic of industrial mass society, which values conformity over individuality,' new media follows the logic of the postindustrial or globalised society whereby 'every citizen can construct her own custom lifestyle and select her ideology from a large number of choices. Rather than pushing the same objects to a mass audience, marketing now tries to target each individual separately.'

## THE RISE OF FEDERAL REGULATION

Unlike newer communications technologies, broadcasting was born into an unregulated environment. Wireless communications had existed for almost a quarter of a century, but the first commercial broadcast did not occur until 1920. Consequently, existing law related principally to maritime uses of radio. With the November 2, 1920 transmission of election returns by station KDKA in Pittsburgh, commercial broadcasting began, and along with it, the justification for a whole new field of regulation.

Once initiated, commercial broadcasting grew quickly. By the beginning of 1922, the Department of Commerce had authorised 30 radio stations. That year, however, an additional 600 stations took to the air. In 1922, 1 in every 500 U.S. households was equipped with a radio receiver, but in 4 short years the number rose to 1 in every 6 households. The rapid proliferation of both transmitters and receivers led to a chaotic situation that promoted numerous calls for federal legislation. The growth of broadcasting accelerated in 1926, prompted in part by the decision in United States v. Zenith Corporation that the Secretary of Commerce lacked the authority to assign wavelengths or deny broadcast licenses. Congress responded by passing the Radio Act of 1927—the first attempt at establishing a comprehensive regulatory framework for radio, including broadcasting. The Act created the Federal Radio Commission (FRC) staffed with five commissioners charged with the general authority over radio broadcasting, regulating the medium in ways that would promote the public interest, convenience or necessity. The public interest standard for broadcast regulation—a concept borrowed from the regulation of railroads—was not defined in the Radio Act. Rather, the FRC was mandated to perform various tasks, including classifying radio stations, describing the type of service to be provided, assigning frequencies, making rules to prevent interference, establishing the power and location of transmitters, and establishing coverage areas in a way that maximized the public good. course, this begged the essential question of what constitutes "the public good."

The FRC took the position that the Supreme Court eventually would define the public interest on a case-by-case basis. Nevertheless, the Commission outlined the primary attributes of the public interest in its policy statements and licensing decisions. The Radio Act was superseded by passage of the Communications Act of 1934. In addition to consolidating the government's regulation of radio, the new law created the FCC to succeed the FRC. The Communications Act simply re-codified many of the essential features of the Radio Act, including the public interest standard. Other than a few general directives, as noted later, the Communications Act continued to leave the term public interest undefined. Congress purposefully left the regulatory standard open, with the detailed filled in by the FCC over time.

This had much to do with the fact that radio was a new and complicated technology. The FCC's broad powers were based on the assumption that "Congress could neither foresee nor easily comprehend...the highly complex and rapidly expanding nature of communications technology". This approach has not lacked critics. As one court noted, "the Act provides virtually no specifics as to the nature of those public obligations inherent in the pubic interest standard. Some have taken the pragmatic view that the public interest means nothing than what a majority of commissioners say it means at any given point in time. Nevertheless, shortly after the Communications Act was adopted, the Supreme Court ruled that the open-ended public interest approach was sufficiently precise to withstand constitutional scrutiny. In FCC v. Pottsville Broadcasting Co., the Court called the public interest standard "as concrete as the complicated factors for judgement in such a field of delegated authority permit," and labeled the approach "a supple instrument for the exercise of discretion." Despite the lack of a categorical definition of the public interest, various provision of the 1934 Act operationally defined what Congress intended. For example, the 1934 Act directed the FCC to provide, to the extent possible, rapid and efficient communication service; adequate facilities at reasonable charges; provision for national defence and safety of lives and property; and a fair, efficient and equitable distribution of radio service to each of the states and communities. In 1983, Congress added to this list of objectives by adopting a new section establishing "the policy of the United States to encourage the provision of new technologies and services to the public." This new provision created a presumption favouring increased competition in the communications marketplaces.

The reliance on competition in the communications marketplace as a determinant of the pubic interest brought to the surface a notion that had always been implicit in the public interest standard: Media economics help define the public good. Although this is not quite the same as saying "what is good for NBC is good for the nation," one broadcaster summed up the industry by saying "there's been a lot of about money. You guys like to talk about the public interest. To us, it's the same thing." Or, as FCC Commissioner Sherrie Marshall explained to an audience at the 1990 National Association of Broadcasters Convention, there is often a "harmonic convergence" between the public interest and a given applicant's private interest. Indeed, economic issues permeate virtually every category of FCC decision making. Under the 1934 Act, the Commission was responsible for allocating radio spectrum to various services, assigning licenses to competing parties, and otherwise managing the usage of the assigned frequencies. It is essential that the agency take into account economic factors when choosing which service should receive an allocation of increasingly scarce and valuable spectrum. Similarly, the marketplace phenomena can be important when deciding which applicant should receive a grant of a federal radio license. Moreover, regulatory choices, once made, are not necessarily permanent. Economic conditions often determine the shape of the pubic interest.

## ECONOMICS AND CHANGING REGULATIONS

The changing fortune of AM and FM radio provide a clear example of how market adjustments result in regulatory changes. Edwin Armstrong invented FM radio in the 1930s as a way of overcoming interference problems associated with AM service. FM (frequency modulation) is a means of encoding information on a carrier wave by varying the frequency. AM(amplitude modulation) encodes information by varying the strength of the carrier signal. AM is more susceptible to interference because outside sources of energy—atmospheric static, electric motors, or other devices—interact with the carrier wave to produce static. FM is not affected by such phenomena because the amplitude of the carrier remains constant and outside energy fluctuations do not affect the frequency. The net result of this technical difference is that FM made possible a system superior to the one that developed during the first decade of American broadcasting.

AM broadcasting currently occupies 535-1705 kHz on the broadcast frequency spectrum and FM occupies 88-108 MHz. After Armstrong secured patents for his FM system in 1933, he was invited to test his invention at RCA's

Empire State Building facilities. Once he proved the superiority of his system, Armstrong believed that his friend David Sarnoff, head of RCA, would use the new technology to revolutionise the radio industry. Although initial test were more successful than even Armstrong expected, RCA was slow at promoting the new system. In fact, Sarnoff opposed allocation of spectrum for FM broadcasting at FCC hearings in 1936. Instead, Sarnoff urged that the spectrum be reserved to test television. The reasons underlying RCA's position were not difficult to understand. Promoting FM service would undermine the company's investment in AM facilities. Moreover, FM was in competition with television for spectrum location and RCA owned television patents.

One historian has noted that "in almost every overt and covert action, it can be seen that RCA was trying to forestall something that would either cut down, or cut out, their operation". The FCC finally allocated spectrum for commercial FM service in 1941. Four years later, however, the Commission moved FM service to another part of the frequency band. Justified as a means of avoiding interference caused by sunspots, the move was supported primarily by AM interests and adopted over the objections of the FCC's engineering staff. In a single order, all existing FM receivers were rendered obsolete. This action, along with several intervening regulatory measures, helped keep FM a second—class radio service for decades. By 1964, FM radio was not in good financial shape.

Many of the existing 1,300FMstations were largely dependent on the revenues of more successful co-owned AM stations for their survival. As a result, the FCC initiated a rulemaking proceeding designed to promote FM as an independent service. This led to a rule prohibiting FM stations from duplicating more than 50 per cent of the programming of co-owned AM stations in the same local area. The regulation was designed to serve two goals. First, it sought to strengthen FM service by forcing the creation of an independent programming service. Second, the Commission believed that a separate programming service would encourage consumers to buy and use FM receivers. Ten years later, the FCC revisited the AM-FM duplication rules because the number of independent FM stations had increased, as had their revenues and the number of FM receivers.

The economic advances of FM service led the Commission to strengthen the non-duplication prohibition. It limited the FM station of an AM/FM combination to not more than 25 per cent duplication of either station in communities of 25,000 population or larger. Further upheavals in the radio marketplaces led to even more profound changes. In 1986, the FCC found that "FM service is now a fully competitive and viable component of the radio industry" and that FM had captured more than 70 per cent of the radio audience. The number of FM stations had tripled between 1964 and 1986, far eclipsing the growth of AM service. Indeed, the FCC determined that "many heretofore profitable AM stations are now experiencing economic difficulties as a result of the shift of listeners to FM stations". After examining the "structure and market conditions that have occurred in the radio industry in recent years" the Commission concluded that "the programme duplication rule no longer appears necessary or desirable". Consequently, it eliminated non-duplication rules because they were no longer necessary to foster independent FM service. The FCC also sought to help the now-ailing AM stations.

In 1991, the FCC suggested that it might re-impose the non-duplication rule as part of a package to save AM radio from economic demise. As part of a comprehensive set of changes, the Commission proposed weeding out marginal AM stations, in part by perhaps depriving stations of their ability to cut programming costs by simulcasting the FM signal of co-owned stations. The FCC subsequently eliminated the duopoly rule in 1994, to allow for an owner to have more than one AM station per market, and raised national ownership caps. With this proposal, the FCC came full circle with regulations originally adopted in 1964—suggesting changes born entirely of the economic state of the industry.

## THE CARROLL DOCTRINE AND RELATED POLICIES

Many times economic considerations force the FCC to choose between applicants for the same broadcast service. The classic statement of this approach was presented in Carroll Broadcasting Co. v. FCC, decided by the United States Court of Appeals for the District of Columbia in 1958. In that case, Carroll Broadcasting Company had opposed the grant of a radio station license in a community 12 miles from Carrollton, GA, the location of the Carroll station. The station licensee alleged that authorisation of another station in such close proximity would impair its ability to serve the public adequately. Although the Supreme Court had established in Federal Communications Commission v. Sanders Brothers Radio Station that economic injury to an existing station was not grounds for denying a new application, Carroll argued its loss would be so significant as to deprive the public of service.

*The Court of Appeals agreed, noting:*

- Whether a station makes $5,000, or $10,000, or $50,000 is a matter in which the public has no interest so long as service is not adversely affected; service may well be improved by competition. But, if the situation in a given area is such that available revenue will not support good service in more than one station, the public interest may well be in the licensing of one rather than two stations. To license two stations where there is revenue for only one may result in no good service at all. So economic injury to an existing station, while not in and of itself a matter or moment, becomes important on the facts when its spells diminution or destruction of service. At that point, the element of injury ceases to be a matter of purely private concern.

This decision forced the FCC to adopt a procedure for assessing the economic harm from its new licensing decisions. Thus, under what became known as the Carroll doctrine, when an existing licensee offered proof of detrimental economic effect from a proposed new broadcasting station, the Commission was required to consider the issue, and, if sufficient evidence was presented, conduct a nearing and make findings on the issue. The petitioner in such cases had to provide sufficient statistical evidence "to enable the Commission to make an informed judgement as to the overall market revenue potential". The element of such a showing typically included information concerning the number of businesses in the area, the total volume of retail sales, other advertising media, and other data regarding the economics of broadcasting in the specific market. As a direct result of the Carroll decision, the FCC was required to reconsider its decision regarding West Georgia Broadcasting Company—the potential competitor to Carroll Broadcasting. After examining the record and weighing the "speculative injury to the public interest," however, the FCC concluded that Carroll had not met its burden of proof on the economic injury issue and granted West Georgia's application. Despite this inauspicious beginning, existing licensees routinely pleaded a Carroll issue when confronted with a new station applicant in its market.

Although such tactics offered little chance of actually preventing competition, the required Commission review served to at least delay and drive up the cost of competition. Indeed, although the FCC applied the Carroll doctrine for a 30-year period, it never once denied a new license on the basis that a new station would result in a net loss of service. In 1960, the Commission initiated a policy—the UHF television impact policy—protected UHF stations from economic loss associated with the licensing of new VHF television stations. This policy was enacted because VHF signals had a technical advantage over UHF signals. In contrast to the Carroll doctrine, the UHF impact policy protected UHF stations as a class, and not just individual stations, and, at least for a time, was applied rigourously by the FCC. Market conditions prompted the FCC to reevaluate both policies in 1988.

The Commission found that changes in the media marketplace undermined whatever validity had ever existed for the economic theories that supported the Carroll doctrine and the UHF impact policy. The numbers of radio and TV stations had more than doubled, and newer communication technologies such as cable television had proliferated. Most importantly, studies indicated that the advertising market was continuing to expand, and that new stations tended to draw their advertisers from new sources rather than take business from existing ones. Given these findings, the Commission concluded that the Carroll doctrine should be eliminated. It thus held "that the underlying premise of the Carroll doctrine, the theory of ruinous competition, *i.e.*, that increased competition in broadcasting can be destructive to the public interest, is not valid in the broadcast field". At the same time, because studies revealed that many UHF stations were now operating at a profit, the Commission also eliminated the UHF impact policy.

## MEDIA AND COMMUNICATION

Communication is the procedure, which we use to exchange information by various methods. And media is the medium or instrument of storing or communicating information. Media and Communication system is different in every country depending on its economy, polity, religion and culture. In communist and totalitarian countries like USSR and China, there were serious limitations on the media. Any criticism about the state was repressed. While in America having Bourgeois, people enjoy great freedom in the sphere of media and communication. Few years ago, before the era of Communication Satellites, the national media, both public and private, was the medium of communication all over the world.

With the advent of communication technologies like Satellite Delivery and ISDN, came the transnational media and brought with it the facilities of local TV, global films, and global information system. In the new democratic states, various media associations have been formed to fight for just and open media laws, defend civil rights of journalists and promote industry reforms. In the wake of the rapid growth and independence of the mass media, there arose the need of some laws and regulations. The legal infrastructure of a country determines freedom of the media to perform its functions. The International regulating agency in the arena of media and communications is the International Telecommunication Union, which is the prime agency of the UNO for information and communication technologies. It governs the areas of radio communication, standardization and development. ITU is situated at Geneva, Switzerland, and it includes one hundred and ninety-one member states and more than seven hundred sector members and associates. It promotes the adoption and implementation of fair media laws for the transition from an autocratic to a democratic society. Every democratic nation has respective laws to regulate the various branches of public media and mass media.

## MEDIA AND COMMUNICATION LAWS IN INDIA

The evolution of the Media and Communication Laws in India has been greatly influenced by the history of British colonization in India. The first Media and Communication Law in India dates back to 1799 when Lord Wellesley passed the Press Regulation. It imposed pre-censorship on the newspaper publishing industry. The Press Act of 1835 annulled all the previous repressive laws on media and communication. Then came the gagging Act on 18th June 1857. It introduced compulsory licensing for the owning or running of printing presses, empowered the government to prohibit the publication or circulation of any newspaper, book or other printed material and banned the publication or dissemination of statements or news stories which had a tendency to cause furor against the government, thereby undermining its authority.

The Press and Registration of Books Act was passed in 1867 and till today this Act is in force. The Vernacular Press Act of 1878 was promulgated by General Lord Litton, which authorized the government to repress the publication of seditious writings and to impose punitive sanctions on printers and publishers failing to conform the law. The Newspapers (incitement to offences) Act was passed in 1908 with the initiation of Lord Minto to prohibit publication deemed to incite rebellion.

## MASS COMMUNICATION

Mass communication is the term used to describe the academic study of the various means by which individuals and entities relay information through mass media to large segments of the population at the same time. It is usually understood to relate to newspaper and magazine publishing, radio, television and film, as these are used both for disseminating news and for advertising.

### FIELD OF STUDY

Mass communication research includes media institutions and processes such as diffusion of information, and media effects such as persuasion or manipulation of public opinion. In the United States, for instance, several university journalism departments evolved into schools or colleges of mass communication or "journalism and mass communication". In addition to studying practical skills of journalism, public relations or advertising, they offer Programmes on "mass communication" or "mass communication research." The latter is often the title given to doctoral studies in such schools, whether the focus of the student's research is journalism practice, history, law or media effects. Departmental structures within such colleges may separate research and instruction in professional or technical aspects of mass communication.

With the increased role of the Internet in delivering news and information, mass communication studies and media organizations tend to focus on the convergence of publishing, broadcasting and digital communication.

The academic mass communication discipline historically differs from media studies and communication studies Programmes with roots in departments of theatre, film or speech, and with more interest in "qualitative," interpretive theory, critical or cultural approaches to communication study. In contrast, many mass communication Programmes historically lean Towards empirical analysis and quantitative research — from statistical content analysis of media messages to survey research, public opinion polling, and experimental research. Interest in "New Media" and "Computer Mediated Communication" is growing much faster than educational institutions can assimilate it. So far, traditional classes and degree Programmes have not been able to accommodate new shifts of the paradigm in communication technologies. Although national standards for the study of interactive media have been present in the U.K. since the mid-nineties, course work in these areas tends to vary significantly from university to university.

Graduates of Mass Communication Programmes work in a variety of fields in traditional news media and publishing, advertising, public relations and research institutes.

Such Programmes are accredited by the Accrediting Council on Education in Journalism and Mass Communication. The Association for Education in Journalism and Mass Communication is the major membership organization for academics in the field, offering regional and national conferences and refereed publications. The International Communication Association and National Communication Association (formerly the Speech Communication Association) include divisions and publications that overlap with those of AEJMC, but AEJMC historically has stronger ties to the mass communication professions in the United States.

**The Terms 'Mass' and 'Communication'**

The term 'mass' denotes great volume, range or extent (of people or production) and reception of messages. The important point about 'mass' is not that a given number of individuals receives the products, but rather that the products are available in principle to a plurality of recipients.

The term 'mass' suggests that the recipients of media products constitute a vast sea of passive, undifferentiated individuals. This is an image associated with some earlier critiques of 'mass culture' and Mass society which generally assumed that the development of mass communication has had a largely negative impact on modern social life, creating a kind of bland and homogeneous culture which entertains individuals without challenging them. However, with the advancement in Media Technology, people are no longer receiving gratification without questioning the grounds on which it is based. Instead, people are engaging themselves more with media products such as computers, cell phones and Internet. These have gradually became vital tools for communications in society today.

The aspect of 'communication' refers to the giving and taking of meaning, the transmission and reception of messages. The word 'communication' is really equated with 'transmission', as viewed by the sender, rather than in the fuller meaning, which includes the notions of response, sharing and interaction. Messages are produced by one set of individuals and transmitted to others who are typically situated in settings that are spatially and temporally remote from the original context of production. Therefore, the term 'communication' in this context masks the social and industrial nature of the media, promoting a tendency to think of them as interpersonal communication. Furthermore, it is known that recipients today do have some capacity to intervene in and contribute to the course and content of the communicative process. They are being both active and creative towards the messages that they are conveyed of. With the complement of the cyberspace supported by the Internet, not only that recipients are participants in a structured process of symbolic transmission, constraints such as time and space are reordered and eliminated.

'Mass communication' can be seen as institutionalized production and generalized diffusion of symbolic goods via the fixation and transmission of information or symbolic content. It is known that the systems of information codification has shifted from analog to digital. This has indeed advanced the communication between individuals. With the existence of Infrared, Bluetooth and Wi-Fi, cell phones are no longer solely a tool for audio transmission. We can transfer photos, music documents or even games and e-mail at any time and anywhere. The development of media technology has indeed advanced the transmission rate and stability of information exchange. Characteristics of Mass Communication Five characteristics of mass communication have been identified by Cambridge University's John Thompson. Firstly, it "comprises both technical and institutional methods of production and distribution". This is evident throughout the history of the media, from print to the Internet, each suitable for commercial utility. Secondly, it involves the "commodification of symbolic forms", as the production of materials relies on its ability to manufacture and sell large quantities of the work. Just as radio stations rely on its time sold to advertisements, newspapers rely for the same reasons on its space. Mass communication's third characteristic is the "separate contexts between the production and reception of information", while the fourth is in its "reach to those 'far removed' in time and space, in comparison to the producers". Mass communication, which involves "information distribution". This is a "one to many" form of communication, whereby products are mass produced and disseminated to a great quantity of audiences.

## GOVERNMENT AND MASS MEDIA: THE PROBLEMS

That this conference on Government Communication and Media Policy has come about is, in part, an indication of a problem between government and mass media. That is not necessarily an unhealthy or unnatural thing in a democracy. But clearly, some kind of resolution is hoped for, at least on the government's side. This is of course a conference convened by the office of Deputy President Thabo Mbeki, who is on record as being a frequent critic of the state of mass media in South Africa, judging it from the standpoint of government objectives in transforming this country. Many others in politics have expressed a similar viewpoint, and the frustrations with the media have increased in proportion to growing frustrations with the slow pace of transformation in society and the implementation of the Reconstruction and Development Programme. Government complaints about the mass media cover both omission and commission. There is unhappiness that government affairs are ignored, underplayed or inadequately reported. There appears to be some substance in this. As Mathatha Tsedu, political editor of The Sowetan, has noted, for instance the parliamentary press corps simply cannot cover all the activities taking place within the legislature. Even apart from staff shortages, existing staffs are very poorly trained. And, as US journalist Joe Pierson (1965), once put it, reporters covering government need:

- The patience of a fly fisherman
- The mathematical genius of Einstein (to interpret budgets and spending).
- A law degree
- Diploma from a Dale Carnegie Course (on how to make friends and influence sources). (Cited in Hage et al, 1983:190).

Such features are hard to find in journalists anywhere, let alone South Africa.

Compounding this problem are the demographics of much South African journalism (and indeed professional life in general). Most media owners are still disproportionately white, most journalists are still disproportionately white, most experts cited in the media are still disproportionately white. Little wonder therefore that there is a lack of sensitivity to different life concerns and experiences in much of the media-in contrast to the new situation in politics. There is escalating change in this unfortunate situation, even though not fast enough for many-including the government.

The media then is vulnerable to criticism of the quality of its coverage. In the light of all this, of the problems of having one section of the community trying to report on concerns alien to their experience, not to mention vast array of extremely complicated and specialist kinds of information, a question arises. Could not government experts themselves, then, do a better job than the journos? Perhaps so. Yet it is also precisely the value of the journalist as an experienced communicator that needs to be fostered, rather than bypassed.

Thus, although officials prefer to see stories in the press on their own terms, there is value in their handing over control to journalists. "It is the responsibility of the reporter... to translate the activities of the agency into pertinent information for the reader." The example is given of reporters having to translate terms like "comprehensive modalities of treatment" into simple English like "a range of methods" in a story on health issues.

To play this role properly, to enhance reporting expertise, requires investment in training and more attractive staff conditions. But the media industry, like many other industries in South Africa, has so far shown itself slow to recognise this-and in my view is unlikely to do so in the short term.

What can be done here? Nothing direct by government, I believe, except perhaps to develop a national training policy with incentives for all forms of industry to upgrade staff competence.

On the other hand, and presenting the media point of view, some of the blame for poor press coverage must also be laid at the door of government as well. Even with existing journalists, government could secure far better coverage in areas where the problems derive from its side. Inefficient and slow press liaison, like unstructured rambling press conferences, press statements issued on Friday afternoons, poor access to political figures by the press-these are all areas about which journalists could talk a lot.

It would also help if government's expectations of the mass media were tempered by knowledge of how the media works. News, by nature, is often negative. This is not because journalists are inherently disagreeable individuals or anti-ANC. It is rather because negative news interests people-not surprisingly seeing that it deals with events that impact on them adversely. Good tidings are a bonus to people's lives: bad news can mean an irrevocable setback. For these reasons, it is more important for the public to hear about corruption in the school feeding schemes, than when the same scheme is running smoothly. And the importance of bad news is that it may at least provoke action to halt a worsening situation, which is often a more urgent priority than simply alerting people to improvements. Negativity deals with subtractions, which in life tend to be more significant than additions. Negative events are also characterised typically by other key ingredients of news: drama and conflict. These are the part of the language of (admittedly Western-style) journalism-a mode of communication to which the public has acquired a taste, and which it will buy (directly or indirectly). Most significantly, drama, conflict and negative journalism has historically held a key place in a democracy. From the point of view of the press, then, government needs to understand and accept these characteristics.

A further point sensitising government to the media is the need to be clear on the distinction between criticism by the press itself, and reportage of public criticisms. To blur the two is to begin to blame the messenger for the message, and to embark on a strategy in which the logic is to deal with the manifest symptom, while ignoring the more profound causes. In addition, a further necessary distinction is between the press's responsibility for what is carried, and the part played by the source of that content. If the RDP sends contradictory signals by saying on the one hand that it is not a pot of gold, and on the other hand presents Presidential projects which suggest that there is money to dish out, the press cannot be blamed for public confusion.

Finally, government would do well to understand why the media operates generally with a libertarian political philosophy which entails an element of adversarial relations with government. This arises, of course, out of an international history, combined here with the special circumstances of fighting the extreme authoritarianism of the apartheid state. The riposte to this might be, and Thabo Mbeki has said as much, that the adversarial attitude is anachronistic today, given that there is a government elected democratically and committed to deepening democracy. There is some truth in this-and yet, worldwide experience admonishes journalists to be sceptical. This is reinforced by their experience on a host of post-election issues (ranging from the Defence Ministry's infamous attempt to block articles on the Directorate of Covert Collection in the Weekly Mail and Guardian in 1994, through to gagging orders given out by the courts as in the Dorrenstein case).

Government officials thus need to understand the roots of the adversarial tendencies in the press, and realise that this does have real foundations. "Democracy," as Adv Mojanku Gumbi has said in a slightly different context, "should not depend on the benign nature of the rulers we have." The significance of all this for government communication? If you understand who you see as your adversary, you find a basis for cooperation even if not partnership.

**USING THE MEDIA**

"Government communication has a basic public relations function: to demonstrate that government is functioning well and deserving of popular support," writes De Wet (1988). In his view, "the fact is that the modern democratic state is necessarily and inescapably the propagandist state." (1988) The aim is the management of public opinion. To this end, governments need a policy of "news media diplomacy", which is the "tactful and artful management of the national and international news media by Government officials through give-and-take processes." (1988). While people may object to De Wet's cynical and reductionist views of the aims and nature of government communication, his remarks on "news media diplomacy" are spot on.

To the extent that a government is in an adversarial relationship with the press, it does of course have the right to fight-hopefully with civilised methods. It can "try to withhold information, have secret meetings, to distort information for its advantage, to have its favourite reporters and reward them in various ways, to deal in disinformation and other propagandistic techniques, to subpoena journalists, and restrict their activities in various ways" (Dennis and Merril, 1991). Not all these methods are quite by "gentlemen's rules", and some could well rebound to government disadvantage.

There are less extreme ways of dealing with the media, of course, though not all are without controversy. For many years, the British prime minister's aides have practised a "lobby system" of twice daily off-the-record selective briefings to the press. The result is content attributed to "sources close to the PM", or "senior Government sources". However, several papers have protested against what they regard as press manipulation, and the system has been boycotted by the Independent, The Guardian and the Scotsman. One good bit of advice to frustrated governments, and given originally to the Apartheid regime, is worth repeating. According to De Wet, "Government should "stop shouting at the news media and start whispering to increase the newsworthiness of that which is to be conveyed". This is certainly the case in the USA.

Certainly, in Western Europe, political leaders and parties are increasingly adopting strategies of sophisticated media management and attempted public opinion control (Blumler et al, 1990). This entails an adaptation to the norms and logic of the media, some of which were touched on above in the discussion of the characteristics of news. Sigal (1973) points out that "officials want to disclose the information they want, when they want, and in the way they want." Success, however, depends on an astute understanding of things from the media point of view.

The danger of government and state officials seeing things purely in adversarial terms is that it can lead to efforts to circumvent the press, and to the blind alley of getting directly involved in the communications business, *i.e.* to bypassing the problem instead of tackling it. It makes sense rather to acknowledge that the media is not adversarial all of the time: sometimes it may even be a friend.

The adversary role, typically described as watchdog, looks for improper conduct. But there is also, at least, the media role of performance monitor-where the verdict is not necessarily negative, and also the role of service provider where simply useful information about government and state is supplied.

In this regard, government can do well to ask how much reactive and how much proactive media liaison it performs. Government may berate the press for a lack of coverage or the prevalence of negative coverage: that is a different question from whether officials are doing the kind of sustained press out reach and liaison required to provide their news to increasingly overstretched (and under trained) journalists? The potential for success from proactive media liaison is high: South Africa resembles the situation in the USA, described by Sigal as being such that "news space is still more readily available to high administration officials than it is to spokesmen of any other organization or institution in society".

Government and state can also gain better coverage in the media by increasing access to officials. Government communication needs a policy definition about the level at which information can be released. Holding briefings or issuing statements is usually the prerogative of senior officials or public information officers. But as Sigal warns, lesser people banned from speaking to the press may resort to anonymous leaks, notwithstanding all manner of controls and surveillance mechanisms. Maximum access may be the more advantage policy for the interests of both government and media. This situation prevails at present with the SA Police Services who allow each police officer to speak to the media (provided he or she takes responsibility for what is said), seems preferable. Such a policy is strengthened when effective internal communication with government and state empowers all levels of officials with an understanding of the issues. One wonders at present how much communication there is with South African civil servants about the RDP, public service and press relations, the Bill of Rights, and so on and whether an audit of this would not be useful research.

It should not be that, as in the USA, officials have to look to the media to tell them "what their boss wants, who has power, and 'who's got the action' ".

Whatever the level of access and openness, to use the media effectively requires training for relevant specialist officials. And this is not just training in efficient operational skills, but in understanding the nature of news and deadlines, and the social value of an independent press even when the relationship is an adversarial one. That means understanding that the media are not free agents, but institutions limited by things like their need to be topical, news values which include impact and drama, the dependence of news on events rather than processes. And it means acknowledging the distinct social functions played by government/state and mass media.

## DIRECTION OF COMMUNICATION

If it's considered formal communications as they occur in traditional military organizations, messages have a "one-way" directional characteristic. In the military organization, the formal communication proceeds from superior to subordinate, and its content is presumably clear because it originates at a higher level of expertise and experience. Military communications also carry the additional assumption that the superior is responsible for making his communication clear and understandable to his subordinates.

This type of organization assumes that there is little need for two-way exchanges between organizational levels except as they are initiated by a higher level. Because messages from superiors are considered to be more important than those from subordinates, the implicit rule is that communication channels, except for prescribed information flows, should not be cluttered by messages from subordinates but should remain open and free for messages moving down the chain of command. "Juniors should be seen and not heard," is still an unwritten, if not explicit, law of military protocol. Vestiges of one-way flows of communication still exist in many formal organizations outside the military, and for many of the same reasons as described above.

Although management recognizes that prescribed information must flow both downward and upward, managers may not always be convinced that two-wayness should be encouraged. For example, to what extent is a subordinate free to communicate to his superior that he understands or does not understand a message?

Is it possible for him to question the superior, ask for clarification, suggest modifications to instructions he has received, or transmit unsolicited messages to his superior, which are not prescribed by the rules? To what extent does the one-way rule of direction affect the efficiency of communication in the organization, in addition to the morale and motivation of subordinates? These are not merely procedural matters but include questions about the organizational climate, pr psychological atmosphere in which communication takes place. Harold Leavitt has suggested a simple experiment that helps answer some of these questions.

À group is assigned the task of re-creating on paper a set of rectangular figures, first as they are described by the leader under one-way conditions, and second as they are described by the leader under two-way conditions. A different configuration of rectangles is used in the second trial. In the one-way trial, the leader's back is turned to the group. He describes the rectangles as he sees them. No one in the group is allowed to ask questions and no one may indicate by any audible or visible sign his understanding or his frustration as he attempts to follow the leader's directions.

In the two-way trial, the leader faces the group. In this case, the group may ask for clarifications on his description of the rectangles and he can not only see but also can feel and respond to the emotional reactions of group members as they try to re-create his instructions on paper. On the basis of a number of experimental trials similar to the one described above, Leavitt formed these conclusions.

- One-way communication is faster than two-way communication.
- Two-way communication is more accurate than one-way communication.
- Receivers are more sure of themselves and make more correct judgements of how right or wrong they are in the two-way system.
- The sender feels psychologically under attack in the two-way system, because his receivers pick up his mistakes and oversights and point them out to him.
- The two-way method is relatively noisier and looks more disorderly. The one-way method, on the other hand, appears neat and efficient to an outside observer.

Thus, if speed is necessary, if a businesslike appearance is important, if a manager does not want his mistakes recognized, and if he wants to protect his power, then one-way communication seems preferable. In contrast, if the manager wants to get his message across, or if he is concerned about his receivers' feeling that they are participating and are making a contribution, the two-way system is better.

**Interpersonal Communication**

Another facet of communication in the organization is the process of face-to-face, interpersonal communication, between individuals. Such communication may take several forms. Messages may be verbal (that is, expressed in words), or they may not involve words at all but consist of gestures, facial expressions, and certain postures ("body language"). Non-verbal messages may even stem from silence.

Managers do not need answers to operate a successful business; they need questions. Answers can come from anyone, anytime, anywhere in the world thanks to the benefits of all the electronic communication tools at our disposal. This has turned the real job of management into determining what it is the business needs to know, along with the who/what/where/when and how of learning it. To effectively solve problems, seize opportunities, and achieve objectives, questions need to be asked by managers—these are the people responsible for the operation of the enterprise as a whole.

Ideally, the meanings sent are the meanings received. This is most often the case when the messages concern something that can be verified objectively. For example, "This piece of pipe fits the threads on the coupling." In this case, the receiver of the message can check the sender's words by actual trial, if necessary. However, when the sender's words describe a feeling or an opinion about something that cannot be checked objectively, meanings can be very unclear.

"This work is too hard" or "Watergate was politically justified" are examples of opinions or feelings that cannot be verified. Thus they are subject to interpretation and hence to distorted meanings. The receiver's background of experience and learning may differ enough from that of the sender to cause significantly different perceptions and evaluations of the topic under discussion.

Non-verbal content always accompanies the verbal content of messages. This is reasonably clear in the case of face-to-face communication. As Virginia Satir has pointed out, people cannot help but communicate symbolically (for example, through their clothing or possessions) or through some form of body language.

In messages that are conveyed by the telephone, a messenger, or a letter, the situation or context in which the message is sent becomes part of its non-verbal content. For example, if the company has been losing money, and in a letter to the production division, the front office orders a reorganization of the shipping and receiving departments, this could be construed to mean that some people were going to lose their jobs — unless it were made explicitly clear that this would not occur.

A number of variables influence the effectiveness of communication. Some are found in the environment in which communication takes place, some in the personalities of the sender and the receiver, and some in the relationship that exists between sender and receiver. These different variables suggest some of the difficulties of communicating with understanding between two people. The sender wants to formulate an idea and communicate it to the receiver. This desire to communicate may arise from his thoughts or feelings or it may have been triggered by something in the environment.

The communication may also be influenced or distorted by the relationship between the sender and the receiver, such as status differences, a staff-line relationship, or a learner-teacher relationship. Whatever its origin, information travels through a series of filters, both in the sender and in the receiver, before the idea can be transmitted and re-created in the receiver's mind.

Physical capacities to see, hear, smell, taste, and touch vary between people, so that the image of reality may be distorted even before the mind goes to work. In addition to physical or sense filters, cognitive filters, or the way in which an individual's mind interprets the world around him, will influence his assumptions and feelings.

These filters will determine what the sender of a message says, how he says it, and with what purpose. Filters are present also in the receiver, creating a double complexity that once led Robert Louis Stevenson to say that human communication is "doubly relative". It takes one person to say something and another to decide what he said.

Physical and cognitive, including semantic filters (which decide the meaning of words) combine to form a part of our memory system that helps us respond to reality. In this sense, March and Simon compare a person to a data processing system. Behaviour results from an interaction between a person's internal state and environmental stimuli. What we have learned through past experience becomes an inventory, or data bank, consisting of values or goals, sets of expectations and preconceptions about the consequences of acting one way or another, and a variety of possible ways of responding to the situation.

This memory system determines what things we will notice and respond to in the environment. At the same time, stimuli in the environment help to determine what parts of the memory system will be activated. Hence, the memory and the environment form an interactive system that causes our Behaviour. As this interactive system responds to new experiences, new learnings occur which feed back into memory and gradually change its content. This process is how people adapt to a changing world.

**Communication Approaches in an Organization**

Informal and Formal Communication are used in an organization. Informal communication: Informal communi-cation, generally associated with interpersonal, horizontal communication, was primarily seen as a potential hindrance to effective organizational performance. This is no longer the case. Informal communication has become more important to ensuring the effective conduct of work in modern organizations. *Top-down approach*: This is also known as downward communication. This approach is used by the Top Level

Management to communicate to the lower levels. This is used to implement policies, gudelines, etc. In this type of organizational communication, distortion of the actual information occurs. This could be made effective by feedbacks.

## Research in Organizational Communication

### Research Methodologies

Historically, organizational communication was driven primarily by quantitative research methodologies. Included in functional organizational communication research are statistical analyses (such as surveys, text indexing, network mapping and Behaviour modeling). In the early 1980s, the interpretive revolution took place in organizational communication.

*In Putnam and Pacanowsky's 1983 text Communication and Organizations*: An Interpretive Approach. they argued for opening up methodological space for qualitative approaches such as narrative analyses, participant-observation, interviewing, rhetoric and textual approaches readings) and philosophic enquiries. During the 1980s and 1990s critical organizational scholarship began to gain prominence with a focus on issues of gender, race, class, and power/ knowledge. In its current state, the study of organizational communication is open methodologically, with research from post-positive, interpretive, critical, postmodern, and discursive paradigms being published regularly.

Organizational communication scholarship appears in a number of communication journals including but not limited to Management Communication Quarterly, Journal of Applied Communication Research, Communication Monographs, Academy of Management Journal, Communication Studies, and Southern Communication Journal.

## Current Research Topics in Organizational Communication

The field of organizational communication has moved from acceptance of mechanistic models (*e.g.*, information moving from a sender to a receiver) to a study of the persistent, hegemonic and taken-for-granted ways in which we not only use communication to accomplish certain tasks within organizational settings (*e.g.*, public speaking) but also how the organizations in which we participate affect us.

These approaches include "postmodern", "critical", "participatory", "feminist", "power/political", "organic", etc. and adds to disciplines as wide-ranging as sociology, philosophy, theology, psychology, business, business administration, institutional management, medicine (health communication), neurology (neural nets), semiotics, anthropology, international relations, and music.

*Currently, some topics of research and theory in the field are:*

- Constitution

- Narrative
- Identity
- Interrelatedness
- Power

Constitution

- How communicative behaviours construct or modify organizing processes or products.
- How the organizations within which we interact affect our communicative behaviours, and through these, our own identities.
- Structures other than organizations which might be constituted through our communicative activity (*e.g.*, markets, cooperatives, tribes, political parties, social movements).
- When does something "become" an organization? When does an organization become (an)other thing(s)? Can one organization "house" another? Is the organization still a useful entity/thing/concept, or has the social/political environment changed so much that what we now call "organization" is so different from the organization of even a few decades ago that it cannot be usefully tagged with the same word—"organization"?

**Narrative**

- How do group members employ narrative to acculturate/initiate/indoctrinate new members?
- Do organizational stories act on different levels? Are different narratives purposively invoked to achieve specific outcomes, or are there specific roles of "organizational storyteller"? If so, are stories told by the storyteller received differently than those told by others in the organization?
- In what ways does the organization attempt to influence storytelling about the organization? under what conditions does the organization appear to be more or less effective in obtaining a desired outcome?
- When these stories conflict with one another or with official rules/policies, how are the conflicts worked out? in situations in which alternative accounts are available, who or how or why are some accepted and others rejected?

**Identity**

- Who do we see ourselves to be, in terms of our organizational affiliations?
- Do communicative behaviours or occurrences in one or more of the organizations in which we participate effect changes in us? To what extent do we consist of the organizations to which we belong?

- Is it possible for individuals to successfully resist organizational identity? what would that look like?
- Do people who define themselves by their work-organizational membership communicate differently within the organizational setting than people who define themselves more by an avocational (non-vocational) set of relationships?
- For example, researchers have studied how human service workers and firefighters use humor at their jobs as a way to affirm their identity in the face of various challenges Tracy, S.J.; K. K. Myers; C. W. Scott. Others have examined the identities of police organizations, prison guards, and professional women workers.

**Interrelatedness of Organizational Experiences**

- How do our communicative interactions in one organizational setting affect our communicative actions in other organizational settings?
- How do the phenomenological experiences of participants in a particular organizational setting effect changes in other areas of their lives?
- When the organizational status of a member is significantly changed (*e.g.*, by promotion or expuls-ion) how are their other organizational memberships affected?
- What kind of future relationship between business and society does organizational communication seem to predict?

**Power**

- How does the use of particular communicative practices within an organizational setting reinforce or alter the various interrelated power relationships within the setting? Are the potential responses of those within or around these organizational settings constrained by factors or processes either within or outside of the organization—(assuming there is an "outside"?
- do taken-for-granted organizational practices work to fortify the dominant hegemonic narrative? Do iDndividuals resist/confront these practices, through what actions/agencies, and to what effects?
- Do status changes in an organization (*e.g.*, promotions, demotions, restructuring, financial/social strata changes) change communicative Behaviour? Are there criteria employed by organizational members to differentiate between "legitimate" (*i.e.*, endorsed by the formal organizational structure) and "illegitimate" (*i.e.*, opposed by or unknown to the formal power structure)? Are behaviours? When are they successful, and what do we even there "pretenders" or "usurpers" who employ these communicativemean by "successful?"

## COMMUNICATION STUDIES

Communication studies is an academic field that deals with processes of communication, commonly defined as the sharing of symbols over distances in space and time. Hence, communication studies encompasses a wide range of topics and contexts ranging from face-to-face conversation to speeches to mass media outlets such as television broadcasting. Communication studies, as a discipline, is also often interested in how audiences interpret information and the political, cultural, economic, and social dimensions of speech and language in context.

The field is institutionalized under many different names at different universities and in various countries, including "communications", "communication studies", "speech communication", "rhetorical studies", "communications science", "media studies", "communication arts", "mass communication", "media ecology," and sometimes even "mediology" although this latter is a different area of study. Communication studies often overlaps with academic programmes in journalism, film and cinema, radio and television, advertising and public relations and performance studies. Recently, institutions have migrated towards the common term of "communication studies" to encapsulate and cohere the vast depth and breadth of the field.

In the United States, the National Communication Associ-ation (NCA) recognizes nine distinct but often overlapping sub-disciplines within the broader communi-cation discipline: Communication and Technology, Critical-Cultural, Health, Intercultural-International, Inter-personal-Small Group, Mass Communication, Organizational, Political, and Rhetorical.

The International Communication Association (ICA) recognizes a much larger and evolving list of sections, including among others Communication History; Commun-ication Law and Policy; Ethnicity and Race in Communication; Feminist Scholarship; Gay, Lesbian, Bisexual and Transgender Studies; Global Communication and Social Change; Informa-tion Systems; Instructional/Developmental Communication; Journalism Studies; Language and Social Interaction; Organizational Communication; Philosophy of Communication; Political Communication; Popular Communication; Public Relations; and Visual Communication Studies.

Communication studies is often considered a part of both the social sciences and the humanities, drawing heavily on fields such as sociology, psychology, anthropology, political science, and economics as well as rhetoric, literary studies, linguistics, and semiotics.

The field can incorporate and overlap with the work of other disciplines as well, however, including engineering, architecture, mathematics, computer science, gender and sexuality studies.

The vast breadth and interdisciplinary nature of commun-ication studies has understandably made it difficult for both students and institutions to place it within the broader educational system. Despite intellectual incoherence, the field attracts and sustains large numbers of students, scholarly journals, professional associations, and lively discussions across the academy for researchers, educators, lawmakers, businesses, and reformers.

Broadly understood, the contemporary study of communication *per se* interfaces and overlaps with areas such as business, organizational development, philosophy, languages, composition, theatre, debate (often called "forensics"), literary criticism, sociology, psychology, history, anthropology, semiotics, international policy, economics and political science, among others. The breadth and the primacy of communication in many areas of life is responsible for the ubiquity of communication studies, as well as for the resulting confusion about what does and does not constitute communication. Ongoing debates rage whether commun-ication studies can best be understood as a discipline, a field, or simply a topic. Most U.S. graduate programmes in Communication today trace their history through speech to ancient rhetoric. Programmes in Communication, Communication Arts or Communication Sciences often include Organizational Communication, Interpersonal Communication, Speech Communication (or Rhetoric), Mass Communication, and sometimes Journalism, Film criticism, Theatre, Political science (*e.g.*, political campaign strategies, public speaking, effects of media on elections), or Radio, Television or Film production.

Graduates of formal communication programmes can be found in a wide range of fields working as university professors, marketing researchers, media editors and designers, speech therapists, journalists, human resources managers, corporate trainers, public relations practitioners, and media managers and consultants in a variety of fields including, media production, life coaching, public speaking, organizational, political campaign/issue management and public policy.

Communication is often recognized as a cornerstone of modern society—it would be hard to conceive of modern life without it. However, communication as an English-language field of study and a subject of social thought took off only in the first part of the twentieth century, and is thus a relatively recent and thus unsettled discovery.

In what is sometimes called the "transmission" view, communication is a process by which messages are sent, transmitted, filtered, and received. At core, the transmission view maps closely onto information theory inspired by Shannon's 1948 "a Mathematical Theory of Communication." A more recent "ritual" view, proposed by the late James W. Carey, holds that communication partakes in central daily rituals that forge meaningful human relationships and communities. While transmission proposes a model of communication as transportation (across space, in one time), the ritual model proposes that meaning can be constituted in repeated media events (across times, in one space). The newspaper, for instance, does not only transmit messages to the reader through text, but reminds and reassures the reader through repeated and meaningful events, such as its morning appearance on the doorstep and a familiar page layout. A fuller conceptualization of communication activity, many scholars contend, lies somewhere between and beyond these two views.

## History, pre-20th Century

Various aspects of communication have long been the subject of human study. In ancient Greece and Rome, the study of rhetoric, the art of oratory and persuasion, was a vital subject for students. One significant ongoing debate was whether one could be an effective speaker in a base cause (Sophists) or whether excellent rhetoric came from the excellence of the orator's character (Socrates, Plato, Cicero). Through the European Middle Ages and Renaissance grammar, rhetoric, and logic constituted the entire trivium, the base of the system of classical learning in Europe.

## History, North America

### 1900s–1920s

Though the study of communication reaches back to antiquity and beyond, early twentieth-century work by Charles Horton Cooley, Walter Lippmann, and John Dewey has been of particular importance for the academic discipline as it stands today in the United States. In his 1909 *Social Organization: a Study of the Larger Mind*, Cooley defines communication as "the mechanism through which human relations exist and develop—all the symbols of the mind, together with the means of conveying them through space and preserving them in time."

This view, which has subsequently been largely marginalized in sociology, gave processes of communication a central and constitutive place in the study of social relations. *Public Opinion*, published in 1922 by Walter Lippmann, couples this view of the constitutive importance of communication with a fear that the rise of new technologies and institutions of mass communication allowed for the manufacture of consent and generated dissonance between what he called 'the world outside and the pictures in our heads' on a scale that made democracy as classically conceived almost impossible to realise. John Dewey's 1927 The Public and its Problems drew on the same view of communications, but coupled it instead with an optimistic progressive and democratic reform agenda, arguing famously "communication can alone create a great community". Cooley, Lippmann, and Dewey capture themes like the central importance of communication in social life, the rise of large and potentially powerful media institutions and the development of new communications technologies in societies undergoing rapid transformation, and questions regarding the relationship between communication, democracy, and community.

All these remain central to the discipline of communication studies. Many of these concerns are also central to the work of writers such as Gabriel Tarde and Theodor W. Adorno, which has been central to the development of communication studies elsewhere. The first decades of the twentieth century also saw the development of parallel currents of cultural criticism that drew less on the social sciences and more on the humanities. Though trained as a sociologist, the work of W. E. B. Du Bois on art and spirituals stands out here.

The study of American public address began during this time frame. In 1925, Herbert A. Wichelns published the essay "The Literary Criticism of Oratory" in the book *Studies in Rhetoric and Public Speaking in Honour of James Albert Winans.* ' Wicheln's essay attempted to "put rhetorical studies on par with literary studies as an area of academic interest and research." Wichelns wrote that oratory should be taken as seriously as literature, and therefore, it should be subject to criticism and analysis. Although the essay is now standard reading in most rhetorical criticism courses, it had little immediate impact on the field of rhetorical studies.

**1930s–1950s**

The institutionalization of communication studies in U.S. higher education and research has often been traced to Columbia University, the University of Chicago, and the University of Illinois Urbana-Champaign, where early pioneers and institutionalizers like Paul F. Lazarsfeld, Harold Lasswell, and Wilbur Schramm worked. The Bureau of Applied Social Research was established in 1944 at Columbia University by Paul F. Lazarsfeld. It was a continuation of the Rockefeller Foundation-funded Radio Project that he had led at various institutions from 1937, which had been at Columbia as the Office of Radio Research since 1939. In its various incarnations, the Radio Project had involved Lazarsfeld himself, and people like Adorno, Hadley Cantril, Gordon Allport, and Frank Stanton (who went on to be president of CBS).

Lazarsfeld and the Bureau mobilized substantial sums for research, and produced, with various co-authors, a series of books and edited volumes that helped define the discipline, such as *Personal Influence* which remains a classic in what is called the 'media effects'-tradition. At Columbia, communications studies have traditionally been closely aligned with sociology, and people like Robert Merton and others from the sociology programme were at times involved. The university did only recently, in the 1990s, establish an actual degree-granting graduate programme in communications, illustrating how much important research on communications continues to take place outside the discipline that carries the name. The Bureau, and Lazarsfeld's research more generally, exemplifies the close relations that have sometimes existed between communication studies and the media industries. From the 1940s and onwards, the University of Chicago was home to several temporary but important committees and commissions on communications, programmes that also educated several leading communication scholars. In contrast to what took place at Columbia, these programmes explicitly claimed the name 'communications' for themselves. The Committee on Communication and Public Opinion, also funded by the Rockefeller Foundation, was staffed with, in addition to Lasswell, people such as Douglas Waples, Samuel A. Stouffer, Louis Wirth, and Herbert Blumer, all of whom held positions elsewhere at the university.

They formed a committee that essentially served as a scholarly and educational extension of the federal government's increasing interest in communications during times of war, and was in particular closely linked to the Office of War Information. The committee is a reminder of connection as important as the Bureau's with the industry, namely the connection between communication studies and government interests and funding.

Chicago later provided an institutional home for The Hutchins Commission on the Freedom of the Press and the Committee on Communication. The latter was a degree-granting programme that counted Elihu Katz, Bernard Berelson, Edward Shils, and David Riesman amongst its faculty, and produced graduates like Herbert J. Gans and Michael Gurevitch. The committee also produced publications like Berelson and Janowitz' *Public Opinion and Communication* and the journal *Studies in Public Communication*. The Institute for Communications Research was founded at the University of Illinois at Urbana-Champaign in 1947 by Wilbur Schramm, who was a key figure in the post-war institutionalization of communication studies in the U.S. Like the various Chicago committees, the Illinois programme claimed the name 'communications' and granted graduate degrees in the subject. Schramm, who, in contrast to the more social science-inspired figures at Columbia and Chicago, had a background in English literature, developed communication studies partly by merging existing programmes in speech communication, rhetoric, and, especially, journalism under the aegis of communication. He also edited a textbook *The Process and Effects of Mass Communication* that helped define the field, partly by claiming the Lazarsfeld, Lasswell, Carl Hovland, and Kurt Lewin as its founding fathers.

He also wrote several other manifestos for the discipline, including *The Science of Human Communication* 1963. Schramm and the Institute moved on to Stanford University in 1955. Many of Schramm's students, such as Everett Rogers, went on to make important contributions of their own.

**1950s–1960s**

From the 1950s onwards, communications studies branched out in several new and often very different directions. Numerous new programmes opened up at various universities, and new journals were established. The work of what has been called 'medium theorists', arguably defined by Harold Innis' (1950)

*Empire and Communications* grew increasingly important, and was popularized by Marshall McLuhan in his *Understanding Media*. This perspective informs the later work of Joshua Meyrowitz.

Two developments in the 1940s shifted the paradigm of communication studies in the 1950s and thereafter towards a more-quantitative orientation, or at least the inescapable need to consider such an orientation. One was cybernetics, as formulated by Norbert Wiener in his *Cybernetics: Or the Control and Communication in the Animal and the Machine*.

The other was information theory, as recast in quantitative terms by Claude E. Shannon and Warren Weaver in their *Mathematical Theory of Communication*. These works were widely appropriated to, and offered for some the prospect of, a general theory of society.

The tradition of critical theory associated with the Frankfurt School was, as in Europe, an important source of influence for many researchers. While done out of sociology departments, the work of Jürgen Habermas, the US-based Leo Löwenthal, Herbert Marcuse, and Siegfried Kracauer, as well as earlier figures like Adorno and Max Horkheimer continued to inform a whole tradition of cultural criticism that often focused both empirically and theoretically on the culture industry. In 1953, to address growing needs in industry, Rensselaer Polytechnic Institute began offering a master of science degree in technical writing. In the 1960s, partly because of the need to represent that the degree incorporated training in oral and audiovisual communication, the degree title became technical communication. It was the brainchild of longtime RPI professor and administrator Jay R. Gould.

**1960s–1970s**

In the 1960s Gould and his colleagues experienced increasing demand for doctoral-level studies in technical and business communication. As result, in 1965 RPI began its Ph.D. programme in communication and rhetoric. This Ph.D. degree programme became a prototype for other technologically oriented Ph.D. communication programmes in the United States and other industrialized countries. The 1960s and 1970s saw the development of cultivation theory, pioneered by George Gerbner at the Annenberg School for Communication at the University of Pennsylvania. This approach shifted emphasis from the short-term effects that had been the central interest of many earlier works on the media, and instead tried to track the effect of exposure to, for instance, television over time on viewers' perceptions of reality.

**1970s–1980s**

Neil Postman founded the media ecology programme at New York University in 1971. Media ecologists draw on a wide range of inspirations in their attempts to study entire media environments in an even broader and more cultural fashion than the work done in the Canadian medium theory tradition. This perspective is the basis of a separate professional association, the Media Ecology Association.In 1972, Maxwell McCombs and Donald Shaw published a path-breaking article that offered an agenda-setting theory of media effects that gave new ways of conceptualizing the short-term media effects that earlier work had generally deemed limited. This approach, organized around additional ideas such as framing, priming, and gatekeeping, has been highly influential, especially in the study of political communication and news coverage.

The 1970s also saw the development of what became known as uses and gratifications research, developed by scholars such as Elihu Katz, Jay G. Blumler, and Michael Gurevitch. Instead of looking at communications processes simply as a one-way flow from senders to receivers, this approach began scrutinizing what audiences get out of communications, what they do with it, why they engage with it—especially with mass media.

**History, Germany**

Communication studies in Germany has a rich hermeneutic heritage in philology, textual interpretation, and historical studies. The post-world war II era, however, has seen the rise of a number of new paradigms. Elisabeth Noelle-Neumann pioneered work on the spiral of silence in a tradition that has been widely influential across the world and has proven to be easily compatible with the dominant paradigms in, for instance, the United States.

In the 1970s, Karl Deutsch came to West Germany, and his cybernetics inspired work has been widely influential there as elsewhere. The work of the Frankfurt School has been a cornerstone of much German work on communication, in addition to Horkheimer, Adorno, and Habermas, figures like Oskar Negt and Alexander Kluge has been important in the development of this strand of thought. An important competing paradigm has been the systems theory developed by Niklas Luhmann and his students, such as Dirk Baecker and others.

Finally, from the 1980s and onwards, people like Friedrich Kittler has led the development of a 'new German medium theory', aligned partly with the Canadian medium theory of Innis and McLuhan and partly with post-structuralism.

**Professional Associations**

- National Communication Association (NCA): The main national professional organization covering many of the areas of communication studies in the U.S.
- International Communication Association is the main international association for communication studies, which combines an older focus on quantitatively based social science studies with newer critical and cultural studies of communicative phenomena.

- Association for Education in Journalism and Mass Communication.
- Association for Business Communication (ABC).
- International Association of Business Communicators (IABC).
- Society for Technical Communication (STC).
- Public Relations Society of America (PRSA).
- European Communication Research and Education Association (ECREA) is the main European association for communication studies.
- European Association for the Teaching of Academic Writing (EATAW) is the main European association for writing studies.
- Association for Teachers of Technical Writing (ATTW).
- International Association for Media and Communi-cations Research (IAMCR) is also a large international association for communication studies.
- IEEE Professional Communication Society.

## ASSOCIATION FOR BUSINESS COMMUNICATION

The Association for Business Communication (ABC) is the primary academic organization for the field of business communication scholarship, research, education and practice. The mission statement on its web site reflects this: "The Association for Business Communication (ABC) is an international organization committed to fostering excellence in business communication scholarship, research, education, and practice."Much of the strength of the organization rests in its interdisciplinary nature. Members belong to such varied academic fields as Management, Marketing, English, Foreign Languages, Speech, Communication, Linguistics, and Information Systems. Additionally the organization brings together university academicians, business practitioners, and business consultants.

### Organizational Structure

ABC is an international organization, divided into eight regional divisions, each with its own separate academic conferences. The regions are Europe, Asia and Pacific Rim, Caribbean and Central America, and five North American regions (Canada plus Eastern, Midwest, Southeast, and Southwest United States).

Each year the entire membership meets at the International Convention in October or November. Midyear, two regional conferences are held—one in the European region and the other in one of the North American regions. The Asia and Pacific Rim region holds a conference every two years. At the International Convention and at the regional conferences, members come together to share research in business communication, participate in workshops, and network. A Board of Directors and an Executive Committee lead the ABC. The Board of Directors is directly elected with a Vice President elected from each of 8 regions and 12 directors at large, with staggered terms. The executive committee consists of a permanent position of Executive Director and four officers of the Association. The members of the executive committee serve for four years in rotating capacity, beginning as second vice president in the first year, then first vice president the next, president the next, and past president the last year on the committee.

The organization as a whole elects the second vice president position from among candidates on the Board of Directors.The current Executive Director of the ABC is Dr. Betty S. Johnson of (Stephen F. Austin State University). She took office in 2007, succeeding Robert J. Myers of Baruch College in that position. When she took office, the headquarters of the ABC moved with her from New York City to Nacogdoches, Texas where Stephen F. Austin State University is located.

For 2007-2008 the Executive Committee consists of President Dr. Roger Conaway, First Vice President Dr. James Dubinsky (Virginia Tech), Second Vice President, Deborah Valentine (Emory University, Atlanta, Georgia, USA), and Immediate Past President Dr. Jackie Harrison (AUT University, Auckland, New Zealand).

### *Journal of Business Communication*

*JBC* was founded in 1963. At the time (and for several decades) it remained the only journal devoted solely to business communication theory. In its own words on the ABC web site *JBC* "publishes manuscripts that contribute to knowledge and theory of business communication as a distinct, multifaceted field approached through the administrative disciplines, the liberal arts, and the social sciences."

*JBC* summarizes its research focus as devoted to articles which contribute to knowledge and theory of business communication as a distinct, multifaceted field approached through the administrative disciplines, the liberal arts, and the social sciences. Accordingly, JBC seeks manuscripts that address all areas of business communication including but not limited to business composition/ technical writing, information systems, international business communication, management commu-nication, and organizational and corporate communi-cation. In addition, JBC welcomes submissions concerning the role of written, verbal, non-verbal and electronic communi-cation in the creation, maintenance, and performance of profit and not for profit business. The current editor-in-chief of the *JBC* is Dr. Margaret Baker Graham of Iowa State University. The last several editors-in-chief of *JBC* have been in Iowa State University's English Department, which also devotes office space and resources to *JBC* and to the *Journal of Business and Technical Communication.*

### *Business Communication Quarterly*

*Business Communication Quarterly* was founded in 1937. In its earlier years, *BCQ* was known as the *Bulletin of the ABCA* and later the *Bulletin of the ABC.*

It took on its present name in 1994. In its own words on the ABC web site, *BCQ* is "devoted to the teaching of business communication, which is a broad, interdisciplinary field.

*" BCQ summarizes the focus of its articles as*:

- Discussions of issues and methods for teaching business communication in a variety of settings: two–year college, technical institute, four-year college, university, corporate or agency training programme, and the like
- Case studies of specific classroom techniques
- Tutorials on business communication processes or products, especially innovations in electronic technology that need to be introduced into the classroom
- Research on classroom teaching or assessment
- Summary reviews of literature on teaching business communication
- Book reviews—reviews of both textbooks and other items of interest to teachers
- Reports on strategies for programme development

The current editor of *BCQ* is Dr. Kathryn Riley of Illinois Institute of Technology.

**Standing Committees, Ad Hoc Committees and Interest Groups**

*The ABC has 17 standing committees, as follow*:

1. Association to Advance Collegiate Schools of Business (AACSB) Liaison
2. Business Practices Committee
3. Community College Committee
4. Convention Procedures Committee
5. Diversity Initiative Committee
6. Employment Opportunities Committee
7. Intercultural Communication Committee
8. International Issues Committee
9. Modern Language Association (MLA) Liaison Committee
10. Nominations Committee
11. Publications Board
12. Research Committee
13. Review of the Executive Director Committee
14. Student Competition Committee
15. Teaching Committee 16. Undergraduate Studies Committee
17. Web Board

The ABC has *Ad Hoc* Committees for interests that have not yet warranted a Standing Committee, but may in the future become so. Many of the Standing Committees began as *Ad Hoc* Committees. In 2006 has four *Ad Hoc* Committees:

- Marketing of ABC
- Non-Tenure Track Faculty
- Professional Ethics
- Retired Members

Additionally, ABC members pursue a number of professional objectives through voluntary interest groups. Interest group may be convened by the First Vice President or by members' current interest groups. In 2006, the ABC had the following five Interest Groups:

- MBA Consortium
- Business Practices
- Consultants' Interest Group
- Intercultural Communication
- Rhetoric Special Interest Group

ABC was founded in 1936, beginning with a modest membership of 72 members, all but one from the United States (the only exception being from Canada). The organization, based at the University of Illinois, was then named the "Association of College Teachers of Business Writers." The next year, 1937, that name changed to the "American Business Writing Association."

By the 1960s, the field had grown considerably and became heavily interested in areas well beyond business writing (such as oral presentations, negotiations, and non-verbal communication among others). In 1967, the Board of Directors voted to change the name of the organization to the "American Business Communication Association" to reflect this change.

By the late 1970s, as the membership of the organization grew to include more member from outside the Americas and as the focus of research expanded heavily into the fields of intercultural communication and cross-cultural business communication practice, the term "American" became increasingly inaccurate of both the membership and focus of the organization. In 1985, the Board of Directors voted to change the name to its current "Association for Business Communication."

**International Association of Business Communicators**

The International Association of Business Communicators (IABC) is a leading association for business communication professionals. IABC has approximately 16,000 members in more than 100 chapters in 70 countries.

IABC members hold positions in a variety of communication professions, including: public relations, media relations, corporate communications, employee communi-cations, public affairs, investor relations, government relations, marketing communication, community relations, writing, editing, advertising, graphic design, human resources and teaching. IABC's headquarters are located in San Francisco, California, United States. IABC was founded in 1970 from a merger of the American Association of Industrial Editors and the

International Council of Industrial Editors. Its initial focus was on internal communication. However, IABC expanded its mission after research showed that members would leave after being promoted into positions with wider public relations responsibilities.

### Accreditation

IABC members can seek accreditation as Accredited Business Communicators (post-nominal ABC). Accreditation is offered as an IABC professional development programme. It offers communicators a way of demonstrating their ability to think and plan strategically and to successfully manage those skills essential to effective organizational communi-cation, which could include internal communications, media relations, crisis communications and external relations.

To receive accreditation, applicants must meet education and experience requirements, submit a portfolio that includes work samples with measurable outcomes, and pass both written and oral examinations. Accreditation recognizes communicators who have reached a standard of knowledge and proficiency that is globally accepted among the communication profession.

### Code of Ethics

The organization has a code of ethics for those professionals in public relations. The themes of its values are that business communications must be "legal... ethical, and... in good taste". Members are required to follow the IABC Code of Ethics. However, it has been observed that there is not an enforcement programme in place that can realistically punish breaches of its code.

### Research Foundation

Founded in 1982, IABC Research Foundation serves as the research and development arm of the International Association of Business Communicators. The Foundation supports and advances the practice of organizational communication by providing IABC members with research that bridges the divide between communication theory and practice by offering in-depth knowledge and tools that improve organizational communication performance and strengthen the commun-ication profession as a whole.

### Awards Programmes

Every year, IABC sponsors three levels of communication awards programmes for members and non-members: Bronze Quill awards, Silver Quill awards, and Gold Quill awards.. Communicators can choose to enter their best professional work produced during the prior year in these Quill communications contests.

The specific divisions and categories for each contest can vary, but typical categories include marketing communi-cations, member/employee communications, media relations, crisis communications, social responsibility, writing, graphic design, publication design, social media, interactive/web design, and photography.

Bronze Quill (BQ) awards programmes are hosted by local IABC chapters. The respective chapter's board of directors plans and executes a BQ communications contest open to business communicators working with a specific city and/or a small region of a state/province. Silver Quill is sponsored by regional divisions, such as IABC's Heritage and Pacific Plains regions, and are open to communicators in the respective geographic area.

Open to all communicators worldwide, Gold Quill typically receives entries from over 25 countries. The programme aims to cross communication disciplines and reviews entries from professional communicators, ranging from strategists to tacticians. All Gold Quill Awards winners receive international recognition in IABC's magazine, Communication World; are eligible to participate in an awards ceremony at IABC's annual international conference, are mentioned on the IABC web site, and are considered for publication in IABC's resource materials. In 2008, the programme attracted over 1,000 entries across 26 categories.

IABC awards programmes are open to both members and non-members of the organization. Global Leadership Awards include the Fellow Award and the Chairman's Award. The IABC Fellow designation is the highest honour IABC can bestow on an individual and acknowledges outstanding leadership, professional accomplishment and service to IABC and the communication profession.

Criteria for the Fellow Award include contribution to the organizational communication field and profession; career achievement; authorship, speaking and lecturing; contribu-tions to IABC; and other professional recognition such as community activities and other business-related activities. The Chairman's Award recognizes IABC members who have made selfless contributions and worked behind the scenes at the international level to enhance the association's image, facilitate member development and benefit the communication profession.

### Annual Conference and Networking Opportunities

IABC holds a world conference each year. In 2006, the host city was Vancouver, Canada. In 2007, the host city was New Orleans, Louisiana and IABC partnered with Wells Fargo to volunteer and provide financial support to build homes through Habitat for Humanity for the city's hurricane-damaged Ninth Ward.·The 2008 conference was in New York City, and the 2009 event will be held in San Francisco from June 7 to June 10, 2009. Eurocomm 2009 will be held in Lugano, Switzerland February 9 - 10, 2009

IABC's world conference is open to communicators, regardless of membership. As a professional association, IABC offers networking opportunities for students and other people entering the industry. As the United States Department of Labour notes, IABC "provides an opportunity for students to exchange views with public relations specialists and to make professional contacts that may help them find a full-time job in the field."

## NEW COMMUNICATION TECHNOLOGIES

### WHAT ARE NEW COMMUNICATION TECHNOLOGIES?

As the name itself implies, new communication technologies are those which are of more recent origin. Interactivity is their distinguishing feature. For the purpose of this unit, new communication technologies can also be understood as those which are capable of a much higher degree of interactivity than that offered by the traditional communication technologies. Writing, printing and electronic media like radio and television ax examples of traditional technologies which are essentially one-way in nature. Therefore, their interactive capabilities are very limited. Besides, this limited interactivity occurs after considerable delay. For example, a newspaper which depends on the traditional technology for print can be said to be interactive to the extent that it publishes readers' letters in its 'letters to the editor' column. Similarly, a radio station too is interactive in that it broadcasts programmes which carry responses to audience queries. We can, therefore, say that interactivity is at best a marginal property of traditional communication media. In the new communication technologies, on the other hand, interactivity is the main property. The use of computers in one form or the other, as an integral part of their system, is what enables them to be interactive. In the following sections, we will take up for study some of the main technologies under this category.

*Computer Networks :* The idea of interlinking and communicating with the aid of computers was as old as the mainframe computers of the 1970s. Owing to their prohibitive price, the mainframes came to be owned only by mega-establishments like governments, big business houses, universities etc. Individuals could not afford them for personal use. At the same time, the high cost of the mainframes required their owners to find ways and means to maximize their utilization in order to make them cost effective. The networking of computers, it was found, allowed simultaneous access to a single mainframe by any number of users. Naturally, this development suited owners and users alike. Computer networks thus emerged as a kind of public utility to help users communicate with a central computing facility such as a database, and retrieve information too. In the decades that followed, computer technology advanced by leaps and bounds. This resulted in the invention of much smaller computers that displayed greater capabilities at just a fraction of the price.

At present the use of computer networks for various specialized and general purposes has become quite common, even in the less developed parts of the world. In our own country, computer networks are widely used by public sector organizations, big business houses, government department etc., for their day-to-day transactions. Indian Airlines, Indian Railways and a few state undertakings own computer networks dedicated to managing their operations. Such real-time flow of information enables planners and other decision makers at the headquarters to decide on appropriate policies, taking into consideration the latest statistics. In the absence of such computer networking in the past, it is said that vital decisions at the national level had to be taken with the help of data which were at least a decade old! Apart from helping administrators, NICNET is also said to be regularly used for other application like exchange of expert medical advice by specialists to doctors working in remote areas. On a global scale, INERNET is the largest computer network which permeated almost all parts of the world. Composed of thousands of interconnected networks initially in the united states, INTERNET can offer you an immense range of information services such as electronic mail file transfer, databases and multi-media INTERNET also provides connectivity to mobile receivers through a wireless broadcasting service operating on satellite links. Computer networks have several advantages over interpersonal communication. Asynchronocity that is the flexibility inherent in the system to enable information exchange without the need for the sender and the recipient to be present simultaneously, is one such advantage. However, it also suffers from various drawbacks like the lack of a human touch. Communication engineers constantly endeavour to improve the so-called 'user friendliness' of the system concerned by approximating it to interpersonal interaction.

*Teleconferencing :* Teleconferencing is a mean by which individuals or groups located at different places can exchange data, speech, visual materials like graphs or diagrams, or moving pictures of themselves and any other relevant information. Teleconferencing is made possible by the integration of computers and communication in such a manner as to form a holistic system which can work in real-time. Depending on the particular application, scope and complexity involved, Teleconferencing can be classified under the following types:

- *Computer conferencing*: in the case, only computer data can be exchanged among multiple locations. Real time interaction among the location is possible, but only the extent of computer data. The physical linkages among the several computers can be in the form of telephone wires or though wireless means as in the case of microwave or satellite.
- *Audio conferencing*: In this participant can actually talk to one another as if in a face to face situation facilities are provided for any one

location to talk any other or all of them simultaneously. In addition, audio teleconferences also enable exchange of computer data on the same physical link (telephone cables or wireless). Audio teleconferencing enables real time exchange of information without losing the human touch.

- *Audio Graphic conferencing*: This is a more advanced form of audio teleconferencing in which, in addition to audio and computer data, still graphics like drawing, maps etc, can also be exchanged. Further refinements in technology enable even slow scan video pictures to be exchanged as a part of the audio teleconferencing system. The same pairs of telephone wires would suffice to carry all the above 'Bandwidth Compression' techniques which are technically known as ISDN (integrated data network services).
- *Video conferencing*: This is the highest form of teleconferencing in which a two-way exchange of moving pictures is possible without any restriction, in addition to audio and data. The telecommunication links required for such conferencing system prove to be very costly because of the fact that moving pictures need very wide bandwidths. Hence, a lower version of video teleconferencing which is called 'one-way video and two-way audio is gaining currency. In the latter case, the main location (typically the headquarters of an organization) will have facilities for sending audio as well as video which are received by all the remote locations. But the remote locations will have facilities for sending only audio, and not video. In other words, while the remote locations can receive both—pictures and voices—they will be able to respond only through voice. Teleconferencing of this kind has been widely experimented with by many organizations in India using satellite links.

Already, Teleconferencing has been an accepted form of technology in advanced countries, especially for business communications. It is only a matter of time before this technology becomes popular in countries such as ours, because the necessary infrastructure like telephone links and satellite are already available. Teleconferencing is gaining popularity due to the minimal physical travel demanded of its participants. The time-saving involved in this process is also a significant factor. The experience of advanced countries has been that, apart from economizing on time and travel, teleconferencing also help in improving corporate efficiency and participatory management.

*Teletext :* Teletext is a form of broadcast technology by means of which several 'pages' of textual information (say, latest weather reports, stock exchange figures, airline train reservations etc.) Can be transmitted on an already existing television channel. The teletext information is encoded in the so called 'vertical blanking interval' of the television screen which is invisible in the normal course of television viewing. However, when activated by a teletext 'decoder' at the receiving end, the television screen starts displaying the-teletext information in lieu of the normal TV programme. Facilities exist in teletext to enable viewers to choose a particular page of teletext containing relevant information which serves their needs, and recall that particular page. Thus, a businessman wanting to know the latest trend in the stock exchange can press his decoder for the particular page containing stock market news, and get the display on' his TV screen instantly. He will be able to view that page as long as he wishes, or he can turn over to some other page or revert back to the normal TV programme as per his wish. TV stations equipped with a teletext service, normally update the information at regular intervals, say every half an hour, for the benefit of the viewers. About 300 teletext pages (a page means one TV frame containing information) can be accommodated per TV channel and a collection of these pages goes by the name of 'teletext magazine'. The pages of a teletext magazine can incorporate illustrations like graphs, bar charts etc., in addition to simple text. The Delhi Station of Doordarshan provides a teletext service on the second channel; access to it is possible with the help of a decoder. The magazine contains specific pages earmarked for national and international news, travel information, sports, local announcements, weather reports etc. A few main pages of the magazine are also put out in the 'picture mode' *i.e.,* on the main channel itself for the benefit of use not equipped with decoders. It is possible to extend this service to other Doordarshan stations for the benefit of viewers all over the country: Teletext is a simple technology which can be used to advantage for public communication. The advantages inherent in broadcast media such as instant and widespread teach, to an unlimited clientele, are applicable to teletext as well. Different countries have teletext services which conform to different technical standards, and a universal code of transmission is yet to be invented. Its essential simplicity, instantaneous dissemination of messages and ease of updating information make it a worthwhile technology with myriad applications.

*Radio Text :* Better known by the term 'Radio data systems' (RDS), Radio text is a technology similar to Teletext but with the important difference that it works in conjunction with FM Radio (frequency Modulation) while Teletext works on television. While conventional radio broadcasts on medium wave and shortwave bands have the advantage of larger service areas for a given radio station, the severe congestion of radio stations in these bands in recent years has forced the use of higher frequency bands for radio transmission. Use of these higher frequency bands as in the case of the FM Radio, however, would mean restricting the reach of a radio station essentially to line of sight range which is about 30 km radius. FM stations are ideal as local radio stations, as they can offer programmes of local community interest, high fidelity music, local news etc., to the public. Radio text is to be seen as a value-added service on FM Radio. This technology essentially consists of transmitting data and other textual material piggyback on the FM carrier so that the listeners/viewers who are equipped with a radiotext 'decoder' can extract this signal from an ongoing FM transmission and watch the same on a computer screen which forms a part of the radiotext receiving system. Facilities are available in a decoder to select either the radiotext or the normal FM transmission at will. In addition, the listeners or viewers, as in the case of teletext, will be able to select the particular page of information of their interest and hold on to it for any length of time. Audio signals of speech quality (*i.e.*, of restricted bandwidth) can also form part of a radiotext signal. This would mean that institutions like Open Universities can transmit their audio lessons or radiotext, while simultaneously transmitting portions of their print material. Experiments of thin kind are already underway with the joint 'collaboration of All India Radio and Yashwantreo Chavan Maharashtra State Open University, Nasik. An important deterrent for widespread use of Radiotext of such applications, however, is that the receiving system works out to be several times costlier than the FM Radio set itself. Moreover, FM Radio is still in its infancy in our country and the availability of FM radio sets is rather rare. Under the circumstances, the widespread use of Radiotext in our country will be unlikely in the near future.

*Videotext :* Videotex (please note the absence of 't' at the end of the word) is another form of interactive communication technology which is in wide usage in several advanced countries. While the teletext operates on television and radio text on FM radio, Videotext works with the help of the public telephone network. The home computer, telephone connection and the domestic TV set/ computer screen form integral components of a Videotext system. Customers provided with Videotext facilities can make use of it for such varied applications as electronic shopping, access to databases, tele-banking, or exchanging messages with friends. As Videotext is essentially interactive it has much more to offer than teletext or radio text in terms of selective information exchange and retrieval. However, a well developed and reliable telephone network is essential for operating a Videotext service. For this reason, as of now, Videotext services are popular only in advanced countries. With gradual improvements taking place by way of digital telephone exchanges and replacement of conventional telephone wires with optical fibres, the reliability as well as capacity of telephone systems everywhere are bound to increase in due course. Value-added services like the Videotext too are expected to gain in popularity alongside such developments.

*Interactive Cable Distribution Systems :* Dissemination of television programmes via cable to a community of households started in the 50s. To begin with advantages of cable distribution was seen as improving the reception conditions of television in isolated mountainous-regions. Later on, TV signals received via satellite were put out on cable distribution systems, thus offering many more TV channels for the viewers. With this, the popularity and spread of cable distribution systems grew dramatically. Concurrently with the distribution of satellite channels, facilities like 'pay TV' in which individual viewers have the choice of receiving programmes of their preference at a price, have also been introduced. In other words, the cable systems have been endowed with interactive properties. Advancements in digital technology and fibre optics have resulted in further improved versions of cable distribution. For example, viewers in the advanced countries can now make use of the cable for receiving programmes of their choice at the press of a button. The selected programme is then down-loaded by the cable company onto the viewer's terminal as a compressed 'digital packet' in a matter of seconds. The programme is then held in the electronic memory of the receiving terminal which can be viewed straightaway or some time at leisure. The asynchronocity of interactive cable distribution systems is a unique advantage in the gamut of new communication technologies.

*Communication Satellites :* Transnational television, *i.e.,* transmission of television programmes from one country to, another, became a reality with the development of Communication Satellites. These satellites are stationed in an orbit above the earth's equator at a height of about 36,000 km. called the geo-stationary orbit. All satellites parked in the geostationary orbit have a period of rotation equal to 24 hours and hence, appear stationary to an observer on the earth. Besides, the great distance of the orbit also offers the advantage of the satellite to 'see' as much as one-third of the earth's surface thus enabling it to cover such a vast area. Communication Satellites are owned by various individual nations as well as collectively by groups of nations to cater for several applications like broadcasting, television and telecommunications. INTELSAT (International Telecommunications Satellite Consortium) is an international body consisting of more than 90 member countries of which India is one. The satellites commissioned by INTELSAT cater to, the collective needs of the member countries as per a mutually agreed tariff structure. Ground terminals (these are known as earth stations) for receiving/sending signals from/to the satellites are located in several places in the member countries. In India, two such earth stations have been established for the INTELSAT network—one near Pune and the other near Dehradun. Most of the international telecommunications traffic and exchange with other countries of live coverage of events takes place via the INTELSAT network. India is credited with taking several major initiatives in the field of satellite communications. The famous SITE experiment (Satellite Instructional Television Experiment) during 1975-76, in which about 2400 remote villages in the country were served by television programmes via satellite, is a case in point. The experiment has proved the efficacy of satellite communications as a cost effective means for countrywide dissemination of educational and developmental TV programmes.

Gradually, our country has developed its own satellite system, INSAT (Indian National Satellite System). INSAT is a multi-purpose satellite service catering to telecommunications, radio and TV transmission and weather forecasting. The second generation of INSAT satellites which are currently in operation, have a larger number of transporters which can be used for further expansion of satellite communications. In particular, regional telecasting can be extended in all language zones and new services like teleconferencing introduced. Mushrooming of satellite-based transnational television in recent years is a cause for concern as well as hope. The sudden spurt in the availability of satellite channels all over the country from across our borders would mean a potential threat to our own national broadcast media. The virtual absence of any legal mechanisms to check or control these transmissions of extenlal origin can jeopardize our own priorities in the communication sector and divert the attention of the populace away from important information on developmental activities. On the other hand, the competitive presence of external channels call motivate the local broadcasters to become more professional and quality conscious. Direct Broadcast Satellites (DBS) are specially designed for broadcast applications so that the signals transmitted from them can be directly received by home receivers equipped with a small dish antenna (typically half a meter diameter) and an interfacing unit. Use of such satellites obviates the need for land based retransmitting stations (called LPTs). DBS is in extensive use in Europe, the USA and Japan. As mentioned earlier, the application areas to which multi purpose satellites like the INSAT can be put to use are many and varied. Satellite communications have in fact become so common that we take then for granted. Whenever you dial a long distance telephone call, say from India to the USA, your voice and that of the person you have called travel via some satellite route or the other, most probably via the INTELSAT network. You may notice in such cases, a very small but clearly discernible delay of a fraction of a second in receiving the response of the other person. A similar delay will be felt by the person at the other end while receiving your voice. This is because of the extraordinarily long journey of thousands of kilometres which the voice signals have to traverse on the satellite route. Of course, such delays are common not only to telephone conversations but also all other traffic taking place through satellite communications. Many national newspapers which are published simultaneously from multiple locations take advantage of satellite communication for instant transmission of their pages from one publishing centre to another. For example The Hindu has arrangements for publishing its Delhi edition by transmitting pages from Madras to Delhi through INSAT.

## COMPARISON OF NEW COMMUNICATION TECHNOLOGIES

In the foregoing sections, we have surveyed the salient features of some of the new communication technologies individually. It is to be noted, however, that real-life situations often employ the simultaneous use of more than one technology in a given situation. For example, the STAR TV programmes that you receive on your home TV set, reach you by means of satellite communications up to the point of your cable operator's terminal, and from then on, via cable. Similarly, a long distance telephone call may get connected via microwave or a submarine cable for part of the route and via satellite for the rest of its journey. Such combinations, however, usually do not affect the technical quality of the communication in question. So, the users for the most part remain unaware of the details of the technology mix involved. Nevertheless, every technology has its distinct attributes, advantages and disadvantages, because of which an optimal technology selection is possible for any given application. Some of these have already been discussed in the concerned sections earlier; what follows is a relative assessment of the various technologies with regard to communication parameters like interactivity, asynchronocity and demassification.

*Interactivity :* While interactivity is a property in which the new communication technologies, as a rule, excel over the traditional ones, some of them are evidently much more interactive than others. Teleconferencing and video teleconferencing can be cited as the most interactive while, teletext or radiotext can be placed at the other end of the interactivity scale. Even in the traditional communication media, the ordinary telephone is a very good interactive device. The strength of the new technologies in this regard, is that their interactivity is much more extensive and is not necessarily limited to just two individuals as in the case of the telephone.

*Asynchronocity :* The term asynchronocity refers to that property of the medium whereby the simultaneous presence of all the participants in a communication exercise is not compulsory. For example, in a computer network, facilities like "store and forward" enables the message to be retrieved at a convenient time other than the one at which the message has actually been sent. Thus, while real time exchange of communications is possible through such a technology, it offers the added flexibility of asynchronocity. The degree of asynchronocity varies from one technology to the other. It can be said to be the highest where only computers are required to interact without live human intervention, as in the case of Electronic Mail, or computer data are only kind of teleconferencing. It is least in a two-way video teleconferencing.

*Demassification :* Traditional media like press, radio or television are instances of 'one-to-many' kind of communications. Therefore, they are unsuitable where the communication needs are more individualized. Demassification refers to the extent to which a given technology can lend itself to such individualized communication. The normal telephone system is an ideal example of a technology endowed with a high degree of demassification. New communication technologies in general possesses this characteristic while at the same time enabling communication among large groups or individuals dispersed over large areas. In other words, the new communication technologies are the reverse of the traditional technologies. Teleconferencing or computer communication is high in their demassification while teletext is at the lower end of the demassification ladder.

## SOCIAL ISSUES

As we have noted earlier, the new communication technologies have not yet penetrated sufficiently in Third World countries like ours. Therefore, we will not be able to determine their likely impact on our society with any degree of certainty. What we can conjecture in this regard is by studying the experience of developed countries like the USA which have been using these technologies over a considerable period and by extrapolating the impact of some of the present technologies like television. Noted communications scholar, Everett Rogers, says that the new communication technologies have a marked social impact in the following respects, especially during their adaptability stages.

- As newer technologies are relatively costlier and knowledge-intensive, they will be adopted only by the higher echelons of society at first, who can really afford them. Thus, ironically, communication gaps would widen among several sections of society because of the new communication technologies. This phenomenon is, of course, not unique for the new technologies. When television was introduced, a similar thing has happened as only the rich could embrace this medium in the beginning. As the ownership of TV sets gradually increased, the initial imbalances to have become less pronounced. A similar situation is expected in the case of the new technologies. Despite initial imbalances, however, overall information flow in the society is bound to go up.
- What happens by way of information imbalance within a society is also true of situations among countries at large. Advanced countries which are already information-rich tend to become richer, thereby widening the information gap between countries. This may lead to an unfavourable situation for the Third World countries which are already at the receiving end of the technological supremacy of the First World.
- Information overload is likely to happen, which in turn poses problems of coping with selective retrieval of required information, from heaps of randomly accumulated information. Here again, the new technologies themselves are likely to come to our rescue, as for example special computer software which may enable users to obtain such selective display of information as is relevant to them.
- Unemployment may abound in certain sectors as the new technologies

would eliminate or render surplus certain traditional jobs and occupations. Some new jobs and new occupations may be created in their place, but not in numbers sufficient enough to compensate the loss of traditional jobs. Displacement of jobs may be felt more acutely during the introductory phase of the new technologies, than when the technologies in question get integrated fully into society.

- The universal presence of computers and easy access to them via networks is likely to raise problems concerning privacy and security of communications. Use of special passwords and the like are of course an obvious protection, but they too have their limitations. Clever use of special software may also enable computer miscreants/hackers to break the secret passwords and get at the classified information straight away.
- Greater use of the new technologies may enable the organizations concerned to become more decentralized in their decision making and other functions. Here again, an exact opposite may be possible as the new technologies permit much tighter monitoring on the movements and performances of subordinate staff thereby bringing about a 'Big-Brother' kind of centralized control. Much depends on the way the managements want to use the new technologies.
- It is feared the gender-inequality will increase. Though unfounded, the apprehension is prevalent that boys rather than girls will adapt themselves faster and more easily to things like computer programming, due to their supposedly inherent superiority in mathematical skills. This is of course a debatable point. However, in the initial stages of adoption of the new technologies, social pressures may be generated bemuse of gender inequalities.

From the above discussion, you may be inclined to think, that since these new technologies have certain undesirable effects on society, they might as well be avoided entirely. Such thinking, however, would be too short sighted and technophobic to be true.

The history of technology is replete with instances of social. Instability and resistance upon introduction of major technological innovations. Eventually, however, as the society adapted itself to these new innovations and assimilated their full impact, the initial resistances were found to have melted away. Not only were those, the new technologies themselves found to be instrumental in finding solutions to the very problems what they had generated in the first place.

In case any particular technology was found unable to conform to the above pattern, sociological forces would automatically tend to relegate such a technology into oblivion. The case of the new communication technologies that we have discussed in this unit, can be no exception to this overall trend.

## NEW MEDIA AS A TOOL FOR SOCIAL CHANGE

Social Movement Media has a rich and storied history that has changed at a rapid rate since New Media became widely used. The Zapatista Army of National Liberation of Chiapas, Mexico were the first major movement to make widely recognized and effective use of New Media for communiques and organizing in 1994. Since then, New Media has been used extensively by social movements to educate, organize, share cultural products of movements, communicate, coalition build, and more. The WTO Ministerial Conference of 1999 protest activity was another landmark in the use of New Media as a tool for social change. The WTO protests used media to organize the original action, communicate with and educate participants, and was used an alternative media source. The Indymedia movement also developed out of this action, and has been a great tool in the democratization of information, which is another widely discussed aspect of new media movement. Some scholars even view this democratization as an indication of the creation of a "radical, socio-technical paradigm to challenge the dominant, neo-liberal and technologically determinist model of information and communication technologies." A less radical view along these same lines is that people are taking advantage of the internet to produce a grassroots globalization, one that is anti-Neo-liberal and centred on people rather than the flow of capital. Of course, some are also skeptical of the role of New Media in Social Movements. Many scholars point out unequal access to new media as a hindrance to broad-based movements, sometimes even oppressing some within a movement. Others are skeptical about how democratic or useful it really is for social movements, even for those with access. There are also many New Media components that activists cite as tools for change that have not been widely discussed as such by academics.

New Media has also found a use with less radical social movements such as the Free Hugs Campaign. Using websites, blogs, and online videos to demonstrate the effectiveness of the movement itself. Along with this example the use of high volume blogs has allowed numerous views and practices to be more widespread and gain more public attention. Another example is the ongoing Free Tibet Campaign, which has been seen on numerous websites as well as having a slight tie-in with the band Gorillaz in their Gorillaz Bitez clip featuring the lead singer 2D sitting with protesters at a Free Tibet protest. Another social change seen coming from New Media is trends in fashion and the emergence of subcultures such as Text Speak, Cyberpunk, and various others.

### NATIONAL SECURITY

New Media has also recently become of interest to the global espionage community as it is easily accessible electronically in database format and can therefore be quickly retrieved and reverse engineered by national governments.

Particularly of interest to the espionage community are facebook and twitter, two sites where individuals freely divulge personal information that can then be sifted through and archived for the automatic creation of dossiers on both people of interest and the average citizen.

**Interactivity and New Media**

Interactivity has become a key term for number of new media use options evolving from the rapid dissemination of Internet access point, the digitalization of the media, and media convergence. In 1984, Rice defined the new media as communication technologies that enable or facilitate user-to-user interactivity and interactivity between user and information. Such as Internet replaces the "one-to-many" model of traditional mass communication with the possibility of a "many-to-many" web of communication. Any individual with the appropriate technology can now produce his or her online media and include images, text, and sound about whatever he or she chooses. So the new media with technology convergence shifts the model of mass communication, and radically shapes the ways we interact and communicate with one another. Vin Crosbie described three communications media in "What is new media?". He saw Interpersonal media as "one to one", Mass media as "one to many" and, finally New Media as Individuation Media or "many to many".

When we think of interactivity and its meaning, we assume that it is only prominent in the conversational dynamics of individuals who are face-to-face. This restriction of opinion does not allow us to see its existence in mediated communication forums. Interactivity is present in some programming work, such as video games. It's also viable in the operation of traditional media. In the mid 1990s, filmmakers started using inexpensive digital cameras to create films. It was also the time when moving image technology had developed, which was able to be viewed on computer desktops in full motion. This development of new media technology was a new method for artists to share their work and interact with the big world. Other settings of interactivity include radio and television talk shows, letters to the editor, listener participation in such Programmes, and computer and technological programming. Interactive new media has become a true benefit to every one because people can express their artwork in more than one way with the technology that we have today and there is no longer a limit to what we can do with our creativity.

Interactivity can be considered as a central concept in understanding new media, but different media forms possess different degree of interactivity, even some forms of digitized and converged media are not in fact interactive at all. Tony Feldman considers digital satellite television as an example of a new media technology that uses digital compression to dramatically increase the number of television channels that can be delivered, and which changes the nature of what can be offered through the service, but does not transform the experience of television from the user's point of view, as it lacks a more fully interactive dimension. It remains the case that interactivity is not an inherent characteristic of all new media technologies, unlike digitization and convergence.

Terry Flew (2005) argues that "the global interactive games industry is large and growing, and is at the forefront of many of the most significant innovations in new media". Interactivity is prominent in these online computer games such as *World of Warcraft*, *The Sims Online* and *Second Life*. These games, developments of "new media", allow for users to establish relationships and experience a sense of belonging, despite temporal and spatial boundaries. These games can be used as an escape or to act out a desired life. Will Wright, creator of *The Sims*, "is fascinated by the way gamers have become so attached to his invention-with some even living their lives through it". New media have created virtual realities that are becoming mere extensions of the world we live in. With the creation of Second Life people have even more control over this virtual world where anything that a participant can think of in their mind can become a reality in Second Life.

New Media changes continuously due to the fact that it is constantly modified and redefined by the interaction between the creative use of the masses, emerging technology, cultural changes, etc.

### The Industry

The new media industry shares an open association with many market segments in areas such as software/video game design, television, radio, and particularly movies, advertising and marketing, which seeks to gain from the advantages of two-way dialogue with consumers primarily through the internet. The advertising industry has capitalized on the proliferation of new media with large agencies running multi-million dollar interactive advertising subsidiaries. Interactive websites and kiosks have become popular. In a number of cases advertising agencies have also set up new divisions to study new media. Public relations firms are taking advantage of the opportunities in new media through interactive PR practices.

### Fluffpose

As new media searches for revenue pools, it crosses paths with old media and vice versa. One of the latest strategies is the "fluffpose" piece. Part expose, part fluff, this article is paid for directly from an advertiser and contains some form of exposure to bring in the readers, but at its heart is an advertisement.

## BRAVE NEW MEDIA WORLD

Possibly the greatest testament to the media's power over mass consciousness is its ability to rewrite and even erase history. As the world plunges headlong into what's been labeled the Information Age, for example,

Western-dominated mass media-with the sometimes unwitting assistance of new Internet-based enterprises-have so far convinced most of their avid consumers that we're dealing with unique issues and a revolutionary new environment that makes old debates about mass communication irrelevant. In reality, it's just a case of media-induced amnesia.

Concern about press responsibility and information policy actually dates back to the 1890s, particularly after the impact of media propaganda was dramatically demonstrated during the Spanish-American War. In 1922, the president of General Electric warned Europe about the downside of radio, urging nations to stop hurling insults at each other "in furious language." Five years later, the League of Nations passed a resolution opposing "obviously inaccurate, highly exaggerated, or deliberately distorted" news, urging the press not to undermine international peace. By the early 30s, an International Federation of Journalists had established a tribunal to deal with information that promoted hate and violence.

From the start, however, the US opposed or remained aloof from proposals designed to impose sanctions or promote balance, even though its leaders recognized the danger of a European news cartel and, later, the power of fascist and Nazi propaganda. The US stand, then as now, was that only private-sector ownership could ensure the so-called "free marketplace of ideas." The fact that commercially-based media are subject to abuses and distortions was ruled irrelevant, while arguments for a "new international information and communication order," one that would be democratic, support economic development, enhance the exchange of ideas, share knowledge among all the world's people, and improve the quality of life, was called demagoguery, the leading edge of a plan to impose a global socialist state.

In the early 80s, this battle came to a head in the US effort to discredit the UN Educational, Scientific, and Cultural Organization (UNESCO), established in 1945 to promote the worldwide exchange of thought and ideas in hopes of promoting peace and prosperity. Although never completely comfortable with this agenda, the US went along until the late 70s, when calls for a New International Information Order (NIIO) directly challenged the West s "cultural imperialism." Information flows shouldn't be one-directional, all nations should have equal access to information and international transmission channels, the power of existing transnational media monopolies should be reduced, and additional media voices should be heard-these were some of the NIIO's lofty goals.

Not surprisingly, the response from the US government and corporate media was negative and savage, using all the power at their disposal to derail this challenge to the "free marketplace" gospel. Once Ronald Reagan became president, the Heritage Foundation, a conservative think tank that developed many of Reagan's policies, led the charge. Now, the goal was not only to squelch any talk about media reform, but also to discredit UNESCO and the entire UN system. Mainstream media pitched in, casting the issue as a power play by Third World dictators to destroy the "free press"-a widely accepted euphemism for media in private hands, largely financed by advertising, and not subject to government controls or demands for social responsibility.

At the same time, they played the technology card. In response to complaints about information flow imbalances, cultural dependence, unequal facilities, and distorted coverage, government and business leaders asserted that high tech would eliminate age-old gaps and even enable under-developed countries to "leapfrog" into a post-industrial future. The argument was persuasive, but the record since then shows that the main beneficiaries have been corporations and the US military-intelligence-industrial complex. The communications revolution has dramatically enhanced the mobility of capital, while helping the military to impose a global surveillance regime that would shock George Orwell. The attack on UNESCO climaxed with the US withdrawal in 1985. After that, hopes for a "new world information and communication order" evaporated. Some critics suggest that the approach was doomed anyway, since it was promoted by political and intellectual elites, and focused on the role of states rather than individuals and civil society. In short, they argue that such a campaign for "democratization from above" would empower only governments, and likely produce new forms of censorship and control.

Today, the information superhighway, like other media, is mainly driven by the market, which defines what services consumers get and how much they'll pay. Those lacking sufficient bucks-a group that includes the vast majority of the world's population are simply shut out. The companies investing in this highway want control of access to consumers to recoup their investments. The Internet-at this point still largely a public meeting place where people exchange information, search databases, play games, and chat-has clearly attracted the attention of the international business community. Once its effectiveness as a vehicle for advertising and sales is further refined, this public, relatively un-regulated, un-censored, pluralistic network may become essentially a global electronic shopping mall.

A century after the power of global communications was first acknowledged, we're still being fed the same old line: The market best protects the free exchange of information, and is certainly preferable to any form of state or global intervention. There is another point of view, though not one our corporate gatekeepers have deigned to mention. It's embodied in the People's Communication Charter (PCC), a global initiative developed by Third World Network in Malaysia, the Centre for Communication and Human Rights in Amsterdam, the US-based Cultural Environment Movement, and the World Association of Community Radio Broadcasters. The PCC articulates essential rights and responsibilities that ordinary people should have in relation to their cultural environment. "All people are entitled to participate in communication, and in making decisions about communication within and between societies," it asserts. "The majority of the world's peoples lack minimal technological resources for survival and communication. Over half of them have not yet made a single telephone call. Commercialization of media and concentration of media ownership erode the public sphere and fail to provide for cultural and information needs, including the plurality of opinions and the diversity of cultural expressions and languages necessary for democracy. Massive and pervasive media violence polarizes societies, exacerbates conflict, and cultivates fear and mistrust, making people vulnerable and dependent."

In 18 articles, the charter outlines a set of principles that provide the basis for a campaign to transform global communications. Building on existing treaties and the Universal Declaration of Human Rights, it calls for broad rights to access and literacy, international protection of journalists, and the right of all people to "reply and to demand penalties for damage from media misinformation." It addresses the issues of cultural identity, language diversity, and protecting children from harmful media products. In addition, it focuses on privacy rights, equitable use of cyberspace, protection of consumers from promotion disguised as news or entertainment, and accountability through self-regulatory bodies, based on the standards outlined in the charter.

Finally, reflecting its focus on "democracy from below," the PCC also deals with the vital question of independence. The right to participate in and benefit from self-reliant communication structures, it explains, "requires international assistance to the development of independent media; training Programmes for professional media workers; the establishment of independent, representative associations, syndicates or trade unions of journalists and associations of editors and publishers; and the adoption of international standards."

At this point, corporate media's response has been to ignore that there's anything to discuss, aside from some self-indulgent hand wringing about whether the press focuses too much on polls and conflicts and not enough on content. Of course, we know what they're really focused on-ratings-which, in the end, means money. Still, the charter's agenda does go straight to the heart of what worries most people about our brave new media world. The questions are whether, this time, enough people will see through the "free marketplace" spin-and whether civil society will seize the initiative before it's too late.

# 5

# International Media Proceedings in India

## INTRODUCTION

This focuses on perceptions of televised global beauty pageants among business and media professionals in India who organized, sponsored, and supported the Miss World beauty contest. The 1996 Miss World pageant, which was held in Bangalore, a cosmopolitan city in South India, proved to be highly controversial due to protests expressed against the pageant by religious leaders, conservative women's groups, feminist activists, and political parties. My analysis of discourses on Miss World that circulated among professionals in the Indian culture industry is based on data gathered from ethnographic fieldwork in Mumbai and Bangalore. Informants' statements about the televised Miss World revealed that categories of nation and gender deeply influenced local producers' interpretations of the benefits that accrue to India through the practice of hosting global media events.

In selecting a logo for Miss World, organizers and sponsors had to carefully negotiate local religious and gender politics as well as global fashion and beauty standards. Organizers' motives in holding the pageant in India demonstrated the launching of new configurations of global cultural flows that highlight Third World culture industries' desires to manage and control their own projects of globalization. The study shows that the selection of a venue for Miss World was shaped by struggles to challenge regional hierarchies within India. In conclusion, I consider the implications of this qualitative research on local producers' interpretations of Miss World for studies of media globalization, nationalism, and gender.

The staging of international beauty contests in non-Western countries is an integral part of the process of economic and cultural globalization that has intensified in the last two decades. Two recent developments that have aided the transnational traffic in consumer products, rituals, and practices commonly referred to as "global culture" inchide the internal liberalization or deregulation of developing countries' economies and the imperatives of Euroamerican multinational firms seeking new and larger middle-class markets). In the case of India, since the government launched a series of economic reforms in the late eighties that were designed to promote a free-market economy and facilitate the entry of multinationals, the presence of global culture has manifested through a variety of such consumerist signifiers as the Barbie doll, McDonald's fast food, Coca Cola, MTV, Baywatch, and most recently, the Miss World contest. When the Miss World pageant was held in India in 1996, it was the first time that a region in South Asia became the setting for a global contest. This monograph analyzes the 1996 Miss World pageant as a significant global media event that captured, exacerbated, and created tensions among discourses of gender, nationalism, regionalism, and modernity in postcolonial India.

While beauty pageants have long existed in various regional and national forms in India, Belize, Tibet, Sri Lanka, and Nicaragua, international contests have only recently turned their attention to non-Western locations, contestants, and audiences. Donald Trump and the CBS corporation jointly own the Miss Universe contest, which was founded in 1952. Although Miss Universe contests were held in Puerto Rico and the Philippines in the seventies, since 1992, this contest has traveled to numerous developing countries-Thailand, Peru, Namibia, Mexico, Trinidad and Tobago, and Cyprus. When Miss Universe was held in Bangkok in 1992 for the first time, a New York Times article "Where Beauty Queens Pre-en, No Eyesores Please" reported that thousands of the urban poor were evicted from the streets to avoid offending pageant contestants, tourists, and contest spectators.

The Miss Universe contest held in Manila in 1994 created controversy when some politicians in high office protested the large sums of money the state had agreed to invest in the pageant. Similarly, the Miss World contest, launched in 1951 by an English couple, Eric and Julia Morley, has also shifted its venues over the last decade from London to lesser-known cities. Miss World was held in the United Kingdom for thirty-nine years before the founders began shipping it to Eastern Europe, Asia, South America, and Africa. Before Miss World was held in India in 1996, the South African resort location, Sun City, was home to this global pageant on four occasions. Since the early nineties, judges in the Miss World contest have included performers, media moguls, and celebrities from Latin America and Asia and increasingly, women of colour dominate the pool of finalists and winners of the contest.

Bangalore, a cosmopolitan city and the capital of the state of Karnataka in South India, was the venue for Miss World on November 23, 1996. Along with an estimated live attendance of 25,000 people, the pageant was attended by many of Asia's business elite and entertainment celebrities, and by international personalities like the Sultan of Brunei. The communications company, Amitabh Bachchan Corporation Limited (ABCL), organized the pageant in India. ABCL was founded in 1994 in Mumbail by the famous Indian celebrity icon and actor Amitabh Bachchan.

The event was sponsored chiefly by one of India's largest manufacturers of consumer products, Godrej, which produces soaps, detergents, food and hair products, electronic appliances, and office furniture. Other commercial sponsors for the event included national and multinational corporations: Mastercard, Citibank, Europcar, Coca Cola, Omega Watches, Welcom Group of hotels, Modi Revlon, Lakme cosmetics, Air India, and Reva Automobile. After considering bids from several countries, Miss World founders, Eric and Julia Morley, chose ABCL to host and manage the pageant in India, a task that included selecting a site for the live performance of the contest, producing publicity materials, securing media coverage, negotiating with the Indian government for licenses, and ensuring the financial support of commercial sponsors. As an ambitious business venture that was estimated to cost ABCL Rs. 10 crore (approx US$2.25 million), the Miss World pageant was hailed as an economic milestone for the Indian entertainment, advertising, and tourism industries. Business Today labeled Miss World and the Michael Jackson concert in Mumbai, which preceded the pageant by two weeks, as two of the biggest entertainment events hosted by the country.

Leaders in the Bangalore fashion, film, performance, and art worlds marveled at the entrepreneurial spirit of ABCL because the televised version of the pageant was estimated to be viewed by an audience of 3 billion in over 112 countries. The advertising revenue of Rs. 20 crore (approx US$4.5 million) raised by ABCL for the thirty minutes of air time allocated to commercials during the two and a half hour long televised pageant was referred to as a "new benchmark for Indian television, which surpassed records for any previous event of this kind".

Bangalore city officials, who were convinced that Miss World had the potential to increase tourism and foreign investments, were prepared to incur expenses of over Rs. 10 crores in funding renovations, providing security, and offering a state-owned public venue for the live performance of the pageant. The Godrej company, which invested Rs 8.75 crores (approx US$2 million) in Miss World as the major sponsor of the event, claimed that the national publicity would aid in reversing declining sales of its well-known soap brands Cinthol, Ganga, Marvel, Crowning Glory, and Shikakai.

Foreign and Indian investment analysts argued that the international pageant symbolized the tremendous growth potential for the multinational cosmetics industry in the recently liberalized Indian economy. The cosmetics market had doubled in a short span of six years and with a projected annual growth of 20 per cent, total sales of cosmetics in 1998 was estimated to be in the region of US $27 million.

As the disagreements among state officials over the 1994 Miss Universe contest in Manila demonstrated, the arrival of globalization in the form of beauty pageants in Asia has sometimes generated conflict, opposition, and heated debate. Much to the dismay of Miss World's founders, organizers, and sponsors, the 1996 pageant in Bangalore provoked strong resistance and special-interest group mobilization.The pageant became highly controversial due to vigorous public protests expressed by a wide range of conflicting factions. Members of protest groups organized marches and demonstrations, called for boycotts and strikes, distributed pamphlets and brochures at public places, performed street plays and skits, and vandalized offices of commercial sponsors, Reasons for these public protests against the Miss World pageant included charges that global beauty contests promoted cultural and economic imperialism, sexism, Western standards of beauty, immorality, and modes of consumption inappropriate for a Third World country where the vast number of its people still lived in extreme poverty.

Although globalization, particularly the possible impact of global media on local cultures in Third World settings, has attracted much theoretical musing, there is little empirical research that can illuminate the contradictory, heterogeneous, and conflicting responses to global culture. Examining the current contributions of scholars to research on globalization, anthropologist Janet Abu-Lughod expresses discomfort with the high level of abstraction in current theories of global culture. Concerned that theories of globalization lack adequate grounding in specific studies of localization, Abu-Lughod urges scholars to "capture the ambiguities and nuances of the concrete" because "the field, if not controlled, can degenerate into what we might call `global babble'".

In providing a case study of the 1996 Miss World pageant in India, this monograph aims to reduce "global babble" by concretely mapping the shifting qualities of meanings, which were attributed to a global media event that has come to signify the advent of Western modernity in many local settings.

The purpose of this study, which focuses on the Indian culture and media industries, is to examine the Miss World contest as a media event where the global and local intersected to produce, reinforce, and challenge relations of sameness and difference, gender and power, tradition and modernity, and centre and periphery.

How do indigenous capitalist enterprises harness discourses of gender and nationalism in embracing global media culture and legitimizing their commercial goals for the consumption of local audiences? How do organizers and producers negotiate local tensions and cultural politics in marketing globalization to local and transnational media audiences? Does the presence of global culture in local settings always imply relations of economic and cultural dependence between centre (West) and periphery (non-West)? Are local media corporations in non-Western locations deploying Western rituals and spectacles to produce new flows of media culture that do not originate in the First World?

How can local agents in non-Western nations seek out global culture to challenge regional hierarchies and hegemonies? In considering these questions, the scope of this monograph's analysis is restricted to the perspectives of professionals in the entertainment, media, and beauty industries in India.

In privileging fieldwork data gathered from informants who were involved in managing, sponsoring, and supporting Miss World, this monograph does not address contestants' motives for participating in international pageants, the histories of global or national pageants, the changing aesthetics of international beauty queens' bodies over time, or audience responses to the televised pageant.

I do not provide specific textual analyses of media coverage accorded to pre-pageant events, the pageant itself, or public protests.

The first section of this monograph briefly reviews studies of beauty pageants to provide insights into what we can learn from examining beauty contests as public sites where social and economic structures of gender, class, age, race, and nation are captured in a spectacular fashion. The following section briefly sketches the representations of Miss World that appeared in the media and outlines the relevance of current theoretical speculations on global-local interactions for this study of the culture industry in India. The next section provides a brief overview of my methodology and fieldwork in India.

The five sections that follow the discussion of methodology contain an extended analysis of fieldwork data, which demonstrates that organizers' and sponsors' perceptions of the mediated staging of Miss World contest in India reinforced and challenged national, regional, global, and gender identities.

I begin by examining local media and advertising professionals' views on the positive impact of Miss World on India's image in the global public sphere. I then analyse informants' opinions on the links between the recent global visibility of successful Indian beauty queens and the arrival of the 1996 Miss World contest in Bangalore. Exploring the cultural politics of gender and religion in India that organizers had to maneuver, the next section analyzes ABCL's strategies in designing a logo for Miss World.

The following section addresses organizers' motives for hosting Miss World in India and the last and fifth section of analysis investigates the internal, behind-the-stage process that led to the selection of Bangalore, a city in South India, as the venue for the live performance of Miss World.

In conclusion, I debate the implications of my qualitative research on the localization of Miss World in India for studies of media globalization, nationalism, and gender. I argue that debates over patriotism, loyalty to cultural traditions, and local women's empowerment do not occur only within the discourses of activism or state politics-such cultural conflicts and tensions also suffuse the imaginary landscape that guides local producers' involvement in capitalist cultural production.

## METHODOLOGY: FIELDWORK IN INDIA

This monograph's analysis is part of a larger project that interrogates the controversial 1996 Miss World pageant in India as a mass-mediated ritual that provoked vigorous debate over the impact of global culture on gender, modernity, and tradition in India. The research data gathered for this study is based on five months of fieldwork in the cities of Bangalore and Mumbai in India.

The qualitative research techniques I used included informant and ethnographic interviews, participant observation, focus group sessions, and textual analysis of media coverage accorded to the pageant. The analysis of ethnographic fieldwork data in this monograph focuses on the perspectives and views of organizers, sponsors, advertisers, and other supporters of the Miss World pageant.

As defined by Thomas Lindlof, informant interviews are two- to three hour-long interviews with select key members of groups that represent different and sometimes competing social and economic interests, and can thus offer a variety of insights into a research problem. Informant interviews elicit responses to specific domains of information about a cultural phenomenon, and researchers conduct these interviews with prepared questions at pre-set times and places.

I conducted thirty five informant interviews with former and current employees of the firm Amitabh Bachchan Corporation Limited who were responsible for managing the pageant; sponsors and advertisers; public relations directors and assistants at the firm that handled publicity and promotion for the Miss World pageant; editors, reporters, and writers at English-language newspapers, newsmagazines, women's magazines, and popular vernacular magazines. Based on the preferences of informants, these interviews took place at homes, offices, restaurants, public parks, and lobbies of office buildings.

Although most interviews were conducted in individual sessions where I interacted with one informant at a time, in certain cases, at the request of employees who worked for the same organization, I interviewed them in small groups of two or three. In recording informant interviews, I used a combination of writing fieldnotes and audiotaping conversations. With the exception of two, all informants agreed to be taped, and fully transcribed interviews were provided to all those who requested copies of interview transcripts. To preserve informants' anonymity and confidentiality in this monograph, I use job titles or pseudonyms for those who specifically requested that I mask their identity.

Lindlof defines ethnographic interviews as "informal conversational interviews" that occur more spontaneously in the course of conducting pre-planned research. Ethnographic interviews are "sensitive to the needs and nuances of the moment" and do not require a special site or much preparation.

In the process of conducting informant interviews, I was referred to numerous other individuals who had been closely involved with the pageant. As a result of these recommendations and referrals, I conducted ethnographic interviews with government officials at the Karnataka State Tourism

Development Board; administrative staff at the Windsor Manor Hotel (where beauty contestants from over ninety countries and the founders of the Miss World contest, Eric and Julia Morley, stayed); fashion coordinators; and staff at the cricket stadium where the pageant took place. None of the ethnographic interviews was taped; however, all these interviews were documented with fieldnotes.

## SOUTH INDIA APPEARS MODERN AND TRENDY

Describing the contentious and argumentative deliberations that took place at ABCL over the selection of a venue for the pageant, employees reported that financial expenses and concerns over negative images of urban decay and poverty had been their primary concerns. While ABCL managers' first choice was Mumbai, the entertainment and business centre of India, they had quickly ruled it out due to the high costs of luxury hotel accommodations, exorbitant rental fees for public venues, and large numbers of slum and street dwellers whose presence could detract from the image of a clean and safe tourist location. As one public relations assistant, who worked for the Godrej company in Pune, a smaller city close to Mumbai, remarked:

Bombay is the place you see on Mira Nair's film, which won all those awards-it's Salaam Bombay. It shows all those street children and poverty, and that's why we rejected Calcutta too. Calcutta to the world is the black hole, the place that people have seen in that Patrick Swayze's film City of Joy-full of diseased lepers and poor people.

Yet another advertising accounts executive, a native of Calcutta whose family members had participated in protests against the filming of City of Joy in Calcutta, complained that Hollywood had ensured that Calcutta could never be considered a venue for Miss World even though the city was well known in India for its lively art, film, and theater culture.'" Although New Delhi, the capital of India had a cleaner image than Mumbai and Calcutta, some informants ruled out the capital city because they feared that the central government's sluggish bureaucracy would delay legal permissions and licenses.

The final decision to hold the pageant in Bangalore, a city in South India, was largely due to the pivotal role played by two South Indian ABCL employees, who had decided that this event would highlight South India's receptiveness to modern culture. While Delhi was being seriously considered, one young sales manager in Mumbai, who had grown up in Chennai, the capital city of one of India's southernmost states, had proactively introduced the possibility of holding Miss World at a venue in South India: "When I brought up South India, some people thought I was nuts. Those who don't know the South have these strange notions about us. It's because Hindi movies show South Indians as clowns with no sense of fashion or style." Nodding his head, this executive's South Indian friend agreed with him and then shared further details about how they had decided upon Bangalore: "Chennai was seen as too conservative even though it is the largest city in the South. Other South Indian cities like Hyderabad and Trivandrum were not large enough, and there was no doubt in our minds that Bangalore was perfect." Discussing the image of Bangalore within and outside India, he said:

Bangalore has been in the news a lot. It is a clean city without the crime and poverty of cities like Bombay, so retired people like it. It is already a global city because so many multinational computer firms have their Indian offices there. The college women are trendy and fashionable-not as conservative as Hyderabad or Chennai. Those cites will change too but that will take some time.

Determined that South India needed more recognition and a new image that could challenge stereotyped representations in Hindi films and sitcoms, these two executives contacted tourism officials at the Karnataka State Tourism Board in Bangalore to gauge their interest.

Sensing potential for increasing tourism and business opportunities, state officials began to lobby for Miss World. To the excitement of the two South Indians in Mumbai, tourism officials responded with enthusiasm when they were informed about the possibility of bidding for the pageant. They offered to contact the Karnataka Chief Minister's office to confirm other high-level state administrators' willingness to support the event.

The Chief Minister's office also responded positively and suggested that ABCL could hold the inaugural press conference at the impressive, palatial State Legislature building called the Vidhana Soudha. Describing ABCL's reaction to the offer, Akhil Maiyar, the former Chennai resident stated, "That was the turning point. The city of Goa had just approached us, but the offer of the Vidhana Soudha mansion in Bangalore was just too tempting. ABCl knew our inaugural event in that huge building would look very impressive on TV." The state of Karnataka's eagerness to host Miss World was motivated by an interest in propelling Bangalore beyond its global profile in the high-tech business world to new arenas in the beauty, fashion, and entertainment industries. In her analysis of Bangalore's recent evolution as an ideal city for global sports and entertainment events, which had the potential to enrich the city's cosmopolitan image as India's Silicon valley, Smriti Srinivas wrote:

The pageant was surely one of the most important spectacles in the city that year. In fact, several newspaper articles claimed that henceforth, for tax purposes, the definition of entertainment should be changed in the state .... The articles argued that the beauty contests should rightfully be included under the category of entertainment along with sports and films to bring greater revenue to the state.

In enumerating the reasons for the state of Karnataka's positive response to Miss World, one Tourism official in Bangalore pointed to the difficulties in reaching large audiences in India due to the fragmentation of television viewers by cable networks: "We knew Miss World could get people together as much as anything on TV can do it anymore. Bangalore could get so much out of Miss World."

South Indian ABCL executives' views about the South as an ideal "trendy" space for global culture that had not received its due recognition from the rest of India was echoed by others in the business world. Heralding South India as the new "Sexy South," the region in India that had the fastest growing middle-class and the best facilities for enjoying an upper-class lifestyle, Business World, one of India's largest-circulation business magazines, declared, "Junk all the stereotypes; the south as comprising languid backwaters, and southerners as idli [rice cake]-consuming take-it-easy plodders. In fact the South is looking seductive".

Parodying and mocking stereotypes of South Indians as dull and stodgy, the cover of the magazine displayed a nerdy, religious South Indian man in traditional attire sporting designer dark glasses and cowboy boots, and holding a Pepsi can. The cover story indicated that although there was a time when the rest of India had pejorative names for South Indians, the image of South India was rapidly changing. Business World proposed that a stable and growing middle-class, a greater sense of professionalism and ethics in the workforce, a growing demand for lifestyle products among consumers, and a high degree of media penetration had transformed South India into an attractive region for many international and domestic companies. Indian business managers from Volvo, Revlon, Maruti, Whirlpool, and Hyundai, who were interviewed by Business World, discussed their growing investments in major urban centers in South India.

The Miss World pageant was thus eagerly sought after by South Indian ABCL executives and the State of Karnataka to serve local concerns-to challenge the stereotype of South India as the conservative, slow-paced region caricatured in mainstream Hindi films and culture. When ABCL announced its final decision to hold the pageant in Bangalore, other South Indian employees at ABCL, who had joined the campaign to select a venue in South India, celebrated ABCL's decision as a symbolic victory for all South Indians.

## INDIAN BEAUTY QUEENS BRING MISS WORLD TO INDIA

The timing of the Miss World pageant's arrival in India, according to some interviewees, was the result of the representational power of mediated images of beautiful Indian women that had appeared on television and the Internet in the nineties. Some advertisers and media managers argued that were it not for the significant media presence of former Indian beauties who had brought the country great name recognition, the Morleys would not have chosen India as a site for the 1996 Miss World contest.

Although these business professionals conceded that the Indian government's recent economic reforms and the increasing market share of multinational companies in the beauty industry (cosmetics, chemicals, media) contributed to the Morleys' decision to stage Miss World in Bangalore, they maintained that India would not attracted attention, had it not been for the visibility of Indian beauty queens on global television.

Since the early nineties, a series of Indian women have become prominent in the international beauty scene of fashion shows and beauty pageants. In 1992, a virtually unknown Indian woman named Madhu Sapre, came perilously close to winning the Miss Universe title, an event which one writer proposed made the "world and the fashion mavens of India sit up and take notice".

In 1993, a Miss India winner, Namrata Shirodkar, was second runner-up in the Miss Universe pageant. In 1994, a year when a series of Indian women reigned as beauty queens, the first victory for India was Sushmita Sen's crowning as Miss Universe.

Sushmita Sen's victory, as one writer put it, was the "logical culmination of India's quest to wrest a title that until now was the prerogative of a club of esoteric Western nations only." Shortly after Sushmita Sen's success, Sheetal Mallar was crowned in 1994 as the international model of the year at a modeling contest organized in Ibaza, Spain.

Finally, Aishwarya Rai became the first Indian woman to win the Miss World title at Sun City in South Africa. Commenting on the unprecedented amount of media coverage and political endorsement that Sen and Rai received, Corrine Scott writes:

The media reacted as if this were a momentous event in Indian history, providing front-page feature news coverage and numerous TV interviews. Sushmita and Aishwarya were received by the then Prime Minister and President of India in a style more appropriate to important foreign dignitaries.

Aishwarya Rai's and Sushmita Sen's victories at these international pageants caused a frenzy of national media attention in India and even the normally sedate government-owned television channel, Doordarshan, devoted prompt and frequent news coverage to the success of these two women throughout the two days after their crowning.

Informants interpreted the implications of Indian women's new successes and visibility in the global beauty and fashion worlds for India's national image in the global public sphere in explicitly gendered terms. Indian beauty queens were praised because they had finally compensated for Indian men's failures in global athletic events and their invisibility in the widely popular, hyper-masculine (physical, combative, contact) sports world of American football and basketball.

In recounting their reactions to the victories of Indian women in Miss World and Miss Universe, some media professionals contended that these beauty queens' television appearances projected images that transported India into the glamorous and sophisticated worlds of fashion and beauty, and conveyed the message that Indians were now competitive in the global arena. Discussing his feelings of embarrassment whenever he watched the Olympics on television, one young ABCL staffer commented:

I was surprised and happy when I heard that ABCL managed to win the Miss World account. I think Sushmita and Aishwarya did it for us.

Whenever I used to watch the Olympics on television, it was as though it was not even meant for Indians to watch. We're nowhere in any of the sports. My friends and I used to pick other countries to support. These Indian guys cannot even win a bronze medal. Nowadays with these beauty pageants, we're at least there, we're being noticed and even winning. We're beating places like China and Japan-they're always winning in swimming and gymnastics on the Olympics.

Another executive at the Indian branch of L'Oreal cosmetics in Mumbai, a company that was part of ABCL's pageant organizing committee, similarly said:

Unlike those developed countries, our men have not been able to compete in world sports-maybe it's lack of training? Indian women, on the other hand, seem to have an edge. Madhu, Sushmita, and Aishwarya are like our cultural ambassadors when they appear on television. They do so much for our international image and bring international events like the Miss World pageant to India.

One executive from the Welcom Group Hotels, who had played hockey for India, asserted that Indian women's participation in global beauty pageants and ABCL's decision to host Miss World were significant because they signaled India's willingness to speak the common language of global consumerism promoted by the staging of pseudo media events.

According to the Welcom Group executive, Indian men's successes or failures in hockey and cricket mattered little because most people across the world watched American football and basketball, sports in which India would not be able to compete because very few Indian men could meet the standards for strength, endurance, and height. Capturing the spirit of such comments that exalted Indian beauty queens as emblems of national pride, Times of India columnist Jug Suraiya wrote that the victories of Rai and Sen proved that Indians had at last "triumphed over our own unplumbed potential, largely unexplored for lack of self-confidence and self-esteem".

These ideas about the power of Indian women's mediated beauty, a globally mobile product that could command Western culture to embrace India, and critical comments about Indian men's lack of strong, athletic masculinity offer rich insights into the gendered spaces of global representation within which Indians gain currency. Challenging and reversing such discourses of nationalistic pride that celebrated Indian women's successes in the feminine sphere of beauty pageants, the chairperson of the National Commission on Women, Mohini Giri, was reported to have urged the state government to rechannel funds that were originally allocated to city beautification for Miss World into the training of Indian women for the Olympics.

The adulation expressed by professionals in the entertainment and consumer industry for Indian beauty queens as media icons is inextricably linked to the economic boom in the global beauty business in India and to the hypervisibility of the "New Indian Woman" in the nineties as the ideal consuming subject.

In India's recent phase of economic liberalization, the Indian beauty business, which was dominated by Lakme in the eighties, witnessed a flurry of interest among multinational cosmetic giants-Revlon, Oriflame, Avon, L'Oreal, and Benckiser-that began clamoring for a competitive share of the growing Indian middle-class market. With an investment of $1.7 billion and highly publicized tours of supermodels Cindy Crawford and Claudia Schiffer, Revlon, which was launched in India in November 1995, a year before the Bangalore Miss World, secured an 18 per cent share of the cosmetics market in one year.

Former Indian Miss World Aishwarya Rai was hired by Lakme to promote its line of cosmetics, and after their victories, Rai and former Miss Universe Sen have become popular heroines commanding high billings in the Indian film industry. Numerous beauty parlors and beauty shops in Indian cities and villages, several named after the two international Indian beauty queens, now offer a dazzling array of beauty treatments with imported cosmetic products. The multinational cosmetics, fashion, and consumer industries (personal hygiene, household products, cookware, and soft drinks in particular) in India have become actively involved in sponsoring beauty pageants at school, college, community, district, and state levels.

As marketing professionals in this study argued, the awarding of beauty titles has become a costeffective and grass-roots method of building brand awareness and market loyalty. journalists and feminist activists report increases of 30 to 40 per cent in women's memberships in fitness clubs and requests for plastic surgeries have leaped by 20 to 30 per cent from 1990 to 1995.

Simultaneously, the confident and modern middle-class Indian superwoman easily straddling home, work, and marketplace has become ubiquitous in television and print media commercials, sitcoms, and films. As Shoma Munshi reports, the savvy Indian homemaker in commercials is represented as being far more educated about the marketplace than her husband; she reads the fine print about product features, knows more about fashion trends and sophistication, and gathers information on the most nutritious diets and healthy lifestyle choices for her family.

Conflating the power of Indian beauty queens with the consuming potential of the discerning Indian middle-class female consumer, one executive for a cosmetics firm suggested, "Aishwarya and Sushmita showed on television that Indian women can compete and win in anything they want. The Indian woman wants to be the best.

She is demanding the best products. We have to compete for her attention, get her respect, and deliver excellence." In the context of a developing nation, mediated representations of international beauty pageants, fashion parades, Indian beauty queens, and women consumers, wrapped within the package of Western style cosmopolitanism and individualism, have come to constitute the most visually alluring public face of economic globalization.

Contrary to widely accepted notions of beauty queens as organic and spontaneous cultural emissaries of their nations, the patriotic sentiments that global beauty contest participants have voiced as national ambassadors can be traced in part to routine beauty training and grooming. When Indian beauty queens have won titles, their first response, as the Indian contestant, Yukhta Mookhey, Miss World 1999, is reported to have expressed in a BBC news report, is to talk about the glory they have brought their country.

In India, Femina magazine organizes the national Miss India contest and arranges additional training for the winners of the national contest because these "Miss India" winners are automatically selected to compete in Miss World. Femina's chief editor proudly declared that her magazine's training programme for beauty queens guided Aishwarya Rai's response to journalists when she won the Miss World title in 1994: "We [Indians] have conquered the world." Citing this quote, which was widely reproduced in national and international newsmedia, she said, "We have to teach them [Indian contestants] about the power of the media, how to take full advantage of the media moment when they are announced as winners. Without the media, the contestants and the countries they represent cannot get the publicity they want."

Informants' persistent comments about the Bangalore Miss World contest as an accomplishment for India that was facilitated by media images of Indian beauty queens is a reflection of the new emphasis on media training in beauty contestants' grooming Programmes. While fashion experts, women's magazine editors, and business executives agreed that achieving beauty, poise, and glamour had always required commitment, discipline, and diligence, several men and women proposed that the new and evolving terrain of training for international contestants was the task of preparing them to perform for the media.

Media training sessions for Miss India Universe and Miss India World included media orientation lessons; speech, voice, and accent sessions; and lectures on media practices and media audiences. Sharing details about media orientation lessons, the chief editor of Femina magazine revealed that she urged contestants to rise above their selfish and short-term motives for winning the crown of Miss World. Contestants for international beauty, fashion, and modeling events were urged to use the media as a vehicle for promoting India to foreign investors, advancing the prospects of future Indian women contestants, and gaining the support of Indian businesses and Indian citizens.

Speech and voice pathologist Sabira Merchant emphasized that fluent English-language speaking skills were one of the most important criteria in selecting the Indian Miss World contestant, "English is the language of the world. When Miss World contestants from over 100 countries came to Bangalore, they were so pleased that Indians could speak English." In English accent training for the media, Merchant taught Indian contestants to minimize their native regional accents and instead cultivate a more upperclass British accent. Similarly, in his research on beauty contests in Thailand, Callahan also notes that a fluent ability in the English language had become an unwritten qualification for contestants in the national Miss Thailand contest.

As one Thai beauty contest judge he interviewed said, "The beauty queen who cannot speak English will be a dumb-mute beauty queen" . Finally, contestants also learn from Indian news professionals that the electronic media favour consistent, pleasant, and succinct spoken responses. In mock media interview sessions that were taped and reviewed, contestants were exposed to a range of interview questions and techniques. The editor of Women's Era, who had served as media trainer in many grooming Programmes, suggested that the Moneys' decision to select India as a venue for Miss World proved that media training of Indian beauty queens had yielded rich benefits.

Discussing the implications of Indian women's victories at global beauty pageants, Sarah Banet-Weiser comments that the recent crowning of non-Western women as beauty queens indicates that these women have now proven to the world that they can "successfully enact Western disciplinary practices of femininity". Echoing the arguments of protests groups in Bangalore, Banet-Weiser points to the limitations of narratives that construct global beauty pageants as empowering rituals for women of colour, and cautions that as beauty queens, South Asian women are now legitimated by hegemonic, Western standards of beauty.

Countering such academic and activist critiques of global pageants, most executives argued that the Miss World pageant's arrival in India, following in the wake of Indian beauty queens' victories, meant that Indian women could not only meet Western standards of beauty, but in fact exceed and transform these standards.

A few informants proposed that successful Indian beauty queens could raise standards of beauty in Miss World and Miss Universe to new levels that would include non-Western concepts of ideal feminine beauty. In the eyes of many fashion designers, cosmetics firm owners, and women's magazine editors, the Miss World pageant in India signaled the power of Indian women's beauty as possessing unique qualities that surpassed and challenged White, European standards of beauty. The editor of Femina and the manager of special events at ABCL argued that Sushmita Sen's and Aishwarya Rai's successes as beauty queens drew attention to the kind of feminine attractiveness that India valued-beauty that transcended physical attributes to include warmth, grace, charm, intelligence, and personality. Dismissing charges that Miss World's recent relocation to Third World countries offered evidence only of the global beauty industry's profit-making goals, another advertising coordinator for Godrej suggested that Indian beauty contestants were culturally hybrid citizens of the world, who could easily traverse different geographic and cultural spaces:

That's such a negative view of why Miss World came to India. How about thinking in a more positive sense that foreigners are beginning to understand that Indian women are just as and even more sophisticated than Western women. Our women know how to live in both worlds-how to be Indian and how to be Western-so in fact they're even better. They know how to belong in both cultures.

Drawing on discourses of transnational multiculturalism that emphasize exotic and colorful difference in aesthetic and consumer practices, one fashion designer offered, "People are bored with seeing only White faces and Western locations, Indian women's beauty is novel and striking. We have the same features as Westerners, but we are also very different." Yet another manager at a cosmetics company asserted, "Our girls sparkle. On camera, they have the most beautiful and expressive eyes, the best smiles, and when they speak, they sound so cultured and intelligent. We have no dumb blondes."

Informants' assertive comments about the superior qualities of Indian women's beauty and their opinions about Indian beauty queens as active agents who bring success and fame to India are not new discourses about women as idealized cultural representatives of the nation.

These statements that suggest intersections between notions of womanhood and nationhood in informants' interpretations of India's encounters with global culture also influenced early anti-colonial, Indian nationalist discourse. As numerous postcolonial scholars including feminists have argued, one crucial strategy through which Indian male social reformers and nationalists in the 19th century confronted British colonialism was to assert the moral superiority of Indian women as ideal mothers, wives, and national citizens. Partha Chaterjee locates the 19th century idealization of Hindu women as pure and virtuous within the ideology of Hindu nationalism, which constructed a powerful distinction between the home (inner)/private world and the material (outer)/public world. Hindu women, who were seen as part of the home, the world that had not been contaminated by British imperial culture, became the symbols of Indians' superior spiritual and moral inner life.

With the dramatic entry of Indian women into the public sphere of beauty pageants and the recent legitimization of fashion and beauty contests as a part of India's cultural landscape, Indian women continue to function as the "ground" for negotiating Western culture, although the terms of cultural bargaining have changed.

As organizers of the pageant and others testified, the new terrain for establishing the superiority of Indian culture is based not on the virtue or moral character of Indian women, but on Indian women's abilities to compete confidently in the gendered world of global material culture by mastering commodified forms of femininity. Mediated images of modern, cosmopolitan Indian women, who can function as synecdoches for the nation, and spectacular events that represent India as receptive to public displays of women's sexuality become routes to overcome contemporary Western culture's colonial images of India as backward, static, and traditional.

Employing strategies based in gender that echoed the discourses of 19th century Indian nationalists, informants emphasized the celebration of Indian womanhood in the global arena as central to the task of building a modern nation.

Additionally, some informants' comments about the failure of Indian men to display the hypermasculinity that American sports demand is also a discourse that was found in debates over the "weak" masculinity of Indian men in early British colonial discourse. In countering the threat of rebellion from educated Indians who were beginning to question colonial rule, British administrators and intellectuals began to characterize Indian men as the passive, effeminate, and emotional "other," whose subjectivity was contrasted with the strong, assertive, and logical masculinity of British men.

Some informants argued that the Miss World pageant's arrival in India did not signify the dominance of White standards of beauty because Indians' pride in their culture could overcome the power of Western images. One ABCL executive, who previously worked as advertising manager at Cosmopolitan's office in Mumbai, was particularly defensive about the protests against the pageant. In this executive's view, conservative activists' protests about the Miss World pageant as a symbol of cultural imperialism, were not based on the reality of Indian consumers' responses to global images:

Everyone in the advertising, fashion, and media industries knows that Indian consumers have rejected the wholesale import of anything Western. Just because the Miss World pageant comes and brings along with it some beautiful White women, Indian men are not going to forget that our women are very pretty too.

Indian women are also too confident of our culture to buy into those White women's images. When I worked at Cosmopolitan in Bombay, the American management there did a lot of research-- surveys and interviews-and found out that Indian women readers preferred Indian models on the covers. We're not like Japan or Turkey where Cosmo uses only White women on their covers. The public relations director of the agency in Bangalore that ABCL hired to manage local media relations for the Miss World pageant suggested that Aishwarya Rai's and Sushmita Sen's victories (former Miss World and Miss Universe respectively) would command the rest of the world to come to India to learn about what Indian culture values as beautiful:

All the foreign contestants in Miss World wore Indian clothing, the bindis on their foreheads, and got to see traditional Indian beauties. These contestants saw how much we value our culture. India is the only country maybe in the world where women are still proud of our traditional clothing-sarees and shalwar kameezes-everywhere in Asia women wear Western clothing. Another fashion photographer and mother of two girls argued that organizers had done their best to localize Miss World for Indian audiences. Drawing on her parenting experiences to explain Indian consumers' loyalty to their own culture, she said, "My girls were excited about Miss World but they don't hate Indian culture. For example, they like their Barbie dolls in saris the most. Unlike other countries, Barbie did not sell in India until Mattel put her in a sari."

These statements seem to offer evidence of the localization of global culture in India, that is, of local audiences' indifference Towards standard Western products and images.

Scholars have shown that multinational corporations have needed to modify and "Indianize" their cultural products to appeal to Indian consumers.

On the one hand, Indian consumers' preferences for localized versions of transnational products such as Barbie or beauty pageants demonstrates that consumption practices are mediated by ethnic, racial, and national differences. On the other hand, these preferences also reveal the transnational commodification of multiculturalism and the growing obsession with "ethnic chic" within India.

As Indrepal Grewal writes, certain sections of the urban elite in India consume Indian folk and rural art, food, and clothing in upscale retail stores along with Western products to experience their identities as global consumers, yet retain a sense of authenticity, distinction, and difference from the rest of the world.

Additionally, as Nilanjana Gupta writes, although Indian consumers of television have shown strong preferences for indigenous programming in the midst of a wave of foreign programming, most of the popular music Programmes, sitcoms, and soaps borrow liberally from Western formats.

Informants' defensive arguments about Indian consumers' appreciation for authentic Indian beauty and Indian values, even as they expressed enthusiasm for the Miss World pageant as a symbol of Western modernity, captures the complexities of transnational culture that weaves the local into the global.

## THE CULTURAL SIGNIFICANCE OF BEAUTY PAGEANTS

While numerous feminist scholars have studied cultural ideals of feminine beauty in advertising and popular culture, beauty pageants have only recently begun to attract academic attention. Although cultural studies scholars have challenged many earlier distinctions between high and low culture, beauty pageants continue to function as a form of "low culture," yct to be awarded the kind of "hip" and current academic interest in popular television culture such as the X-Files, Ally McBeal, Simpsons, The Jerry Springer show, or Seinfeld. Pointing to the difficulties she encountered in being considered a serious scholar of gender and contemporary culture because she wanted to study beauty pageants, Sarah Banet-Weiser notes the dearth of scholarly work on beauty pageants and writes, "...these events are often and easily dismissed as frivolous, meaningless, or carnivalesque and therefore unworthy of serious and sustained intellectual scrutiny".

This study's analysis of international beauty pageants in the non-- Western world as multi-layered global media events that narrate stories about gender, nationalism, the politics of religion, and regionalism echoes recent feminist approaches to beauty pageants in the United States. Going beyond early radical feminist critiques of pageants as events that embody the patriarchal and sexist objectification of women's bodies, scholars have instead begun examining contests as rituals that are also deeply entangled with discourses of race, class, nation, and ethnicity. Combining a historical approach with empirical data gathered from interviews with producers and beauty contestants, Sarah Banet-Weiser shows that the Miss America pageant is a cultural site that encapsulates notions of White upper-class respectability, corporate multiculturalism, and U.S. nationalism.

Analyzing archival documents and oral history interviews, Judy TzuChun Wu (1997) explores the historical significance of the Miss Chinatown USA pageant in San Francisco. Focusing on written and spoken discourses about beauty contestants' roles within the Chinese community, she argues that the pageant became a ritual for Chinese Americans to express assimilation and difference.

Chinese Americans viewed the pageant as a performance of Western modernity that would allow them to become a part of White America, yet retain their own distinct cultural identity by using the pageant to promote Chinese traditions and values. Similarly, Pamela Thoma (1999) studies "Miss India Georgia," a video documentary of interviews with prospective Indian-American beauty contestants, to illustrate the complex diasporic experiences of second-generation immigrant women whose identities oscillated among their life experiences as East Indians, American citizens, and minority women of colour.

An important argument underlying the studies of Banet-Weiser, Tzu-Chun Wu, and Thoma is their insistence on analyzing women's participation in and consumption of beauty pageants as activities that incorporate more than a sense of false consciousness or passive submission to ideologies of patriarchy or capitalism. As these feminists argue, pageants include and draw upon cultural narratives of women's empowerment, liberal notions of individual achievement and equal opportunity, and progressive ideas of diversity and pluralist tolerance.

Anthropologists have been far ahead of media scholars in studying the significance of beauty pageants in non-Western locations. In a pioneering collection of essays in the book Beauty Queens on the Global Stage, folklorists and cultural anthropologists examine community queen contests in Guatemala, Nicaragua, and rural Minnesota and national pageants in Thailand, Belize, Tonga, and Tibet to reveal the ways in which beauty contests are embedded within and epitomize struggles over regional, national, global, and gender identities.

Avoiding the simplistic assumption that beauty pageants offer evidence only of hegemonic Western cultural imperialism, the essays in Beauty Queens on the Global Stage pay careful attention to the harnessing of global culture in non-Western contexts to debate and contest various local identities within national boundaries. This study of the Miss World pageant in India adopts these authors' nuanced approach to the cross-cultural popularity of imported Western rituals and artifacts in the developing world.

Political scientist William Callahan's essay on the Miss Thailand contest is the only study of pageants that pays attention to the electronic media's role in transforming beauty contests into large scale public spectacles.

Employing a semiotic and historical approach, Callahan analyzes the changing local political and economic contexts of the national Miss Thailand contest to illustrate the different meanings that various competing forces-the nation state, elite upper-class groups, and capitalist organizations-mapped onto the figure of Miss Thailand.Emphasizing the role of the mass media in shaping non-Western audiences' experiences of Western modernity, Callahan writes, "Television promoted Miss Thailand and Miss Thailand promoted television; one of the prizes for the winner of the contest was a television set ...".

Callahan's proposition that the relationship between electronic media and popular rituals is a dialectic and dialogic process-the spectacle of beauty pageants affects television's visual power and the audiences of television in turn influence the form and content of beauty pageants-- underlies this study's analysis of Miss World in India.In building upon the growing body of research on beauty pageants, this ethnographic study of the Indian culture industry's views on the televised Miss World contest contributes to international communication research on media globalization and feminist media studies.

My analysis of interviews with organizers, sponsors, and other supporters of Miss World reveals that the social construction of beauty pageants as rituals of modernity is inseparable from perceptions and impressionistic images about the power of global media. In taking a feminist approach to the ethnographic data on media representations of beauty pageants, my research shows that gender-debates over femininity, feminism, and modernity-mediates local reception to globalization.

## GLOBALIZING BOLLYWOOD

When actor Amitabh Bachchan founded the Amitabh Bachchan Corporation Ltd. (ABCL) in India in 1993, one among the many goals that he had envisaged for the corporation was to shape the company over the nineties into India's top event-management company. He wanted ABCL to become the leader among firms in India that managed domestic and international events.

The Miss World pageant was the first international media event that the company decided to host in India to gain a national reputation and announce the grand scope of ABCLs vision for the future. Gaining name recognition for his company in event management was, however, only part of Bachchan's plans for ABCL because he had even greater ambitions- eventually, through his company's media ventures he intended to become India's local version of the media mogul Rupert Murdoch.

The Miss World pageant's popularity since the late eighties has decreased among its earlier traditional audiences in the United Kingdom and the United States, and has moved on to newer pastures in Latin America, China, Russia, Eastern Europe, South Asia, and Africa.

It was precisely because of Miss World's increasing popularity in these new regions that the founder decided it would be appropriate for ABCL to seek out the pageant as its launching pad. Discussing the grand game plan behind the founding of ABCL, Bachchan's chief assistant shared with me the long-term plans Bachchan had outlined to his employees in order to ensure that ABCL gained prestige as an excellent communications company.

The Miss World contest was the ideal event to announce Bachchan's vision because ABCL's longterm goal was to manage the distribution of Hindi films, Indian television Programmes, and popular Indian music (Indypop) within India and abroad.

In the last ten years, films produced in Bollywood, as the city of Mumbai is referred to in a parody of Hollywood, have become popular among non-Indians in the Middle East, Africa, Russia, Eastern Europe, Fiji, and the Philippines, and among the South Asian diaspora in Europe and the United States. Among the Bollywood film stars who are well known in these parts of the world, Bachchan continues to have the highest name recognition despite the appearance of a wave of new film stars since the late eighties. Describing Bachchan's popularity in many countries across the world, Carla Power and Sudip Mazumdar (2000) write:

Tom Cruise didn't make the list, Marilyn Monroe finished ninth, and Sir Laurence Olivier was runner-up. In a worldwide BBC Online poll last year on the millennium's biggest star, the winner was 57-year old man born in Allahabad, India. Amitabh Bachchan or `the Big B' to millions of Indian film fans has been a megastar for three decades. His devotees found everywhere from Rajasthani villages to Australian cities are a passionate lot.

As his employees reported, Bachchan's idea to start a communications company grew out of his travels abroad when scores of Indian and Non-Indian fans lined up to greet him in Russia, Egypt, Cameroon, and Mauritius. These fans often called out to the celebrity star using his film names from the popular Hindi films (easily over two hundred) in which he had played the role of the romantic, rebellious, and strong hero.

Several informants claimed that ABCL, as a corporate citizen committed to advancing India's economic growth, was founded to aid the Indian popular culture industry to maintain control over its production and distribution systems. As one ABCL executive put it, "Bachchan's goal was to bring professionalism, discipline, and order to a very undisciplined film industry that was producing popular films for non-traditional areas of the world.

" The "undisciplined film industry" he referred to is the world's largest film industry-Hindi film production based in Mumbai and other new locations in India. One entertainment executive from Sony Music, who had worked for ABCL during Miss World, said:

It was a very good sign when ABCL appeared on the scene because it meant that we Indians were getting our act together to systematically manage the unruly entertainment industry in India. And it was even better when they decided to announce this with the Miss World event. It showed their commitment to an international vision, to being ambitious, and you know, to taking India to a new level in the entertainment industry.

According to a judge in the 1996 Miss World pageant, the founders/ owners of the Miss World pageant, Eric and Julia Morley, were well aware of Bachchan's popularity as a film star and a media celebrity, and hence they were confident that ABCL was the best company in India to manage the Miss World event. In fact, the Moneys had invited Bachchan the previous year to be a judge in the 1995 Miss World contest in Sun City in South Africa.

Framing Bachchan's goals in founding ABCL and in bringing the Miss World pageant to India as efforts to infuse Bollywood with a new image of professionalism, one executive at the cable channel Zee TV talked about the Miss World pageant as "clean and fun" entertainment, a wholesome image of confident and beautiful women that would serve ABCL well in India because the Bollywood film industry had traditionally been financed and run by "goondas" (gangsters).

However, this Zee channel executive's enthusiastic endorsement of ABCL's bid to host Miss World as their firm's first international event was not a unanimous, seamless response articulated by all Indian business and entertainment professionals. In some quarters, reception to Bachchan's choice of Miss World as his inaugural media venture reflected intergenerational differences and class-based, nationalistic responses to pageants as a form of rejected "low culture" that Western multinationals were dumping into the Third

World. Some older male informants at Godrej and Air India suggested that despite their admiration for Bachchan, they were reluctant to approve their younger colleagues' decision to sponsor Miss World.

One employee, who had worked at Godrej over thirty years, expressed his disappointment on two levels, "I was shocked that Bachchanji wanted to do this. His father was a famous literary figure, a high-class poet. And then I was surprised that my company's highly educated management thought this was a good idea." A government official at Air India clearly denounced Miss World as a project unworthy of Bachchan, a larger than life media figure in India, who should have diplomatically rejected the Morleys' offer to host Miss World after the protests began, "I know he wants to make money, but he should also wonder why foreigners, the Moneys, want to bring pageants to India.

He has become an unwitting pawn of these multinationals." As Outlook magazine reported, some older actors and directors in the Indian entertainment industry thought Bachchan had in fact "cheapened" his image by associating himself with a beauty pageant, a trivial event that only "girls" watched anymore. Such debates surrounding Bachchan's decision to host Miss World indicate that semiotic struggles over gender, modernity, and culture take place not only among scholars, intellectuals, or activists, but also within the culture industry itself.

Challenging the role of "greedy, money-hungry-businessman" that some Indian actors, artists, and directors imputed to Amitabh Bachchan, his current and former employees argued that the superstar had not founded his business solely to make money.

These informants proposed that Bachchan's lofty goal as a visionary was to ensure that Indians did not lose control over their own culture in the process of globalization. Bachchan had hoped that ABCL's hosting of Miss World would convince Indian entertainment and media companies that they did not need an experienced Western multinational to distribute and manage their media products.

Protesting charges from his fans and followers within the industry that he had become a ruthless capitalist, who could ignore ethics, cultural traditions, and patriotism in his pursuit of profits, Bachchan evoked nationalism when he passionately defended himself:

The idea wasn't to make money with the Miss World pageant. It was a vision. I wanted Indians to see that ABCL could do this and more even. ABCL was to launch India to the rest of the world and if we didn't do it ourselves, foreigners would do it for us ... they would move in..

In an interview with Telegraph and Outlook magazines, Bachchan stated that his objective in accepting the assignment to manage Miss World pageant in India was to utilize the profits from the pageant to initiate Indian film and popular music distribution ventures that might otherwise be taken over by

American multinationals. Despite his lifelong career in the film industry, Bachchan, a savvy media entrepreneur, resisted the notion of using his celebrity status to promote Miss World among middle-class Indian youth, an audience that advertisers and sponsors were eager to target. ABCL executives had wanted Bachchan to concentrate on courting young, urban cosmopolitan Indians among whom they felt Miss World was bound to be much more popular than older audiences.

These executives had encouraged the actor to reach out to younger Indian audiences because unlike older Indians in the 30-50 age group, who had grown up watching famous blockbuster Bachchan movies, young Indians were not as familiar with Bachchan's films. One young public relations director argued that young Indian audiences' low awareness of the actor's contributions was linked to new practices of consumerism and global media consumption that distinguished television-savvy Indians from the older film-watching generation:

Young people in our country are Westernized-they are MTV, Cosmo, Coca Cola kids. They watch lots of TV, not just films. Amitabh had a hard time understanding that he had to make an effort to reach out to them-to give interviews, appear on TV with his children, and associate more with younger film stars like Aamir Khan, Sharukh Khan, and Aishwarya Rai on TV. To promote Miss World, he had to let young people know that he was a famous international star and let them know that through managing ABCL, he was going to improve India's economic power.

ABCL employees and their colleagues in the media industry offered two reasons for Bachchan's reluctance to promote Miss World on television; his ignorance of media marketing and branding strategies and his inability to understand the performative aspects of his role as Miss World's Indian spokesperson for television.

Based on the advice of management consultants, Bachchan had brushed aside his wife's fears over the invasion of her family's privacy and agreed to name his communications company after himself so that his media venture could gain instant awareness and recognition. However, his vision of the Miss World contest's ability to translate his fame and celebrity status into a brand name for ABCL did not go beyond this initial effort.

One ABCL marketing executive suggested that Bachchan, son of famous Indian poet Harivanshrai Bachchan and friend of India's former prime minister Rajiv Gandhi (grandson of Jawaharlal Nehru), was confident that his literary upper-class background, political connections, and fame as a superstar ensured that he did not have to court the news and entertainment media to publicize Miss World.

This executive argued that although Bachchan had earned more money than any other Indian film star, the actor was woefully naive about money matters and business practices of building and expanding fledgling enterprises,

"Bachchan is more of an artist than a businessman. His family members and managers took care of everything his whole life. Miss World proved that when he was suddenly thrown into the corporate media ocean, he could not cope." Others claimed that Bachchan's shy and reserved off-screen personality that starkly contrasted with his emotional on-screen performances surprised reporters and television audiences because it mistakenly conveyed a remote arrogance and lack of warmth.

Even before he founded ABCL, Bachchan had developed a reputation among film and entertainment reporters and celebrity columnists as an inaccessible and emotionally difficult interview candidate. ABCL executives and their PR agency employees disclosed that one of the most difficult tasks they undertook was training Bachchan for his promotional public appearances and press conferences, "We had to teach him to speak in soundbites, to be enthusiastic, to recite dialogues from his films, and to smile more often."

Paradoxically, despite Bachchan's assiduous efforts to overcome his repugnance for public appearances and commodify himself as a brand for Miss World and ABCL, his managers discovered that Indian audiences' responses to these promotional images were lukewarm, less than enthusiastic, and in some cases, hostile. After Miss World, the actor continued to market his celebrity status by appearing in television commercials where he endorsed BPL's electronic goods and Pepsi's beverages.

In a cover story on the superstar's failed attempts to brand himself for Miss World, Outlook magazine argued that the aging actor, adored by millions of Indian fans, had degraded himself by trying to gain cheap publicity. Offering comments that scorned the media strategies of ABCL's management professionals, who were eager to transform Bachchan's cultural capital into economic gains, Outlook reporter Saira Menezes suggested that it was impossible to transform Bachchan's magical, godlike aura of superhero masculinity into a brand:

For simply too many people, if not all, Bachchan was the supreme embodiment of life's most incredible possibilities. He could rouse you to anger, move you to tears, and dissolve you in smiles as consummately and completely as any real life experience. It was the fantasy trade millions around the country made everyday, as they paid up at theaters to live out a heightened and intensified life cycle in three short hours. The faceless and soulless money managers who gathered around him made the mistake of convincing him he was a brand. He is not. He is magic.

Reinforcing Menezes' views about Bachchan's mistakes in pursuing the mundane arena of television after a grand history on the awe-inspiring canvas of films, Graphiti magazine indicated that Bachchan had erred by suddenly offering numerous media interviews in 1996. Veteran film reporter Vir Sanghvi remarked that Bachchan's enormous popularity was related to the actor's decision to quietly stay behind the scenes, conduct himself with "impeccable dignity," and allow his on-screen persona to conduct the real work of performance and artistry.

Comparing Bachchan's enduring prestige and fame with other actors (Rajesh Khanna and Vinod Khanna), whose well-publicized, sensational personal lives had exposed their weaknesses and failures, Sanghvi remarked, "What could be done when the warrior became a deviant selling beauty pageants, television sets, and cold drinks? The warrior began to make the hero on a white charger look increasingly like a half-wit on a flea-ridden horse craving petty profits".

## GLOBALIZATION AND LOCALIZATION

In considering beauty contests as rich sites for ethnographic study, Beverly Stoeltje, a feminist ethnographer and folklorist, argues that pageants, much like the spectacular rituals of pre-modern societies, are ritualistic cultural performances of our modern world. Stoeltje writes that as mediated spectacles, beauty pageants offer scholars three sites for cultural analysis: the evolution of the event's form, the organization of the event's production, and the discourse in which it is embedded.

One important discourse that shapes the production and reception of global pageants among local media and culture industries is the promise of the potential visibility that these media events offer contestants, sponsors, advertisers, and the nations and cities that host these contests. Analyzing the staging of global pageants in locations outside of Western metropolitan centers, Banet-Weiser suggests that in bidding for the pageant, state officials and local event management firms seek out the constructed media representation of their host countries as desirable places to visit, invest, and conduct collaborative business.

A critical aspect of marketing rituals of global culture in today's mediasaturated world is ensuring that newsmedia, magazines, and local and national television build anticipation and excitement prior to the staging of the live media event. Organizers of the Miss World contest began generating print and video news releases about the contestants, history of the pageant, and the format of the live performance six months prior to the live event. Advertisers and members of the hospitality and tourism industries also promoted their involvement in supporting the pageant.

For example, a lengthy feature story in India's roost reputable financial newspaper, The Economic Times, titled "Colonial ambience, Indian warmth for beauties" explained the preparations that the Windsor Manor hotel in Bangalore had undertaken to ensure a memorable lodging experience for the contestants, many of whom were visiting India for the first time.

This chapter contained details about decor modifications-special furnishings, plants, lighting, and landscaping-and cuisine arrangements ("delicious but not fattening") that the Windsor Manor hotel staff had planned to welcome and host Miss World's founders and participants. Suruchi Rai, the senior housekeeping manager of the hotel conducted several guided tours for television and print reporters and writers during the month of October. Miss World's founders, Eric and Julia Morley, visited India in July 1996, four months before the scheduled live performance, to promote the pageant as "Beauty with a Purpose" at local charity events in Mumbai.

Not all audiences in local cultures greet international beauty pageants and other rituals of globalization with the enthusiasm and excitement expressed by state officials, advertisers, and members of the entertainment industry. The city of Bangalore witnessed an unprecedented flurry of public protests that intensified during the months of October and November 1996.

Members of women's groups-Mahila Jagran Samiti, Mahila Jagruthi, Vimochana, the All India Women's Democratic Forum, and the National Commission on Women-courted local and global media. To gain publicity, the All India Women's Democratic Forum hosted a mock pageant, a satirical commentary on Miss World, that was covered on the front pages of newspapers and in local and national television news; at a large, centrally located public park, feminists crowned mock women contestants as "Miss Poverty, Miss Homeless, and Miss Landless."

Numerous columns authored by feminist academics, activists, and journalists appeared in the Deccan Herald, Indian Express, Times of India, and The Hindu.

Competing with ABCL for news coverage, leaders of political parties including the Communist Party of India (Marxist), the Bharatiya Janata Party, and the state's peasant group, the Karnataka Rajya Raitha Sangha, actively cultivated journalists, gave interviews, and provided provocative quotes.

State of Karnataka residents, who were members of the protest group, the Kannada Agitators Forum, dressed as demons of Hindu mythology and carried a nude cutout of Amitabh Bachchan, owner of ABCL. During the week of the pageant, as the protests became increasingly vocal and violent, CNN, BBC, The New York Times, the Los Angeles Times, and the Washington Post zoomed their journalistic lenses on Bangalore.

On November 23, 1996, CNN World View anchor Jeanne Meserve and CNN's Indian correspondent Anita Pratap described the live performance of the pageant and summarized the reasons for the protests during the prime time news slot at 7 p.m.

The 1996 Miss World contest in India thus highlights the media's crucial role in representing the agendas of different competing groups in the global public sphere. At the most fundamental level, mass media create the conditions of possibility for media events such as beauty pageants that rely on consumer desire for spectacle to attract the support of capitalist enterprises. However, the very same media that serve the commercial goals of advertisers and sponsors also enable activist and community organizations to enlist public support for their causes. The discourses of organizers, sponsors, and protesters disseminated by the media transformed the pageant into an ideological space in which numerous social and commercial entities voiced their opinions on India's gradual incorporation into the global economy. This ethnographic account, which unravels perceptions of the media's representational power among local agents in India, who had the greatest investment in the success of Miss World, considers recent theoretical propositions regarding the tensions and contradictions that arise during the process of globalization.

Revising earlier models of cultural imperialism, interdisciplinary scholars of globalization have begun speculating on alternative ways of studying and theorizing transnational relationships between the West and the non-West. Instead of envisioning globalization as a binary encounter where the global is the agent of cultural destruction and the local is the site of pristine cultural authenticity, Ien Ang and Ulf Hannerz suggest that the global and local are complexly articulated in mutually constitutive ways.

Extending this argument further, Robertson argues that we cannot always assume the idea of locality to be synonymous with forms of local resistance to the hegemonically global, that is, locality cannot simply be seen as the pitting of non-Western subalterns against dominant Western forces.

As Robertson comments, discourses of globalization cannot be effective unless they actively participate in the production of locality-the cultural adaptation of global commodities, rituals, and ideologies to persuade local audiences to become loyal fans and consumers. For effective localization, multinational producers and distributors therefore need the services and resources of local cultural agents who can shape the ideological, material, and historical contours of global culture for local consumption.

In the case of the Miss World pageant in India, protests by cultural, traditional, and activist groups against the pageant comprised one element of the local; however, another aspect of the local that preceded the protests was the goals of Indian commercial enterprises-ABCL, Indian advertisers, women's magazine editors, and professionals in the fashion and beauty industry-to collaborate with the Moneys in organizing and producing the pageant in India. Significantly, one common critique of numerous protests launched against the staging of the pageant in Bangalore addressed the collusion of local Indian producers in transnational projects of globalization.

Given the context of local activism against globalization, what roles do organizers of pageants construct for local producers of mediated global culture? How do professionals in local culture industries legitimize their coproduction of allegedly imperialistic narratives?

Addressing the discursive indigenization of international pageants in their new locations in Asia and Eastern Europe, Banet-Wesier (1999) suggests that despite the overt layer of Westernization, internal categories of nationalism and sexuality permeate local renderings of Miss World and Miss Universe. What media strategies of crisis containment based in local cultures and histories did producers devise to indigenize Miss World?

Analyzing the production of locality, Arjun Appaduari (1996) argues that ethnographies of global-local interactions must shift from merely describing the local to analyzing the imaginary landscape that informs the mediation of globalization by local historical subjects.

Appaduari also contends that the experience of locality is a relational achievement, that is, the global becomes intelligible to local actors through the discursive generation of historical, geographic, and ideological contexts that frame and provide meaning to participation in global projects. With the recent focus on media reception, the local is often conflated with audiences and consumers' responses to global culture; however, local producers, individuals who are part of the wider culture and share its values, are rarely subjects of ethnographic study.

As local actors in the production of international pageants, what contexts and historical events influenced Indian media and business professionals' endorsement of India's association with globalization? Did they express their enthusiasm for the televised global pageant vis-a-vis the imaginary construction of the First World? Did other neighborhoods, closer to India, constitute contexts against which the mediated Miss World became a source of power and modernity?

Most research on globalization has exclusively focused on the impact of Western culture on national, racial, and ethnic identities. Reviewing studies of political economy and audience reception in non-Western cultures, Anabelle Sreberny-Mohammadi questions the glaring absence of analyses that take into account categories of gender and class in studying media globalization. Gender, a crucial site of difference that organizes global consumerism, has become a resource for global and local producers of media culture to shape their persuasive messages for local audiences.

Indrepal Grewal sketches the gendered context of cosmopolitan consumerism in urban India where the boom in the beauty and vanity industries, following economic liberalization, has reinforced and reshaped existing gender and class relations.

Grewal notes that English-language magazines such as Verve targeted at middle-class Indian women project their ideal readers as hybrid, cosmopolitan female consumer subjects-contemporary urban women with Indian roots and Western exposure.

Mining state and activist discourses on Indian women's empowerment, proliferating advertising images in media discourses simultaneously exalt traditional roles even as they construct Western style consumption practices as alternative modes of experiencing individualized freedom and resistance. With regard to Miss World, what imaginary notions of gender relations and female subjectivity guided local producers' visions of global pageants?

Globalization also cannot be envisaged solely in terms of existing centre-- periphery models because the new global cultural economy has begun to reveal numerous overlapping zones of cultural production and consumption. Suggesting that globalization need not always imply Americanization, Appadurai argues that new nodes of globalization emerging in Asia may draw from Western discourses of modernity, but the desire to produce and consume American culture and emulate Western practices of consumerism cannot itself be viewed as evidence of cultural and economic capitulation.

Did the arrival of the Miss World contest herald more than India's steady incorporation into the global marketplace? What economic imperatives drove ABCL, a fledgling media production and distribution firm in India, to seek out the assignment of hosting Miss World?

Exploring local producers' perceptions of imported Western rituals and commodities could also demonstrate the complex appropriation of global culture in non-Western contexts to reinforce and challenge local hierarchies and power relationships. Original producers of transnational culture in First World settings may or may not always be able to envision the heterogeneous, semiotic negotiations that take place over the incorporation of global culture into local structures.

As len Ang writes, much to our surprise, we may find that "local cultures tend to reproduce themselves precisely, to a large extent, through the appropriation of global, mass-mediated forms and technologies". For instance, what cultural factors compel different cities within host nations to offer competing bids for international pageants? Why was Miss World held in Bangalore in South India and not in the wellestablished, larger metropolitan cites of Mumbai, New Delhi, or Calcutta?

## HARNESSING THE POWER OF THE GLOBAL IMAGE

By the time the 1996 Miss World pageant came to the city of Bangalore, global television had become fairly entrenched as a part of leisure culture in urban India. Commenting on the widespread availability of global television networks like CNN, which have today extended their reach to many non--Western locations, len Ang (1996) writes in her book Living Room Wars, "The transnational dissemination of mass mediated culture is, given the strength of global capitalism in today's world economy, an irreversible process that cannot be structurally transcended".

One recent development, which visibly proclaims the arrival of the global economy in India is the advancing intrusion of global television into the imaginary worlds of Indian consumers; numerous cable channels including CNN,

MTV, Discovery, and STAR have become popular within a largely middle- and upper-class urban Indian market. In her comprehensive study of the growth of television in India, Nilanjana Gupta (1998) writes that although cable TV had very slow growth in the late eighties, by 1993, with the advent of satellite television, several major Indian cities witnessed a dramatic increase in the number of cabled households. The demand for cable television networks in Mumbai that offered CNN, as Sevanti Ninan documents, increased in leaps during and after the Persian Gulf War in January-February 1991.

Although many informants in Mumbai and Bangalore appreciated CNN as a valuable educational resource that enabled Third World audiences to gain knowledge about the world and become global citizens, a majority argued that the positive potential of global television news was undermined by its persistent, ethnocentric representations of India.

Interviews with business and media professionals and observation of television's place in their everyday lives indicated that subscribing to cable television services, particularly those that offered news networks like CNN and BBC, was not considered an indulgence or luxury. The central space occupied by the television set in living rooms, the scheduling of interviews to accommodate informants' news viewing practices, and parents' insistence on exposing their children to CNN and Discovery pointed to these upwardly mobile informants' strategic use of cable television as a commodity that could enhance their access to global cultural capital in a changing economy.

One meeting with three executives who had worked for ABCL during the Miss World pageant took place at the home of Rajan Mehta, a resident of Malabar Hills, an affluent neighborhood in Mumbai where a large number of India's well-known entertainment and business élite lived. Gesturing towards a large screen television that dominated one wall of the lavishly furnished living room, Mehta offered, "It's the magic window that shows us the world."

Responding to his remark, his friend and former colleague quickly said, "Yeah, but the window does not always show reality." As the interview proceeded, the context and meaning of the second comment, which alluded to the inability of global television news to accurately portray reality, became a crucial subtext that lurked beneath informants' enthusiasm for the Miss World contest.

All three men including Mehta spoke animatedly about the world now appearing in their homes and of being privileged to routinely receive live news coverage of world events; however, they also became involved in a heated debate about the marginalization of India and Indians in Western media. Arguing that ethnocentric Western news producers could not imagine middle-class Indians as intelligent audience members, who expected accurate and complete coverage of India, one executive spoke at length about the images of India he had frequently seen on CNN and Discovery: Whenever India is on the television, my children will usually shout and ask me to hurry up so I can catch what they're showing. They're very proud of course that India is on foreign TV. But whenever India is on foreign channels, it is either the plague, shortage of onions, nuclear war, famine, or snake charmers. That's what they had on Discovery the other day. Snakes in India. Think of India and you can predict what will be on screen.

Interrupting, the third executive, who had received his MBA degree in the United States, voiced similar sentiments, although he focused on the representations of Indian women in a broader range of media including newspapers, newsmagazines, and television news:

Whenever they show Indian women in any foreign media - New Yorker, CNN, Time magazine, National Geographic, New York Times - it is always poor abused widows, child brides who are exploited, women who are aborting girl babies, ... that journalist for the New York Times - yes, Barbara Crossette, she always writes only negative stories about India. When I lived in the United States, Americans would often ask me what I thought of how Indian men treated their wives and mothers.

Suggesting that global media's representations of its new audiences in Asia lagged far behind its ambitious goals of geographic expansion, an advertising accounts executive for the Godrej company (chief sponsor of the pageant) said:

It is as though world news is for those people, those who live in Europe and the United States. We in Asia watch TV too you know. They forget I think that people in countries like India get BBC, CNN-when they show India on the news now, I want to tell them, hey watch out, Indians are watching their own country on your news.

Two other advertising managers (one represented a large garment retailer and the other a hair products company), who had persuaded their CEOs to release funds for advertising space during the live broadcast of Miss World, expressed similar resentment over Western representations of India-not just in the news, but also in Hollywood films like Indiana Jones and the Temple of Doom and City of Joy.

These comments illustrated the contradictory experiences of transnational audiencehood for consumers of global news and popular culture in developing countries such as India. While Indian television viewers feel empowered as global citizens through easy and instant access to news of the world. they also have to routinely endure Western media's recycled catalog of stories on India that emphasize exotic customs, natural disasters, poverty, and ancient forms of oppression.

It is against this context of global television news from the West, which in the words of my informants, continues to code and interpellate the Euroamerican consumer as the ideal viewer, that television coverage of the Miss World pageant became a powerful tool for ushering in change. The televised Miss World contest in Bangalore presented a crucial opportunity for

Indians to gain media access and produce modern images that could counteract the negative discourse of global newsmedia. Informants described the power of Western modernity associated with Miss World not in the concrete terminology of global audiences or its appeal among Euroamerican viewers, but as inherently contained in the history and spectacular form of the pageant itself.

The pageant's power as a performance of Western cosmopolitanism was conflated with the material presence of the grand stage, a loquacious and entertaining commentator, the panoply of dances and performances, live media coverage, confident women enthralling large audiences, and the indisputable origins of beauty pageants in Western metropolitan locations. Describing Miss World as a historic media event that could harness the representational power of television for India, one ABCL executive discussed the excitement in his office when upper-management formally announced their decision to host the pageant:

Our boss told us it was a great honour for us. On the day when he announced the names of the people on the team that would be working on the pageant full-time for six months, we were all told that this was just the beginning of India's major appearance on world television and for once it would not be famine or poverty, trains crashing, or female children being killed.

Comparing the inclusiveness and popularity of the pageant to other sports events in India that have also claimed the aura of an international appeal, his friend joined in and remarked:

We've had other events you know like World Cup Cricket and International Test Matches but those are just bogus titles-these events are not really world or international. It's just a few countries that were ruled by the British. Now the Miss World pageant was a real world event, with close to 100 contestants, from Europe, Africa, South America, Mexico. It is the world that was coming to India and television can announce that to many.

Arguing that the Miss World pageant enabled the creation of positive news about India, one ABCL executive's comments echoed the sentiments of non-aligned and Third World nations' leaders, who crafted the New World Information Order Policy to explicitly address and reduce imbalances in information flows between developing and developed nations.'

Advising Indians to aggressively pursue visibility on television, he suggested, "We must become the creators of news-otherwise nothing will change. Indians are ignoring the power of television. We need to be active, and participate as people of the world, not just as Indians. We must set the record straight." Finally, hailing the Miss World pageant as a major milestone in India's television history and progress towards Western modernity, one ABCL television producer explained: When the Asiad sports event came to India in the eighties we went to colour TV because we wanted to present the event with all its excitement to Indian audiences who were proud that the Asiad was being held in India. The Miss World pageant is even better than the Asiad because it has been around longer. It will show people who watch television that India can have live large-scale events. People will learn that we're modern, that India is changing and joining the world.

Such local discourse about the power of beauty pageants to project media images of modernity also becomes a strategic defence for producers of global culture to gain support among the elite in Third World locations. In promoting Miss World in local media in Bangalore, Julia Morley, president of Miss World Ltd., drew on resentment among the urban Indian middle- and upper-classes over India's image as a Third World country to persuade city residents to ignore protest groups' demands that the pageant be banned.

Morley is reported to have said to the Bangalore edition of the national newspaper Indian Express, "I find this concept of the Third World very distasteful. When there is talk of one world, how can you polarise and divide it like this".

An important element of the Miss World pageant's symbolic value was its association with specific geographic locations that were compared to India in terms of their progress Towards global modernity. Discussing the potential of Miss World to disrupt the dominant Western image of India as a country beset by "backwardness," one young manager at the public relations company that was responsible for promoting the pageant argued:

The Miss World pageant has gone to Venezuela three times because they [the Venezeulans] are smart. It has even gone to Thailand, I think in 1992. They know that this will get them on TV, and we should be doing it too. When you say the word "Third World" anymore, I know people think of India or Rwanda-we're the same as Rwanda. That's not okay. Even Thailand is probably not considered as Third World as we are. We have to move forward and do what these countries are doing.

According to the manager of the Windsor Manor hotel in Bangalore where the contestants stayed, the Miss World pageant's appearance on television would showcase India's dynamic, urban, cosmopolitan culture in contrast to representations of rural India that suggested stagnation and lack of economic and cultural change. He claimed that media representations of Bangalore as a location where modern, glamorous, and confident women from all over the world could come and perform, would set India apart from other "backward" nations in South Asia:

Think about it. This Miss World pageant used to be held in London and now it's coming to India. Do you think Eric and Julia Morley would even think about going to places like Pakistan or Bangladesh? When people think of Pakistan the only things they can think of are guns, dictators, Mullahs [Islamic priests] and women who cannot even go to college. India is different-we're a secular democracy-and people know we have freedom, our women have the freedom to do many things.Lampooning this widespread urge to construct Pakistan as the demonic "other" in India, newspaper columnist Raj Kamal Jha wrote in a satirical essay that among the top ten reasons for India's hosting the Miss World pageant, the number one reason was, "we're so scared that if we don't, ooooooh, Pakistan might." Mediated representations of Miss World were thus viewed as possessing the power to distinguish India as a modern nation; as similar to ultra-metropolitan spaces in the Western world and newer, modernizing "tourist" nations like Thailand, but different from other Islamic states like Pakistan that are often vilified in mainstream Indian and global media.

According to some interviewees, moving the nation Towards the path of modernity was not a task that the nation state, the Indian government, could accomplish because it was inefficient, corrupt, and lacked entrepreneurial initiative. As one media manager for ABCL argued, it was only due to the visionary spirit of private business that Miss World, a largescale international media event, had arrived in India in 1996, less than a decade after the state's programme of economic liberalization was launched.

Vikram Scindia, the primary special events manager for ABCL, framed the pageant as an event that announced the success of private enterprise in India to the outside world loudly and clearly:

The Miss World pageant is the best special event any country could host to show that they are ready and receptive for multinational companies. We had to pull together three resources-the media, theatre and fashion experts, and the contestants-to create this event. Although the government provided a stadium and security for the pageant, they would not have bidden for Miss World. The government is not capable of doing anything like that because they have no imagination and lack brainpower. All the government wants is easy money-bribes and cutbacks.

In constructing the Miss World pageant as a repository of modernity, another ABCL executive in charge of generating media coverage for the pageant in the English-language newsmedia, argued:

Eric and Julia Morley came to India only because they were confident that ABCL, a private communications company, did not have the hierarchical and corrupt structure of the Indian government. Yes, the government has decreased regulations but that is not enough. You have to communicate to multinationals thatIndia, which is thought of as a Third World country, will support the creation of markets here just like in any developed country.

The chief editor of Femina, a popular women's magazine, bemoaned the lack of commitment and integrity in Indian political leaders since the demise of Jawaharlal Nehru, the first prime minister of India, who actively employed the media to promote Western science and technology as the means to India's modernization. She explained that the Miss World contest represented a milestone in private enterprise's successful intervention into enriching the scope and potential of Indian television: Putting modern images, new and creative images in the media is the responsibility of the private sector. I remember as a child watching the movie Mother India and looking at images of big dams being built within the plot, and it made a huge impact on me. The decision to do that was made by the director who wanted India to make progress. The Miss World contest can do the same-- it can tell people that we are no less than any other country. Today we have liberalization but no real action because the Indian politician lacks imagination and sophisticated thinking.

These charges and complaints from private sector employees about a corrupt Indian government that lacked initiative in seeking out creative media outlets to advertise India's entry into a global economy is part of a larger ongoing and tense relationship between the Indian state and private business interests. As Hilton Root argues, economic liberalization in many Asian countries was proposed by local economists as one among a series of solutions to end political corruption, but the cure for corruption promised by a more free-market economy has yet to be realized.

According to Root, the tense relationship between the private and public sectors in India has only been further exacerbated in the nineties when private firms, hoping for a better business environment, instead found themselves compelled to continue earlier practices of maintaining secret contacts with bureaucrats, cultivating personal connections with politicians, and avoiding tax payments to compensate for high licensing fees.

Informants' association of Miss World with the energy and force of private capitalist enterprise is part of a longer history of beauty pageants in India, which have always been organized and sponsored by media corporations. In fact, the national Miss India beauty contest, managed by Femina, an English-language women's magazine owned by the media conglomerate Bennett and Coleman, has widely been viewed as belonging to the exclusive world of the elite Mumbai-based business and entertainment classes.

In contrast to Thailand, where the national Miss Thailand contest was hosted by the state in the early nineteen fifties as an official public relations event to disseminate messages about democratic ideology and to garner support for the military, the national Miss India contest had not attracted the official attention of the Indian state.

Unlike Thailand where the national beauty contest is apart of its official military history, it would have been unthinkable for the government of a newly independent India that had Mahatma Gandhi as its national hero-the image of austerity, spirituality, and anti-materialism-to use the spectacle of beauty pageants to promote nationalism.

William Callahan writes that the organization of the Miss Thailand contest by private business interests in the sixties, eighties, and nineties signaled a shift in the symbolic value of the contest from being a vehicle for public policy to becoming an agent of private advertising and consumption, and hence a symbol of the power of television as a capitalist force.

Given the different construction of the beauty pageant in India as a performance that was accessible primarily to Westernized elite consumers and celebrities for over three decades, the televised Miss World pageant, as the editor of Femina explained, heralded a new frontier for beauty contests as more democratic and public performances because television, unlike print media, could cross boundaries of class and literacy, "I think the Miss World contest on television allowed many Indians, even those who are poor, to be at a beauty pageant. Poor people could not buy tickets but they could watch Miss World on TV."

As a media spectacle, the global beauty pageant's presence in India also announced the managerial public relations abilities of various local commercial groups. Public relations skills including the organization of the live performance, coordination of news conferences and special events, and the production of news releases and other publicity materials testified to India's new capitalist competence in the global marketplace.

Proclaiming the staging of the Miss World pageant in India as a pivotal event that enhanced Femina magazine's reputation as a leader in the beauty business, an assistant editor in charge of event management at Femina argued, "Thanks to Femina's efforts for over fifty years, India could be seen as a place where we are aware of the power of special events as a magnet for the media.

Advertising is old. Public relations is where the action is today. " One media executive for ABCL remarked that the Miss World pageant signaled the beginning of recognition for the profession of public relations in India, "We need to use public relations not just advertising. In advertising, you pay for media space, but in PR you can get the media to cover you for free. Parameshwar Godrej got on the news because she sponsored Miss World-advertising cannot do that for you. "

Ironically, interviewees cast the positive, productive power of global media events and their public relations' potential differently when they discussed various protest groups' attempts to gain visibility in the public sphere. Some ABCL executives and representatives of commercial sponsors expressed anger and frustration at the volume of unexpected, passionate, and public protests that had erupted over their company's decision to host the Miss World pageant.

These protests against the pageant began as early as July 1996, and as protesters' activities gained momentum, organizers had feared that the live performance of the pageant at the cricket stadium in Bangalore on November 23 would be sabotaged. Several ABCL employees and representatives of advertisers expressed bitterness over public protests-marches in business areas, large public meetings, and angry demonstrations-because these forms of activism caused tremendous disruption in the city, resulted in negative publicity for Miss World, and created a stressful crisis management experience for the organizers.When protests against the pageant took on violent overtones, the assistant to the founder of ABCL was quickly assigned the official title of media spokesperson, and was asked to provide consistent, calm responses to the media. Elaborating on his impressions about protesters' motives, this person argued:

I think the protesters just saw the pageant as an opportunity for lot of free publicity, you know, just to get their names into the news-- they're very cheap. The protests were all about getting themselves in the media-not at all about the pageant. We could easily see that because those feminists in Bangalore never protested dirty images of Indian women in Hindi films. Hindi films show women in the worst ways.

Two employees at Windsor Manor hotel, responsible for placating protesters gathered outside the hotel gates, suggested that political parties and special-interest groups opposing the pageant were not sincere because their shouting and chanting grew louder when television cameras arrived. Informants' assessment of feminist protest against the pageant as a blatant display of opportunism to gain media attention surfaced repeatedly.

Some executives pointed out that feminists organized these protests because they were eager to take advantage of the media attention offered by the unusually large number of reporters from national and international media who had convened in Bangalore to cover the pageant.

Statements about opportunistic "publicity hungry" feminists were frequently accompanied by references to other much more "vulgar" and sexist images of women in imported television Programmes-Baywatch and MTV-and in commercial Indian cinema, images that feminists had apparently chosen to ignore. Two young men explicitly stated that feminists in Bangalore would have gained more credibility if they had protested recent vernacular popular films produced in South India that objectified women in far more graphic ways than beauty pageants.

The media thus figured prominently in denunciations of feminist protest, either to present feminists as exploiting the media's desire for sensationalism, or to suggest that certain forms of entertainment media were the far more dangerous enemies of women that feminists should have targeted instead of the pageant.

Global media coverage of feminists' protests was also interpreted as a spectacular form of public embarrassment that only underscored anti--nationalistic, negative stereotypes of India as chaotic, unstable, and unfit for modernity. Invoking nationalist sentiments, some informants framed feminist protest against the Miss World contest as self-centered promotion because it detracted from organizers' vision of the pageant's arrival in India as a collective, shared victory for the nation that transcended self-serving commercial goals.

ABCL's crisis manager declared that the vocal protests of the feminist organization Mahila Jagran Samiti proved these women's incompetence when presented with opportunities beyond their routine local campaigns. He argued that global news images of women protesters could suggest that India was not prepared for the media performance that economic globalization demanded:

"People will think we do not know how to control ourselves in front of foreign media. Samiti women don't fit in anywhere-- they are not prepared to be traditional nor do they want to be modern. They are confused and it showed in their junglee (wild) Behaviour."

## NEGOTIATING THE POLITICS OF GENDER AND RELIGION

An important debate that was part of the process of managing the symbolic representation of Miss World in the media revolved around the selection of a logo, an iconic image that would be consistently reproduced on press releases, posters, advertisements, and banners. ABCL executives, in charge of supervising the public relations agency they hired, wanted to ensure that the pageant was packaged as a hybrid of Indian and Western culture because this dual branding strategy would facilitate the effective marketing of Miss World to a wide range of consumers in different countries including the Indian diaspora now scattered in diverse locations. In selecting a logo, ABCL executives first considered the idea of using a well-known goddess image drawn from Hindu mythology, but eventually decided against this strategy after a meeting with their public relations agency:

Some of us wanted an image of the goddess Saraswati, but we were so happy when someone from the agency quickly warned us against it because just two years ago the famous Indian artist M.F. Husain, actually a Muslim too, painted the goddess Saraswati naked. And then the controversy was amazing because many Hindus, not just the fundamentalists, were so angry that he, a Muslim, would choose a Hindu goddess to do that. It was all over the front pages. I didn't realise Saraswati was such a hot subject now.8

Recalling memories of the same meeting, the public relations agency director, a man in his early thirties, talked about how difficult it was to persuade older ABCL executives that Indian culture was not only about Hindu goddesses: "I knew it would be trouble because some people think of pageants as vulgar, and even after being so careful about everything we had all these protests. Could you imagine how much more trouble we would have had if we used a goddess image?" As the PR director volunteered, yet another reason to avoid the image of the goddess Saraswati-the goddess of learning, arts, and performance-was because Jaya Bachchan, wife and partner to the founder of ABCL, reminded them that ABCL owned another television software company by the name Saraswati.

She expressed the fear that this company could inadvertently be "dragged into some gadbad (battle, dispute)" that could have erupted over the use of goddess Saraswati as a logo for the pageant. Another ABCL executive talked about the long hours they spent agonizing over which specific image among a range of historical and mythological icons was safe and appropriate for the logo given the divisive politics surrounding religious identity in India.

Public relations consultants advised ABCL to choose a logo that would not ignite religious controversies, which could escalate into major crises with serious implications for the failure of Miss World. These difficulties that ABCL managers experienced with regard to finding a safe logo indicated that local producers experienced difficulties in locating a secular, pan-- Indian cultural symbol for the pageant that would appeal to all religious communities.

Their struggles over the ideal cultural representation of Miss World reflected the tensions around religion, communalism, and culture that have become highly public issues in India, particularly since the early nineties with the outbreak of violence and rioting between Hindus and Muslims during the Babri Masjid incident.

The Babri Masjid or Ramajanmaboomi incident took place on December 6, 1992, when a mob of Hindus belonging to various political and religious groups destroyed a mosque in the city of Ayodhya in Uttar Pradesh, claiming that the mosque had been built by Muslim invaders on a site that was the original birthplace of the Hindu god Ram.

Since the Babri Masjid incident, and the rise in the political and social power of the Bharatiya Janata Party, the Hindu nationalist party, and other associated Hindu revivalist organizations, religious minorities-Indian Muslims and Christians-have experienced increasing marginalization, violence, and exclusion from the public sphere.

To ensure that the logo for Miss World would appeal to a wide range of consumers without provoking controversy, ABCL sought input from influential business, cultural, and media professionals and social elites in India. Although ABCL employees had first thought that they would leave the decision about the logo to the public relations agency they hired, eventually, after many discussions, they decided to set up a panel of judges who would offer their opinions on the best symbol that could capture the global and local essence of the pageant. Reflecting on that decision, the chief assistant to the founder of ABCL (the actor Amitabh Bachchan), said:

I think that was a very good decision. Amitabhji decided that Miss World's logo had to be a careful decision even though he was in a hurry to get things going. We set up a panel of judges from different professions and different religions-journalists, magazine editors, cosmetics industry experts, actresses and actors, and even two politicians.

Ultimately, the logo that ABCL selected as their final choice was the reproduction of a woman's image, a Buddhist inspired painting of a female figure representing a heavenly apsara (a dancer). The painting was part of a 5th century

AD fresco from the walls of the Ajanta caves in the Western part of India, close to Mumbai.The Buddhist inspired cave painting was viewed as a familiar and recognizably "Indian" symbol yet secular and unlikely to offend any religious group. Elaborating on the reasons for choosing a Buddhist symbol, the PR agency director offered:

Hinduism, Islam, or Christianity, none of these matched the comfort we felt with the Buddhist symbol. Christian symbols would not have been good because Christianity is not an Indian religion, and Islamic symbols may have upset the Mullahs-(Islamic priests). Nobody has so far created any public outcries about anything Buddhist.

A manager from the Godrej company (chief sponsor of the pageant) and the editor of Femina magazine, both who had traveled in other parts of Asia, explained that Buddhism was one of India's best exports, and that the Buddha, one of India's most revered prophets, was known for his message of equality, peace, and harmony in India and outside.

The Buddhist painting was thus viewed as a symbol that was outside of the rather controversial politics that has besieged Hindu-Muslim relations in India. Furthermore, the painting was viewed as an ideal international symbol for Miss World because audiences in Malaysia, Thailand, China, and Japan where Buddhism spread widely could relate to the Buddhist-influenced artwork.

Once the logo was finalized, a creative director at a large advertising agency in Mumbai suggested that they add a well-known national symbol to the figure of the apsara in the painting to enable Indian audiences to instantly connect Miss World with their country. In the logo's final version, which was unveiled at a news conference in Bangalore on October 31, 1996, by Amitabh Bachchan and Parameshwar Godrej, a headdress with a large peacock feather that was not a part of the original painting, was added as an ornamental decoration. "We added the peacock feather at the last minute because someone thought that would really reflect what is Indian about the Miss World pageant. Indian TV audiences would appreciate a feather from their national bird appearing on the logo," explained Sharat Sharma, who was responsible for organizing the news conference where the official logo was first displayed.

In addition to the politics of religion and nation that had to be carefully considered in crafting the official logo for Miss World, yet another layer of representational meaning that influenced decisions about this symbol revolved around gender and ethnicity.

The woman in the logo appeared slender and androgynous with a dark skin tone, a long neck, and a calm face with large serene eyes. She represented a very different image from the images of women in Hindu-inspired art and sculpture that can be found in the famous Kajuraho temple carvings where the sculpted women's voluptuous bodies suggest fertility and overt sexuality with their wide hips, slightly bulging abdomens, narrow waists, and large breasts.

Discussing the feminine body aesthetic in a logo that would be the best match for Miss World, two fashion designers proposed that the slender and small-breasted body of the woman in the Ajanta cave painting was more appropriate for the pageant than the voluptuous female figures that were common in classical Hindu sculpture found in many historic sites in India.

According to these two women, the female bodies in Hindu sculpture would not have captured the global fashion and advertising aesthetic for feminine bodies-the androgynous waif look-that is currently popular. The apsara's dark skin tone fulfilled the Morleys' desire to revive the popularity of Miss World by marketing it is an exotic and ethnically diverse contest. Despite the widespread cultural marginalization of dark skinned women within India, an ABCL media executive remarked that in the international marketplace of multicultural media images, the dark skin of the woman in the logo would aid in consolidating the new image of the Miss World contest as a ritual that affirmed global ethnic diversity.

In describing the logo, one informant cleverly negotiated feminist critiques of beauty pageants as sexist rituals that are residual forms of such patriarchal practices as prostitution, which sells women's bodies as commodities. For this informant, the empowering potential of the logo and modern beauty pageants could be traced to the coterminous ascent of the new female body and the rise in the economic power of the Indian female consumer. The chief editor of Femina magazine carefully distinguished the pornography aesthetic from the fashion aesthetic in her account of the logo's ability to capture the mission of the pageant. Employing the language of liberal feminism, which espouses equality for women within existing social and economic structures, she argued:

The Miss World event is for modern women, and those of us in the fashion business in India are aware of what's going on-the thinner look is in. Those images of women in Indian sculpture are for men who watch pornography. The new image of the beautiful woman we see in the Miss World pageant, the image we wanted to convey in the logo, is about speaking to women who watch the Miss World pageant-not just men. The Miss World pageant signals the power that women in India have today.

The very same editor was also quoted in the Indian newsmagazine Sunday as saying, "India is now more receptive to and aware of the international look. We have adapted ourselves over the years and are now in tune with international standards".

Discourses on Indian women's accomplishments and empowerment that cocooned the crafting of the logo for Miss World also permeated organizers' and sponsors' responses to the media when protests erupted against the pageant. Women's protests in Bangalore captured a diverse array of opinions that spanned conservative religious beliefs on the traditional roles of Indian women, socialist feminist perspectives on women's commodification and sexual objectification, and liberal feminist views on women's equal participation in the public sphere. The women's organization Mahila Jagran Samiti, affiliated with the Hindu nationalist Bharatiya Janata Party, received the most media coverage for their protests against the pageant as an offensive ritual of Western culture that had the potential to corrupt the purity of the traditional Indian woman, a wife and mother, who exposed her body only for the gratification of her husband.

The vocal spokesperson of the right-wing Jagran Samiti, Shashikala, threatened to sneak into the stadium along with fourteen other women members to commit a public suicide in which she and her supporters planned to burn themselves during the live performance of the pageant.

A few renowned female artists-dancers, classical singers, and folk performers-endorsed the Jagran Samiti's view of Miss World as an assault on Indian culture; however, certain artists like singer Gangubai Hangal emphasized that Miss World would corrupt ancient Indian artistic and performance traditions along with Indian women's morality. Socialist feminists represented by Subashini Ghai and Brinda Karat of the All India Democratic Women's Association, Madhu Reddy of Vimochana, and numerous other independent feminist writers like Ammu Joseph and Sudha Sitaraman wrote lengthy commentaries in the media where they distanced themselves from the conservative women's groups' agendas.

Advocating against conservative activists' call to choose tradition as the moral ground to protest the onslaught of Western culture in India, these feminists drew attention to the poverty of India's vast majority of women and suggested that it would be more fruitful to examine beauty pageants as examples of the consumerist class divide created and reinforced by globalization.

Educated and secular middle-class women's voices were widely represented in the media as endorsing and supporting Miss World in Bangalore because it offered Indian women a new space along with Indian men for expressing their individuality.

Summing up the opinions of a group of professional Indian women, who had marched in support of the pageant, Santosh Rajagopalan argued that Miss World's organizers should be "lauded for promoting substantial social upheaval by bringing about a change in the perceptions of women's roles". Well-known women personalities and spokespersons for social causes-film actress Shabana Azmi and dancer Vani Ganapathy-joined supporters of the pageant because they strongly objected to the disruptive methods of protest chosen by rightwing and left-wing women's groups.

In responding to the protests of conservative women's organizations, the Moneys, the Godrej company, and ABCL held up Miss World's logo, traditional performances they planned to stage during the live performance, and the participation of foreign beauty contestants in Hindu rituals as evidence of Miss World's commitment to Indian women's authentic cultural traditions.

In their first press release bearing the signature logo of the Buddhist apsara in bright yellow, blue, and green colors, which was issued in response to the protests, ABCL argued, "The thought behind the logo is to depict the kind of land India is and our way of appreciating women's beauty in India. Our apsara is shown wearing jewelry, which all Indian women value and cherish.

The butterfly on the crest of her crown is a symbol of the free spirit and grace of every Indian woman." ABCL also claimed in a press release that the pageant's rules, which did not allow married women to participate, showed the respect that Bachchan and the founders of Miss World had for local traditions and family values; organizers did not want the rigorous training, hectic schedule, and travel commitments of Miss World's contestants to disrupt Indian women's marriages and result in the neglect of their children.

In countering the charges of commodification from leftist feminist groups, ABCL's press releases touted their Miss Personality and Miss Talented contests, performances in which they claimed judges evaluated contestants for their sense of humor, oratory skills, and artistic talents. ABCL also organized a press conference where former Indian Miss World and celebrity film star Aishwarya Rai lectured on the history and tradition behind the logo.

Endorsing the opportunities that Miss World offered the average middle-class Indian woman, Rai shared the numerous monetary and travel benefits she had accrued after her 1994 crowning, and pointed to the charity efforts she and the Moneys had become involved with since her return to India.

## NATIONALISM, GENDER, AND GLOBAL MEDIA EVENTS

Some scholars have predicted that the advancing reach of globalization in its standardized and commodified forms will steadily reduce the significance of local structures of nation, tribe, and community for local cultural production and reception. Daniel Dayan and Elihu Katz proposed that the spread of global media events anticipates the demise of nationalism and national borders as structuring elements in audiences' experiences of their identities.

Barber argued that globalization "contributes to shrinking the world and decreasing the salience of national borders" and that the popularity of global culture announced a "considerable victory over factitiousness and particularism". Contrary to such predictions, this monograph demonstrates that nationalist sentiments suffused local producers' visions of Miss World's impact on India's image in the global public sphere.

While organizers' and sponsors' creative production of Miss World attempted to go beyond national boundaries, this media event was also simultaneously crafted as a nationalistic project.

The culture industry in India sought to incorporate cultural and historical ideas of the nation-India and Indianness-into the ideological, discursive, and material manifestations of the mediated global pageant. Organizers' vision of the Miss World pageant's potential to challenge the Third Worldness of India in global media, Amitabh Bachchan's desire to ensure that Indians not foreigners gained control over global Indian entertainment, and the patriotic sentiments that Indian beauty queens were trained to express at global contests illustrate the continued symbolic strength of the concept of nation within the trajectories of transnational culture.

In the process of becoming indigenized or localized, discourses of globalization thus invoke contradictory impulses and allegiances. On the one hand, multinationals encourage the widespread consumption of global culture in different localities by standardizing cultural products and rituals to transcend the limits of national identity.

On the other hand, in order to ensure acceptance within a wide range of social, political, and economic groups within local settings, global culture resorts to the recuperation of national identity.

Urging scholars of transnational culture to map out the different ways in which global consumption is linked to the cultural imaginary of nationalism, Indrepal Grewal argues that global culture could "resuscitate the nation-state while simultaneously reducing its compass".

Producers, advertisers, and media professionals involved in Miss World claimed that the Miss World pageant did not represent an imperialistic Western discourse that could destroy Indian culture because they intended to harness the pageant to promote India's latent potential as a culturally rich nation that was eager to modernize its economy.

In a paradoxical fashion, local producers and sponsors of Miss World in Mumbai and Bangalore argued that supporting and participating in international contests enabled Indian citizens to experience their Indianness more intensely; the global spectacle was thus ideologically constructed as a means to enhance and strengthen the local.

A double-spread advertisement promoting ABCL corporation and the Miss World pageant in The India Magazine, an upscale publication targeted at the urban English-educated elite in India, vividly echoed informants' packaging of the global within the semiotics of the local. Celebrating ABCL's successful bid to host Miss World, the advertisement showed a pensive Amitabh Bachchan addressing the globallyminded Indian reader by posing a series of questions: "Why do we (Indians) have a need to impress all foreigners?,

Why do we feel good when others say India has potential? Why are we down in the third world, when we could be up there?" The advertisement ended by suggesting that the staging of Miss World in India represented the assertion of Indians' independent, far-reaching, and entrepreneurial spirit that could transform the nation and its citizens' low self-esteem into vigorous patriotic pride and confidence. Following cultural critiques offered by postcolonial feminist scholars, my analysis of local organizers' and sponsors' discussions about mediated representations of the Miss World pageant shows that gender plays a crucial role in shaping and legitimizing the modernization projects of globalization. The explicit invoking of gender politics in organizers', sponsors', and public relations personnel's understanding of Miss World became apparent in the following: criticisms targeted at representations of Indian women in global newsmedia; comparisons drawn between women's lives in India and Pakistan; expressions of admiration for the globally legitimized beauty of Indian women offset by the denigration of Indian men's failures in world athletic events; and arguments that Indian women, as hybrid subjects who could confidently traverse Eastern and Western cultures, exemplified ideal global femininity in a multicultural world.

Perceptions of Miss World expressed by members of the culture industry in India indicates that gender-the trope of the feminine-operates as a strategic cultural resource to announce local producers' commitment to modernity's progressive impact on traditional local cultures. Postcolonial feminist media scholars have explored the multiple forms of interpellation that girls and women encounter in India's intensely mediated culture of the nineties.

Shoma Munshi argues that in India's current climate of economic liberalization, consumerist discourses are incorporating ideologies of femininity, feminism, and nationalism to synthesize a post-feminist image of the "New Indian Woman."

In her analysis of consumer advertising in India, Munshi notes that advertisers have incorporated accommodationist forms of resistance to traditional patriarchy in their images by representing the New Indian Woman as a wife, mother, and daughter-in-law who can control, manage, and manipulate patriarchy through clever and educated forms of consumption.

Producers and sponsors of the Miss World pageant take such commodified incarnations of women's resistance in the media further when they argued that Miss World with its public representations of female sexuality offered a representational space that countered the limitations of local patriarchy's restricted codes for ideal womanliness.

Editors of women's magazines, women fashion designers, and trainers in Femina's beauty contestant grooming Programmes viewed Miss World as a ritual that had the potential to catapult Indian female subjectivity beyond the patriarchal roles of sex object and wife, daughter, and mother.

For local organizers of Miss World, battling protest groups' demands to ban the pageant, the elaboration of feminist discourses of women's empowerment within the mediated fabric of the pageant constituted a strategic response of crisis containment.

ABCL employees and sponsors exalted the pageant as a sign of progressive shifts in traditional gender relations and constructed Indian women as free agents to convince local audiences to embrace the individualized ideologies of freedom and class mobility that guide the imaginary realms of late capitalist economies. By closely examining the rhetoric of feminist empowerment among members of the culture industry in India who organized and supported Miss World, we can appreciate the complex articulation of female agency in global consumerism where patriarchy and capitalism intersect to offer women positions of domination and resistance.

Contrary to theories of power that construct discourses of global capitalism as non-conflictual and harmonious spaces that are outside of progressive activism, nationalism, and polemics of struggle, this analysis of Miss World shows that local producers negotiate and strategize multiple subjectivities for women, which include more than the interpellation of women as passive consumer subjects.

Informants' conjoining of Miss World to feminist notions of resistance against patriarchy demonstrates the necessity for a Foucauldian approach to the hegemonic character of modern structures of global capital.

The power of global consumerism is not necessarily exercised by one dominant group over another non-dominant group, that is, in a top-down fashion, rather, consumer modernity's ideological messages manifest in multiple locations and utilize mechanisms of domination and subordination to secure consent among local audiences. Amitabh Bachchan's strategy of using the televised Miss World contest to advertise ABCL's competence as an enterprising manager and distributor of Indian films in various locations abroad draws attention to new circuits of global culture that are beginning to appear in the nineties.

These emerging flows of global culture challenge the paradigm of globalization as always and only being synonymous with Americanization.

Critiquing earlier models of cultural imperialism, recent scholars of globalization have pointed out the limitations of envisaging centre-periphery relationships as cultural flows that begin at the centre (the developed world) and gradually penetrate the periphery (the developing world), with the peripheral nation typically viewed as possessing little control over the invasion of its indigenous culture.

Ostensibly, the 1996 Miss World pageant's appearance in India (the periphery) implied the flow of a cultural form that evolved and originated in Euroamerican culture (the centre), yet the purpose behind this visible sign of Western culture was to strengthen an Indian company's own goals of globalization.

The Miss World pageant was part of a start-up package for Bachchan's communications company. Bachchan's goal, as many executives explained, was to be an early pioneer in managing the globalization of the increasingly popular Indian entertainment industry's media products. ABCL's hosting of Miss World in India demonstrates that rituals of Western modernity can be deployed to announce the emergence of regional networks of global media culture that encompass more than the obvious, well-rehearsed scenario of First World-Third World interaction. Commenting on the newer configurations of global culture in the nineties, Power and Mazumdar (2000) write:

The West may have the biggest stalls in the media bazaar, but it's not the only player. Globalization isn't merely another word for Americanization-and the recent expansion of the Indian entertainment industry proves it. For hundreds of millions of fans around the world, it is Bollywood-India's film industry-not Hollywood that spins their screen fantasies.

Typically, the developing world's encounter with a ritual of Western modernity-a beauty pageant-is viewed as a process that involves binary top-down relationships between the Euroamerican World and the Third World. However, as ABCL's motives in hosting Miss World demonstrates, private businesses and entrepreneurs in non-Western locations can use global media events to inaugurate their own media globalization projects.

Advocating a nuanced view of cultural imperialism that recognizes the pluralization of new cultural production centers around the world, John Tomlinson argues that scholars abiding by undialetical centre-periphery models should be cautious about assuming that the ubiquitous presence of Western culture indicates lack of competition in the global media market.

Conflating the local with only the national may conceal other struggles taking place within the space of the global. Anabelle Sreberny-Mohammadi writes that national agendas may not always represent or coincide with the heterogeneous variations of the local, "In international relations, the national level may be local vis-a-vis the global level, but in domestic relations, the national is itself a site of struggle, with a variety of local identities and voices in contention".

South Indian executives' pursuit of Bangalore as the site for Miss World showed their resistance based in their regional identities to hegemonic North Indian representations of South Indians as culturally backward.

Miss World presented an opportunity for South Indians to challenge the dominant discourse that casts Mumbai or New Delhi as ideal locations to symbolize the nation as cosmopolitan and modern. South Indian ABCL executives' deployment of Miss World to challenge regional hierarchies of representation also illustrates Ien Ang's theoretical proposition that global culture can be strategically manipulated to serve the interests and agendas of specific local constituencies.

Finally, this monograph offers insights into the multiple layers of media and cultural intercontextuality that characterize the performances of global media events in different locales.

The Miss World pageant represented organizers' and advertisers' efforts to enter the zone of public culture in India, an arena that Arjun Appadurai and

Carol Breckenridge characterize as a field of consumption that is a "shifting array of texts and experiences, which constitute evolving contexts for one another".

Public modernity in its mediated form, as Breckenridge and Appadurai argue, is an interlocular field that is "structured so that each site or setting for the socializing and regulating of the public gaze is to some degree affected by the experiences of other public sites".

Their example of one such event that exemplifies the experience of the interlocular in India is the world of cricket where leisure practices, desire for spectacle, narratives of stardom, and nationalist sentiments intersect to produce masculine achievement as global culture.

As a ritual form of public culture that illustrates Appaduari and Breckenridge's approach to mediated modernity in South Asia, the Miss World pageant represented an interlocular event that informants interpreted against and within numerous cultural contexts and relationships.

Pageant organizers' selection of a Buddhist logo as the least controversial embodiment of Indian culture demonstrated the influence of religious politics on the localization of global culture; however, their choice of a dark-skinned, thin woman in the logo revealed their efforts to globalize the logo in order to satisfy transnational consumer appetite for commodified multiculturalism.

Informants' discussions about covers of Cosmopolitan magazines in India, vulgarity in vernacular Indian films, the indigenized clothing of Barbie dolls, MTV consumption among Indian youth, stereotypes of India in Hollywood films, and caricatured images of South Indians in North Indian popular culture highlighted the media intertextuality that permeated local producers' interpretations of Miss World. ABCL's promotion of Amitabh Bachchan's superstar image revealed the interweaving of celebrity stardom as a local and global branding strategy into the mediated fabric of the pageant. Ultimately, these multidimensional and intercontextual interpretations of the televised Miss World contest in India underscore the profound embeddedness of local cultural production within concrete, heterogeneous, and complex historical and cultural conditions.

# 6

# Alternative Media

## AN INTRODUCTION

Alternative media are defined most broadly as those media practices falling outside the mainstreams of corporate communication.

Proponents of alternative media often argue that the mainstream media is heavily biased, criticizing their pretended objectivity as a dissimulation of class biases. Causes of this bias include the political interests of the owners, government influence or the profit motive. This criticism, paradoxically, springs from observers of all political orientations. The concentration of media ownership, as well as the concentration of the publishing industry are other causes of economical censorship. While sources of alternative media are also frequently highly (and sometimes proudly) biased, the bias tend to be different, hence 'alternative'. Alternative media outlets often engage in advocacy journalism and frequently promote specific political views, often dissident views (or, again paradoxically, views considered "dissident" from whatever the perceived mainstream; contributors to Democratic Underground and Free Republic are diametrically opposed to each other politically, and both are likely to consider themselves dissidents from an oppressive mainstream).

Authors such as Louis Althusser and Noam Chomsky have written in detail about the problems of the mainstream press, and their writings have inspired the creation of many alternative press efforts. Many current alternative press sources share values on copyright with the open source movement.

For a medium to be considered "alternative", it must possess some kind of counter-hegemonic quality. The counter-hegemony should be represented through at least one of the following parameters:

- Content – what is being "said"
- Aesthetical form – the way it is being said
- Intention – the point of success
- Organizational structure – how the media are being run
- Process - the relationship between production and consumption of information

Examples of alternative media: The following is a list of news sources considered to be part of an alternative media, in both print and electronic forms:

- Information Clearing House
- LA Freewaves
- Taking Aim
- World Independent News Group
- American Free Press
- The French Connection
- CounterPunch
- WorldNetDaily
- Infowars.com
- Democracy Now
- COA News
- Z Magazine
- Traditions Magazine
- Earthhope Network
- Adbusters
- Great News Network
- Eagle World News
- Indymedia
- undercurrents (news)
- What Really Happened
- Altermedia
- Commondreams
- The Raw Story
- Drudge Report
- Drudge Retort
- Haiduts.net
- The Common Language Project
- CitizenShift
- Townhall.com
- Frequency The Snowboarder's Journal
- Northern Alliance Radio Networks
- People associated with the alternative media
- Christopher Bollyn
- Matt Drudge
- Joseph Farrar
- Lisa Guliani
- Alex Jones
- Jason Leopold
- Michael Collins Piper
- Jeff Rense

- Michael Rivero
- Michael Ruppert
- Ralph Schoenman
- Daryl Bradford Smith
- Victor Thorn
- Hugh Hewitt

**Underground Press**

The phrase underground press, especially underground newspapers (or simply underground papers) is most often used in reference to the alternative print media, independently published and distributed, associated with the countercultural movements of the late 1960s and early 1970s.

This movement borrowed the name from previous *underground presses* such as the Dutch underground press during the Nazi occupations of the 1940s. The French resistance also published an underground press and prisoners of war (POWs) published an underground newspaper called *Pow wow*. Those predecessors were truly "underground," meaning they were illegal, thus published and distributed covertly. While the countercultural "underground" papers frequently battled with governmental authorities, for the most part they were distributed openly through a network of street vendors, newsstands and "head shops," and thus reached a wide audience.

The underground press in the 60s and 70s existed in most countries with high GDP per capita and freedom of the press; similar publications existed in some developing countries and as part of the *samizdat* movement in the communist states, notably Czechoslovakia. Published as weeklies, monthlies, or even "occasionals", and usually associated with left-wing politics, they evolved on the one hand into today's alternative weeklies and on the other into zines.

## ALTERNATIVE NEWS/INFORMATION DISTRIBUTION SYSTEM

### ADVANCEMENT OF COMMUNICATION TECHNOLOGY AND THE GROWTH OF THE INFORMATION SYSTEMS

The post-second world war era was marked by revolutionary technological advancement in the field of the telecommunications. The information explosion provided the impetus for this technology to disseminate news and information across national boundaries. The electronics and computer systems have vast potential for information storage, retrieval, and delivery. Naturally, it revolutionized the media in the developed world in Europe, North America, and Japan. With the introduction of the communication satellites in outer space, the TV, and the transistor, the impact of information revolution could be felt in the remotest villages in the Himalayas and the Sahara. The scientific and technological revolution led to the borderless outflow of information to the Third

World countries, and the advanced industrialized nations, grasping the scope of this technological advancement, have set up controls over information flows.

*The Dominance Syndrome:* The countries of North and South are separated by an enormous gap in their respective communication capacities. The developed countries continue to exercise considerable political, economic, and technological control on information flows. Let us first examine the quantitative dimension of the concept of dominance and dependence. Over 5.5 billion people on this planet own over one billion radio receivers and 500 million television sets. The world receives information from 150 major news agencies, 30,000 radio and television stations and 8,200 daily newspapers with a total of 446 million copies a day. This global picture hides major regional imbalances. For instance, there are only 4.5 newspapers per 100, and one television set for 3,000 Africans. This is several times less than the corresponding figures for the Europeans and Americans. What is worse is that eight African countries publish no newspaper at all, 113 have only one each.

As a rule, the print order of the largest of these newspapers does not exceed 16,000 in Mica. The Television is non-existent in nearly 30 Asian, African and Latin American nations. Further, 18 African and 16 Asian nations have no news agencies of their own. Asia, Africa and Latin America, where about two-thirds of the world population lives, account for only 5 per cent of the world television sets, and 12.5 per cent of world's newspapers. The hegemony is also exercised through the publication of encyclopedias and other reference books, which interpret the experience and the history of the Third World countries in a deliberately biased and distorted way so that it serves the interests of the richer or technologically advanced countries. Nearly 80 percent of the information disseminated in the world originates from five largest transnational news agencies *i.e.*, the AP, UPI, Reuters, AFP and ITAR-TASS.

You have already learned about the extent and significance of the operations of these news agencies, in the earlier units. About 15 great media corporations dominate the production of the radio sets, television sets and printing equipment including printing devices, radio, and television communication satellites, paper, inks, and other elements of mass media technological infrastructure, ten of these corporations belong to the United States of America. The statistical details cited above might have changed to some extent, but one should try to see the truth beyond the facts. These figures are noted to provide you a feeling of the extent of the disparities that exist, and the dominance of the North in the field of information, thus making the countries in the South depended on them.

*Consequences of Dominance and Dependence:* You may wonder what happens if there is Western dominance. Some might say that anyhow, we are getting news and information, which, otherwise, we in the developing countries, could not aspire to, given the limited capacity of our media systems. Of course, this could be true, if we did not understand the polemics behind it. Due to our dependence on the media delivery systems of the West, we also become dependent on the west. To understand this, we shall now discuss the various forms of dominance in the information flow with a couple of concrete examples. You may study, on your own, several such instances in your daily exposure to foreign news.

- *Example 1*: During the British war with Argentina over their claim on the Falklands Islands, several developing countries supported the Argentinean claim, but 'their newspapers were receiving the stories put out by the transnational news agencies, which were biased in favour of Britain. The newspapers in these developing countries could not afford to send their own correspondents to cover the Falklands war.
- *Example 2*: The Gulf War provides a classic example of how dependence on the West for news and information can distort the news content of the Third World media.

During the Gulf War, India's language dailies had no capacity to cover the war events through their own correspondents. Almost all the newspapers depended upon the news originating from the Western news agencies. Interestingly, the usage of words in the news dispatches became a form of psychological warfare during the so-called "Gulf War". To build up the image of the US-led multinational forces, the label 'Allied Forces' was used, a reminder of the Second World War.

The Indian dailies published all these news items. The control over news flow in the Indian print media could be shown by citing the example of the news of 600 Iraqi soldiers, buried under the sand by the tanks of the Allied Forces, which was suppressed by the Western media. No Indian newspaper carried the news item. How the big agencies take the Third World press for granted can be understood by looking at the coverage of the incidents at Tiananmen Square in China. Even in covering the incidents in a neighbouring country and on the issues the coverage of which in all possibilities might be distorted by the Western agencies, the Indian Press did not take an independent stand, but, instead, toed the line of the Western monopolistic agencies. A recent study revealed that newspapers in Asian countries published 76.4 percent of news on the Third World supplied by the big four news agencies.

This survey was done by the Bangladesh Press Institute of Newspapers of six South Asian countries. Similar studies, done elsewhere in other developing countries, also revealed that the media of these nations were still highly dependent on the foreign especially the Western, news agencies for news and information about the other countries including their own neighbours. By now, you must have got a fairly good idea of the concept of dominance and dependence in news and information distribution. With this, you might be convinced of the need for achieving self-reliance in news and information distribution.

## NEED FOR SELF-RELIANCE

Self-reliance in news and information distribution, both in disseminating news to the outside world, or in getting news and information from various places in the world, for internal consumption, is essential for the following reasons:

- To provide the media a national identity and personality,
- To facilitate the analyses of the world events not from the perspective of the West but from the 7 national perspective,
- To foster better understanding among the developing countries, which is far more essential now than ever before,
- To prevent the unwarranted entry of foreign and alien ideas, cultures, and lifestyles, that always tend to contribute to shaping public opinion in favour of foreign countries, particularly of the West, and
- To provide an objective account of the news and developments that were considered newsworthy by the indigenous media.

*The Role of NAM:* The first important step towards achieving some self-reliance in news collection and dissemination was the effort made by some of the non-aligned nations. First, the call for New World Economic Order was articulated from the non-aligned centres as a reflection of the movement's general antipathy to the former colonies. This was evident from the first statement on information endorsed by the fourth summit of the Movement in Algiers, in 1973, and there could be no doubt about such an orientation in the documents on information endorsed by the fifth summit in Colombo, in 1976. Ultimately, it was the New Delhi Declaration of NAM which said:

- "The present global information flows are marked with inadequacy and imbalance. The means of communicating information are concentrated in a few centres. The majority of countries is reduced to be passive recipients of information, which is disseminated from a few centres.
- This situation perpetuates the colonial era of dependence and domination. It confines judgments and decisions on what should be known, and how it should be made known to a few.
- Just as political and economic dependence are legacies of the era of colonialism, so is the case of dependence in the field of information, which, in turn retards the achievements of political and economic growth.
- In a situation where the means of information are dominated and monopolized by a few, the freedom of information really comes to mean the freedom of these few to propagate information in the manner of their choosing and the virtual denial to the rest, and of the right to info-and being informed objectively and accurately. The enunciation of the Non-aligned Movement's New Delhi Declaration is perhaps

the running thread that continues in all the NAM documents for information. These statements are precisely the philosophy of the Non-aligned Movement is regarding information flows. Its efforts to combat the existing information imbalances emerge from this understanding.

*Formation of Non-aligned News Pool:* As per the directives of the UNESCO to establish a new pool or a consortium of news agencies, the "Pool" of news agencies of the non-aligned countries were formally launched in July, 1976, at the New Delhi Conference of Information Ministers and Representatives of the news agencies of the non-aligned countries. According to a statement of the Conference, the objective of the Pool is to expand the mutual exchange of information among the non-aligned countries in a spirit of collective self-reliance. The former Prime Minister of India, the late Mrs. Indira Gandhi, in her address to the Conference, called upon the non-aligned countries to know one another directly, not through the eyes and ears of the Western media. Besides the creation of optimum possibilities for the exchange of information, the tasks of the Pool, as formulated at its General Conference in Belgrade, in 1979, were mainly a programme for training the journalists working in this service, and also the creation of bilateral regional and multi-national communications systems and their linkup to the overall communication systems of the non-aligned countries. The Conference stressed that the creation of a communication network of the non-aligned countries is one of the main long term aims of the Pool.

*Restraints on Growth of the Pool:* The biggest obstacle to the broad development of information and news exchanges among the non-aligned countries through the Pool have been:

- *Communication Restraints*: Many of the developing countries do not have an extensive and elaborate telecommunication network. In some other countries, higher tariffs are major barriers. Hence, it is clear that the development of the communication Systems in the non-aligned countries is imperative to their overall development. It should also be understood that the optimum information exchange also depends on the level of development of communication systems in the individual non-aligned countries. It is worth noting here the statement of the former Director General of the UNESCO, Arthur M'Bow, who said: "The creation of the widespread communication system of the non-aligned countries are intrinsically linked to the overall development of these states.
- *News Flow*: According to a study by J.S. Yadava, a few years ago, about 85 per cent of the news items receive by PTI from the Pool partners were spiked. The reasons for this were given as delay in news reception, poor quality, low news value, or propaganda material.

- *Lack of Training*: The lack of proper training among the non-aligned journalists and their inability to match the professional standards of the journalists of the transnational news-agencies, are the reasons for the poor quality of material put out by the Nonaligned News Agencies Pool.
- *Political Constraints*: Due to the totalitarian and despotic governments in many non-aligned countries, the news agencies are under the strict control of the governments in these countries. The first casualty of such a solution is the objectivity of the news and information put out by their agencies. For instance, the news agencies in Pakistan or Sri Lanka, which are the partners of the Pool, hardly provide any objective news, either about their own news events, issues, and problems, or those of other countries. Even the coverage of the movement for democracy in their own countries lacks objectivity, and are highly lopsided and biased. Should the Indian news media publish or use these materials, just because they have to foster cooperation and exchange among the non-aligned countries?
- *The Media's Lukewarm Attitude*: The editors of privately-owned newspapers in the democratic countries like India, either are not convinced of the need for such an inter-regional cooperation or they do not respect the news coverage of several agencies, which are participants of the Pool.

## INTER-REGIONAL COOPERATION

In the first part of this unit itself, we have dealt at length with the Non-aligned News Agency Pool. We shall now broadly discuss the problems and bottlenecks in the process of inter-regional cooperation. The essence of any inter-regional cooperation in the field of information is to bring about a new sense of common destiny, and unite news agencies operating under different levels of development. The UNESCO played the role of more than a catalyst in fostering inter-regional cooperation in the field of information. The fundamental problem in the inter-regional news networks and cooperation is that the participating news agencies in the networks being, essentially, domestic agencies are geared to serve purely national needs in their news coverage. This has often been quoted as the reason for the non-descript coverage of the Pool News. Another area is about the issue of relevance.

Most of them are editorially ill-equipped to produce copy for the consumption of the other agencies in the region. They are mostly irrelevant to each others needs. Further, in most of the networks, almost all agencies are, in principle, committed to producing a regional file containing news reports and features, especially prepared for the consumption of the readers outside their national frontiers. However, the tendency that persists is to move copy originally written for a domestic readership for the network transmission without necessary rewriting. A great deal of information may be missing in such reports for the readers abroad, or much more than necessary is included. For instance, proper designation of a politician in the story, the conversion of local currency into internationally known monetary units, is absolutely essential when the story is disseminated abroad. But, criticism on several agencies, which are part of such networks, is that they do not make amendments and changes in the news reports, keeping in view the requirements of the readers abroad. Another severe criticism is that a large majority of reports transmitted in these networks is hard news, which rarely attract the attention of the editors in other countries. On the other hand, the transnational news agencies with their speedy transmission and professionally more competent stories and spicy writing, obviously overwhelm the inter-regional networks. Especially in the case of spot news, the networks lag behind the transnational agencies like the AP, UPI or Reuters, etc. When we look at the small degree, of the success of the Pool and similar such efforts, we see that inadequate facilities and improper planning continue to be an impediment in strengthening inter-regional cooperation. Several countries, though involved in such regional bodies articulate their resolve to strengthen mutual cooperation, but hardly take any steps to achieve their goals. Mutual distrust continues to remain a major obstruction, in addition to the allurements dangled before these poor countries by the advanced and developed countries, in the shape of aid and help.

For instance, can any meaningful exchange of news or other information be possible between the media of Pakistan and India, when there is a tension between the two countries with both being tempted by the rich Western powers to tilt towards them? Under such conditions and relations that exist among different countries in the same region, any inter-regional cooperation will, at best, prove to be a mechanical exchange of information rather than a medium of one country enjoying the confidence and credibility of the media of another. Suppose, the Pakistani news agency, the Associated Press of Pakistan (APP), sends a report on the situation in Sindh, and the Press Trust of India (PTI), as a nodal agency in the inter-regional cooperation among the SAARC nations, disseminates that news report fed by the APP to all Indian newspapers. What will happen to that news item? You can easily imagine the possible fate of such a report in the editorial offices of the Indian Newspapers.

## TOWARDS SOUTH-SOUTH COOPERATION

Whatever may be the Third World's criticism in the West for the latter's dominance in the field of information, at the same time, one has to understand the underlying reality. On the news collection and dissemination front, the threat from transnational agencies is of a qualitative nature. Hence, improving the quality and increasing professionalism of the indigenous media systems in the developing countries is very essential. This needs cooperation and a spirit of sacrifice. One of the most important suggestions made to remedy the situation is to develop infrastructure. Elaborate infrastructural facilities, like telecommunication network with reduced tariff structure, proper news-gathering facilities, sharing satellite time, etc., should be developed. The editors have to be convinced of the importance of expanding the news network abroad. For instance, it is ironic that most of the major Indian newspapers are able to afford to have correspondents in Western capitals, but does not have their own men in the neighbouring countries. As a result, the two neighbouring countries have to know each other through the eyes of a biased Western press. This was amply proved between India and Pakistan on the issues of Ayodhya and Kashmir. It has also been suggested that inter-regional cooperation should not confine to just the governmental level, but, such an exchange and cooperation should be encouraged at the media-to-media level, between newspapers, journalists, editors, etc. Efforts are to be intensified to foster mutual confidence by providing easy access at the people-to-people level. All artificial barriers existing in the way of the free movement of the journalists should be bridged. A recent interaction between the SAARC journalists, held at Hyderabad, recommended doing away with visa regulations among the seven South Asian countries. Proper training should be imparted to the journalists in these countries. Finally, while these efforts are going on, what we need to see is that the editors and decision-makers in the different media are "educated" on the need for such a cooperation in the South-South level by removing their firm belief that the "West is the best". These steps would lead to the establishment of an alternative news and information system suited to the needs of the developing countries and relevant to the conditions existing in these countries.

## ALTERNATIVE NEWS DISTRIBUTION SYSTEMS

While there has been a continuous effort to establish an alternative news and information distribution systems in the world, the recent global changes have had a deep impact on the information scene. This has especially to do a lot with the Third World efforts to usher m alternative information flows, between and among themselves, on the one hand, and with the developed world, on the other. The West has been for a long time using the concept of "freedom of information" as an ideological weapon, and successfully deploying it to deflect the Third World from its pursuit of a new world information and communication order. In the matter of broadcasting, the Western powers insist upon the "open skies" policy, which they claim to be consistent with the principle of freedom of information. On the face of things, this seems a plausible argument. The metaphor of open skies seems to connote a situation of an unfettered information exchange of knowledge flowing freely across the national boundaries. On the contrary, the same Western countries, in a different forum—the multilateral trade negotiations, popularly called GATT (General Agreement on Tariff and Trade) shows a complete disinclination towards free trade by imposing heavy tariffs to protect their own products. However, they link their intellectual property rights, by using Super 301 against countries like India and China. These developments call for a greater unity among the Third World countries to come out of the dependence and dominance in the field of information, and promote self-reliance. So, any emergence of alternative information systems should be understood in this changing world scenario and current concept of a "unipolar" world dominated by the West, particularly the USA. The existing world information order provides an opportunity for the richer nations to use the scarce global natural resources, such as the radio and a satellite frequency range, and exclude the poor nations from using the same. For instance, the radio frequency range and the geosynchronous orbital slots for parking communication satellites are both natural Western monopolies today. Added to this, an attempt is made through the ongoing GATT talks to impose stronger forms of monopoly control over the content of information flows. Let us also examine what the Third World countries are done at the global level on the question of providing access to the communications media. The allocations of the radio frequency spectrum and geosynchronous orbital slots are done through the instrumentality of the World Administrative Radio Conference (WARC), convened every ten years, by the International Telecommunications Union (ITU). A sub-session of the WARC, held in February 1992, marked a new low in the ability of the Third World to influence the international negotiating agenda in matters relating to the utilization of scarce global resources. The Third World underwent a volte face in the WARC. More than a decade ago, in the WARC 1979 Conference, the Third World made a united bid, and could make the West accept the principle of equity in the allocation of radio frequency spectrum. However, to date, this has not been translated into reality.

## THE UNDERGROUND PRESS IN AUSTRALIA

The most prominent underground publication in Australia was a satirical magazine called *Oz* (1963 to 1969), which owed an obvious debt to the UK magazine *Private Eye*.

In London, Barry Miles, John Hopkins and others produced *International Times* which, following legal threats was renamed *IT*.

Richard Neville arrived in London from Australia where he had edited *Oz* (1963 to 1969). He launched a British version (1967 to 1973), which was A4 (as opposed to *IT*'s broadsheet format). Very quickly, the relaunched *Oz* shed its more austere satire magazine image and became a mouthpiece of the Underground. It was the most colourful and visually adventurous of the alternative press (sometimes to the point of near-illegibility), with designers like Martin Sharp. Other publications followed, such as *Friends* (later *Frendz*) , based in the Ladbroke Grove area of London, *Ink*, which was more overtly political, and *Gandalf's Garden* which espoused the mystic path. Neville published an account of the counterculture called *Playpower*, in which he described most of the world's underground publications. He also listed many of the regular key topics from those publications including Vietnam, Black Power, Politics, Police Brutality, Hippies and Lifestyle Revolution, Drugs, Popular Music, New Society, Cinema, Theatre, Graphics, Cartoons etc.

The underground press offered a platform to the socially impotent and mirrored the changing way of life in the UK underground.

Police harassment of the British underground in general became commonplace to the point that in 1967 the police particularly focussed on the "source of the antagonism": the underground press. Harassment had the opposite effect than was intended: if anything, it made the underground press stronger. "It focused attention, stiffened resolve, and tended to confirm that what we were doing was considered dangerous to the establishment." remembered Mick Farren. From April 1967 on, the police raided the offices of *International Times* to try and close the paper down. In order to raise money for *IT* a benefit event was put together, "The 14 Hour Technicolor Dream" Alexandra Palace on 29 April, 1967.

By the end of the decade, community artists and bands such as Pink Floyd, (who later "went commercial"), the Deviants, Pink Fairies, Hawkwind, Michael Moorcock and Steve Peregrin Took would arise in a symbiotic co-operation with the underground press. The underground press publicised these bands and this made it possible for them to tour and get record deals. The band members travelled around spreading the ethos and the demand for the newspapers and magazines grew and flourished for a while.The flaunting of a defiant sexuality within the underground press provoked prosecution. *IT* was taken to court for publishing small ads for homosexuals, despite the legalisation of homosexuality between consenting adults in private. The *Oz* "School Kids" issue, brought charges against the three *Oz* editors who were convicted and given jail sentences. This was the first time the Obscene Publications Act 1959 was combined with a moral conspiracy charge. The convictions were, however, overturned on appeal.

## THE UNDERGROUND PRESS IN THE UNITED STATES AND CANADA

The North American countercultural press of the 1960s drew inspiration from predecessors that had begun in the 1950s, such as the *Village Voice* and Paul Krassner's satirical paper *The Realist.* Arguably, the first underground newspaper of the '60s was the *Los Angeles Free Press*, founded in 1964 and first published under that name in 1965. By 1967, the cooperative Underground Press Syndicate (UPS) was formed at the instigation of the publisher of another early paper, the *East Village Other*. The UPS allowed member papers to freely reprint content from any of the other member papers. Other prominent underground papers included the *San Francisco Oracle,* the *Berkeley Barb* and *Berkeley Tribe* (Berkeley, California); *Fifth Estate* (Detroit), *Other Scenes* (dispatched from various locations around the world by John Wilcox); *The Helix* (Seattle);

The *Chicago Seed*; *The Great Speckled Bird* (Atlanta); *The Rag,* (Austin, Texas); *Rat Subterranean News* (later "Women's LibeRATion") (New York City), *The Inquisition* (Charlotte, North Carolina), and in Canada, *Georgia Straight* (Vancouver). By 1969, virtually every sizeable city or college town in North America boasted at least one underground newspaper. The underground press phenomenon proved short-lived. By 1973, many underground papers had folded, at which point the Underground Press Syndicate acknowledged the passing of the undergrounds and renamed itself the Alternative Press Syndicate. That organization soon collapsed, to be supplanted by the Association of Alternative Newsweeklies. During the 1960s and 1970s there were also a number of left political periodicals with some of the same concerns of the underground press. Some of these periodicals joined the Underground Press Syndicate to gain services such as microfilming, advertising, and the free exchange of articles and newspapers.

Examples include *The Black Panther* (the paper of the Black Panther Party, Oakland, California), and the *Guardian*, New York City; both of which had national distribution. The U.S. Federal Bureau of Investigation (FBI) conducted surveillance and disruption activities on the underground press in the United States, including a campaign to destroy the alternative agency Liberation News Service. As part of its COINTELPRO designed to discredit and infiltrate radical New Left groups, the FBI also launched phony underground newspapers such as the *Armageddon News* at Indiana University Bloomington, *The Longhorn Tale* at the University of Texas at Austin, and the *Rational Observer* at American University in Washington, D.C. The FBI also ran the Pacific International News Service in San Francisco, the Chicago Midwest News, and the New York Press Service.

*Georgia Straight* outlived the underground movement, evolving into an alternative weekly still published today; *Fifth Estate* survives as an anarchist magazine. Most others died with the era. Given the nature of alternative journalism as a subculture, some staff members from underground newspapers became staff on the newer alternative weeklies, even though there was seldom institutional continuity with management or ownership. An example is the transition in Denver from the underground *Chinook*, to *Straight Creek Journal*, to *Westword* , an alternative weekly still in publication. Some underground and alternative reporters, cartoonists, and artists moved on to work in corporate media or in academia.

## ADVOCACY JOURNALISM

Advocacy journalism is a genre of journalism that is strongly fact-based, but may seek to support a point-of-view in some public or private sector issue. It is particularly common in Europe. Corporate crime, government criticism, corruption and social issues are frequent topics of interest. In this way, advocacy journalists serve the public interest in a similar way to muckrakers. Advocacy journalism criticize the objectivity ideal of mainstream press as an ideological dissimulation of class bias, and underline the fact that political censorship can easily be and is often replaced by economical censorship.

*A hypothetical example of advocacy journalism*

- In Anytown, USA, there is public conflict regarding opposition and support for building a large power plant. A local print or electronic media outlet opposed to the plant presents a five part series strongly accenting negative consequences the power plant has for the town. The news outlet reports on the criminal activity of the builder, conflicts of interest between the builder and local politicians, and negative environmental impacts. It gives coverage to local demonstrations and town meetings. The news media outlet presents facts in a compelling, well-researched manner.

Traditionally, advocacy and criticism are restricted to editorial and op-ed pages: a fire-wall exists between the editorial section and the newsroom. *The Wall Street Journal*, for example, has a policy of strict separation between the news desk and the editorial board; most major print and electronic news outlets do as well. However, *advocacy journalism* describes journalism that crosses the line, in which one may observe subtle or obvious editorializing in reports. Even a television news presenter's facial expression, or a radio broadcaster's tone of voice, or other nuance, is interpreted as lending an opinion to what is being reported.

*Advocacy journalism* is often practiced by a broad range of alternative media and special interest publications and Programmes. Many of these media outlets have clearly defined political and editorial positions. The genre may apply to a single article in a publication, such as political stories in *Rolling Stone*; there are also "advocacy journals", or "alternative publications", which are marketed to target groups based on their interests or biases, for example:

- Print media: *The Spotlight*, *The Nation*, *National Review*, *Mother Jones*, *The New Republic*, *The Economist*, *The Weekly Standard*, *L'Humanité*, *Libération*, *Charlie Hebdo*, *Le Canard Enchaîné*.
- Electronic media: Sean Hannity, Rachel Maddow, Rush Limbaugh.

## ADVOCACY JOURNALISM AND U.S. MEDIA BIAS

In the United States, *Advocacy journalism* is part of the nomenclature of questions related to debate over systemic media bias in domestic media. Investigative reporter Greg Palast has said there is "*an electronic Berlin Wall that surrounds the United States,*" with regard to certain political stories, such as the U.S. Presidential election of 2000. In 2005, the board of PBS debated *Advocacy journalism* with regard to its Programmes, and subsequently reduced time and funding for the Programme Now with Bill Moyers, and expanded a show hosted by Tucker Carlson.

In the U.S., complex national and global issues are often covered with the use of simple, key terms *(examples: War on Terrorism, Terri Schiavo, Liberals, Conservatives, Neo-Cons, Weapons of mass destruction, Plame affair, Iran-Contra Affair, Watergate).* In these situations, reports are labeled "Advocacy journalism" by their subjects with the intent to dismiss the news report, attempting to relegate it to a dismissable report using an ad hominem argument. In other words, journalists and the public may observe a key figure dismiss a report as "*advocacy journalism* to cast doubt on the integrity of the reporter or the news media outlet it came from.

In some instances a publication or journalist specifically advocates a particular political figure as part of the staff of a publication, such as Judith Miller's advocacy of the president's position that Iraq had Weapons of mass destruction. There are also paid-for propaganda campaigns, such as Armstrong Williams': he was paid to support the No Child Left Behind education plan of President Bush.

The U.S. government has also made use of video news releases in covert domestic propaganda campaigns. In 2004 and 2005, Jeff Gannon was given access to the whitehouse press corps with the intent that he ask questions crafted to assist the White House spokesperson, Scott McClellan, and the president, to give favorable answers which were understood to be the answer to be used by media outlets advocating the White House's overall public relations plan. These are examples of a highly unethical form of "advocacy journalism" trying to pass itself off as objective news.

## PERSPECTIVES FROM ADVOCACY JOURNALISTS

One writer for the " alternative" journalism collaborative, the Independent Media Center, writes the following in a call to action:

Classic tenets of journalism call for objectivity and neutrality. These are antiquated principles no longer universally observed.... We must absolutely not feel bound by them. If we are ever to create meaningful change, advocacy journalism will be the single most crucial element to enable the necessary organizing. It is therefore very important that we learn how to be successful advocacy journalists. For many, this will require a different way of identifying and pursuing goals.

In an April 2000 address to the Canadian Association of Journalists, Sue Careless gave the following commentary and advice to advocacy journalists, which seeks to establish a common view of what journalistic standards the genre should follow

- Acknowledge your perspective up front.

- Be truthful, accurate, and credible. Don't spread propaganda, don't take quotes or facts out of context, "don't fabricate or falsify", and "don't fudge or suppress vital facts or present half-truths"
- Don't give your opponents equal time, but don't ignore them, either.
- Explore arguments that challenge your perspective, and report embarrassing facts that support the opposition. Ask critical questions of people who agree with you.
- Avoid slogans, ranting, and polemics. Instead, "articulate complex issues clearly and carefully."
- Be fair and thorough.
- Make use of neutral sources to establish facts.

Sue Careless also criticized the mainstream media for unbalanced and politically biased coverage, for economic conflicts of interest, and for neglecting certain public causes. She said that alternative publications have advantages in independence, focus, and access, which make them more effective public-interest advocates than the mainstream media.

History:The Crisis, the official magazine of the NAACP, was founded in 1910. It describes itself as inheriting the tradition of advocacy journalism from *Freedom's Journal*, which began in 1827 as "the first African-American owned and operated newspaper published in the United States."

Muckrakers are often claimed as the professional ancestors of modern advocacy journalists; for example: Nellie Bly, Ida M. Tarbell, Lincoln Steffens, Upton Sinclair, George Seldes, and I.F. Stone.

French newspapers *Libération*, *Charlie Hebdo*, *Le Canard Enchaîné* and *L'Humanité* all recuse what they consider pseudo-objective journalism for a purposeful explicited political stance on events. They oppose *Le Monde* neutral style, which doesn't impede it, according to those critics, from dissimulating various events or from abstaining to speak about certain subjects. On the other side, a newspaper like *Le Figaro* clearly assumes its conservative stance and pool of readers.

Objectivity: Advocacy journalists may reject the principle of objectivity in their work for several different reasons. Many believe that there is no such thing as objective reporting, that there will always be some form of implicit bias, whether political, personal, or metaphysical, whether intentional or subconscious. This is not necessarily a rejection of the existence of an objective reality, merely a statement about our inability to report on it in a value-free fashion. This may sound like a radical idea, but many mainstream journalists accept the philosophical idea that pure "objectivity" is impossible, but still seek to minimize bias in their work. Other journalistic standards, such as balance, and neutrality, may be used to describe a more practical kind of "objectivity".

"Alternative" critics often charge that the mainstream's media claims of being "bias free" are harmful because they paper over inevitable (often subconscious) biases. They also argue that media sources claiming to be free of bias often advance certain political ideas which are disguised in a so-called "objective" viewpoint. Critics may contend that the mainstream media reinforce majority-held ideas, marginalizing dissent and harming the larger political and cultural discourse.

The proposed solution is to make biases *explicit*, with the intention of promoting transparency and self-awareness that better serves media consumers. Advocacy journalists often assume that their audiences will share their biases (especially in politically charged alternative media), or will at least be conscious of them while evaluating what are supposed to be well-researched and persuasive arguments.

Some who believe that objective (or balanced, neutral, etc.) reporting *is* possible, or that it is a laudable goal, do not find that striving for objectivity is *always* an appropriate goal, perhaps depending on the publication and the purpose at hand. For example, it might be argued that when attempting to expose a waste, corruption, or abuse, a neutral position would "get in the way" of the exposition, and a "bias" against this kind of criminal activity would be quite acceptable to the intended audience.

Many advocacy journalists claim that they can reject objectivity while holding on to the goals of fairness and accuracy, and claim that corporate journalists often lack both.

## ADVOCACY JOURNALISM AS INVESTIGATIVE REPORTING

In some instances, *advocacy journalism* is the same as investigative journalism and muckraking, where these serve the public interest and the public's right to know. Investigative reports often focus on criminal or unethical activity, or aim to advance a generally accepted public interest, such as government accountability, alleviation of human suffering, etc. It might be argued that the journalist is assuming a point of view that public action is warranted to change the situation being described. The most famous example of this was Edward R. Murrow's 'See it Now' series of reports on Sen. Joseph McCarthy.

### *Criticism of advocacy journalism*

Professional journalists and members of the public critical of the term assert that with the sacrifice of a measure of journalist objectivity you have bad journalism: reporting that does not serve the public interest. This is essentially editorializing or sensationalizing on the news pages or during electronic news media presentations. The editorializing is not announced but only advocated by the intrinsic structure of the report.

The term might also indicate a serious breach of journalistic canons and standards, such as rumor mongering, yellow journalism, sensationalism or other ethically flawed reportage — for example, the 2004 revelations created by a press leak in the Plame affair, where a leak was used to help an office holder's political position. Some fear the activity of *advocacy journalists* will be harmful to the reputation of the mainstream press as an objective, reliable source of information. Another concern is that undiscriminating readers will accept the facts and opinions advanced in advocacy pieces as if they were objective and representative, becoming unknowingly and perhaps dangerously misinformed as a result.

Advocacy journalists vary in their response to these criticisms. Some believe that mainstream and "alternative" outlets serve different purposes, and sometimes different audiences entirely, and that the difference is readily apparent to the public. Many believe that the mainstream press is *not* an objective and reliable source of information, and so doesn't deserve the reputation it seeks to maintain.

## CONTEMPORARY TRENDS IN MEDIA AND INTERNATIONAL RELATIONS

With the end of the cold war between the Soviet Union and the United States of America, there seems to be a new, more relaxed and more cooperative environment prevailing in the world politics. But this situation is very deceptive. Developments in the US, on the domestic front, and their balance of payment position, and, in Russia, on the political and economic front, have dampened the dominant outlook presented at the beginning of the current decade. The fight to influence the developing countries has ended. Most of the communist countries are now desperately trying to get aid and cooperation possible fare restructuring their own countries. In India, the new economic policy has been formulated, and is being implemented now. The economy is opening up for the participation of the foreign companies. But this is not shaping up as planned, and already there are misgivings, internally, and fears expressed about the stability of the country by the foreign investors. Ironically, in such a fluid situation, the experts from both the West and Third World countries, like India, are discussing such issues-like environment protection, AIDS, NPT, etc., to salvage mankind from being wiped off from the face of the earth. This contradiction needs to be resolved before any meaningful effort could be made to reverse the trend in the Third World. All these issues are reflected in the television and radio programmes, Satellite communication has wired the whole earth. People sitting in any town in any country can hook their TV sets to the satellite and watch programmes of their choice. Due to the speed with which things are happening, decades or even centuries could be compressed in a few years time. In the Third World, there is a sharp decline in autocratic and dictatorial rules. The military-led regimes in South American, African and Asian countries have gone back to the barracks. The popular governments are taking over be reins of running their countries. There is a marked visibility of people at the grassroots level participating in government. What we are witnessing is a phase of maturity in the former colonies of the imperialist powers. The media of the Third World does realize this change in the national and international political and economical spheres. The exchanges of the TV programmes, especially educational programmes, are quite frequent, though the flow is still imbalanced, because more western programmes are seen on the TV screens of the Third World countries. At the recently concluded International Film Festival in New Delhi, the quality of the movies from the West left much to be desired. This revealed the status the West still gives to such an important country like India. Thus, despite the large-scale changes brought about by technology, imbalance persists in the media and coverage of the developed West vis-a-vis the developing countries of the Third World.

## NEW WORLD INFORMATION AND COMMUNICATION ORDER

### DEBATES AND DEVELOPMENTS

We have already familiarized you with the essentials of the international communication the monopolization of news and information flow by a handful of transnational media giants, such as AP, AFP, Reuters, UPI, ITAS-TASS, VISNEWS. International organizations and regulatory bodies like ITU; and the imbalances in news and information flow arising out of the monopoly by transnational media conglomerates and the guiding principles of 'free flow' of information. A major consequence of the monopoly of news and information flow was the 'one-way flow' of news and information, generally from the developed to the developing world. The nature of flow, as the eminent journalist, D.R. Mankekar, describes, was "imbalanced, iniquitous, sometimes even biased and West-oriented, impervious" to the needs of the developing world. As this was detrimental to their interests in more than one way, the developing nations attacked the free-flow concept and its concomitant—the transnational media empires. For they believed that the monopolistic media empires of the west created and sustained distorted pictures of the world that were far away from the reality. These developing nations campaigned for a 'new order' in the field of international information and communication, which would facilitate a 'free and balanced flow' of information capable of breaking through the stereotypes created and nurtured for over 50 years by the Western media empires. The new order, they maintained, would create a new international information climate that would foster a closer and better understanding among nations and individuals. The ensuing debates in the international forum lasted for nearly a decade, beginning from the early 1970s. This period is reckoned as a watershed in the history of international communication. Indeed, it was a period of many significant developments. First, the developing nations, under the Non-aligned umbrella resolved to address themselves to the international communication issues. Second, to offset the ill effects of One-way flow, alternative means of exchange for meaningful and relevant news and information among the non-aligned nations took roots. The most important step in this direction was the hunching of the Nonaligned News Agencies Pool, in 1975, followed by the establishment of many other news distribution systems at national, regional and international levels. Third, notable revisions also occurred in the concepts and thoughts governing international communication. The 'free-flow' concept was amended to 'free-and balanced flow', when a declaration on the role of the media in the promotion of international understanding and peace was approved by the UNESCO, in 1978. Commensurately, the corollary doctrine, the 'the right to know' was transformed into 'the right to communicate'. Fourth the new order debates led to the setting up of an International Commission for the study of communication problems better known as the "MacBride Commission", whose report was accepted by UNESCO, in 1980. Fifth, resolution 4.19 of the 21 UNESCO General Assembly, held in 1981, outlined the basic character and content of the 'new order'. Sixth, in the same year, the International Programme for the Development of Communication (IPDC) was set up to provide assistance for the development of the communication infrastructure in the developing countries.

*Nomenclature:* Before we proceed further, please note that there has been no uniformity with regard to the nomenclature of the 'new order' concept. The non-aligned nations coined the phrase, New International Information Order (NIIO), The MacBride Commission broadened the schism by substituting the term 'word' for 'international' and incorporating 'communication' along with 'information'. Since then the phrase the 'New World Information and Communication Order (NWICO), or its shortened form the NWICO, has been widely used. In this unit the nomenclature NWICO is used. Also note that the terminologies of the Third World and Developing World, and the First World and Developed World are used interchangeably.

*News Flow Controversies:* Most of the scholars trace the origin of the demand for new international information and communication order to the cold war era, and the emergence of the Third World consciousness in the 1950s. Some of the contentions and problems aired now by the mind World that a handful of media-rich countries determined the nature and kind of news and information flow between nations, that the international news and information business operations benefited only the media-rich nations, and that such operations are detrimental to the interest of media-poor countries, were as fundamental to the media controversies of the early decades of the 20th century as to the 1970s new order debates. Ever since the birth of the international news agencies, the monopolistic practices in the international news business have been in evidence. First, their home regions came under their monopoly. Subsequently, through the cartel agreements of the 1870s the European agencies extended their monopoly in regions under the influence of their home countries. But, in several aspects, the relationship among the cartel members was unequal. In terms of territory, Britain's Reuters had an area as vast as the British empire, spread across Africa, Asia, America, Australia and Europe, covering almost one-fifth of the globe. In terms of influence too, it was the Reuters that mattered. Its extensive network supported by Britain's control of the world's transoceanic cables, helped it to become the most powerful agency in the world. The monopoly of the international news business by the European triumvirate was not to continue unchallenged in the fast changing political climate of the 20th century. Much of the resistance to the European agencies came from the US, which, by the end of World War I, was switching its role from an international debtor to that of a major creditor. Its increasing control over transoceanic cables and an expanding medium at home provided the much needed muscle power to its agencies to challenge the European cartel. Many in the US had come to realize the advantage that would accrue out of the international news business. At this juncture, the AP synthesized its commercial interest with diplomatic interest of the US by stressing how the Reuters, through European news cartels, controlled all foreign news sent into the US, and all American news to the rest of the world, and how such practices promoted Britain's interests while affecting the interests of both the US and the AP. Finally, the AP ceded from the cartel, in 1934, and independently went into the business of news collection and distribution around the world, heralding the impending domination of the US in the coming years.

*Free Flow Ideas:* A major factor that helped the growth of US agencies was the wireless transmission technology, perfected at home, which reversed the world communication imbalance to the overall advantage of the American interest. Yet another forum responsible for the growth of the US communication network abroad was a general realization in the US of the advantages that world communication controls bestowed on foreign trade and commerce. Following such realizations, ideas on the unrestricted flow of communication between nations began to crystallize in the US. Fit, the American Society of Newspaper Editors adopted a resolution urging the political parties to support freedom of information and unrestricted flow of communication throughout the world. Subsequently, with the Democrats and Republicans adopt these aims, the free flow doctrine became an integral part of the US political ideology and foreign policy. The UN too came under its influence. Its declaration on Freedom of Information, issued m 1946, made the first reference to the free flow of information:

- "All states should proclaim policies under which the free flow of information, within countries and across frontiers, will be protected. The right to sell and transmit information should be insured in order to enable the public to ascertain facts and appraise events."

The US was also successful in incorporating some of its viewpoints in the Universal Declaration of Human Rights, which was passed by the UN General Assembly in 1948. Article of the declaration reflects the American concept of free flow. It reads:

- "Everyone has the right to freedom of opinion and expression; this right includes freedom to hold opinions and to seek, receive and impart information and ideas through any media regardless of frontiers."

With its lead in communication technology, the US had everything to gain from the free flow doctrine. In about two decades, its grip on international communication was complete.

## INFORMATION IMBALANCES BETWEEN DEVELOPED AND DEVELOPING COUNTRIES

Before going into the issue of information imbalance, one has become familiar with concepts that are central to international communication. International communication, at a simple level, could be conceptualized as a communication process between two or more national and cultural systems. Theoretically, nations are free to assume any role in this process. But the ground realities are different. The status of a given nation and its media institutions in the international news flow system is determined by the role a national media system is destined to play: the role of a producer-distributor or that of a consumer-buyer. Economics determines the ability of a nation to establish its own infrastructures for newsgathering and transmission. The importance of the Technology factor hardly needs any emphasis. Those having access to modern communication technology as the 'producer-distributor' of media products. The UNESCO was made a willing tool in promoting the interests of the 'producer-distributors' of the media products and technology. In 1961, the UNESCO proposed that for each 100 inhabitants of a country, the minimum standard be, at least, 10 copies of daily newspapers, 5 radio receivers, and 2 television sets. Lacking the financial resources, manpower and technology, the new nations had no other option but to be "consumer-buyers" of what the Western media produced and distributed worldwide in terms of hardware and technology, and software programmes. The major implications of such a domination are that :

- These agencies determine the very nature of the news flow in the world,
- The news consumers everywhere view the world as these agencies report it,
- The news flow, by-and-large, is one-way from the developed nations to the developing nations,
- In the one way flow, the developing nations are under-reported and, when reported; they are presented in a bad light.

These are the consequences of the spread of the Western media, in general, and the US media, in particular, it was not surprising that in the early 1970s a large number of new nations began to complain about the ill effects of the monopoly of international communication. In the Pre-eminent position of the US and a few of her allies, a threat to 'national sovereignty' was seen in the US export of cultural products such as books, films, the TV programmes and magazines, a growth of a new kind of imperialism, 'cultural imperialism', was perceived, and the free-flow doctrine was accused of having promoted one-way flow, from the US to the rest of the world.

## THE DEMAND FOR NWICO

*The following overlapping and mutually complementing factors are at the base of the demand for a new order in the field of information:*

- The emergence of new nations following the dissolution of the colonial empires after World War II.
- The asymmetrical economic relationship between the new nations and the Western industrialized nations which, while strengthening the latter's wealth and power, perpetuated the new nation's dependency, not merely economic but political and cultural as well.
- The coming together of the new nations under the umbrella of non-alignment in the wake of aggressive bloc-building by the US and the USSR.
- The new nations' realize that their under-development was related to their dependence on rich nations followed by a firm resolve to assertive actions to correct imbalances in world trade and commerce, and cultural exchanges.
- They're gaining in strength in international organizations, such as the UN and the UNESCO.

Four stages can easily be identified in the history of the NWICO. The first stage, from 1973-76, marked the evolution of a new order. The second stage, from 1976-79, saw the accumulation of data and empirical evidences to give credence to the new order demand. The third stage followed the publication of the MacBride report in 1980. The fourth stage is the period following the adoption of the NWICO Resolution in the UNESCO, and the setting up of IPDC. Generally, the evolution of the new order concept is credited to the Non-aligned Movement WAM). However, the contribution of the UNESCO cannot be ignored but in the early years the UNESCO also played the willing tool role to the hilt. It propagated the doctrine of the free flow of information because of its domination by the West. But, with the continual addition of newly-freed status to the UN in the 60s and 70s, the UNESCO underwent changes not only in its structural makeup, but also in its concerns, policies, and programmes in several areas including communication. Much of the credit for the enlarging communication agenda of the UNESCO in the 1970s goes to the Non-aligned Movement, which saw communication, at least in the early 70s, as a means to an end, the end being economic development of the poor nations. It was in this context that it laboured at the international level for the formulation of the UN Anti-colonial Declaration, for the launching of the UN development decade in 1964, for the creation of the UNCTAD in 1964, the UNDP in 1965 and the UNIDO in 1976, and also adopted Western development models in which development was to be achieved through modernization and industrialization. Very soon, it realized that the development was not forthcoming; most of the newly independent nation remained where they were. This failure, which led to a process of re-examination, eventually culminated in the demand for a New International Economic Order (NIEO). Soon followed its natural corollary, new order in the field of international information and communication, the NWICO.

*The Algiers Summit:* From the viewpoint of the NWICO history, the Algiers Summit of the non-aligned countries, held in 1973, is a major landmark, for it was here that communication concerns were addressed directly in more than one paper in the context of their economic development programmes. Around this time, the UNESCO was in the midst of a crisis, which had arisen out of a resolution moved by the Soviet Union, with the support of the Third World, at the 17th General Conference of the UNESCO, held in the 1970s, calling upon the UNESCO Director General to prepare a declaration on the Fundamental Principles Governing the Use of the Mass Media, with a view to strengthening of peace and understanding, and combating War, Propaganda, Racialism and Apartheid, hereafter referred to as the Mass Media Declaration (MMD). This resolution was to influence significantly the tone and tenor of the information flow debates.

While it provided an opportunity for the Third World to bring forth its views on the free-flow concept and its consequences of inadequacies and imbalances in international news and information flow, it opened a new chapter in the East-West struggle, which was to last until 1978. To avoid further deepening of the crisis, the 19th UNESCO General Conference postponed the consideration of the draft on the MMD to its next session to be held in 1978, and adopted a resolution inviting the Director General to undertake a review of the problems of communication in modem society. In response to this, the Director General constituted a 16-member Commission for the study of Communication Problems under the chairmanship of Sean MacBride, a distinguished diplomat and winner of both Nobel Peace Prize and Lenin Peace Prize. The Commission's work, a major landmark in the international communication history, is one of the major outcomes of the NWICO debates. The 20th UNESCO general conference, held in 1978, was marked by a spirit of compromise. The behind the scene negotiations for reconciliation bore fruit: the new MMD text now retitled as 'Declaration on Fundamental Principles Governing the Contribution of the Mass

Media in Strengthening Peace and International Understanding and in Combating war Propaganda, Racialism and Apartheid' were approved. The six-year long controversy finally ended. The new text satisfied all. It must, however, be made clear that though the declaration called for a free-flow and better-balanced dissemination of information, it did not define the new order, and thus, in reality, the issue remained unresolved. Non-etheless, the Third World was very clear about the meaning of the NWICO. What is wrong with the existing system? Why a new order? And what measures need to be taken to bring about a new order? The answer to these could be found in Mustapha Masmoudi's paper, 'New World Information Order', submitted to the MacBride Commission, which presents a complete catalogue of the Third World complaints against the Western nations and their media empires, and also outlines the measures needed in the political, legal, and technical-financial spheres for the realization of the new order.

Masmoudi's indictment of the international communication system and exposition of the essentials of the hew order did not go unquestioned in the West. For many, Masmoudi's new order was restrictive in character and content. Prof. Elie Abel, a member of the MacBride Commission, while agreeing to the presence of gross imbalances in the international communication system, attributed this to the historical process resulting in an uneven spread of development. Denying Masmoudi's allegation that foreign news agencies imposed unsuitable Western values and perspectives upon the less developed countries, he pointed out that, in most developing countries, the, subscriber is the government or government controlled agencies, since newspapers or broadcasting stations are not allowed to subscribe directly to the foreign agency services. Prof. Abel also opposed Masmoudi's suggestion that restrictions be placed on rights such, as the right of free circulation of information and of access to information so as to eliminate imbalances. The only constructive approach, according to him, was a "massive international effort to increase the capacity for communication at every level-the individual, the community, the nation, and among nations".

## THE MACBRIDE REPORT

The most important outcome of the NWICO debates of the 1970s was the formation of the International Commission for the Study of Communication Problems as per the decision of the 1976 general conference of UNESCO. The 16-member commission comprised experts representing world's diverse ideological, political, economic and geographical zones. Popularly known as the MacBride Commission, it met eight times at the UNESCO headquarters in Paris for facilitating discussion among its members. In addition, it organized four round table discussions in Sweden, Yugoslavia, India and Mexico, received some one hundred background papers from professionals and scholars around the world, and investigated the new order issues more thoroughly than any previous from had done. Its final report, published as Many Voices, One World, stands out as a complete source of information on communication in today's and tomorrow's world. The Commission viewed communication as a basic social need of individuals, communities and nations with an inseparable relationship with politics, as an economic force, with decisive influence on development, as an educational tool, and as an integral part of the culture. Thus, any change in any aspect of communication within and among nations would call for changes in all these aspects of communications. The issues of imbalances and inequalities were fully recognized by the Commission. Attributing the imbalance to a historical process of unequal growth of nations and complex political, economic and social-cultural realities, the Commission supported the view that 'free flow' was nothing more than 'one-way free flow', and also that the principle, on which it was based, should be restated so as to guarantee 'free and balanced flow'. It identified imbalances in the flow between the developed and developing countries. The Commission took note of imbalances in the flow of news through the instruments of technology.

The developed world, which have access to modern technology, has had both positive and negative influences on the Political, economic, socio-cultural fabric of their home regions and other nations, which have come to depend on them for their news and information needs. A positive influence was that they extended facilities for cultural development. Their negative effect was the promotion of alien values across cultural frontiers. Thus, they were practicing cultural imperialism through their control of communication infrastructure, news circulation, cultural products, educational software, books, films, equipment, and training. The Commission concluded that the primary factor in imbalance and inequalities was an economic one. It said that the one way-flow of communication is basically a reflection of the world's dominant political and economic structures, which tend to maintain or reinforce the dependence of the poor countries of the rich nations.

# 7

# Status of Press Freedom Worldwide

## WORLDWIDE PRESS FREEDOM

Every year, Reporters without Borders establishes a ranking of countries in terms of their freedom of the press. The Worldwide press freedom index list is based on responses to surveys sent to journalists that are members of partner organisations of the RWB, as well as related specialists such as researchers, jurists and human rights activists. The survey asks questions about direct attacks on journalists and the media as well as other indirect sources of pressure against the free press, such as pressure on journalists by non-governmental groups. RWB is careful to note that the index only deals with press freedom, and does not measure the quality of journalism.

In 2003, the countries where press was the most free were Finland, Iceland, the Netherlands In 2004, apart from the above countries, Denmark, Ireland, Slovakia, Portugal and Switzerland were tied at the top of the list, followed by New Zealand and Latvia. The country with the least degree of press freedom was North Korea, followed by Burma, Turkmenistan, People's Republic of China (mainland only), Vietnam, Nepal, and Iran.

### NON-DEMOCRATIC STATES

According to Reporters Without Borders, more than a third of the world's people live in countries where there is no press freedom. Overwhelmingly, these people live in countries where there is no system of democracy or where there are serious deficiencies in the democratic process.Freedom of the press is an extremely problematic problem/concept for most non-democratic systems of government since, in the modern age, strict control of access to information is critical to the existence of most non-democratic governments and their associated control systems and security apparatus. To this end, most non-democratic societies employ state-run news organizations to promote the propaganda critical to maintaining an existing political power base and suppress (often very brutally, through the use of police, military, or intelligence agencies) any significant attempts by the media or individual journalists to challenge the approved "government line" on contentious issues. In such countries, journalists operating on the fringes of what is deemed to be acceptable will very often find themselves the subject of considerable intimidation by agents of the state.

This can range from simple threats to their professional careers (firing, professional blacklisting) to death threats, kidnapping, torture, and assassination. Reporters Without Borders reports that, in 2003, 42 journalists lost their lives pursuing their profession and that, in the same year, at least 130 journalists were in prison as a result of their occupational activities. In 2005, 63 journalists and 5 media assistants were killed worldwide.

- The Lira Baysetova case in Kazakhstan.
- In Nepal, Eritrea and China (mainland only), journalists may spend years in jail simply for using the "wrong" word or photo.
- The Georgiy R. Gongadze case in Ukraine (information needed, spammer removed information)

According to the Press Freedom Index for 2007, Iran ranked 166th out of 169 nations. Only three other countries - Eritrea, North Korea and Turkmenistan - had more restrictions on news media freedom than Iran. The government of Ali Khamenei and the Supreme National Security Council had imprisoned 50 journalists in 2007 and had all but eliminated press freedom. Reporters Without Borders (RWB) has dubbed Iran the "Middle East's biggest prison for journalists."

**Poland**

Freedom of Press laws are first passed in the Commonwealth in 1532.

**Sweden**

The world's first Freedom of the Press Act was introduced in Sweden in 1766.

**Denmark-Norway**

Between September 4, 1770 and October 7, 1771 the kingdom of Denmark-Norway had the most unrestricted freedom of press of any country in Europe. This occurred during the regime of Johann Friedrich Struensee, whose first act was to abolish the old censorship laws. However, due to the great amount of mostly anonymous pamphlets published that was critical and often slanderous towards Struensees own regime, he reinstated some restrictions regarding the freedom of press a year later, October 7 1771.

**England**

The Glorious Revolution of 1688 in England established parliamentary sovereignty over the Crown and, above all, the right of revolution. A major contributor to Western liberal theory was John Locke. Locke argued in *Two Treatises of Government* that the individual placed some of his rights present in the state of nature in trusteeship with the sovereign (government) in return for protection of certain natural individual rights. A social contract was entered into by the people.

Until 1694, England had an elaborate system of licensing. No publication was allowed without the accompaniment of a government-granted license. Fifty years earlier, at a time of civil war, John Milton wrote his pamphlet *Areopagitica*. In this work Milton argued forcefully against this form of government censorship and parodied the idea, writing "when as debtors and delinquents may walk abroad without a keeper, but unoffensive books must not stir forth without a visible jailer in their title." Although at the time it did little to halt the practice of licensing it would be viewed later a significant milestone in press freedom.

Milton's central argument was that the individual is capable of using reason and distinguishing right from wrong, good from bad. In order to be able to exercise this ration right, the individual must have unlimited access to the ideas of his fellow men in "a free and open encounter." From Milton's writings developed the concept of the open marketplace of ideas, the idea that when people argue against each other, the good arguments will prevail. One form of speech that was widely restricted in England was seditious libel, and laws were in place that made criticizing the government a crime.

The King was above public criticism and statements critical of the government were forbidden, according to the English Court of the Star Chamber. Truth was not a defence to seditious libel because the goal was to prevent and punish all condemnation of the government.

John Stuart Mill approached the problem of authority versus liberty from the viewpoint of a 19th century utilitarian: The individual has the right of expressing himself so long as he does not harm other individuals. The good society is one in which the greatest number of persons enjoy the greatest possible amount of happiness. Applying these general principles of liberty to freedom of expression, Mill states that if we silence an opinion, we may silence the truth. The individual freedom of expression is therefore essential to the well-being of society.

Mill's application of the general principles of liberty is expressed in his book On Liberty: "If all mankind minus one, were of one opinion, and one, and only one person were of the contrary opinion, mankind would be no more justified in silencing that one person, than he, if he had the power, would be justified in silencing mankind".

**Nazi Germany**

The dictatorship of Adolf Hitler largely suppressed freedom of the press through Joseph Goebbels' Ministry of Public Enlightenment and Propaganda. As the Ministry's name implies, propaganda did not carry the negative connotations that it does today (or did in the Allied countries); how-to manuals were openly distributed by that same ministry explaining the craft of effective propaganda. The Ministry also acted as a central control-point for all media, issuing orders as to what stories could be run and what stories would be suppressed. Anyone involved in the film industry — from directors to the lowliest assistant — had to sign an oath of loyalty to the Nazi Party, due to opinion-changing power Goebbels perceived movies to have. (Goebbels himself maintained some personal control over every single film made in Nazi Europe.) Journalists who crossed the Propaganda Ministry were routinely imprisoned or shot as traitors.

**India**

The Indian Constitution, while not mentioning the word "press", provides for *"the right to freedom of speech and expression"* (Article 19(1) a). However this right is subject to restrictions under sub clause (2), whereby this freedom can be restricted for reasons of "sovereignty and integrity of India, the security of the State, friendly relations with foreign States, public order, preserving decency, preserving morality, in relation to contempt, court, defamation, or incitement to an offense". Laws such as the Official Secrets Act and Prevention of Terrorism Act (PoTA) have been used to limit press freedom. Under PoTA, person could be detained for up to six months for being in contact with a terrorist or terrorist group. PoTA was repealed in 2006, but the Official Secrets Act 1923 continues. For the first half-century of independence, media control by the state was the major constraint on press freedom. Indira Gandhi famously stated in 1975 that All India Radio is "a Government organ, it is going to remain a Government organ..." With the liberalization starting in the 1990s, private control of media has burgeoned, leading to increasing independence and greater scrutiny of government. Organizations like Tehelka and NDTV have been particularly influential, *e.g.* in bringing about the resignation of powerful Haryana minister Venod Sharma however this freedom of speech and expression is automatically canceled during emergency. The word Reasonable was not present in the original article 19(1)(a. But this was later on added to this article, and presently in India there are number of organizations who are really influential.

## THE CONCEPT OF PRESS FREEDOM

A free press is a cornerstone of (liberal) democracy. It is essential for holding government accountable, and for citizens to get informed, to communicate their wishes, to participate in the political decisionmaking. In principle, and on the analogy of democracy, press freedom has been accepted worldwide as the norm. The Soviet mass media enjoyed, in contrast with 'bourgeois' mass media and on the analogy of 'real democracy', 'real freedom'.

Hence, media were freed from the obligation to be profitable: 'Freedom of the press was equated with freedom from private ownership: being freed from the profit motive, the media were free to do their duties as instruments of the state and the Party'. The communist model embraced the notion of the so called 'positive freedom', namely the freedom to, whereas in the liberal view, common in the West, the concept of 'negative freedom' or freedom from, prevailed: freedom from external goals (eg. building of a communist society, class homogenization) and external control and pressures (eg. government, parties, industry).

A free press, in other words, is an autonomous press: free to determine its own tasks and policies. In line with this view of freedom, 'traditional free press theory lacks a prescriptive character. It does not in its simple and most basic form say anything of what the press ought to do'. Media autonomy, or independence, implies that the media are clearly separated from state and political institutions and free from/of inhibiting forms of economic, political or other dependency. Karol Jakubowicz (2000) distinguishes three levels of media independence:

- External independence of media organizations, that is freedom to establish and operate media outlets without legal, political, or administrative interference or restraint.
- Internal independence of editorial staff, that is editorial autonomy, respected by owners, publishers and managers.
- Personal/professional independence of media practitioners, both management and journalists, which implies their impartiality and detachment from social, political and economic interests in their performance of journalistic duties and a sense of high professionalism and dedication to journalistic ethics.

Whereas laws, codes and institutions can contribute a lot to the first two levels of independence (media institutions and editorial staff) – one could speak of a 'formal press freedom' in accordance with the notion of 'formal democracy' – the third level, that is the individual level, is situated more on the field of (political) culture (i.e. attitudes, norms, values). And whereas the first two levels can be possibly realized without the third, absence of the third level on the other hand makes external and internal independence to a large degree meaningless. In other words: as democracy, press freedom is not considered a dichotomic but a continuous variable.

The choice is not between press freedom or no press freedom but between more or less press freedom. In every country and every system one can distinguish factors that spur press freedom on the one hand and factors that curtail press freedom on the other hand. The American organization Freedom House (2002) concentrates on the external factors that endanger press autonomy as the most measurable criteria: laws, regulations and administrative decisions that influence media content, political pressures and controls on media content, economic influences over media content and repressive actions (censorship, physical violence, arrests, killing of journalists). On the basis of these criteria Russia enjoys a 'partial press freedom'. Very often the issue of 'press freedom' is linked to the issue of 'press responsibility' or 'social responsibility'.

Together with Freedom House (2002) we want to stress the demand for 'freedom' above the demand for responsibility. Hence, the issue of 'press responsibility' often is voiced to defend governmental control of the press. It is linked more with the concept of 'positive freedom' than with the concept of freedom as such ('negative freedom'). Another frequently made association is that of press freedom with 'freedom of information' and the 'right to know'. This aspect is crucial indeed and complementary to press freedom as it relates to the perspective of the citizen. We'll come back to it later.

## THE PARADOX OF DEMOCRACY AND PRESS FREEDOM: THE POLITICIAN'S SIDE

The process of democratization in Russia paradoxically became a justification to curtail press freedom and to keep the media instrumentalized. The instrumental use of the mass media in postcommunist Russia is a continuation of the communist past. Although the external (societal) goal has changed from the building of the communist society into support for the democratic society, the mobilization of the mass media as a means to a goal remained unchanged. Gorbachev considered the mass media main instruments in promoting his politics of glasnost and gaining support for his reforms. As before, mass media mobilized people for the ideology of socialism but now in a more dynamic way. Yassen Zassoursky, dean of the Faculty of Journalism of the Moscow State University, has labelled the media model in the glasnost era (1985-1991) successively the 'glasnost-model' and the 'instrumental model'.

The first label (glasnost- model) points out an element of change, namely the break with the previous 'administrative-bureaucratic model'. Also in this model, however, Zassoursky points at the instrumental use of the mass media. In the name he later used (instrumental model), this aspect of continuity is brought to the forefront. The first Yeltsin-years received from Zassoursky the label of 'fourth power model'. The expectations, however, were pitched too high, and from 1995-'96 onward this label was changed in for that of 'authoritarian-corporate model'. It seems that the press could not meet the requirements for being called an independent 'Fourth Power'.

'Whatever good or bad happened to the Russian media in the 90s was directly tied to Yeltsin's views and acts in the information sphere', states media law specialist Andrei Richter. Yeltsin presented himself as the self-constituted personal guarantor of democracy and press freedom. While it is obvious that

Yeltsin 'allowed' more freedom than any of his predecessors, he never questioned his presumed right to allow such freedom. And in exchange he expected loyal support from the mass media for his policy.

Yeltsin embodied the belief that in order to improve the democratic procedures one has to step 'beyond' these procedures. In the name of democracy he fired upon Parliament in October 1993 and banned opposition newspapers. In the name of democracy he ruled largely by decree thus ignoring a whole series of 'horizontal checks'. In times of elections - 'the lifeblood' of democracy– the mobilization of mass media reaches a peak. In the name of democracy Yeltsin blatantly expected the mass media to support and arrange his re-election as President in 1996.

The mass media were committed to an anti-communist crusade. The whole election campaign was reduced to a duel between President Yeltsin and oppositional candidate Zhuganov, between the future and the past, between democracy and communism, between press freedom and press control. The tone of the campaign was set by the sacking on 15 February 1996 of Oleg Poptsov, head of the state-owned television station RTR. The right to appoint and dismiss media functionaries are one of the most powerful means of direct influence in the media for the executive. The President appoints the chairman of the 'public' television channel ORT and the government channels RTR and Kul'tura.

The government appoints the chairmen of the central radio channels. Another way of direct control are the state organizations directly subordinated to the executive, especially the Media Ministry but also an ad hoc institution such as Boris Yeltsin's 'Federal Information Centre of Russia' or an institution with no direct authority over the media such as the Security Council. The possibilities for indirect control are even greater. There is the reliance of many media outlets on economic sponsorship, either through state subsidies or by businesses, either open or secret. There is the use of courts as weapons deployed against journalists (esp. libel and slander). There is the dependency on the Kremlin – instead of an independent agency – for the issuance and revoking of broadcast and publishing licenses.

There is the dependency on state facilities such as printing houses, transmission facilities, and distribution systems. There is the accreditation of journalists and the unequal access to information. There is the use of violence against journalists. To this we can add the legal insecurity caused by the rapid succession of decrees, government orders and procedures, and the unpredictable changes in policy and practice of, for example, tax collection (eg. massively tolerated tax-evasion, followed by repressive controls on a large scale).

The paradox of democracy and press freedom: the media's side It does not appear fair to exclusively blame the authorities for the described system. The label 'authoritarian-corporate model' implies next to the 'authoritarian' aspect (that is, the media subordinated to the authorities) also the 'corporate' aspect (that is, the cooperation and alliances). The distinction comes down to the question whether the media are 'forced' rather than 'free' partners of the authorities. The question of quilt is inappropriate. We can only observe and conclude. In the early years of the Russian Federation, marked by the conflict between President and Parliament, 'most of the Russian media appeared to adopt a strongly pro- government stance'.

A content analysis of central television Programmes in the run-up to the referendum of 25 April 1993, showed 'the obtrusive partisanship of state television'. The majority of media voluntarily opted for the new, hence democratic partiality. Their leaders approached Yeltsin on their own initiative for protection and promised loyalty (read: partiality) instead. In the presidential elections of 1996, the majority of journalists and media professionals rallied behind Yeltsin again and voluntarily agreed with the mobilization function of the media. As Shevelov, vice president of television channel ORT, stated: 'you can only refer to pressure if there is resistance. There is none.'

The journalists adhered to partisanship not only for material reasons but also out of normative considerations. Igor Malashenko, president of the private television station NTV, who joined the Yeltsin re-election campaign in April 1996 as chief media advisor, explained this logic as following: if the private media provided "unbiased, professional, and objective" campaign coverage, Zyuganov would win the election, and journalists would lose their freedom permanently. Better to become a temporary "instrument of propaganda" in the hands of the Kremlin, Malashenko argued. Partijnost' was justified for the protection of democracy and consequently for press freedom. In the name of democracy the journalists voluntarily gave up their autonomy and their freedom.

Elections in general, and the 1996 elections in particular, can be considered critical but not atypical periods. Hence, it is not possible to treat the electoral period as being distinct from the context in which media normally operate. Quite the reverse, if we may believe Brzezinski: 'A perceptive formula is easier to articulate in a moment of special stress. (..) The situation of crisis permits sharper value judgments'. In general, and apart from election context, research has shown that many Russian journalists do not reject the paternalistic character of power and therefore accept its tutelage in mass communication. The journalist considers himself, in line with the tradition, a missionary of ideas, not a neutral observer or autonomous information disseminator.

The concept adhered to is that of the active or participant journalist as described by the Hungarian writer Janos Horvat: someone who wants to influence politics and audiences according to his political beliefs. The restriction to the presentation of mere facts is even commonly regarded as a devaluation of the profession of journalist. The attitude of the individual journalists suits the media-owners who like to use the argument of press freedom to protect their own freedom and their particular interests. As the majority of media-holdings form part of larger financial-industrial groups and as money is still made through political connections, political, economic and media-interests go closely together.

Political and economic elites try to secure via the media their own positions. Oligarchs and media magnates like Boris Berezovsky and Vladimir Gusinsky are the classic examples. When the media outlets of Vladimir Gusinsky became the target of prosecution, Gusinsky immediately alarmed that press freedom and in extension even democracy was endangered. His alarm was taken over by other journalists in Russia as well as in foreign countries (the USA in the first place).

There were, however, also skeptical voices. Robert Coalson (2000) wrote in a column in The Moscow Times: 'Gusinsky has shown very little genuine concern for press freedom. Like the other oligarchs, he only appears when his own interests are directly at risk'. In the same way Sergej Markov noticed with reference to a rally on freedom of speech, organized in connection with the NTV-case: '.. all speeches by NTV stars were about NTV's freedom. Such egoism could not inspire champions of freedom of expression'. Also in line is the following reflection: 'Where were the voices of protest from this 'independent' press when Yeltsin attacked the legitimate Russian parliament with military force, when the Soviet Union became dissolved by the signatures of a few officials, when the country's resources passed into the hands of a few oligarchs, and when corruption allowed Yeltsin's chosen family and friends to suddenly acquire wealth and transfer this wealth out of the country? That 'independent' press manipulated a government that served its interests.'

'The concept of freedom of speech has become hackneyed after Gusinsky and somewhat awkward to use' concludes the however not neutral General Director of Gazprom-Media, Alfred Kokh (2001: 20) and the public? As Price and Krug (2000: 4) state: 'for free and independent media to 'work', the community in question must value the role that the media play'. The public however seems to accept the 'Russian interpretation' of press freedom. Or, in any case, is adapted to it. The people react to mass media information by asking themselves not 'is this true' but 'komu eto vygodno?' (to who's advantage ?). News is interpreted in function of the news source, whether 'Berezovsky's channel', 'Gusinsky's channel' or 'the government's channel', or whether Potanin's newspaper, LUKoil's newspaper or the Communist Party's newspaper.

It is telling that 'independent' media in Russia are identified with 'opposition' media. Media independence is considered illusory, and partisanship the norm. Many Russians endorse the proposition that the mass media have the obligation to support 'the system'. A poll at the end of 2000, for example, shows that 34% of the Russians agree that the mass media have to give 'full support' to the President and that opposition is not desirable. 'In today's Russia, media freedom is not the most fashionable and popularly supported notion' declared television presentator and journalist Evgeny Kiselev in an interview with Jeremy Drukker. And Elena Androunas (1993: 35) points to the absence of 'freedom as a state of mind'.

## FREEDOM OF OPINION, NOT OF INFORMATION

The result is a pluralist but not an independent (autonomous) press. Pluralist, in the sense of representation in the media system of a broad range of political expression, opinions and interests. In this sense, postcommunist Russia is hardly less pluralistic than older democracies and probably even more, as it is not hindered to the same degree by 'political correctness' or 'la pensée unique'. Peter Humphreys (1996: 312) points in his book on media policy in Western Europe at a systematic decline of pluralism in the 20st century, caused by a de-ideologization of the traditional politics and commercialization, standardization and concentration of the media.

While the Russian media system is characterized by a high degree of concentration as well, this concentration is not at all linked with depolitization: 'money in the CIS is still made through connections in the government, and in this game it helps to own newspapers and stations as instruments of political influence'. Ivan Sigal (1997) has named Russian news coverage 'a part of politics'. 'In such circumstances', says Izvestiya-journalist Sergej Agafonov, 'a free independent press is doomed, but an unfree and dependent press can flourish'. Alexei Pankin speaks of a unique result: 'a genuinely pluralistic unfree media'.

However, a pluralism that derives the right to exist from the presence of different power groups in society is an uncertain pluralism. Hence, when the different power groups join forces because they feel threatened in their positions, as was the case in the 1996 presidential elections, this pluralism dies. The greatest victim of this kind of pluralism is the (factual) information. Every newspaper and every television channel brings its own versiya of the facts. In order to get an accurate picture of what happened, one has to read daily about six newspapers and watch several television stations, claims Andrei Fadin (1997). But who does? 'What we have is not freedom of information, and this 'freedom' is not exhaustive stimulating readers to buy half a dozen newspapers, but rather discouraging them from reading anything other than gossip columns and cheap sensations, and even more importantly, from organising their own actions on the basis of information received' reacts Alexei Pankin (1997).

The skepticism of the public is illustrated by its small confidence in the media: down from 70% in 1990 to only 13% in 2000. To fulfil their information function, the media need not only to break with the view of journalism as 'politics conducted with other means'. They also are in need, more concretely, for guaranteed access to information and transparency of governance. Press freedom presumes that, though independent, the press is not shielded away from government and industry. Worldwide, a correlation is determined between press freedom and transparency, and consequently between transparency and democracy: 'Information gathering is a vital component of freedom of information.

Without access to information, journalists are engaged primarily in the presentation of opinions. And while openness in the statement of opinions is an important element of democratic society, it is not sufficient for its development and maintenance. The possibility for an informed citizenry depends on the ability of journalists to have access to sources. Without this kind of journalistic effectiveness, a society can have free and independent media, but their utility Towards advancement of democratic institution-building might be severely limited.'

A climate of open access clings to the principle of information as a universal right, adjudged to everyone on an equal basis according to laws and procedures (universalism) whereas a culture of secrecy considers information a privilege, dependent on position or connections (particularism). Laws concerning transparency include those that recognize and guarantee public access to government-controlled information and institutions, with limited exceptions for national security, protection of personal privacy, crime prevention, and other goals. Laws concerning the licensing and accredititation of journalists also relate to his question. Russia has always been characterized by a culture of secrecy rather than transparency.

Always in Russian history, information was considered a privilege not a universal right - a property of the 'elite' who could dispose of it arbitrarily. In the Soviet Union, access to news sources depended on one's hierarchical (Party) position. The privileges of the nomenklatura 'first class' citizens not only included material goods, such as high salaries, access to 'diplomatic' shops, country houses, and the like, but also enhanced access to information: from the right to see foreign movies, or to read books, declared unsuited for general distribution to the receipt of special foreign news bulletins, on a daily basis compiled by TASS and distributed on paper of different colors according to the degree of detail and the intended public.

Though the high-placed functionaries received significantly more information, they too received their information on a 'need-to-know' basis. The result of this information policy was an information deficit: information became one of the most sought after commodities in the Soviet Union. Informal networks and rumours filled the vacuum. Parallel to the official information circuit, and on the analogy of the 'black market', an unofficial information circuit (*e.g.* samizdat) was functioning. The use of personal networks and informal contacts for obtaining scarce information, services or goods is indicated in Russian by the word blat or the term ZIS (znakomstva i svyazi). In the Soviet

Union, the use of informal information networks primarily had an economic function, namely the survival in an economy of scarcity. In the transition to a free market economy, privileged access to information played a key role in the process of privatizations, which became indicated as 'insider privatizations'. Personal (particularistic) relations (*e.g.* corruption, loyalties, privileges) continue to dominate the post-communist Russian economy and politics alike. Postcommunist leaders continue to see secrecy as a method to control the information flow. The panelists that IREX brought together to discuss the media situation in Russia agreed unanimously that 'access to some publicly relevant information is not free: authorities continue to view information as their property, and want to control access.' Defence-related security topics that are not state secrets have the status of classified information.

As a result 'obtaining publicly relevant information has become an increasingly challenging and dangerous job for Russian journalists, especially in cases of investigating authorities' abuses, corruption, fraud during election campaigns, and the war in Chechnya'. Banai sums up the three most efficient processes of information gathering in Russia as 'trust, relationship and integration'. Authorities still offer privileges to some periodicals and journalists. Mikhail Gulyaev names as 'privileged media' under President Yeltsin the news agencies ITAR-TASS and Interfaks, the newspapers Kommersant' and Izvestiya, and the weekly Argumenty i Fakty.

More recent examples support the enduring culture of secrecy. The way in which the Kremlin handled the disaster with the sunken submarine Kursk in the summer of 2000 fuelled speculations that the government was trying to withhold information from the public. Media coverage of the disaster was restricted, only state-controlled television channel RTR was granted full access to the disaster scene. The dissemination of false and misleading information led to confusion and government officials provided obscure answers to justified questions. The adoption by the Security Council of the 'Doctrine of the Information Security of the Russian Federation' on September 9$^{th}$, 2000 roused fear that the government intended to limit the free flow of information and conceal information from the public.

Among others, the doctrine promotes a feeling of distrust towards the foreign press whereas the unrestricted access to foreign media nowadays is guaranteed by the Russian mass media law of 27 December 1991. The Russian mass media law gives the citizens only an indirect right to information that is they have the right to efficient reception through the mass media of correct information on the activities of state organs, societal organizations and their functionaries. Mass media however have guaranteed access to government and administration information. Unlawful refusals from government or administration functionaries to communicate information requested upon are punishable by law. In reality however, refusal of information remain a problem. Since 1993, the Glasnost

Defence Foundation draws up an inventory of all infringements of the rights of journalists and mass media. The majority of violations are tied up with precisely the refusal and restriction of access to information. What's more, the number of infringements increases throughout the 90s. Very few journalists however, claim their rights before court. Again, we have to conclude that the existence of laws alone is not a sufficient condition for their implementation. Kathryn Hendley (1999) points out that the 'demand for law' lags behind the 'supply of law'. The demand for law implies respect for the law and trust in law, or, in other words a 'juridical culture'. We started from the common understanding that presses freedom and democracy are closely associated concepts. Both concepts, however, are not unequivocally defined.

Democracy implies participation of the citizens in the decision making process, at the least in the election of the government. But gradations are legion. Press freedom implies media autonomy, freedom from external goals and controls. Again, gradations are numerous. Having said that, the correlation seems to exist: in the sense that there was 'no democracy' and 'no press freedom' in the Soviet Union and only 'partial democracy' and 'partial press freedom' in post-communist Russia.

A third concept should be added, crucial to both press freedom and democracy, namely the right to know or the right to information coupled up to transparency of governance and administration. Information has to be considered a key concept in democracy and, at times, an antidote to opinion. The close integration of democracy with press freedom and in extension of politics with mass media has to be considered not only in terms of manipulation and force but also in terms of sharing a common political and information culture. Hence, the same values underly both 'cultures'.

All observations come down to the same conclusion: laws and institutions alone are not sufficient. Attitudes and values do play a role - whether named juridical culture, political culture, information culture, or culture tout court. The concept of culture suggests some communality of values: politicians, media workers and public alike share the same political culture and in extension the same information and communication culture. The concept of culture also suggests some continuity over time: not only over the communist and postcommunist period but also dating back to the time of the czars.

Culture is not unchangeable, but too high expectations concerning the role of media as triggers of democracy are doomed to fail. Media and society's development go together in coherent patterns. Howie Severino raises an interesting question in his latest blog post: how can a country that supposedly enjoys so much press freedom, such as the Philippines, be so corrupt? Isn't sunshine the best disinfectant? If we are a nation of tattletales, how come many are still stealing and cheating? Howie cites data that suggest that countries with high press-freedom rankings are less corrupt.

The conventional wisdom is that a free and courageous press exposes, thus helps to eliminate, corruption. One of the exception, Howie points out, seems to be the Philippines. We all have our own theories on why this is so. I'm not about to offer mine, except to point out my disagreement with the premise of this whole democracy-equals-press-freedom thing in the context of the Philippines. Press freedom, as we all know, does not exist in a vacuum. In a truly functioning democracy, press freedom should flourish. It is a gauge of democracy's efficacy. Without genuine democracy, it would be impossible for press freedom to exist.

The key word in that last sentence is "genuine." If we define democracy by its classic meaning — that people are free to choose their leaders and chart their own political course - then it would seem that what the Philippines have is indeed a democracy. But Philippine democracy has gone through a lot of permutations ever since the Americans introduced the concept to us more than a century ago. (It was, to be sure, an alien idea, which is probably why for much of the period since then, we were merely experimenting with democracy, not quite sure what to do with it, not quite fully grasping its potential.)

We have been told, since 1986 at least, that a military coup d'etat that is subsequently backed by a throng of people rushing to Edsa is democracy in action. We were told about this again in 2001. Today, we tend to equate democracy in action with the upheavals of a mob - a well-meaning mob, sure, but a mob just the same. The bastardization of democracy continues to this day. Every election time, we are told that a few select families ruling over us for years and years is democracy in action.

An elite political family is good for us, we are told. Political dynasties in the Philippines are the antithesis of democracy and yet we are relentlessly made to accept them as part of our democratic way of life. Never mind that the evidence that elections in the Philippines are far from democratic has always been plain for all to see: the fraud, the vote buying, the violence, the manipulations, to name a few. The consequence of this bastardization, of course, is the poisoning and emasculation of our democratic institutions. This allows politicians to easily steal elections and make us all believe - through the media — that that is the work of God.

We have a Commission on Elections that has shown its capacity to be the chief agent not in upholding democracy but in subverting it. We have a judicial system that tends to favour the rich and those in power. We have an executive branch that is populated by a few select families who Harbour a sense of entitlement to the positions that they had either stole or bought. Not surprisingly, we have had a media that, through all these years, has served the cause of the elite, the rich and the powerful more than they do the common man. The Philippine press, with a few exceptions, has not changed since the end of World War II, which is to say that it remains either a weapon or a plaything by those rich or influential enough to literally buy a newspaper or a broadcast network or pay off reporters, editors and news managers. Filipino journalists work on pittance wages, if at all, making them the most abused of professionals. As such, they are easily corrupted not just by the owners of their newspapers or stations but by those who have the money to buy them and influence how they write or present the news. Again, there are exceptions but these exceptions are not significant enough to empower the press to function properly and professionally.

Perhaps with the exception of the mosquito press during the martial-law years, the Philippine press has never quite shown us why it deserves to be called the "fourth estate," supposedly a vanguard for the people that would come to democracy's rescue if the other three estates — the executive branch, the legislative branch and the judiciary — failed. So what we have now is a democracy that is not quite the democracy that many of us may have wished for. And what we have is a media that is an outgrowth of this anomaly of democracy, a corrupted and incompetent press so weak it cannot function as the sunshine to disinfect the rot in our system.

## FREEDOM OF THE PRESS

Freedom of the press or freedom of the media is the freedom of communication and expression through mediums including various electronic media and published materials. While such freedom mostly implies the absence of interference from an overreaching state, its preservation may be sought through constitutional or other legal protections. With respect to governmental information, any government may distinguish which materials are public or protected from disclosure to the public based on classification of information as sensitive, classified or secret and being otherwise protected from disclosure due to relevance of the information to protecting the national interest. Many governments are also subject to sunshine laws or freedom of information legislation that are used to define the ambit of national interest.

The Universal Declaration of Human Rights states: "Everyone has the right to freedom of opinion and expression; this right includes freedom to hold opinions without interference, and impart information and ideas through any media regardless of frontiers" This philosophy is usually accompanied by legislation ensuring various degrees of freedom of scientific research (known as scientific freedom), publishing, press and printing the depth to which these laws are entrenched in a country's legal system can go as far down as its constitution. The concept of freedom of speech is often covered by the same laws as freedom of the press, thereby giving equal treatment to spoken and published expression.

## FREEDOM OF THE PRESS IN THE UNITED STATES

Freedom of the press in the United States is protected by the United States

Constitution. John Hancock was the first person to write newspapers in the British colonies in North America published "by authority," that is, under license from and as the mouthpiece of the colonial governors. The first regularly published newspaper was the *Boston News-Letter* of John Campbell, published weekly beginning in 1704. The early colonial publishers were either postmasters or government printers, and therefore unlikely to challenge government policies.

The first independent newspaper in the colonies was the *New-England Courant*, published in Boston by James Franklin beginning in 1721. A few years later, Franklin's younger brother, Benjamin, purchased the *Pennsylvania Gazette* of Philadelphia, which became the leading newspaper of the colonial era.

During this period, newspapers were unlicensed and could freely publish dissenting views, but were subject to prosecution for libel or even sedition if their opinions threatened the government. The notion of "freedom of the press" later enshrined in the United States Constitution is generally traced to the seditious libel prosecution of John Peter Zenger by the colonial governor of New York in 1735. In this instance of jury nullification, Zenger was acquitted after his lawyer, Andrew Hamilton, argued to the jury (contrary to established English law) that there was no libel in publishing the truth. Yet even after this celebrated case, colonial governors and assemblies asserted the power to prosecute and even imprison printers for publishing unapproved views.

During the American Revolution, a free press was identified by Revolutionary leaders as one of the elements of liberty that they sought to preserve. The Virginia Declaration of Rights (1776) proclaimed that "the freedom of the press is one of the greatest bulwarks of liberty and can never be restrained but by despotic governments." Similarly, the Constitution of Massachusetts (1780) declared, "The liberty of the press is essential to the security of freedom in a state: it ought not, therefore, to be restrained in this commonwealth." Following these examples, the First Amendment to the United States Constitution restricted Congress from abridging the freedom of the press and the closely associated freedom of speech.

John Locke's ideas had inspired both the French and American revolutions. Thomas Jefferson wanted to unite the two streams of liberalism, the English and the French schools of thought. His goal was to create a government that would provide both security and opportunity for the individual. An active press was essential as a way of educating the population. To work freely, the press must be free from control by the state. Jefferson was a person who himself suffered great calumnies of the press. Despite this, in his second inaugural address, he proclaimed that a government that could not stand up under criticism deserved to fall.

Jefferson said: "No experiment can be more interesting than that we are now trying, and which we trust will end in establishing the fact, that man may be governed by reason and truth. Our first object should therefore be, to leave open to him all avenues of the truth".In 1931, the U.S. Supreme Court decision in *Near v. Minnesota* used the 14th Amendment to apply the freedom of the press to the States. Other notable cases regarding free press are:

- *New York Times Co. v. United States' (1971): The Supreme Court upheld the publication of the Pentagon Papers.*
- *New York Times Co. v. Sullivan* (1964): The Court decided that for written words to be libel they must be, first of all, false.

## RANKING OF UNITED STATES PRESS FREEDOM

The United States are, as of 2009, joint 20th in the Reporters Without Borders Press Freedom Index. This is a measure of freedom available to the press, encompassing areas such as government censorship, and not indicative of the quality of journalism. In 2009 the United States climbed 16 places from 36th in 2008 with a score of 4.00, with Denmark, Finland, Ireland, Norway and Sweden tied for first place with 0.00 and Eritrea bottom of the list with 115.50. In the Freedom of the Press 2009 report, published by Freedom House the United States is ranked fourth in the Americas, and joint 24th globally. This reports from 0 (free) to 100 (not free), with the United States scoring 18 compared to Iceland (top of the list) on 9 and North Korea (bottom of the list) on 98.

### Notable Exceptions

- In 1798, not long after the adoption of the Constitution, the governing Federalist Party attempted to stifle criticism by means of the Alien and Sedition Acts. (It was notable that the Sedition Act made criticism of Congress, and of the President, a crime, but not criticism of the Vice-President. Jefferson, a non-Federalist, was Vice-President at the time the Act was passed.) These restrictions on freedom of the press proved very unpopular in the end and worked against the Federalists, leading to the party's eventual demise. Thomas Jefferson was among those who opposed the Acts, and did so vehemently, and he was elected President in the election of 1800. Jefferson then pardoned most of those convicted under the Acts. He made it a principle not to ask what they had done, but only whether they had been charged under the Acts. In his first Inaugural Address in 1801 he reiterated his longstanding commitment to freedom of speech and of the press: "If there be any among us who would wish to dissolve this Union or to change its republican form, let them stand undisturbed as monuments of the safety with which error of opinion may be tolerated where reason is left free to combat it."
- The Espionage Act of 1917 and the Sedition Act of 1918, which

amended it, imposed restrictions on the free press during wartime. It carried fines of $10,000 and up to 20 years imprisonment for people publishing "... disloyal, profane, scurrilous, or abusive language about the form of government of the United States or the Constitution of the United States, or the military or naval forces of the United States..." In Schenck v. United States (1919), the Supreme Court upheld the laws, setting the "Clear and present danger" standard. Congress repealed both laws in 1921, and Brandenburg v. Ohio (1969) revised the "Clear and present danger" test to the "Imminent lawless action" test, which is less restrictive.

- 1988: *Hazelwood v. Kuhlmeier*: The Supreme Court upheld that the principal of a school has the right to review and block controversial articles of a school paper funded by the school and published in the school's name.
- In the United States in 2005, interpretation of the Bipartisan Campaign Reform Act may consider political statements as being the equivalent of campaign donations. Because access to Internet statements are weakly controlled, the campaign value of statements is not known in advance and a high ultimate value may trigger large fines for violations. This particularly threatens Internet statements by individuals, and ambiguous definitions of membership in *the press* make the possible effects ambiguous.
- 2008: Wikileaks was forcefully censored by the United States. Wikileaks was given only hours notice "by e-mail" prior to the hearing. Wikileaks pre-litigation California council Julie Turner attended the start of hearing in a personal capacity but was then asked to leave the court room. After appeal, however, all the court of appeals threw out the case, restoring access to Wikileaks.

## LIMITS ON FREEDOM OF THE PRESS

The First Amendment of the United States Constitution states with majestic simplicity: "Congress shall make no law...abridging the freedom of speech, or of the press..." Supreme Court decisions over the years have interpreted this unadorned sentence to bar government generally, including state or local governments, from taking official action to abridge freedom of the press. But that same Supreme Court has been equally clear that the First Amendment is not an absolute, that in certain circumstances "freedom of the press" must yield to other constitutionally-protected values, such as national security and the right of a defendant to an unprejudiced fair trial. The history of the First Amendment's press clause has thus been one of shifting lines back and forth along the broad frontier of freedom. There are four basic stages at which freedom of the press has been or can be limited: (1) access to information;

(2) prior restraint on publishing information (censorship, injunctions); (3) liability for publishing (libel and invasion of privacy suits, fines and imprisonment); and (4) requiring reporters to testify or otherwise disclose sources or materials gathered in the course of their employment. While this fourth category technically does not abridge freedom of the press—it does not bar access or prevent or punish publications—the "chilling effect" it has upon the ability of reporters to function and to gain their sources' confidence certainly merits its inclusion.

**Access**

Even after Richmond, infra, there is no constitutional guarantee of access to most places or information, though several justices have strongly suggested that the First Amendment would be violated by a complete ban on access to a governmental facility like a prison. And the Supreme Court has held in a series of decisions that the press has no right of special access to places or information not shared by the public generally. Houchins v. KQED, 438 U.S.1 (1978); Pell v. Procunier, 417 U.S. 817 (1974); Saxbe v. Washington Post Co., 417 U.S. 843 (1974).

This having been said, however, the courts have also emphasized that members of the press are protected by constitutional rights to evenhanded treatment. This has been required, for instance, in decisions as to which persons receive White House passes and which do not, Sherill v. Knight, 569 F.2d 124 (C.A.D.C.; 1978); and in which an "underground newspaper" had been denied access to police department records available to other media, Quad-City Community News Service, Inc. v. Jebens, 334 F. Supp. 8 (D. Iowa; 1971).

Legislation, of course, is one appropriate vehicle for securing access. The classic statute of this sort is the Freedom of Information Act, both state and federal, discussed elsewhere in this book. Dependence on legislation for any press right, however, is a chancy business at best. For what this year's legislature gives, next year's might take away; and the right based upon legislative pleasure is always a precarious one.

In one area, however, the courts have increasingly recognized a constitutional right of the press and public to access. That area is to the courts themselves. Since the 1980s, the law has been clear that the First Amendment guarantees a right of the public and the press to attend civil and criminal trials, Richmond Newspapers, Inc. v. Virginia, 448 U.S. 555 (1980) and pre-trial proceedings (such as probable cause hearings in criminal cases), Press-Enterprise Company v. Superior Court, 478 U.S. 1 (1986).

Before any such hearing may be closed, the court must hold a hearing on the closure motion—even if both parties to the case agree to closure—and the court must hear evidence showing why closure is necessary. The press must be given an opportunity to present contrary evidence. Closure is permissible only if, based upon evidence presented, the court makes specific findings on the record that closure is essential to preserve values higher than those underlying public access and that the closure is narrowly tailored to serve that higher interest. Press-Enterprise, supra; Globe Newspapers v. Superior Court, 457 U.S. 596 (1982).

If the "higher interest" sought to be served by closure is to ensure an accused person a fair trial, closure is permissible only if the court, based on evidence presented to it which the press has an opportunity to rebut, makes specific findings demonstrating (1) that there is a "substantial probability" (not just a "reasonable likelihood") that the accused's right to a fair trial will be prejudiced by publicity that closure would prevent (as opposed to situations where there has already been so much publicity that whatever prejudice might exist already exists); and (2) reasonable alternatives to closure—such as questioning of potential jurors, changing the jury panel, changing the date or site of the trial, clear instructions from the trial judge—cannot adequately protect the accused's fair trial rights. Press-Enterprise, supra. It is not enough for a court to find that those alternatives would be expensive or cumbersome. If they are "not beyond the realm of the manageable," they must be considered before closure can be justified. Richmond, supra. And courts have held that while an accused is entitled to an impartial jury, he or she is not entitled to one that has never heard of the accused or the charges against the accused. Murphy v. Florida, 421 U.S. 794 (1975).

The Globe case, supra, held unconstitutional a law barring the public and press automatically in all cases involving minors as witnesses as to certain crimes. The Supreme Court emphasized that in each case closure must be decided on a record based on the facts of that particular case, after a hearing of the sort discussed above. Globe raises serious questions about the constitutionality of laws such as those that mandate closed hearings in "juvenile" cases. In addition, other courts have held that due process requires there to be some sort of notice given to the public and the press —even if it is just a written notice on the court's docket or bulletin board—alerting them whenever someone is going to try to close court proceedings. United States v. Criden, 675 F.2d 550 (3 Cir.; 1982); In re Application of the Herald Company, 734 F.2d 93 (2 Cir.; 1984).

The requirement that any closure that is ordered be "narrowly tailored" to meet the need inspiring closure means that the court must be careful to close only as much of the proceeding as the court finds access to it would harm the accused's right to a fair trial. If that means only one witness's testimony, or only a portion of that witness's testimony, that is the only portion that may be closed. Open courts are the rule; closure is the rare exception.

Connecticut has supplied the public with a unique tool to protect its right of access to court proceedings. Since 1980—even before Richmond, supra, was decided —Conn. Gen. Stat. § 51-164x has provided that the effectiveness of any court-order closing a court proceeding will be delayed for seventy-two hours; and if within that time anyone (a newspaper, a reporter, a member of the public) appeals to the appellate court, the order is further stayed until the appeal is decided. The law also provides for a speedy appeal process. Thus, in the highly unusual situation where a court has ordered closure, the factual and constitutional issues will have an opportunity to be fully analyzed by the highest courts before this extraordinary remedy is invoked.

While courts have not held that the electronic media (radio and television) have a constitutional right to record, tape or broadcast live courtroom proceedings, the Supreme Court has ruled that an accused's constitutional right to a fair trial is not violated by a court rule or statute that does allow such access. This has encouraged many if not most states to permit radio and television equipment to record and tape courtroom proceedings, usually under carefully crafted rules designed to minimize the intrusive effect of the equipment and its operation upon the proceedings. In Connecticut the "broadcasting, televising, recording or photographing" of most— but not all—civil and criminal court proceedings is authorized and governed by Connecticut Practice Book § 1-10 and 1-11.

Courts increasingly have also recognized that the public and the press have a First Amendment right of access to inspect and copy court files, including exhibits introduced into evidence; and that before access to such files can be denied, a court must hold the same kind of hearing and make the same kind of findings required for closure of courtrooms.

One reason the battleground has recently shifted to access is that it is so difficult to prevent publication. In a series of decisions the Supreme Court has held that the press is free to publish anything it sees or hears, even if there is a law designed to prevent it from seeing or hearing the information. Here again, however, there are no absolutes. Obscenity, difficult as it may be to define, can be restrained from publication. Also, national security has been recognized as a legitimate basis for banning publications, though what the standards of this basis are (only during wartime? The quantum of clear, certain and immediate danger required) remain murky at best. The Progressive, 467 F. Supp. 990 (W.D. Wisc.; 1979), dismissed, 610 F.2d 819 (7 Cir.; 1979); (the "hydrogen bomb case"). The situation of the electronic media with respect to prior restraints is inextricably intertwined with the fact that radio and television stations are licensed by the Federal Communications Commission ("FCC") and those licenses must from time to time be renewed. The underlying justification for licensure—that the broadcast spectrum is limited, that it is a public resource, that its scarcity requires allocation by government to licensees who operate to further the public interest—has been found to justify two types of prior restraint by government: prohibitions on broadcasting certain types of matter and a requirement that certain other kinds of matter be broadcast. Red Lion Broadcasting Co. v. FCC, 395 U.S. 367 (1978); FCC v. Pacifica Foundation, 438 U.S. 726 (1978); National Broadcasting Co. v. United States, 319 U.S. 190 (1943).

The nature and variety of FCC restraints would take far more space than is here afforded to discuss intelligently. That FCC right, however, is not without limitation. The First Amendment does serve to place certain broadly defined parameters around the right of government to dictate content to the electronic media. Columbia Broadcasting System, Inc. v. Democratic National Committee, 412 U.S. 94 (1973); FCC v. League of Women Voters of California, 468 U.S. 364 (1984).

Once data has been published, the publisher and reporter become potentially liable for what they wrote or said. For while the public has received the benefit of the dissemination of information—thus fulfilling a major purpose of the First Amendment—people may have been hurt as a result, and the law recognizes their right to be compensated.

Criminal sanctions are rare, of course. If, however, a court has issued a gag order barring publication, a reporter or publisher can have appropriate sanctions—fine, imprisonment for contempt of court—imposed upon him or her for violating that court order, even if a higher court later finds the order was wrong. United States v. Dickinson, 465 F.2d 496 (5 Cir.; 1972); but see In re Providence Journal, 820 F.2d 1342 (1 Cir.; 1987), cert. dismissed, 485 U.S. 693 (1988) (discussing "transparently invalid" court orders).

The two primary legal remedies for illegally published material, however, are civil suits for invasion of privacy and libel. The former is treated elsewhere in this book. Suffice it here to be said that Connecticut's courts recognize all four of the separate types of invasion of privacy actions: (1) intrusion (whether by physically entering property without permission or by bugging or secretly recording, photographing or taping); (2) publication of embarrassing facts even though truthful if the matter would be highly offensive to a reasonable person and not of legitimate concern to the public; (3) false light, if highly offensive to a reasonable person and if the publisher knew of the falsity of the publication and the false light or acted in reckless disregard of truth or falsity; and (4) misappropriation of name of likeness (e.g, using someone's photograph without permission in an ad).

By far the best known remedy is a "libel suit". A "libel" in Connecticut has been defined as a false and malicious publication concerning a person which exposes him or herself to public ridicule, hatred or contempt, or hinders virtuous persons from associating with him or her. Burns v. Telegram Publishing Co., 89 Conn. 549 (1915). Ever since the Supreme Court decision in New York Times v. Sullivan, 376 U.S. 254 (1964), however, the law of libel has become "constitutionalized;" and while libel law continues to retain great vitality, it must always be judged by its effect upon First Amendment press rights.

Specifically, no person who is a public official or a "public figure" may succeed in a libel suit against a publisher about an article relating to his or her official conduct or public figure status unless he or she proves "actual malice"—that is, that the publication was false and that when printed, the publisher did so in reckless disregard of whether it was false or not. Mere negligence is not enough fault where a public official or "public figure" is concerned.

While this standard may seem clear, it has proven to be anything but in practice. For one thing, the phrase "actual malice" is a misnomer. It has nothing to do with the traditional "malice"—hatred, spite, ill will or improper motive. A reporter can hate the subject of his or her story and write it hoping to cause hurt; but if the story is true, or if the story is false but the reporter thought it was true or tried his or her best to make certain it was true, there is no "actual malice." In order for a plaintiff to prove "actual malice," the plaintiff must prove by "clear and convincing evidence" (not just the usual "preponderance of evidence") that the defendant either knew that the statement was false or, in fact, entertained serious doubts about its truth, or that the source on which the reporter relied was inherently unreliable. This is a very difficult standard to meet. There has been a continuing debate in the Supreme Court over who is a "public figure." Clearly Muhammad Ali is. But is Oliver Sipple, the ex-Marine who saved President Ford's life in San Francisco and then had his private life exposed nationwide? Some people are public figures for all purposes; anything written about them is probably subject to the "actual malice" test if they sue for libel. Other "public figures" are only limited-pur-pose public figures; the mother who leads the fight to prevent a school from being closed may be a public figure only so far as the stories concern her fight for the school, but not her qualities as a wife, mother, daughter or registered nurse. Which status a person occupies becomes important because status determines how difficult it will be for him or her to win a libel suit. The more "public" a person is, the more he or she is assumed to have taken the risk of publicity, and the greater his or her burden in proving a libel case.

A decision by the United States Court of Appeals for the District of Columbia attempts to devise some tests for who is a public figure, and what kind of public figure he or she is. Waldbaum v. Fairchild Publications, 627 F.2d 1287 (D.C. Cir.; 1980), cert. den., 101 S.Ct. 266. Usually, one who is an "all purpose public figure" (like Muhammad Ali) also has access to the media if defamed. Thus, he or she has a means of responding to defamation other than merely a lawsuit: he or she can generate publicity him or herself. Also, usually, he or she is a person who voluntarily came to public prominence (Ali, as opposed to a vacationer who leaps into the ocean to save a drowning child.)

Those who are not public figures for all purposes may be limited issue public figures—persons who "have thrust themselves to the forefront of particular public controversies in order to influence the resolution of the issues involved." Such a person is "an individual who voluntarily injects himself or is drawn into a particular public controversy and therefore becomes a public figure for a limited range of issues." What qualifies as a "public controversy" is a ripe subject for debate. The court in Waldbaum says a "public controversy is not simply a matter of interest to the public; it must be a real dispute, the outcome of which affects the general public or some segment of it in an appreciable way." "If the issue was being debated publicly and if it had foreseeable and substantial ramifications for non-participants, it was a public controversy."

The fight to save a school from being closed would thus clearly qualify as a "public controversy." But what about debate on the best solution for the Arab-Israeli impasse? How about whether Shakespeare's works were written by Bacon, Marlowe or the Earl of Oxford? With so narrow and precise a definition as suggested by the Waldbaum court, the task becomes both more difficult and more artificial and, inevitably, subjective. One thing the Supreme Court has held in this regard, however, comes as somewhat of a surprise. It has held that publicity surrounding litigation does not by itself elevate the parties to the status of public figures even if they could anticipate the publicity, unless they are using the court as a forum for espousing their views in other controversies (*e.g.*, a crusading atheist who sues to have "In God We Trust" eliminated from U.S. currency). Wolston v. Reader's Digest Ass'n, 443 U.S. 157 (1979); Time, Inc. v. Firestone, 424 U.S. 448 (1976), wherein a socially prominent wife of a Firestone heir, who herself held press conferences and kept a clipping service, was held not to be a public figure for purposes for an item in Time about her divorce suit.

To be a public figure with respect to a public controversy, the plaintiff "either must have been purposely trying to influence the outcome or could realistically have been expected, because of his position in the controversy, to have an impact on its resolution," says the court in Waldbaum. Thus, presumably the leader of the protest march, but not necessarily every picket, would be a public figure (assuming that they were marching about something that was the subject of real public debate and controversy, whatever that might mean). The haziness of these definitions becomes abundantly apparent when one reviews the Waldbaum case itself. In a five-sentence item about Waldbaum's dismissal as president of the second largest consumer cooperative in the world, a trade publication stated that the co-op had been "losing money the last year and retrenching." After elaborately explaining the need and tests for "public controversy" and active participation, the court held Mr. Waldbaum to be a public figure because "he was the mover and shaper of many of the co-operative's controversial actions. He made it a leader in unit pricing and open dating. He supervised, or at least approved, the consumer-oriented views that appeared in Co-op Consumer...He became an activist, projecting his own image and that of the cooperative far beyond the dollars and cents aspects of marketing."However much one may agree that Mr. Waldbaum ought to have been a public figure, it is difficult to draw the conclusion by applying the court's own tests. The article in question was a five-sentence item about Waldbaum's dismissal. So far as the court's opinion discloses, this dismissal generated no "public controversy" no "real dispute, the outcome of which affects the general public or some segment of it in an appreciable way." There was no "issue...being debated publicly" which "had foreseeable and substantial ramifications for non-participants."

Waldbaum displays in one case setting the extraordinary difficulty in determining who is or is not a public figures based on these Gertz tests. Far easier, and far more intelligent in the view of many, was the now rejected test set forth in Rosenbloom v. Metromedia, Inc., 403 U.S. 29 (1971), which focused on the nature of the event, rather than the status of the plaintiff. Rosenbloom held that any plaintiff had to show "actual malice" when suing for libel about a defamatory falsehood "relating to his involvement in an event of public or general concern." The Rosenbloom justices (a plurality, not a majority) reasoned as follows:

If a matter is a subject of public or general interest, it cannot suddenly become less so merely because a private individual is involved, or because in some sense the individual did not "voluntarily" choose to become involved. The public's primary interest is in the event; the public focus is on the conduct of the participant and the content, effect and significance of the conduct, not the participant's prior anonymity or notoriety.

That view, as noted, was rejected by Gertz, which established the "all purpose" and "limited purpose" public figure categories, relegating all other non-public officials to private figure status, (though the Supreme Court later revived it in setting standards of proof for presumed or punitive damages. Dun and Bradstreet, Inc. v. Greenmoss Builders, 472 U.S. 749 (1985)). The advantage of being a private figure is, of course, that his or her burden of proof is less in libel cases. A private figure must still prove that the statement was false and that it was defamatory, (a false but flattering statement would usually not be actionable). And he or she must still show some element of fault; the mere fact of having published a false and defamatory statement will not suffice for liability. But the degree of fault is significantly less than "actual malice." Precisely what it is up to each state, by court decision or statute, to decide. Some states have adopted "gross negligence" as a standard.

Others have adopted simple negligence. Connecticut's Supreme Court has not yet had the occasion to deal with this issue, but one superior court decision has assumed that simple negligence would be what plaintiff must prove. And even damages for "actual injury" are available only where the substance of the defamatory statement warns a reasonably prudent editor of its defamatory potential. In addition to constitutional defences such as "actual malice," a defendant in a libel case may have other defences that have developed in the common law. For example, an accurate report of the proceedings of executive, legislative, administrative and judicial bodies is absolutely privileged from liability, even if what is quoted from these proceedings is false and defamatory.

In the absence of a state shield law, a reporter can be subpoenaed to come to court and to testify or supply materials gathered in the course of covering a story under certain circumstances. Branzburg v. Hayes, 408 U.S. 665 (1972) held that reporters have no constitutional right to disobey grand jury subpoenas and to answer questions relevant to an investigation into the commission of a crime. This general holding has been interpreted to include criminal trial juries as well. The inquiry must be conducted in good faith, however, and the questions must be relevant and material and not asked for purposes of harassment or disrupting the reporter's relationship to his or her news sources.

As Justice Powell stated in his concurring opinion: If the newsman is called upon to give information bearing only a remote and tenuous relationship to the subject of the investigation, or if he has some other reason to believe that his testimony implicates confidential source relationships without a legitimate need of law enforcement, he will have access to the court on a motion to quash and an appropriate protective order may be entered.

The law in this state is further amplified by Baker v. F and F Investment, 470 F.2d 778 (2 Cir.; 1972) which held that before a reporter (in a civil trial, at least) could be required to divulge the identity of his or her source, the person seeking the answer had to show he or she had exhausted other sources that could supply the same information and that the information the person sought to elicit went to the heart of the case. The reasoning of Baker was adopted by the superior court in Connecticut in Conn. Labour Relations Board v. Fagin, 33 Conn. Sup. 204 (1976).

What may be protected unless this test is met are not only the identity of a reporter's confidential sources, but his or her nonconfidential sources as well, and also a reporter's notes, tapes and other materials gathered or prepared as part of the reportorial or newsgathering work. von Bulow v. von Bulow, 811 F.2d 136 (2 Cir.; 1986), cert. den., 107 S.Ct. 1891 (1987). When a reporter is a witness in a libel action in which plaintiff is a public figure and must thus bear the heavy burden of proving "actual malice," the Supreme Court in Herbert v. Lando, 441 U.S. 153 (1979) has held that the reporter may be compelled to disclose the "editorial process"—discussions that occurred about what to include and leave out, which source was credible and which was not, and the reporter's thoughts and impressions.

## INDIAN PRESS FREEDOM

The Indian Constitution, while not mentioning the word "press", provides for "the right to freedom of speech and expression" (Article 19(1) a). However this right is subject to restrictions under sub clause (2), whereby this freedom can be restricted for reasons of "sovereignty and integrity of India, the security of the State, friendly relations with foreign States, public order, preserving decency, preserving morality, in relation to contempt, court, defamation, or incitement to an offense". Laws such as the Official Secrets Act and Prevention of Terrorist Activities Act (PoTA) have been used to limit press freedom. Under PoTA, person could be detained for up to six months for being in contact with a terrorist or terrorist group. PoTA was repealed in 2006, but the Official Secrets Act 1923 continues.

For the first half-century of independence, media control by the state was the major constraint on press freedom. Indira Gandhi famously stated in 1975 that All India Radio is "a Government organ, it is going to remain a Government organ..." With the liberalization starting in the 1990s, private control of media has burgeoned, leading to increasing independence and greater scrutiny of government.

Adherence to ethical norms and self-restraint shown by the Indian media on the cartoon controversy does not mean they are controlled or regulated by an external agency. The media enjoys substantial freedom in the country; the exceptions being in contempt of court, defamation and privilege of the Parliament and state legislatures. The Constitution of India provides freedom of speech and expression, which gives freedom to the media. Expect during the Emergency in 1971, when censorship was imposed by the then government, the press in India is free to carry out their constitutional and social obligation.

The freedom enjoyed by the media can be understood from what Jawaharlal Nehru. said: "I would rather have a completely free press with all the dangers involved in the wrong use of that freedom, than a suppressed or regulated Press." Another former Prime Minister, Rajiv Gandhi reaffirms importance of the press freedom later. He says (Hima Lawrence), "Freedom of the press is an article of faith with us, sanctified by our constitution, validated by four decades of freedom and indispensable to our future as a nation."

Even though the Indian media enjoys substantial freedom there are instances that the media organisations were attacked or harassed by the government, political parties and fanatic religious groups. Newspapers and TV channels pursuing investigative journalism are often being attacked by the affected parties including the government. There are also instances were court cases initiated to harass the media taking advantage of the provision of defamation suits provided in the constitution. Factors such as ownership, editorial policy, financial situation, and political leniency also have its own impact on journalism.

Government policies related to advertisement as well as newsprint import have also influence the freedom of the Press. Legislations such as 'The Official Secret Act' prevent the media from getting information on several sensitive aspects of the governance. At the same time the new legislation, The Right to Information Act, passed by the government has been seen as a revolutionary step making transparency as a guiding principle for governance. According to this law any citizen can collect information on all aspects of governance except few sensitive areas like defence from the designated information officer by submitting an application along with a nominal fee. The concerned officer will be liable for punishment if he fail to provide the information within the stipulated time stated in the act. Journalists and advocacy groups have started gathering information from the government on controversial matters by using the provisions in the new legislation. With the enactment of the 'Right to Information Act' many laws have become redundant including the 'Official Secret Act'. It has been reported that the Government is contemplating to withdraw or amend the outdated laws.

**News Values Versus Restraint**

Many European media including BBC reproduced the cartoons citing the high news value. A section of academicians also supported the publication of the cartoons because of their news value. Professor Jane Kirtly, Silha Professor of Media Ethics and Law at the University of Minnesota and Director of Silha Centre told the Minneapolis Star Tribune of United States that,"it is up to the public to make a judgment on these cartoons, and the media should absolutely repudiate the suggestion that violence should lead to the suppression of free speech. ....given the high news value of the cartoons, United States papers should publish them, but not on their front pages on the editorial pages, and not with out including careful context, such as commentary from Muslim leaders. It can be argued that the public is the ultimate judge and the journalist should not be a gatekeeper when it comes to the public right to know. The reproduction of the cartoons can also be justified by citing the users and gratification theory. But at the same time one should not forget that matters related to religion are very sensitive and it is impossible to predict the reaction of the public. The public may not be wise enough to make a choice when it comes to emotional issues. It should also be remembered that political and communal organizations often take advantage of such situations. As happened in the case of the cartoon controversy, there can be widespread violence. It can also lead to transnational conflict.

There is no point in preaching freedom of the press or gratification of the audience when the world is burning. Media organisations should desist it self from becoming a pliant tool of politicians or communal elements. Paul Solvic cautions the journalists about the unpredictable risk and argues for regulation in order to avoid putting mankind in to danger. He says, (1987), "risk may be understood better when we consider two factors: how unknown the risk is and how dreaded it is". Solvic presents these two factors on axes and suggests that 'when a risk is both unknown and dreadful, people are much more likely to want it regulated.' The Press Council of India directs the journalist to be vigilant and restrained when dealing with issues of communal clashes. In the aftermath of the Gujrat communal carnage the Council revised the 'norms for journalistic conduct' by saying, "the role of media in such situations [Gujrat Carnage] is to be peacemakers and not abettors, to be troubleshooters and not trouble makers". The Council adds, "there is a greater moral responsibility on the media to do their best to build national solidarity and to recement communal harmony at all levels remembering the noble role they had played during pre-independence days." Considering the sensibility and freedom of faith, the Council also prohibits the portrayal of religious figures and characters in bad light.

In the 'norms for journalistic conduct' it says, Newspapers should not publish any fictional literature distorting and portraying religious characters in an adverse light and offending the religious susceptibilities of large sections of society who hold those characters in high esteem, invested with attributes of the virtuous and lofty.

The Council also rejects the argument of 'news value' for the reproduction of any objectionable material. It says, the 'publication of defamatory news by one paper does not give licence to others to publish news/information reproducing or repeating the same.'

**Truth as Defence**

Journalists often face challenges with regard to ethical decision making. Upholding values and principles, journalists have the responsibility to report the truth to their audience. Gordon et al, (1996:82) says, "..truth telling is the first principle, to the where if choices must be made, truth must be given primacy over any other ethical concern." Kant (1986), in his famous essay On the Supposed Right to lie Out of Humanity advocates the fundamental validity of telling the truth, even if there is a conflict of duties: Tell the truth whether it is convenient or inconvenient, regardless of the consequences". Considering these views, it can be argued that the publication of the cartoons by the Jyllands-Posten was the true representation of the reality prevails in the world.

It can also be argued that the reproduction of the controversial cartoons by other media was the true representation of the day's event and it was the responsibility of the journalists to bring such issues before the public. At the same time it has also been argued that the publication of the truth is not advisable when there is a possibility of communal violence and social anarchy. The Press Council of India says, the "truth is no defence for publishing derogatory, scurrilous and defamatory material against a private citizen where no public interest is involved." John Calson of the Pew Forum on Religion and Public Life suggests that even 'lies can be justified if they serve the higher public good'. Sissela Bok (1978:45) also rejects the absolutist position about truth telling and she argues that "..there are some situation where lie would be warranted, especially those were innocent lives are at risk, and where only lie can defend the danger. Therefore, the publication of the cartoons by the Jylland-Posten cannot be justified as per the notion of true representation of the reality.

**Freedom Versus Social Responsibility**

While enjoying freedom, the media should also be responsible to society, nation and world at large. There is no freedom without responsibility. Press freedom imposes a corresponding responsibility upon the press, involving the acceptance and compliance with high ethical standards by editors and journalists. Freedom of the press is not absolute, unlimited and unfettered at all times and in all circumstances as this would lead to disorder and anarchy. The US Commission on Freedom and the Press also emphasize the huge responsibility of media organizations. In its report, the Commission says (1947: 87), "we insist that, morally considered, the freedom of the press is a conditional right, conditional on the honesty and responsibility of writer, broadcaster, or publisher."

The Jyllands-Posten has been defending the publication of the cartoons and the culture editor of the newspaper in an article published in the Critique, says, I commissioned the cartoons in response to several incidents of self censorship in Europe caused by widening fears and feelings of intimidation in dealing with issues related to Islam. And I still believe that this is a topic that we Europeans must speak out. The Idea wasn't to provoke gratuitously—and we certainly didn't intend to trigger violent demonstrations throughout the Muslim world. Our goal was simply to push back self-imposed limits on expression that seemed to be closing in tighter.

According to Rose, the newspaper did not intend to provoke the Muslim world but challenge the European media to abandon its self-imposed regulations. Even though, the intention of the newspaper was not to provoke the Muslim community, the ultimate result of the publication was protest and violence. The newspaper can argue that there was no protest or violence for three months and the atmosphere began to change when politicians and extremist elements started taking advantage of the situation. Media organizations have also played a role in escalating the matter further by asking comments from the Muslim leaders about the controversial cartoons.

The cartoons were uploaded on the Internet making it accessible to all. The Jyllands-Posten can argue that the Muslim community was not provoked by it but by the after effects of the publication of the cartoons. But it has to be remembered the basic issue behind the protest was the publication of the cartoon by the Jyllands-Posten. It has also been alleged that the cartoons were uploaded in the Internet by the Muslim fanatics to take advantage of the situation and divided the world but that would not justify the editoral decision of the Jyllands-Posten. Even if that is true, the newspaper should be blamed for becoming an instrument of the communal elements by making dangerous editorial decisions.

**Was it Necessary?**

Even if one has agreed with the idea of challenging the European media to push back the self-imposed limits was in good spirits, there is no ethical justification for the publication of the caricature of Prophet Mohammed. It can be argued that all sections of the Muslim community are not against the publication of the image of Prophet Mohammed. It can also be argued that the images of the Prophet Mohammed exist in different parts of the world and many occasions media published Prophets images. But these arguments do not justify the publication of the cartoons by the Jylland-Posten where the Prophet was portrayed in bad taste. Even though all cartoons published by the Jylland-Posten were not offensive some were highly objectionable.

It has been argued that non-Muslims are not bound by the Muslim laws and therefore, the Jyllands-Posten was well within its right to publish the cartoons. But the question is whether it was necessary to portray Prophet Mohammed in bad light to achieve the limited objective of criticising the self-regulation of the European media. It should be remembered that the ordinary Muslim community is not responsible for the so called self-regulation. It is only a section of the Muslim community which terrorizes the world. It is also important to note that the so called self regulation has nothing to do with Muslim community but, it is simply a decision by the media organization. Rose, argues that the self-regulation by the European media "...is a popular trick of totalitarian movements: Label any critique or call for debate as an insult and punish the offenders." If that is the case, why did Jyllands-Posten publish the cartoons of the Prophet Mohammed along with its article "Do we still have press freedom?" instead of simply criticising the media. The newspaper could have written editorials against the European media. They could have published cartoons portraying the European media in bad light. It could have also criticized the Muslim community without publishing the cartoons of the Prophet Mohammed. The newspaper has the right to disagree with the Muslim community but there is no justification in putting the blame on the Prophet. One cannot blame Jesus Christ for the wrong doings of Christians. Moreover, it has been reported that the Jylland-Posten had actually received anti-Christian cartoons but had not used them for fear of upsetting Christians. If that is true it totally rejects all justifications put forward by the Jyllands-Posten for publishing the cartoons and exposes its double standard.

It can be argued that the reason behind the self-regulation of the media is because of fear and not that of public interest as in the case of Boston Phoenix.

The Boston Phoenix did not reproduce the cartoons and confessed that it is because of fear. It says,...Out of fear of retaliation from the international brotherhood of radical and bloodthirsty Islamists who seek to impose their will on those who do not believe as they do. This is frankly, our primary reason for not publishing any of the images in question. Simply stated, we are being terrorized and as deeply as we believe in the principles of free speech and a free press, we could not in good conscience place the men and women who work at the Phoenix and its related companies in physical jeopardy.

The stand taken by the Boston Phoenix is unjustifiable. The newspaper believes in something and behaves in a different way. It is simply a compromise and it defeats the very purpose of journalism. One must remember that newspapers world over have passed through tough situations facing tremendous challenges but survived. There are golden examples from India to Africa of suffering during their freedom struggle. It is not advisable to surrender the ethical standards due to fear or any other reason. Considering the journalistic ethics and principles, the stand taken by Jyllands-Posten as well as the Boston Phoenix is not justifiable.

**Press Freedom vs. Public Interest**

The Jyllands-Posten apologized for hurting the feelings of the Muslim Community but was not ready to change the earlier stand regarding the right to publish the cartoons. Rose (2006) says, "I acknowledge that some people have been offended by the publication of the cartoons, and Jyllands-Posten has apologized for that. But we cannot apologise for our right to publish material, even offensive material. You cannot edit a newspaper if you are paralysed by worries about every possible insult."

When Rose says that the newspaper has the right to publish even offensive material it contradicts his earlier stand. Offensive material always provokes the affected party and there was no doubt that the controversial cartoons would be an insult to the Muslim community. The newspaper was not bothered about the outcome of the publication of the cartoons. They simply wanted to prove a point at the cost of universal peace and harmony. It not that media should not publish any offensive material but any such decision should be taken only after considering the possible fallout of that action. Any possible risk regarding the publication of any kind of offensive material should be weighed against the public interest. It is imperative on the media to asses the possible impact of the publication of any material on its readers. In this case, was the publication of the cartoons by the Jyllands-Posten in public interest? Was it prudent to put society in danger in order to achieve the limited goal of provoking the European media regarding self-regulation? The Jyllands-Posten should answer these questions. The irresponsible and short-sighted Behaviour of the press often puts society in danger and there could be irrecoverable damage. While pointing out the importance and possibilities of the modern media the US Commission on the Freedom of the Press cautions about the danger of irresponsible and unregulated media. In the report it (1947) says,

The modern press itself is a new phenomenon. Its typical unit is the great agency of mass communication. These agencies can felicitate thought and discussion. They can stifle it. They can advance the progress of civilization or they can thwart it. They can debase and vulgarize mankind. They can endanger the peace of the world; they can do so accidentally, in a fit of absence of mind. They can play up or down the news and its significance, foster and feed emotions, create complacent fictions and blind spots, misuse the great words, and uphold empty slogans. Their scope and power are increasing every day as new instruments can spread lies faster and farther than our forefathers dreamed when they enshrined the freedom of the press in the First Amendment to our constitution. Media organizations have the primary responsibility of creating an informed citizenry in order empower society and strengthen democracy. Media should also play an active role in enhancing social and religious harmony and the upliftment of the poor and the needy. It has to fight against corruption and social injustice. At the same time media has to perform its responsibility with out challenging the harmony and peace. If it fails to protect the interest of the public or challenges the law of the land, other regulating agencies come to play including the government and the court. The Press Council of India says,

Newspapers shall, as matters of self-regulation, exercise due restraint and caution in presenting any news, comment or information which is likely to jeopardize, endanger or harm the paramount interests of the state and society, or the rights of individuals with respect to which reasonable restrictions may be imposed by law on the right to freedom of speech and expression under clause (2) of Article 19 of the Constitution of India.

## PRESS FREEDOM IN DOMESTIC PHENOMENON

In the preceding section, we have looked at press freedom as a domestic phenomenon in each country as if it were independent of the world system. Such an interpretation, often reflected in the Western assessments of world press freedom such as those of Freedom House, ignores the fact that the whole (the world system as a single unit) is more than the sum of its parts—an integral principle associated with Oriental philosophy (excluding Buddhism) and the world system theory.

I have argued that to ascertain the degree of freedom of opinion-outlets and expression (a broader concept that includes freedom of the press), one has to focus on three levels—the world system, the nation-state, and the individual (Gunaratne, 2000d). By so doing, one can derive the answers to the following: Can the world system inject news and opinion into a nation-state despite restrictions on endogenous (or internal) opinion-outlets—a term more inclusive than press or media—in that nation-state? Can individuals within nation-state access exogenous (or external) opinion-outlets despite restrictions on endogenous opinion-outlets in a nation state? To the extent that the answers to these two questions are in the affirmative, the measures of press freedom based on internal restrictions distort the reality.

The tendency in the West has been to associate press freedom with the characteristics of Siebert's so-called libertarian theory of the press or the CHAOS—competition, heterogeneity, autonomy, openness, and selfishness—paradigm (Merrill, 2000). The purpose of a libertarian press is "to inform, entertain, [and] sell—but chiefly to help discover truth, and to check on government". Within this context, the press enjoys negative rights to publish as it pleases with no concomitant responsibilities. Peterson's formulation of the social responsibility theory of the press, following the Hutchins Commission report, looks at press freedom as a positive right that entails concomitant responsibilities. The Hutchins Commission (Commission on Freedom of the Press, 1947) has observed: "Freedom of the press is not a fixed and isolated value, the same in every society and in all times. It is a function within a society and must vary with the social context". Hocking (1947), in one of the five special studies done for the commission, emphasized the very point that the concept of the free press "cannot mean the same in every society and at all times". If this were the case, then measuring freedom of the press on the basis of a set of criteria relevant to one society at a given time is bound to produce questionable results. This view agrees with the contemporary debate on relating press freedom to Asian values and other social values outside Western society.

Freedom House, however, has been conducting press freedom surveys worldwide since 1979 classifying the media as free, partly free, or not free depending on the "degree to which each country permits the free flow of information" It claims that the survey uses universal criteria starting with the most "universal unit of concern: the individual". Freedom House asserts that it merely applies the basic thrust of Article 19 of the Universal Declaration of Human Rights (*i.e.*, "everyone has the right to freedom of opinion and expression") in assessing press freedom. (Freedom House measures only the extent to which the endogenous print and broadcast media can keep their content free from the influence of laws and regulations, political pressures and controls, and economic influences. It gives a score of 0 to 15 to each of the two types of media in relation to each of these three criteria. A fourth criterion, repressive actions, is scored 0 to 5 for each of the two media types. Thus the maximum possible score for a country is 100, with 0-30 defined as free, 31-60 as partly free, and 61-100 as not free. Freedom House admits that its survey is not a measure of press responsibility.)

Nordenstreng (1999), however, argues that under international law, the subject and "owner" of the "right to freedom of opinion and expression"—a right that "carries with it duties and responsibilities"—is the individual, not the press or media organizations. Thus Nordenstreng makes a distinction between freedom of the press and freedom of individual expression thereby contending that press freedom is not a human right.

The International Commission for the Study of Communication Problems (MacBride Report, 1980) has pointed out the need to devote special attention "to obstacles and restrictions [that] derive from the concentration of media ownership, public or private, from commercial influences on the press and broadcasting, or from private or governmental advertising". The commission also drew attention to the 1952 Convention on the International Right of Correction, thereby expressing its desire to place the right to communicate at the world system level. The concept of the right to communicate includes the right to be informed, the right to inform, the right to privacy, and the right to participate in public communication (Recommendation 54). Gunaratne (1998) has elaborated on the parallels between the views of the Hutchins Commission and the MacBride Commission on press freedom and responsibility. Two decades after the MacBride Report, the concentration of media ownership has become more pronounced as a result of several developments accentuating capital accumulation, *e.g.*, the demise of the socialist bloc, and the U.S.-led worldwide promotion of free-market philosophy.

At the beginning of the 21st century, the global media market has come under the domination of a dozen or so mega-media conglomerates, including AOL Time Warner (CNN), AT&T Broadband, Bertelsmann, Disney (ABC), General Electric (NBC), News Corp. (Fox TV), Sony (Columbia Pictures), Viacom (CBS), and Vivendi-Universal. Freedom of the press, contrary to what the framers of the First Amendment most likely had in mind, has moved away from the individual to the media conglomerates. As Curran and Park (2000) point out, under free-market conditions, a close alliance of big business, press, and government is poised to engender new systems of power inimical to the general public.

At the world system level, these mega-media conglomerates, as well as government-funded opinion-outlets (*e.g.*, Voice of America, BBC, Radio Moscow, Radio Beijing, Deutsche Welle, Radio France Internationale, and Radio Cairo) use satellites, cables, and airwaves to inject information and opinion into every nation-state. The world system pays particular attention to reach individuals in the most authoritarian countries. Western measurements of freedom of the press at the nation-state level take a negative view of government involvement with the press while discounting the effects of commercial interests on opinion and information censorship. Because big business and governments are highly involved in running opinion-outlets at the world-system level, doubts arise about the extent of freedom of opinion-outlets and expression at this level as well. (Although the Internet provides a means for the individual to impart and receive opinion at the world system level, the large majority of people in the world do not have access to the Internet because of telecommunication poverty.) In general, the Western measures of freedom of opinion outlets appear to overestimate the freedom in Western countries and underestimate the freedom in non-Western countries.

## FREEDOM OF SPEECH AND GOVERNMENT FUNDING

The Supreme Court has held that Congress, incident to its power to provide for the general welfare, may attach conditions on the receipt of federal funds, and has repeatedly employed the power "to further broad policy objectives by conditioning receipt of federal moneys upon compliance with federal statutory and administrative directives."... The breadth of this power was made clear in *United States v. Butler*, 297 U.S. 1, 66 (1936), where the Court... determined that "the power of Congress to authorize expenditure of public moneys for public purposes is not limited by the direct grants of legislative power found in the Constitution."

This means that Congress may regulate matters by attaching conditions to the receipt of federal funds that it might lack the power to regulate directly. However, the Court added, "other constitutional provisions may provide an independent bar to the conditional grant of federal funds." One of these other constitutional provisions is the First Amendment. The Court has held, in fact, that the government "may not deny a benefit to a person on a basis that infringes his constitutionally protected interests — especially, his interest in freedom of speech."

Similarly, in *Federal Communications Commission v. League of Women Voters*, the Court declared unconstitutional a federal statute that prohibited Non-commercial television and radio stations that accepted federal funds from engaging in editorializing, even with Non-federal funds. Congress would have the authority to prohibit television and radio stations from using the federal funds they accept to engage in editorializing, as the Court would view Congress in that case not as limiting speech, but as choosing to fund one activity to the exclusion of another.

"A refusal to fund protected activity [*i.e.*, speech], without more, cannot be equated with the imposition of a 'penalty' on that activity." In *Rust v. Sullivan*, the case in which this quotation appears, the Court upheld a "gag order" that prohibited family planning clinics that accept federal funds from engaging in abortion counseling or referrals. The Court found that, in this case, "the government is not denying a benefit to anyone, but is instead simply insisting that public funds be spent for purposes for which they were authorized."

In *Rust v. Sullivan*, the Court also indicated that it will allow Congress to condition the receipt of federal funds on acceptance of a limitation on the use of Non-federal funds as well as of federal funds, but apparently will not allow

Congress to limit the use of Non-federal funds outside the project that accepts the federal funds. Justice Blackmun, dissenting, feared that, "[u]nder the majority's reasoning, the First Amendment could be read to tolerate *any* governmental restriction upon an employee's speech so long as that restriction is limited to the funded workplace."

The Court also "recognized that the university is a traditional sphere of free expression so fundamental to the functioning of our society that the Government's ability to control speech within that sphere by means of conditions attached to the expenditure of Government funds is restricted by the vagueness and over breadth doctrines of the First Amendment." In *National Endowment for the Arts v. Finley*, the Supreme Court upheld the constitutionality of a federal statute requiring the NEA, in awarding grants, to "take into consideration general standards of decency and respect for the diverse beliefs and values of the American public."

The Court acknowledged that, if the statute were "applied in a manner that raises concern about the suppression of disfavored viewpoints," 191 then such application might be unconstitutional. The statute on its face, however, is constitutional because it "imposes no categorical requirement," being merely "advisory." "Any content- based considerations that may be taken into account in the grant-making process are a consequence of the nature of arts funding.... The 'very assumption' of the NEA is that grants will be awarded according to the 'artistic worth of competing applications,' and absolute neutrality is simply 'inconceivable.'"

The Court also found that the terms of the statute, "if they appeared in a criminal statute or regulatory scheme... could raise substantial vagueness concerns.... But when the Government is acting as patron rather than as sovereign, the consequences of imprecision are not constitutionally severe." In *Legal Services Corporation v. Velazquez*, the Court struck down a provision of the Legal Services Corporation Act that prohibited recipients of Legal Services Corporation (LSC) funds (*i.e.*, legal-aid organizations that provide lawyers to the poor in civil matters) from representing a client who seeks "to amend or otherwise challenge existing [welfare] law."

This meant that, even with non-federal funds, a recipient of federal funds could not argue that a state welfare statute violated a federal statute or that a state or federal welfare law violated the U.S. Constitution. If a case was underway when such a challenge became apparent, the attorney had to withdraw. The Supreme Court distinguished this situation from that in *Rust v. Sullivan* on the ground "that the counseling activities of the doctors under Title X amounted to governmental speech," whereas "an LSC-funded attorney speaks on behalf of the client in a claim against the government for welfare benefits."

Furthermore, the restriction in this cases "distorts the legal system" by prohibiting "speech and expression upon which courts must depend for the proper exercise of the judicial power," and thereby is "inconsistent with accepted separation-of-powers principles." In *United States v. American Library Association*, the Supreme Court followed *Rust v. Sullivan*, and upheld the Children's Internet Protection Act, which requires schools and libraries that accept federal funds to purchase computers used to access the Internet to block or filter minors' Internet access to visual depictions that are obscene, child pornography, or "harmful to minors"; and to block or filter adults' Internet access to visual depictions that are obscene or child pornography. Blocking or filtering technology may be disabled, however, "to enable access for bona fide research or other lawful purpose."

The plurality noted that "Congress may not 'induce' the recipient [of federal funds] 'to engage in activities that would themselves be unconstitutional.'" The plurality therefore viewed the question before the Court as "whether public libraries would violate the First Amendment by employing the filtering software that CIPA requires." Does CIPA, in other words, effectively violate library *patrons* rights? The plurality concluded that it does not, as "Internet access in public libraries is neither a 'traditional' or a 'designated' public forum," and that therefore it would not be appropriate to apply strict scrutiny to determine whether the filtering requirements are constitutional.

But the plurality also considered whether CIPA imposes an unconstitutional condition on the receipt of federal assistance — in other words, does it violate public *libraries'* rights by requiring them to limit their freedom of speech if they accept federal funds? The plurality found that, assuming that government entities have First Amendment rights (it did not decide the question), CIPA does not infringe them. This is because CIPA does not deny a benefit to libraries that do not agree to use filters; rather, as in *Rust v. Sullivan*, the statute "simply insists[s] that public funds be spent for the purposes for which they were authorized." "CIPA does not 'penalize' libraries that choose not to install such software, or deny them the right to provide their patrons with unfiltered Internet access.

Rather, CIPA simply reflects Congress' decision not to subsidize their doing so." The Court distinguished *Velazquez* on the ground that public libraries have no role comparable to that of legal aid attorneys "that pits them *against* the Government, and there is no comparable assumption that they must be free of any conditions that their benefactors might attach to the use of donated funds or other assistance." In *Rumsfeld v. Forum for Academic and Institutional Rights, Inc.*, the Supreme Court upheld the Solomon Amendment, which provides that, in the Court's summary, "if any part of an institution of higher education denies military recruiters access equal to that provided other recruiters, the entire institution would lose certain federal funds."

FAIR, the group that challenged the Solomon Amendment, is an association of law schools that barred military recruiting on their campuses because of the military's discrimination against homosexuals. FAIR challenged the Solomon

Amendment as violating the First Amendment because it forced schools to choose between enforcing their Non-discrimination policy against military recruiters and continuing to receive specified federal funding. The Court first rejected an interpretation of the Solomon Amendment that would have avoided the constitutional issue; under this interpretation, "a school excluding military recruiters would comply with the Solomon Amendment so long as it also excluded any other employer that violates its Non-discrimination policy."

The Court instead construed the Solomon Amendment to require schools to allow the military the same access as *any* other employer, including employers who do not discriminate and whom the schools allow on campus. Interpreting the Solomon Amendment as such, the Court concluded: "Because the First Amendment would not prevent Congress from directly imposing the Solomon Amendment's access requirement, the statute does not place an unconstitutional condition on the receipt of federal funds." The Court added: "The Solomon Amendment neither limits what law schools may say nor requires them to say anything.... It affects what law schools must *do* — afford equal access to military recruiters — not what they may or may not *say*."

The law schools' conduct in barring military recruiters, the Court found, "is not inherently expressive," and, therefore, unlike flag burning, for example, is not "symbolic speech." Applying the *O'Brien* test for restrictions on conduct that have an incidental effect on speech, the Court found that the Solomon Amendment clearly "promotes a substantial government interest that would be achieved less effectively absent the regulation." The Court also found that the Solomon Amendment did not unconstitutionally compel schools to speak, or even to host or accommodate the government's message. As for compelling speech, law schools must "send e-mails and post notices on behalf of the military to comply with the Solomon Amendment...

This sort of recruiting assistance, however, is a far cry from the compelled speech in *Barnette* and *Wooley*.... [It] is plainly incidental to the Solomon Amendment's regulation of conduct." As for forcing one speaker to host or accommodate another, "[t]he compelled speech violation in each of our prior cases... resulted from the fact that the complaining speaker's own message was affected by the speech it was forced to accommodate."

By contrast, the Court wrote, "Nothing about recruiting suggests that law schools agree with any speech by recruiters, and nothing in the Solomon Amendment restricts what the law schools may say about the military's policies." Finally, the Court found that the Solomon Amendment was not analogous to the New Jersey law that had required the Boy Scouts to accept a homosexual scoutmaster, and which the Supreme Court struck down as violating the Boy Scouts' "right of expressive association." Recruiters, unlike the scoutmaster, are "outsiders who come onto campus for the limited purpose of trying to hire students — not to become members of the school's expressive association."

## COMMERCIAL SPEECH

"The Constitution... affords a lesser protection to commercial speech than to other constitutionally guaranteed expression." Commercial speech is "speech that proposes a commercial transaction." That books and films are published and sold for profit does not make them commercial speech; *i.e.*, it does not "prevent them from being a form of expression whose liberty is safeguarded [to the maximum extent] by the First Amendment." Commercial speech, however, may be banned if it is false or misleading, or if it advertises an illegal product or service. Even if fits in none of these categories, the government may regulate it more than it may regulate fully protected speech. In addition, the government may generally require disclosures to be included in commercial speech; see the section on "Compelled Speech," below. The Supreme Court has prescribed the four-prong Central Hudson test to determine whether a governmental regulation of commercial speech is constitutional. This test asks initially (1) whether the commercial speech at issue is protected by the First Amendment (that is, whether it concerns a lawful activity and is not misleading) and (2) whether the asserted governmental interest in restricting it is substantial. "If both inquiries yield positive answers," then to be constitutional the restriction must (3) "directly advance the governmental interest asserted," and (4) be "not more extensive than is necessary to serve that interest."

The Supreme Court has held that, in applying the third prong of the Central Hudson test, the courts should consider whether the regulation, in its general application, directly advances the governmental interest asserted. If it does, then it need not advance the governmental interest as applied to the particular person or entity challenging it. Its application to the particular person or entity challenging it is relevant in applying the fourth Central Hudson factor, although this factor too is to be viewed in terms of "the relation it bears to the overall problem the government seeks to correct."

The fourth prong is not to be interpreted "strictly" to require the legislature to use the "least restrictive means" available to accomplish its purpose. Instead, the Court has held, legislation regulating commercial speech satisfies the fourth prong if there is a reasonable "fit" between the legislature's ends and the means chosen to accomplish those ends.

The Supreme Court has applied the Central Hudson test in all the commercial speech cases it has decided since Central Hudson, and we discuss the ten most recent below, in chronological order. In nine of these cases, the Court struck down the challenged speech restriction; it has not upheld a commercial speech restriction since 1993.

In its most recent commercial speech case, Thompson v. Western States Medical Centre, the Court noted that "several Members of the Court have expressed doubts about the Central Hudson analysis and whether it should apply in particular cases." These justices believe that the test does not provide adequate protection to commercial speech, but the Court has found it unnecessary to consider whether to abandon the test, because it has been striking down the statutes in question anyway. In Cincinnati v. Discovery Network, Inc., the Court struck down a Cincinnati regulation that banned news racks on public property if they distributed commercial publications, but not if they distributed news publications.

As for the first two prongs of the Central Hudson test, the Court found that the commercial publications at issue were not unlawful or misleading, and that the asserted governmental interest in safety and esthetics was substantial. As for the third and fourth prongs, although banning commercial newsracks presumably advances the asserted governmental interests, the distinction between commercial and Non-commercial speech "bears no relationship whatsoever to the particular interests that the city has asserted."

The city, therefore, did not establish "the 'fit' between its goals and its chosen means that is required by our opinion in Fox." In Edenfield v. Fane, the Court struck down a Florida ban on solicitation by certified public accountants, even though the Court had previously, in Ohralik v. upheld a ban on solicitation by attorneys. The Court found that the government had substantial interests in the ban, including the prevention of fraud, the protection of privacy, and the need to maintain CPA independence and to guard against conflicts of interest.

However, the Court found no evidence that the ban directly advanced these interests, and noted, among other things, that, "[u]nlike a lawyer, a CPA is not 'a professional trained in the art of persuasion,'" and "[t]he typical client of a CPA is far less susceptible to manipulation than the young accident victim in Ohralik." The Court added, more generally, that the government's burden in justifying a restriction on commercial speech "is not satisfied by mere speculation or conjecture; rather, a governmental body seeking to sustain a restriction on commercial speech must demonstrate that the harms it recites are real and that its restriction will in fact alleviate them to a material degree."

In United States v. Edge Broadcasting Co., the Court upheld "federal statutes that prohibit the broadcast of lottery advertising by a broadcaster licensed to a State that does not allow lotteries, while allowing such broadcasting by a broadcaster licensed to a State that sponsors a lottery...." The governmental interest in the statutes was to balance the interests of states that prohibit lotteries and states that operate lotteries. The broadcaster that challenged the statutes was licensed in North Carolina, which does not allow lotteries, but broadcasted from only three miles from the Virginia border, which does allow lotteries.

The broadcaster claimed that prohibiting it from broadcasting advertisements for the Virginia lottery did not advance the governmental interest or represent a "reasonable fit" because North Carolina radio listeners in its area were already inundated with advertisements from Virginia stations advertising the Virginia lottery and because most of the broadcaster's listeners were in Virginia. The Supreme Court upheld the statutes because, even if they did not advance the governmental interest or represent a reasonable fit as applied to the particular broadcaster, they did as applied to the overall problem the government sought to address.

The Court found sufficiently substantial to satisfy the second prong of the *Central Hudson* test the government's interest in curbing "strength wars" by beer brewers who might seek to compete for customers on the basis of alcohol content. However, it concluded that the ban "cannot directly and materially advance" this "interest because of the overall irrationality of the Government's regulatory scheme." This irrationality is evidenced by the fact that the ban does not apply to beer advertisements, and by the fact that the statute *requires* the disclosure of alcohol content on the labels of wines and spirits. In *Florida Bar v. Went For It, Inc.*, the Court upheld a rule of the Florida Bar that prohibited personal injury lawyers from sending targeted direct-mail solicitations to victims and their relatives for 30 days following an accident or disaster.

The Bar argued "that it has a substantial interest in protecting the privacy and tranquility of personal injury victims and their loved ones against intrusive, unsolicited contact by lawyers," and the Court found that "[t]he anecdotal record mustered by the Bar" to demonstrate that its rule would advance this interest in a direct and material way was "noteworthy for its breadth and detail"; it was not "mere speculation and conjecture." Therefore, the rule passed what the Court called the second prong of the *Central Hudson* test.

As for the final prong, the Court found the Bar's rule to be "reasonably well tailored to its stated objective...." In a subsequent case, the Court wrote that, in *Florida Bar v. Went For It, Inc.*, it had "upheld a 30-dayprohibition against a certain form of legal solicitation largely because it left so many channels of communication open to Florida lawyers." In *44 Liquormart, Inc. v. Rhode Island*, the Court, struck down a state statute that prohibited disclosure of retail prices in advertisements for alcoholic beverages. In the process, it increased the protection that the *Central Hudson* test guarantees to commercial speech by making clear that a total prohibition on "the dissemination of truthful, Non-misleading commercial messages for reasons unrelated to the preservation of a fair bargaining process" will be subject to a stricter review by the courts than a regulation designed "to protect consumers from misleading, deceptive, or aggressive sales practices." The Court added: "The First Amendment directs us to be especially skeptical of regulations that seek to keep people in the dark for what the government perceives to be their own good."

It concluded "that the price advertising ban cannot survive the more stringent constitutional review that *Central Hudson* itself concluded was appropriate for the complete suppression of truthful, Non- misleading commercial speech." In *Greater New Orleans Broadcasting Association, Inc. v. United States*, the Court applied the *Central Hudson* test to strike down, as applied to advertisements of private casino gambling that are broadcast by radio or television stations located in Louisiana, where such gambling is legal, the same federal statute it had upheld in as applied to broadcast advertising of Virginia's lottery by a radio station located in North Carolina, where no such lottery was authorized.

The Court emphasized the interrelatedness of the four parts of the *Central Hudson* test; *e.g.*, though the government has a substantial interest in reducing the social costs of gambling, the fact that the Congress has simultaneously encouraged gambling, because of its economic benefits, makes it more difficult for the government to demonstrate that its restriction on commercial speech materially advances its asserted interest and constitutes a reasonable "fit."

In this case, "[t]he operation of [18 U.S.C.] 1304 and its attendant regulatory regime is so pierced by exemptions and inconsistencies that the Government cannot hope to exonerate it.... [T]he regulation distinguishes among the indistinct, permitting a variety of speech that poses the same risks the Government purports to fear, while banning messages unlikely to cause any harm at all." In *Lorillard Tobacco Co. v. Reilly*, the Supreme Court applied the *Central Hudson* test to strike down most of the Massachusetts Attorney General's regulations governing the advertising and sale of cigarettes, smokeless tobacco, and cigars.

The Court first found the "outdoor and point-of-sale advertising regulations targeting cigarettes" to be Pre-empted by the Federal Cigarette Labeling and Advertising Act, 15 U.S.C. 1331-1341. By its terms, however, this statute's Pre-emption provision applies only to cigarettes, so the Court considered the smokeless tobacco and cigar petitioners' First Amendment challenges to the outdoor and point-of-sale advertising regulations. Further, the cigarette petitioners did not raise a Pre-emption challenge to Massachusetts' sales practices regulations (regulations, described below, other than outdoor and point-of-sale advertising regulations), so the Court considered the cigarette as well as the smokeless tobacco and cigar petitioners' claim that these regulations violate the First Amendment.

The Court struck down the outdoor advertising regulations under the fourth prong of the *Central Hudson* test, finding that the prohibition of any advertising within 1,000 feet of schools or playgrounds "prohibit[ed] advertising in a substantial portion of the major metropolitan areas of Massachusetts," and that such a burden on speech did not constitute a reasonable fit between the means and ends of the regulatory scheme. "Similarly, a ban on all signs of any size seems ill suited to target the problem of highly visible billboards, as opposed to smaller signs." The Court found "that the point-of-sale advertising regulations fail both the third and fourth steps of the *Central Hudson* analysis."

The prohibition on advertising "placed lower than five feet from the floor of any retail establishment which is located within a one thousand foot radius of" any school or playground did not advance the goal of preventing minors from using tobacco products because "[n]ot all children are less than 5 feet tall, and those who are certainly have the ability to look up and take in their surroundings." The Court, however, upheld the sales practices regulations that "bar the use of self-service displays and require that tobacco products be placed out of the reach of all consumers in a location accessible only to salespersons."

These regulations, though they "regulate conduct that may have a communicative component," do so "for reasons unrelated to the communications of ideas." The Court therefore applied the *O'Brien* test for incidental restrictions of speech and concluded "that the State has demonstrated a substantial interest in preventing access to tobacco products by minors and has adopted an appropriately narrow means of advancing that interest." In *Thompson v. Western States Medical Centre*, the Court struck down section 503A of the Food, Drug, and Cosmetic Act, 21 U.S.C. § 353a, which "exempts 'compounded drugs' from the Food and Drug Administration's standard drug approval requirements as long as the providers of those drugs abide by several restrictions, including that they refrain from advertising or promoting particular compounded drugs."

"Drug compounding," the Court explained, "is a process by which a pharmacist or doctor combines, mixes, or alters ingredients to create a medication tailored to the needs of an individual patient." The Court found that the speech restriction in this case served "important" governmental interests, but that, "[e]ven assuming" that it directly advances these interests, it failed the fourth prong of the *Central Hudson* test. In considering the fourth prong, the Court wrote that "the Government has failed to demonstrate that the speech restrictions are 'not more extensive than is necessary to serve'" the governmental interests, as "[s]everal non- speech-related means [of serving those interests] might be possible here."

"If the First Amendment means anything," the Court added, "it means that regulating speech must be a last — not first — resort. Yet here it seems to have been the first strategy the Government thought to try." The Court noted that it had "rejected the notion that the Government has an interest in preventing the dissemination of truthful commercial information in order to prevent members of the public from making bad decisions with the information."

In saying that the government failed to demonstrate that the speech restrictions were "not more extensive than is necessary to serve" the governmental interests, the Court was quoting from the fourth prong of the *Central Hudson* test, but nowhere in *Thompson* did it note that it had previously modified the fourth prong to require merely a reasonable "fit" between the legislature's ends and means, and not use of the least restrictive means to serve the governmental interests. Rather, it wrote: "In previous cases addressing this final prong of the *Central Hudson* test, we have made clear that if the Government could achieve its interests in a manner that does not restrict speech, or that restricts less speech, the Government must do so." Yet the Court did not state that it intended to overrule its reasonable "fit" construction of the fourth prong.

## DEFAMATION

Defamation (libel is written defamation; slander is oral defamation) is the intentional communication of a falsehood about a person, to someone other than that person, that injures the person's reputation. The injured person may sue and recover damages under state law, unless state law makes the defamation privileged (for example, a statement made in a judicial, legislative, executive, or administrative proceeding is ordinarily privileged). Being required to pay damages for a defamatory statement restricts one's freedom of speech; defamation, therefore, constitutes an exception to the First Amendment.

The Supreme Court, however, has granted limited First Amendment protection to defamation. The Court has held that public officials and public figures may not recover damages for defamation unless they prove, with "convincing clarity," that the defamatory statement was made with "'actual malice' — that is, with knowledge that it was false or with reckless disregard of whether it was false or not."

The Court has also held that a private figure who sues a media defendant for defamation may not recover without some showing of fault, although not necessarily of actual malice (unless the relevant state law requires it). However, if a defamatory falsehood involves a matter of public concern, then even a private figure must show actual malice in order to recover presumed damages (*i.e.*, not actual financial damages) or punitive damages.

## SPEECH HARMFUL TO CHILDREN

Speech that is otherwise fully protected by the First Amendment may be restricted in order to protect children. This is because the Court has "recognized that there is a compelling interest in protecting the physical and psychological well-being of minors." However, any restriction must be accomplished "'by narrowly drawn regulations without unnecessarily interfering with First Amendment freedoms.'

It is not enough to show that the government's ends are compelling; the means must be carefully tailored to achieve those ends." Thus, the government may prohibit the sale to minors of material that it deems "harmful to minors" ("so called 'girlie' magazines"), whether or not they are not obscene as to adults. It may prohibit the broadcast of "indecent" language on radio and television during hours when children are likely to be in the audience, but it may not ban it around the clock unless it is obscene. Similarly, Congress may not ban dial-a-porn, but it may prohibit it from being made available to minors or to persons who have not previously requested it in writing. In *Reno v. American Civil Liberties Union*, the Supreme Court declared unconstitutional two provisions of the Communications Decency Act (CDA) that prohibited indecent communications to minors on the Internet. The Court held that the CDA's "burden on adult speech is unacceptable if less restrictive alternatives would be at least as effective in achieving the legitimate purpose that the statute was enacted to serve." "[T]he governmental interest in protecting children from harmful materials... does not justify an unnecessarily broad suppression of speech addressed to adults.

As we have explained, the Government may not 'reduc[e] the adult population... to... only what is fit for children.'" The Court distinguished the Internet from radio and television because (1) "[t]he CDA's broad categorical prohibitions are not limited to particular times and are not dependent on any evaluation by an agency familiar with the unique characteristics of the Internet," (2) the CDA imposes criminal penalties, and the Court has never decided whether indecent broadcasts "would justify a criminal prosecution," and (3) radio and television, unlike the Internet, have, "as a matter of history... 'received the most limited First Amendment protection... in large part because warnings could not adequately protect the listener from unexpected programme content.... [On the Internet], the risk of encountering indecent material by accident is remote because a series of affirmative steps is required to access specific material."

In 1998, Congress enacted the Child Online Protection Act (COPA), P.L. 105- 277, title XIV, to replace the CDA. COPA differs from the CDA in two main respects: (1) it prohibits communication to minors only of "material that is harmful to minors," rather than material that is indecent, and (2) it applies only to communications for commercial purposes on publicly accessible websites. COPA has not taken effect, because a constitutional challenge was brought and the district court, finding a likelihood that the plaintiffs would prevail, issued a preliminary injunction against enforcement of the statute, pending a trial on the merits.

The Third Circuit affirmed, but, in 2002, in *Ashcroft v. American Civil Liberties Union*, the Supreme Court held that COPA's use of community standards to define "material that is harmful to minors" does not by itself render the statute unconstitutional. The Supreme Court, however, did not remove the preliminary injunction against enforcement of the statute, and remanded the case to the Third Circuit to consider whether it is unconstitutional Non-etheless. In2003, the Third Circuit again found the plaintiffs likely to prevail and affirmed the preliminary injunction. In 2004, the Supreme Court affirmed the preliminary injunction because it found that the government had failed to show that filtering prohibited material would not be as effective in accomplishing Congress's goals. It remanded the case for trial, however, and did not foreclose the district court from concluding otherwise. On March 22, 2007, the district court found COPA unconstitutional and issued a permanent injunction against its enforcement.

The grounds for its decision were that "COPA is not narrowly tailored to Congress' compelling interest," the Attorney General "failed to meet his burden of showing that COPA is the least restrictive, most effective alternative in achieving the compelling interest," and "COPA is impermissibly vague and overbroad."

**CHILDREN'S FIRST AMENDMENT RIGHTS**

In a case upholding high school students' right to wear black arm bands to protest the war in Vietnam, the Supreme Court held that public school students do not "shed their constitutional rights to freedom of speech or expression at the schoolhouse gate." They do, however, shed them to some extent. The Supreme Court has upheld the suspension of a student for using a sexual metaphor in a speech nominating another student for a student office. It has upheld censorship of a student newspaper produced as part of the school curriculum. (Lower courts have indicated that non-school-sponsored student writings may not be censored.)

A plurality of the justices found that a school board must be permitted "to establish and apply their curriculum in such away as to transmit community values," but that it may not remove school library books in order to deny access to ideas with Board of Education, Island Trees School District v. Pico, 457 U.S. 853, 864 (1982). The Court noted that "nothing in our decision today affects in any way the discretion of a local school board to choose books to *add* to the libraries of their schools."

The Supreme Court has also held that Congress may not prohibit people 17 or younger from making contributions to political candidates and contributions or donations to political parties. Most recently, in *Morse v. Frederick*, the Court held that a school could punish a pupil for displaying a banner that read, "BONG HiTS 4 JESUS," because these words could reasonably be interpreted as "promoting illegal drug use."

The Court indicated that it might have reached a different result if the banner had addressed the issue of "the criminalization of drug use or possession." Justice Alito, joined by Justice Kennedy, wrote a concurring opinion stating that they had joined the majority opinion "on the understanding that

- It goes no further than to hold that a public school may restrict speech that a reasonable observer would interpret as advocating illegal drug use and
- It provides no support for any restriction on speech that can plausibly be interpreted as commenting on any political or social issue, including

speech on issues such as 'the wisdom of the war on drugs or of legalizing marijuana for medicinal use.'"

As *Morse v. Frederick* was a 5-to-4 decision, Justices Alito's and Kennedy's votes were necessary for a majority and therefore should be read as limiting the majority opinion with respect to future cases.

## AVENUES OF ABUSE OF FREEDOM OF THE PRESS

The avenues of abuse of the Press in modern times, should be noticed in. brief: The foremost danger is that since the Press is a most potent instrument of mass communication, newspapers are sought to be used by powerful parties and financial groups or even individuals having vested interests, for purposes of 'propaganda', *i.e.*, to further their private interests to the detriment of the public, as a result of which the Press, instead of creating a free market of ideas, tend to become an instrument for suppression of view, and an agency of monopolistic contrail or eve news and reports.

The basic assumption that freedom of the Press is indispensable to offer to the public all points of view involved in public issues and to give a truthful account of events so that the reader may freely form his considered view on each issue is defeated if every newspaper gives a biased or coloured report of news and advocates only one of the solutions, namely, that advocated by the party or group which conducts that newspaper.

## SAFEGUARDS AGAINST ABUSE OF FREEDOM OF THE PRESS

Though the likelihood of freedom of the Press to be abused is now evident in all modern countries, the remedy of this serious problem is not so easy. The reason is that it is a necessary evil since freedom of the Press is the ' Ark of the Covenant of Democracy' it cannot be dispensed with. Though it "has some disagreeable results, the wholesome ones are greater and more numerous." If that be so, the Press' cannot be suppressed nor does the remedy lie in State monopoly or nationalization of newspaper, because that would be the assumption by the State of the guardianship of the public mind a very antithesis of democracy.

The result would be the same of the State acquires complete control by a system of censorship of day-to-day regulation. That is why Pundit Jawaharlal once said-" I would rather have a completely free press with all the dangers involved in the wrong use of that freedom than a suppressed or a regulated press". The remedy against abuse of.freedom of the Press has, in fact, been provided, in India, by Art of the Constitution itself. In c1.(2) it empowered the State to impose ' reasonable restriction' in the countervailing social interests such as security of the State, public order and the like, which are enumerated in that clause. "The exercise of these freedoms, since it carries with it duties and responsibilities, may be subject to such formalities condition, restrictions or penalties as are prescribed by law and are necessary in a democratic society, in the interests of national security, territorial integrity or public safety, for the prevention of disorder or crime, for the protection of health or morals for the protection of the reputation or rights of others, for preventing the disclosure of information received in confidence or for maintaining the authority and impartiality of the judiciary". Thus, apart from the interest of security of the State, freedom of the Press may have to be controlled to protect an individual from any damage to his reputation, privacy property and the like, by irresponsible publications through the Press.

"The Press is the servant, not the master, of the citizenry and its freedom does not carry with it an unrestricted hunting license to prey on the ordinary citizen". In short, "Without a lively sense of responsibility a free press may readily become a powerful inst5ument of injustice". Classification of the limitation In India, a journalist, a printer, publisher or proprietor of newspaper or an author has to take care that he does not violate any of the restrictions which have been imposed on the freedom of the Press by a number of Statute founded on different aspects of the need for social or public control. Some of these statutes, again, have a constitutional foundation, *e.g.* those which have been passed to enforce the grounds of restriction envisaged by cl. (2) or (6) of Art while others are general laws applicable to the public, including the Press.'

Besides statutory limitations, there are certain limitations which are founded on English common law, and are still uncodified, *e.g.*, those founded on the common law of torts, such as the civil wrongs of defamation breach of confidence, invasion of privacy and the like. Some of the limitations, again founded on reasons of State or public policy, such as 'official secrets', while others are founded on private rights, such as copyright.

## EXTRA LEGAL RESTRAINTS

The need for an institution to ensure a high standard of responsibilities on the part of the Press arises from the fact that the freedom of the Press is likely to be abused by what is called 'yellow journalism', *i.e.*,. the publication of matters which debase public taste or indulge in intrusion into public lives even though such publication may not be punishable under the provisions of the existing law. Almost every modern country has therefore set up a body which could serve as a watchdog over the standards of journalism and at the same time maintain the freedom of the Press against unwarranted government intrusion. In England, the Press Council (1953) is non-statutory body, having no legal powers.

It is composed of representatives of journalists as well as eminent men and academicians who constitute about one-third of the Council, and is headed by a non-political Chairman. In India, the Press Council is a statutory body. It was first established by the Press Council Act, 1965, on the lines recommended by the first Press Commission (1954). In the main, its functions followed the British precedent, to include:

- The preservation of the freedom of the Press.
- To maintain and improve the standards of newspaper in India
- To form a code of conduct to prevent writings which were not legally punishable but where yet 'objectionable'?

The Press Council Act, 1965 was, however repealed during Mrs. Gandhi's regime, by enacting the Press Council (Repeal) Act, 1976. The Press Council was, therefore abolished with effect from January, 1976, on the following grounds offered by the Government while bringing the Ordinance which later become the Act: The Press Council has failed to set out and enforce any code of conduct, as envisaged by the Act of 1965. It also failed to build up any respectable body of case-law because only complaints of comparatively minor importance were dealt with by the Council. After coming into power, the Janata Government enacted a fresh Press Council Act, 1978, to re-establish the Press Council, with a different composition and powers. Censorship which, when imposed by law, operates as a restriction upon the freedom of the Press, ceases to be so when it is self-imposed. In many countries, therefore, newspaper and journals have put their heads together to formulate a code of conduct or guidelines they would observe to prevent abuses of the freedom of these. In U.S.A., for instance, such guidelines have been formulated in many States, by the news media in consultation with the Bar, as to matters which should not be published to the prejudice of an accused in pending or impending trial, *e.g.* confessions, opinions on the guilt or innocence of the accused, statements as might influence the outcome of trial.

In U.K. the Press Council itself is an institution of self-censorship. Its 'adjudication' on complaints received from members of the public against the Press are thus regarded as having moral authority and have thus been developing a code of conduct of journalists. Self-censorship imposed by voluntary restraints must be distinguished from guidelines issued by a Censor, an instance of which was when in India during the 1975-76 Emergency.

Newspaper editors hardly have to be told about the importance of press freedom. Nor do they need to be lectured on the virtues of peace. But surprisingly, few editors seem to be aware of or articulate the strong connection between the two. Quite simply, a free press promotes peace; creating a universally free press would promote universal peace. The bridge between the two is democracy. Only to academics is democracy a complex term requiring elaborate definition. To most people, correctly I argue, democracy is easily defined by certain rights: that of voting and the secret ballot, of being able to run for any political office, including the highest, and of freedom of speech. And the latter, of course, means not only the freedom to publish criticism of the government, but even to advocate revolution. Except in a time of war, censorship and democracy are not only seen as incompatible—they *are* incompatible. This is clear from a survey of governments around the world. For all countries, without exception, as shown by the latest Freedom House survey of freedom, the most democratic have the freest media; the least democratic have the least free media. Indeed, it is inconceivable that it could be otherwise. Plainly, a free press is essential to democracy, but I would put this even in stronger terms: promoting freedom of the press also promotes democracy—a way to democracy is by working to create a free press. I think that most newsmen would agree with this.

Now, on the other side of the coin, research on war and peace has shown the following results. First, democracies do not make war on each other. There has been no war and virtually no threat of violence between two countries that are democratic. The most war occurs between the least free countries. Note that there are 167 sovereign nations in the world today, 60 of them democracies. Not only has there been or is there no war between them, but there is not even the threat of war; none of these democracies arm against each other. Not one. In its long, bloody history, for example, Western Europe is finally at peace. There is not even the expectation of war among these countries. And, it is no accident that Western Europe is also totally democratic.

Second, democracies tend to have the least internal violence (riots, revolutions, guerrilla warfare, civil war); those countries with the least freedom tend to have the most. Finally, democratic governments just do not kill their own citizens for any but the most reprehensible civil crimes, such as executions for murder; the least free tend to kill their citizens by the millions for political, religious, or racial reasons. In many parts of the world, genocide and totalitarianism are almost synonymous. Consider that in this century alone, aside from foreign or domestic wars, totalitarian governments have killed in cold blood more than 115,000,000 people, over three times the number killed in battle in all wars in this century, including the two world wars.

The major perpetuators are well known; disagreement now only exists about the numbers: Hitler may have slaughtered as many as 14,000,000 people, including near 5,000,000 Jews; Stalin surely outdid him by murdering well over 20,000,000; Mao Tse-tung possibly liquidated even more; Pol Pot in Cambodia exterminated around 2,000,000 Cambodians; the Young Turks killed over 1,000,000 Armenians during World War I. And then there were the assorted butcheries in Ethiopia, Vietnam, Syria, Uganda, Rwanda, Burundi, Indonesia, East Pakistan, and elsewhere. A twentieth century, global blood bath of over 100,000,000; over 140,000,000 people when battle-deaths in foreign and domestic wars are included. But not one of these millions were killed in a war or violence between democracies; few, if any, citizen of a democracy have been killed by their own government for other than civil crimes like murder (the number of criminals executed in the whole history of the United State by federal and local authorities up to 1982 is 13,630). It should be clear that democracies are a way to Non-violence. In fact, promoting democracy is promoting world peace. For were democracy universalized, the lesson of history and contemporary events is that international war would be eliminated, domestic violence minimized, and genocide and governmental mass murder of its citizens ended. The conclusion is now manifest. Since advancing freedom of the press furthers democracy, spreading freedom of the press promotes world peace. And the reverse logic is also true. Without democracies, there will be war; without freedom of the press, democracies cannot exist. Newsmen everywhere should realize this simple equation, then. *To foster peace, foster freedom of the press*.

The recent happenings in Tamil Nadu where six journalists were sentenced to 15 days simple imprisonment for alleged breach of privilege and contempt by the state Legislative Assembly brings back the not so pleasant memories of the Emergency. There is a saying that those who forget history are wont to repeat it. The action is condemnable as the intent of those who passed the judgment is, itself, questionable. The threat to freedom of the press in this country or for that matter in all of Asia hangs like the proverbial sword of Damocles. In India, no political party can boast of respecting the freedom of the press. There have been numerous instances of newspaper offices being vandalised and editors and journalists being roughed up by political flunkeys for publishing articles that were critical of their leaders whose credentials were suspect, to say the least. This sorry state of affairs has increased in recent years.

Not long ago, an article published by Alex Perry, a foreign journalist, on Prime Minister Vajpayee's fitness, thereby questioning his ability to lead the nation, considerably angered the ruling party. The press is considered the watchdog of democracy. Sadly, there is scant regard for this truism in a country which is, ironically, the world's largest democracy. Self-discipline, which is so crucial for the survival of any democracy, is fast disappearing from the Indian polity. Tolerance levels are declining and arrogance is all-pervasive. More often than not political power is used to further the cause of the power-hungry rather than to serve the masses. When obedience to the enforceable is itself neglected, obedience to the unenforceable is out of the question. Even after more than five decades of Independence, democracy in India has still not matured and the quality of public life is declining alarmingly.

Today, political leaders are voted to power because of their oratory and manipulative skills and not for their wisdom and virtue. We cannot expect better governance if we continue to elect people with criminal track records and malafide intentions. Fortunately, the Indian citizen can depend on a strong judiciary, which has so often come to the rescue. The press, on its part, should bear in mind that freedom of the press does not mean a license to write anything. This freedom is precious and it has to be used judiciously. When this freedom is misused, public respect for this profession will diminish. The press has to guard against this.

There is a common understanding that democracy and press freedom are strongly connected and mutually reinforcing. Mass media fulfill an essential function in democracy as a link between the citizens and their political representatives. The information and representation function of the media is thought to be best performed if the media are free, that is to say autonomous. In all dissident movements in Eastern-Europe the demand for democracy was accompanied by the demand for a free press. In Russia, Gorbachev stressed the importance of glasnost' (not the equivalent of press freedom but a step in that direction) as a sine qua Non- for democratic reform.

Yeltsin affirmed that he could not conceive of a democratic society 'without the freedom of expression and the press'. And also Putin stressed the relationship: 'without a truly free media, Russian democracy will not survive'. In this paper we discuss the relationship between press freedom and democracy in post- communist Russia. Post-communist Russia represents a unique historical and socio- political setting, which does not readily allow for generalization. Nevertheless, the observations on Russia can contribute to a deeper understanding of the connection between press freedom and democracy in other contexts as well. Although widely used words, the concepts of democracy and press freedom are not uniformly defined.

Different perceptions of democracy cause different perceptions of the role of the media in democracy. In order to avoid confusion of ideas, we start by having a closer look at both concepts. The concept of democracy Press freedom and democracy are words with a highly positive emotional value. Amartya Sen (1999) has pointed out that while democracy is not yet universally practiced, nor indeed uniformly accepted, in the general climate of world opinion, democratic governance has now achieved the status of being taken to be generally right. Because of its positive emotional value the word is highly vulnerable for abuse and 'cooptation' which leads to a shift, and in the end an emptiness, of meaning.

In the Soviet Union a distinction was made between the real 'socialist democracy' and the fake 'bourgeois democracy'. The meaning of the word democracy became even more obscured by the use of the prefixes pseudo-, new-, or 'not consolidated' in combination with democracy. Post- communist Russia has been labelled all of this, due to the gap between its democratic quality and its democratization rhetoric. Other labels have been used that question the genuineness of Russian democracy even more: Russia as 'delegative democracy', 'totalitarian democracy' or 'authoritarian democracy'. With the same half-heartedness, Olcott and Ottaway (1999) speak of 'semi-authoritarianism',

Zhelev (1999) of 'a multiparty authoritarian system', Sergej Kovalev of an 'authoritarian-police regime that will preserve the formal characteristics of democracy and market economy' and the Russian commentator Mikhail Delyagin of a 'liberal dictatorship' and 'manipulative democracy'. Koshkareva and Narzhikulov (1998: 164) speak of a 'nomenklatura democracy'. Diamond (1996) calls this a characteristic of the 'third wave' of democratization: the gap between the so called electoral (formal, political) and liberal (substantial, social) democracies.

At a minimum, democracy is a political system based on free, competitive and regular elections. This 'electoral' democracy presumes space for political opposition movements and political parties that represent a significant range of voter choice and whose leaders can openly compete for and be elected to positions of power in government. The concept of 'liberal' or 'substantial' democracy extends the key element of free competition with a bunch of political and civil rights (freedom of speech, freedom of association, freedom of religion, etc.) and the notions of the rule of law, inclusive citizenship and civil society. The concept of substantial democracy cannot easily be reduced to a set of procedures and institutions but is described as 'a way of regulating power relations in such a way as to maximize the opportunities for individuals to influence the conditions in which they live, to participate in and influence debates about the key decisions that affect society'.

Democracy in this sense is not a dichotomic but continuous variable. The choice is not between democracy or no democracy but between more or less democracy, which comes down very often to 'old' and 'new' democracies. Linz and Stepan (1996) distinguish 'consolidated' and 'transitional' democracies. Consolidation is attained to when democracy became 'the only game in town', constitutionally as well as behaviourally and attitudinally. At this stage, institutions and laws alone are not sufficient anymore, and the element of political culture joins in. The concept of political culture builds largely on the book of Almond and Verba, The Civic Culture, and experiences some renaissance in the last decennia.

The idea however, that one 'culture' - one constellation of values, norms, belief systems, and attitudes - fits democracy closer than the other, is not new. Plato already pointed out that forms of government (oligarchy, democracy, tyranny, aristocracy) differ according to dispositions of men. More recently, Miller, White and Heywood (1998: 66) have expressed this as 'democracies require democrats'. The concept of political culture provides a link between the macro level of the society and the micro level of the individual. The concept of culture also suggests some continuity over time: 'neither an individual's values nor those of a society as a whole are likely to change overnight. Instead, fundamental value change takes place gradually'. The value that has singled out as most contributive to a 'civic' or 'democratic' culture is trust, and more specifically impersonal trust, in contrast with personal trust. In the 'democratic' culture, the individual is considered an end in itself and a rational being, capable of making independent judgments and choices (eg. voting) and able to construct his own 'truth' out of widely divergent messages. 'Authoritarian culture', in contrast, places truth in the hands of a few 'wise men' whereas the common man is distrusted and considered a dependent, irrational being, a 'cog in the wheel', not capable of making independent judgments and choices.

Merrill and Lowenstein (1990: 159-160) speak of a 'democratic orientation' (with examples such as John Locke and John Milton) versus an 'elitarian orientation'. The former can be linked to individualism, pluralism and trust; the latter to collectivism, dominance (unitary truth) and distrust. Russia has traditionally been an elitist country. Tsarist Russia was characterized by a wide gap between the ruling elite and the common men. Communist Russia was, despite its claims to be egalitarian, very elitist oriented. Lenin stressed the role of the Communist Party as a vanguard party.

Hence, the mass lacked class consciousness and organization and had need of the guidance of the Party. According to Kropotkin, Lenin's attitude was dictated by a fundamental distrust in mankind (cited in Krug, 1990: 106). The American journalist Robert Kaiser (1976: 22) has stated it very crude when he wrote: 'The Soviet system is built on the assumption that the citizenry cannot be trusted'. The sharp dichotomy between the Party and the people outlived Lenin. Pavao Novosel speaks of a division of the Soviet society in 'first and second class citizens', formalized through the nomenklatura system. Postcommunist Russia is characterized by a more diversified social stratification but the contrast between the 'elite' (oligarchs and rulers) and 'the people' remains.

The distinction is expressed more frequently than before in terms of money and standard of living, but remains present in the mentality of the Russians as well. Also Zhelev (1996: 7) sees this as a constant between the past and the present: 'the sense that 'we, the people' are of no consequence' and the tension between 'us' and 'them'. Truth has traditionally been unitary in Russia and so was the community, as words like sobornost' (a kind of mystic unity) testify to. In the Marxist interpretation too there was only one right position. Opposition and diversity were considered falsehood and therefore deserved no hearing. William Zimmerman (1995: 631) has called this 'synoptic thinking': 'the view that there is only one correct philosophy'.

This view is diametrically opposed to the pluralistic view of truth and the parliamentarian model that 'by contrast is based on the assumption that the existence of groups or factions that express and defend particular interests in a representative institution is not only natural but its sole justification'.

# 8

# Media and Communication Management in the 21st Century

## COMMUNICATIONS FOR ACCUMULATION, COERCION, AND LEGITIMACY

Marcos took advantage of global political tensions in September 1972 to impose martial law. This was a time of change in U.S. relations with the Third World, during which the superpower needed to adopt a lower profile in managing the affairs of its client states in response to rising nationalist pressures abroad and an unfavourable economic situation at home.

New communication technologies facilitated this shift by permitting political and commercial decision-making to remain centralized while location-specific activities were decentralized. Communication enterprises in the Philippines, such as the international telecommunications companies RCA and ITT (American) and Eastern Telecommunications Philippine Islands (ETPI, a British Cable and Wireless joint venture) could allow Filipinos to take over routine in-country management while preserving worldwide decision-making and policy matters for the metropolis-based parent companies.

This Behaviour of the Philippine state is largely derivative both of world economic and political forces and of collaborative choices made by the Filipino elite going back to the days of the conquistadores. Colonial rule and private American media and telecommunications established in the Philippines the physical infrastructure and standards, technical and political, that led to commercial exploitation of these extremely valuable resources.

In 1867, the Spanish colonial apparatus established the first long-distance telegraph link (Manila-Corregidor), in 1878 the first overseas connection (Manila-Hong Kong as part of Britain's international cable system), and in 1890 the first telephone company in the Philippines (Manila). In 1898, before steaming to confront and destroy the Spanish fleet in Manila Bay, U.S. Admiral George Dewey cut the Hong Kong cable to the Philippines, thereby severing communication with Madrid and subsequently replacing that colonizer with the political, military, and commercial interests of the rising colonial power. In 1903, the U.S. regime permitted a private telephone company to operate in Cebu City, and in 1905 two Americans organized the private Philippine Islands Telephone and Telegraph Co. in Luzon. Other small provincial companies followed, until an American, J. B. Stevenot, got a franchise to set up the Philippine Long Distance Telephone Company, which started up wired and radio long distance communications in 1933, and eventually became the ATandT of the Philippines.

The Commercial Pacific Cable Co. (United States) developed a Shanghai-Manila connection in consonance with U.S. Open Door foreign policy efforts to extend an American economic foothold in China. Broadcast radio, introduced commercially by an American in 1924 (bought out in 1928 by Radio Corporation of the Philippines, a local agent for the sale of RCA radio sets), also followed the social and economic patterns of its colonizer, which together with privately owned, mostly American, newspapers, magazines, and advertising, imprinted bourgeois values on Philippine mass media for the rest of the century.

Commercial media underwritten by advertising revenues helped develop markets for mass consumption goods where economics of scale and marketing skills would prevail. Household products like Colgate toothpaste and Coke became both the standard of modernity and the literal vernacular (as in *xeroxing*) for the types of commodities they represented. To promote the cultural absorption of these products, global marketeers such as J. Walter Thompson and McCann Erickson assumed the leading role in selling consumption as a pastime and in serving as the propagandists of taste.

## DEVELOPMENT COMMUNICATION

Development communications are organized efforts to use communications processes and media to bring social and economic improvements, generally in developing countries. The field emerged in the late 1950's amid high hopes that radio and television could be put to use in the world's most disadvantaged countries to bring about dramatic progress. Early communications theorists like Wilbur Schramm and Daniel Lerner based their high expectations upon the apparent success of World War II propaganda, to which academia and Hollywood had contributed.

Also with World War II came dozens of new, very poor, countries, left by their former colonial overseers with little infrastructure, education, or political stability. It was widely accepted that mass media could bring education, essential skills, social unity, and a desire to "modernize." Walt Rostow theorized that societies progress through specific stages of development on their way to modernity, what he termed "the age of high mass consumption." Lerner suggested that exposure to Western media would create "empathy" for modern culture, and a desire to move from traditional to modern ways. Early development communications, especially that sponsored by the U.S. government, was also seen as a means of "winning hearts and minds" over to a capitalist way of life.

These early approaches made a number of erroneous assumptions, and have been largely forsaken in contemporary approaches to development. Obstacles to development were naively seen as rooted in developing countries, not as products of international relationships. Modernization was presumed to equate to Westernization, and to be a necessary prerequisite to meeting human needs. Development was seen as a top-down process, whereby centralized mass media could bring about widespread change. Producers of development media often failed to ask if the audience can receive the message (television penetration in developing countries is minimal and radio penetration in the early days of development communication was light), understand the message (a problem in countries with dozens of languages and dialects), act upon the message (with the necessary tools or other forms of structural support), and want to act upon the message. And because it was based upon a propaganda model, development communications efforts were often seen as propaganda and distrusted.

Projects embodying these philosophies have enjoyed little success. In the 1970s and 1980s, a new paradigm of development communication emerged which better recognized the process of deliberate underdevelopment as a function of colonialism, the great diversity of the cultures involved, the differences between elite versus popular goals for social change, the considerable political and ideological constraints to change, and the endless varieties of ways different cultures communicate.

But in some instances mass media technologies, including television, have been "magic multipliers" of development benefits. Educational television has been used effectively to supplement the work of teachers in classrooms in the teaching of literacy and other skills, but only in well designed Programmes which are integrated with other educational efforts. Consumer video equipment and VCRs have been used to supplement communications efforts in some small projects.

Some developing countries have demonstrated success in using satellite television to provide useful information to portions of their populations out of reach of terrestrial broadcasting. In 1975 and 1976, an experimental satellite communications project called SITE (Satellite Instructional Television Experiment) was used to bring informational television Programmes to rural India. Some changes in beliefs and behaviours did occur, but there is little indication that satellite television was the best means to that end. The project did lead to Indian development of its own satellite network. China has also embarked on a ambitious programme of satellite use for development, claiming substantial success in rural education. When television has succeeded as an educational tool in developing countries, it is only when very specific viewing conditions are met. For example, Programmes are best viewed in small groups with a teacher to introduce them and to lead a discussion afterwards.

A variety of types of organizations work with local governments to develop communications projects. The United Nations provides multi-lateral aid to governments. Non-profit non-governmental organizations (NGO) conduct development projects worldwide using U.N., government, or private funding. And government agencies, such as the U.S. Agency for International Development (USAID) provide assistance to developing countries, but with political strings attached. There are three common types of development campaigns: Persuasion, changing what people do; Education, changing social values; and Informing, empowering people to change by increasing knowledge. This third approach is now perceived as the most useful. Instead of attempting to modernize people, contemporary efforts attempt to reduce inequality by targeting the poorest segments of society, involving people in their own development, giving them independence from central authority, and employing "small" and "appropriate" technologies. The emphasis has shifted from economic growth to meeting basic needs.

In this new view of development, communication becomes an important catalyst for change, but not its cause. Local folk media, for example, is employed to reduces media's bias Towards literacy and provide information in a traditional, familiar form. Development journalism provides people with information on change in their society, and works at the local level to advocate change. Where mass media is now employed in developing societies, community newspapers and radio prove far more accessible and useful than television.

The rapid spread of entertainment television in the developing world is proving to be more a disruption to traditional social structures than an agent of progress. One emerging genre of television does show promise for contributing to development. The telenovela, pioneered in Brazil, has demonstrated some success in disseminating "pro-social" messages. Such Programmes are now being evaluated in many countries for their effectiveness in contributing to population control, health education, and other development goals.

## DEVELOPMENT JOURNALISM VS. 'ENVELOPMENT' JOURNALISM

It is some what ironical and unfortunate to talk about the need and the possibilities of development communication in an era that is being characterized as the era of communication revolution. And we are precisely doing that. During last several decades means of communication have really been revolutionized and the process still continues, but at the same time the gap between communication media and human aspects of information that relates to common people has also widened in a similar proportion.

It might pain us but the truth is that our communication media have never assumed the crucial responsibility of defining, reviewing and its role with regard to social concerns and people's problems. It simply means that those who claim to assess and examine everyone and everything are oblivious to assessing and examining their own selves. And this is happening at a juncture when these media are in an extremely capable position for collecting and disseminating information in the society owing to technological and communication revolution.

Despite their vast economic resources, the frequency of allegations on them of being insensitive to people's feelings and needs are increasing considerably. The chasm between what is being told by the mainstream newspapers and what is being felt by people across the country, particularly by indigenous populations is increasingly widening everyday.

Power has been decentralized and has even reached to the Panchayats and yet democracy has weakened in the country. It is common knowledge that for a strong democracy, we must have a legislature, an executive and a judiciary that is sensitive and committed to the people. Unfortunately, our legislative bodies and executive have become rampantly corrupt and decayed. The legislature and the executive are in the grip of crime, nepotism, financial scams and there all kinds of allegations against them. Unfortunately, the Fourth Estate responsible for strengthening democracy has also not played its role adequately. Its main focus is on the legislature and the executive. Most of the space in the mainstream media is occupied by news related to the legislature, the executive, social failures, crimes, statements of political leaders and maligning propaganda. Media has no positive thinking and makes no efforts to give the society a new direction. Nor does it underline the successes of the society. If we cherish the dream of an India where there is social justice for all, there is amity and mutual trust among people, there is equal distribution of resources; we need to take the society in to a particular direction. Then, in place of statements that divide people, we'll have to publish and highlight things that create sense of unity among them. We'll have to identify and publish about efforts that promote small initiatives of the people. If media doesn't define and perform its role and social responsibility, it'll have to face people's questions and ire in the future. It'll loose its credibility as the Fourth Estate, the vigilant eye of society.

We must remember that when we talk about communication, we are not talking only about transfer of information only; we also include in it the participation of the society, the community we are communicating about. In a society, social institutions can come into existence and survive only when people participating in them are interlinked through communication. Man is the only creature who needs communication the most for all aspects of his life; and it is for this reason that he is called "Homo Communicator". What he is today and will be tomorrow is because of his ability to communicate with others. It is obvious that culture is communication and communication is culture.

Today, there are unceasing developments in the area of communication; newer kinds of communication medium are coming in to existence and that is really obliterating distinctions between mass and individual communication. It is evident that the trend of communicating the same information or material to diverse communities scattered over the globe is just a passing phase. The change is indicated by the current trend of local editions being brought out by newspapers in India. Hopefully, in the coming days communication on demand will become crucial.

We should also keep in mind that Information Society is evolving at a fast pace. In such a situation, it might be very difficult to demarcate precisely between mass communication and interpersonal communication. It can only happen if we delimit mass communication process only to publishing or broadcasting or telecasting a chosen material or information ignoring the receptors. But in developing countries like India, apart from interpersonal communication, mass communication is also of considerable interest. It is true not only about carrying health campaigns like the one against aids and disseminating information about new discoveries and inventions, but also for communicating information that is important for the civil society. We'll have to accept the simple fact that a modern society characterized by democracy, social and economic justice, national integration, social discipline and economic progress can't be possible without the active and oriented help of mass media; for in a country as vast as India only mass media can communicate information to the inhabitants of the rural regions. A communication system only can ensure that rural populations are consistently kept informed about latest and relevant information and can have a forum for articulating their views. Only it can ensure that the division of country into information rich and information poor regions is gradually eliminated.

Apart from technological progress and economic development, modernization of a society also includes development of democratic institutions by replacing pre-modern and feudal setups. It can only be done by making the poor, the marginalized sections of the society participate in the decision making processes. Development also includes the values of human dignity, equality, social justice and security. Any development that doesn't bring these values in its orbit; that doesn't provide all people equal opportunities is suspect. Mass media can play a very crucial role in it for any transitional period requires new attitudes, a new mind set and a value system in society. Media by its reach, scope and potential can do it very effectively.

For media to play its role as a watch dog, a vehicle of social change needs to be free of the control and interference of the state. It should also not be controlled by either powerful people or companies for that will make it the mouth piece of only these forces. Freedom of press means that it should not be obstructed it in its above mentioned roles. Flow of information shouldn't be controlled. The roles of media enunciated above can be summarized in a succinct term called 'Development Journalism'. It focuses on the needs of the poor, the deprived, the marginalized and emphasizes their effective participation in developmental planning. Or to say it slightly elaborately, this kind of journalism motivates the active participation of the affected people and advocating for their interests, in place of the views of the policy makers and the planners *i.e.* the government. For last 10 years Charkha has been functioning with this concept of journalism as its model.

It has to extent succeeded in generating an interest among a section of media persons towards people's issues. But on the whole, the scene still persists where the mainstream media is not sufficiently focusing grassroots people's initiatives and movements. It is for this reason; activists of mass movements and organizations have initiated efforts for making an interface possible between mass media and such organizations. One illustrious example and fruit of such interface is the Narmada Bachao Andolan. This movement has assumed a nation wide interest not for the reason that it symbolizes people's fight against mega dams, but because it could and is still using mass media in a better and effective way for highlighting itself in the public eye.

There was a time when media would reach to movements for reporting it. But unfortunately now, activists have to do two things simultaneously-carry on with their movements and write news reports about them and also take those reports to newspaper offices for favour of publication.

The sorcerers of the mainstream media don't make any efforts on their own to lend their ears to the stirrings and upsurges at the grassroots level. Consequently, in situations where activists are yet to learn to find a place for their issues, failures and successes in the mainstream media, these remain confined only to their immediate local surroundings and don't reach to a wider audience or readership. In place of our journalism becoming development journalism in the sense defined above; it has become 'envelopment' journalism based on envelopes with press releases reaching newspaper offices. Charkha is a modest initiative in making an interface possible between action at the grassroots level and the mainstream media; an effort for 'spinning action into words'.

We don't make a case against media; we just try to making bridges between people's issues and the media. If they are left with no time to reach down to the issues; we can take these to them. To put it more clearly, we want media's centralized power to be decentralized.

The word decentralization is in vogue now a day. Power has been decentralized to the Panchayat level; but the watch dog who keeps vigil on this power is increasing getting decentralized. Why has it not been decentralized? If power could be handed over to an illiterate rural woman; why can't a literate Youngman or woman of a village be imparted media training? From the enter to the panchayat level, power wants media with and around it and those who are in media want are with and around those who yield power and in this holy or unholy alliance it is finally people who suffer and are marginalized.

## KIND OF DECENTRALIZATION OF MEDIA

Charkha is precisely working for this kind of decentralization of media and is trying to do it at various levels. We start from the Panchayat level. In Rajasthan, Chhattisgarh, U.P., Jharkhand, Uttranchal and Bihar, we conduct Writing Workshops at the tehsil and state levels in which social activists related to Panchayat Raj and Self-governance are given information about media.

For evolving panchayat level media we train these activists in preparing wall newspapers and also in writing reports etc. for newspapers panchayat related issues. Local editors and journalists are also invited to these workshops so that they could familiarize themselves with the ground realities of a village and in future are willing to include these issues in their papers. We also conduct Media Workshops for journalists and free lancers in which the roles of media and people's issues are the focal point of discussion. Social activists are given information about the internal constitution of the media, its way of functioning, pressures on it and its responsibilities; while media persons get an opportunity for developing a deeper understanding of people's issues. In the light of the experiences we have gained in last ten years reveal that though successes on this path are very difficult to achieve, but not impossible.

Normative theories of journalism concern ideal functions of the press, what the press *should* do. These purposes are best understood in relation to larger claims about the *good society*. In principle, there are as many normative theories of journalism as there are political systems, from Marxism-Leninism to diverse conceptions of democracy.

Non-academics as well as academics may express these ideologies, which are relatively coherent conceptions that cluster together specific ideals (such as representation, deliberation, accountability, and the like) in different combinations with varying emphasis (® News Ideologies; News Values; Standards of News). Such broad theories are, to a certain extent, artificial constructs, because no one from politicians to ordinary citizens is entirely consistent in adhering to only one of them. Journalistic practice likewise does not always accord with normative theories of journalism, but these theories remain an important component of professional training. Institutions and the state draw upon theories of journalism, implicitly or explicitly, when shaping media policies that carry real incentives or penalties for deviant Behaviour.

Scholars attempting to classify normative theories, as well as less systematic reflections about media and democracy, have identified non-democratic theories, including authoritarian, totalitarian, Marxist-Leninist, and developmental, as well as democratic theories, including libertarian, social responsibility, democratic elite, democratic participatory, public sphere, and postmodern. *Authoritarian theory* holds that journalism should always be subordinate to the interests of the state in maintaining social order or achieving political goals. At a minimum, the press is expected to avoid any criticisms of government officials and to do nothing to challenge the established order. The press may remain free to publish without prior censorship, but the state retains the right to punish journalists or close media outlets that overstep explicit or implicit limits on reporting and commentary.

## EXTREME AUTHORITARIANISM

Under more extreme authoritarianism, or totalitarianism, a closely censored press pro-actively promotes and extends a totalizing state control over society. In the context of the Cold War, the Soviet-communist theory stood out, an approach perhaps best understood today as a variant of totalitarianism that includes Islamic and other forms of religious fundamentalism. Since the disintegration of the Soviet Union in 1991, versions of Marxist-Leninist, or *Soviet,* theory have survived in North Korea, Cuba, and Vietnam, and to a certain extent in China, as the most coherent, self-consciously elaborated examples. The Soviet normative theory of journalism posits that media should not be privately owned, should serve the interests of the working classes, and most importantly, should provide a complete, objective view of the world following Marxist-Leninist principles, as defined by the communist-party controlled state.

Another non-democratic normative theory is partly a product of western communication scholarship and foreign development projects. *Development theory* is authoritarianism *for a good cause* (® Development Journalism) supporting the economic development and nation-building efforts of impoverished societies. In the context of western dominance in international news gathering and in cable news, the United Nations Educational, Scientific, and Cultural Organization (UNESCO) has also framed development theory in cultural pluralist terms as the right to communicate and, most recently, as the defence of global cultural diversity.

The western press and communication research generally portray these non-democratic theories negatively, as anti-democratic, whatever their potential merits. Outside of the West, however, purely anti-democratic justifications of journalism have grown more rare. The Chinese government, for instance, defends a *market socialist* approach to the media, which combines limited market freedoms with continuing state control (® China). Certain ideals in non-western societies are not necessarily anti-democratic, such as the poetic or literary ideal of the Arabic press (Mellor 2005). Democratic normative theories have been motivating forces behind emerging non-western media outlets such as the Qatar-based Arabic language cable news channel Al-Jazeera. Even in the most repressive authoritarian states, the language of democracy has become commonplace.

Where authoritarianism stresses the importance of maintaining social order, libertarianism aims to maximize individual human freedom. John Locke and other liberal philosophers of the eighteenth century conceived of the libertarian theory, which relates closely with laissez-faire capitalism. In the oft-used metaphor, the press should offer a *marketplace of ideas,* pursuing profits in a natural process believed to support democracy. *Libertarian theory* sees the government as the primary if not only threat to press freedom. Perhaps the best known embodiment of the ideal is the First Amendment to the U.S. Constitution, which specifies that "Congress shall make no law... abridging the freedom of speech, or of the press." This formulation expresses the ideal only in negative terms, as a freedom *from* state intervention. Presumably the press, left to its own devices, will represent diverse voices and hold government accountable, but the only requirement for the press is to pursue its own economic interests. Far from a caricature, this pure form of libertarianism is alive and well in the public pronouncements of many news media owners and managers as well as of some journalists.

Observers and activists who perceive that a pure market orientation does not necessarily support democracy have argued that the press must instead assume *social responsibility.* In the 1947 Hutchins report, the U.S. Commission on a Free and Responsible Press conceived of the chief responsibilities as factual accuracy, promotion of open debate, representation of diverse views, and protection of individual rights by serving as a watchdog that guards against government abuses of power.

Any theory that the press has a voluntary duty to perform positive functions could belong in this category, but social responsibility theory, as originally described, clearly upheld the U.S. journalistic ideal of *objectivity* which stresses factual reporting over commentary, the *balancing* of opposing viewpoints, and maintaining a neutral observer role for the journalist. This ideal has become dominant globally, even among journalists in countries where highly polarized political cultures make it difficult to put into practice.

Social responsibility theory lacks any systematic critique of capitalist media ownership and funding. Most journalistic professional exhortations about *ethics* are social responsibility theories in this sense, including not only traditional defences of investigative journalism but also the recent U.S. movement for civic journalism. Armed with enough courage, individual journalists are assumed capable of performing their democratic responsibilities. Other democratic normative theories also concern social responsibilities, but emphasize some more than others. Legal scholars, philosophers and social scientists, rather than journalists, largely produced these theories, which may not share the assumption against state intervention as a legitimate means to orient journalism democratically. Representative liberal theory (Ferree *et al.* 2002) or *democratic elite theory* (Baker 2002) proposes that democracy works best with highly educated elites and specialized technicians in charge. The primary duties for the press are to chronicle accurately the range of competing elite perspectives, to examine the character and Behaviour of elected officials, and to monitor closely their activities for corruption or incompetence (the *watchdog* function). In other words, the press should adopt a critical, serious tone in covering public affairs, defined as the activities primarily of government but also, in principle, of business or other powerful social institutions. Democratic elite theories tend to be skeptical, however, of whether the press can adequately report and analyse complex issues.

Pierre Bourdieu's (1998) critique of journalism argues for a democratic elite theory from a sociology of knowledge perspective. He values most highly those forms of intellectual and artistic production sheltered from external economic or political pressures. By analogy, his critique esteems the specialized forms of journalism that maintain the greatest *autonomy* from external pressures (® Science Journalism). He would generally prefer that journalism loosen its *monopoly* over public communication so that non-journalist experts could directly transmit their knowledge as they see fit. However, Bourdieu's ideal of complete autonomy could lead journalists (as well as non-journalist experts) to pursue only their own narrow interests and ignore legitimate concerns of wider publics (Schudson 2005).

## POLITICAL INVOLVEMENT OF CITIZENS

In *democratic participatory theory,* journalism is called upon to promote actively the political involvement of citizens. The theory emphasizes principles such as popular inclusion, empowerment, and full expression through a range of communicative styles (Ferree *et al.* 2002; McQuail 1983). Its theorists emphasize diverse viewpoints and active citizen involvement more than the quality of the discourse (whether reasoned, critical, serious, or the like). They disagree on the best means to achieve these goals. Tabloid forms of journalism (® Tabloid Press; Tabloidization), for example, might provide a bridge leading formerly apathetic citizens to an interest in politics (McNair 2000), or the mainstream press might provide news from more perspectives (Gans 2003). In participatory theory, however, small-scale, *segmented* media, commercial as well as non-profit, are best for promoting grassroots citizen involvement (*e.g.*, Keane 1991).

With his ideal of the public sphere (® Public Sphere; Habermas, Jürgen), the German sociologist and philosopher Jürgen Habermas (1989) combines concerns for the quality (reasoned, critical debate) with the quantity (broad representation and participation) of discourse that journalists mediate (Calhoun 1992). However, *public sphere theory,* also referred to as the *discursive* (Ferree *et al.* 2002) or *republican* (Baker 2002) ideal, places the greatest emphasis on quality, narrowly conceived: the press should create a domination-free environment where the better argument can prevail in a quest for social consensus (® Deliberativeness in Political Communication). The public sphere should be free from the state as well as the market (® Coffee Houses as Public Sphere). Societies seem most likely to achieve the ideal during periods of democratic revolutionary effervescence, as in France and the United States at the end of the eighteenth century or in the Soviet Union and east-central Europe during the late 1980s.

By adaptation (and perhaps taming), public sphere theory can fit the conditions in western democracies. Public television, for example, armed with legal guarantees of autonomy from political intervention, may be the best embodiment of the ideal (Garnham 1986). French and other continental European traditions of a journalism of ideas, rather than of raw information, are also consistent (Albert 1998). The ideal inspired the U.S. movement among journalists to redefine their role, from simply providing information to promoting reasoned and civil public debate among ordinary citizens.

Emerging in part as a critique of Habermas, *postmodern* or *constructionist* (Ferree *et al.* 2002) *theory*, like democratic participatory theories, is more tolerant of diverse styles and forms of discourse that journalists mediate. Feminist scholars such as Nancy Fraser say that the ideal of reasoned-critical debate may embody masculine domination and that the ideal of social consensus may suppress ineradicable identity differences (Calhoun 1992). Building on the motto, "the personal is political," postmodern theory privileges personal narratives and emotion over abstract reason, celebrating grassroots media that facilitate the playful search for identity or the articulation of counter-hegemonic interests. A postmodernist ideal is also evident in Kevin Barnhurst and John Nerone's (2001) critique of rationalized, modernist newspaper design form and the hegemonic aspiration of professionalized journalism to map the social world. Postmodern theory insists on a journalism open to the widest range of narrative styles and perspectives, especially those emerging from the margins of society.

Are normative theories of journalism necessary (Hallin and Mancini 2004)? The best-known texts in normative theory, such as *Four Theories of the Press*, may promote ethnocentrism and justify the U.S. model of market-oriented, ostensibly objective, journalism. The assumption that other approaches are inferior has dampened intellectual curiosity about the practice of journalism in other parts of the world. The market model has also influenced international organizations such as the World Association of Newspapers and the Inter-American Press Association. Freedom House, for instance, rates national press systems as free, partly free, or not free, based primarily on political rather than economic criteria. U.S.-centrism, however, is not inherent to normative reflection on and critiques of journalism.

One promising alternative approach, *complex democracy* (Baker 2002), acknowledges the shortcomings of any type of news media in the face of diverse democratic purposes and seeks to encourage the greatest variety of journalistic practices. A working model includes multiple sectors (Curran 2000): a core sector of public service television, a supplementary private enterprise sector, a professional sector under the control of journalists, a civic sector that social organizations including political parties support, and a closely related sector of ideologically or culturally marginal media that operate in the market with partial subsidies from the state.

Through broad reflection on the many strains of political theory, or through comparative research on media systems, normative theorizing can continue to play a key role in communication education and research (® Journalism Education; Professionalization of Journalism). Value judgments guide all research, and it is important to make implicit normative theories explicit. Plural normative *theories* rather than any singular *theory* can help clarify the range of policy and ethical choices available to guide the practice of journalism.

## ROLE OF THE MEDIA IN DEVELOPMENT COMMUNICATION

*The role of media also changes in development communication. It plays the following four responsible roles:*

- Circulate knowledge that will inform people of significant events, opportunities, dangers and changes in their community, country and the world.
- Provide a forum where issues affecting the national or community life may be aired.
- Teach those ideas, skills and attitudes that people need to achieve for a better life.
- Create and maintain a base of consensus that is needed for the stability of the state.

You must be knowing the meaning of 'empathy'. Daniel Lerner used this term with a particular emphasis on the aspirations for a new identity. Suppose, you have a goal of building a decent house so that you can live with the minimum hassles'. You dream about it, you aspire for it. We can say that you empathize with it. Here, Lerner said that people of any given society must think and aspire for a better life.

If they do so, then they are empathetic about a better life. To perform these roles, the media keep the development orientation in its perspective. Three approaches have been identified in relating communication to development. These are empathy, diffusion, and multiplying of information. We shall discuss each separately, individually.

*Empathy:* Daniel Lerner in his book, Passing of Traditional Society, saw the problem of 'modernizing' traditional societies. He saw the spread of literacy resulting from urbanization as a necessary precondition to more complete modernization that would include participatory political institutions.

Development was largely a matter of increasing productivity. And to increase this productivity one must aspire, and it must begin in the psyche of the people. Hence, it is basically "psychological".

> Urbanization → literacy → economic and political participation → the mass media exposure

According to D. Lerner, development failed to because peasants were unable to 'empathize' or imaginatively identify with the new role, and a changed and better way of life and so remained fatalistic –unambitious and resistant to change. Every change in society must originate and begin in the hearts of the people. If the people would like to change, only then the development would begin. What is required is that some means of providing such people with clues as to what better things in life might be. Lerner saw the media as filling this need of promoting interest among the people for a better life. Not only that, he saw the media as machines, inspiring people for better things in life. He said 'empathy' endows a person with the capacity to imagine himself as proprietor of a big grocery store in a city, to wear nice clothes and live in a nice house, to be interested in "what is going on in the world" and to "get out of his hole". He pointed out to the correlation between economic productivity and the media provisions in different countries in support of his theory. The richest country had the most newspapers, the radios and so on, and the poorest, the least.

*Diffusion:* Everett M. Rogers approached this with a perspective that had much in common with Lerner, but differed with him somewhat in emphasis. He saw the diffusion of the new ideas and their practice as a crucial component of the modernization process. According to him, "the mass communication influence appears to operate with a 'two step flow' process through awareness of the mass media, development of favourable attitudes and adaptation by interpersonal channels, particularly, "opinion leaders". We shall discuss this a little more. It has been found that when a message is propagated, a segment of the population adopts it, and develops a positive attitude towards it. This can happen in the case of a product, fertilizer, seeds, ideas, journals, etc. Then, the people who adopt first, directly or indirectly shape the positive attitude of others who remain indifferent to the message. This is true in places where information and literacy levels are low. Simple people would like to get confirmation from the people living in their proximity. You can think about this process in your daily, life. How many times you need information about a product, a book, or about an incident from your friends, classmates, office-mates, neighbours and others. Women, especially, need a lot of confirmation from others before they adopt something. We can go on citing examples.

*Magic Multiplier:* Wilbur Schramm's Mass Media and National Development, which was produced for the UNESCO, became almost a blueprint for development communication. While Lerner and others saw all of the media cut put as having potentially modernizing effects, for Schrarmm it was their content that was the key to their use in development. "Social change of great magnitude is required. To achieve it, people must be informed, persuaded, educated. Information must flow, not only to them but also from them, so that their needs can be known, and they might participate in the acts and decisions of the nation-building; and information must also flow vertically so that decisions may be made. Works should be organized, and skills should be learned at all levels of society for better utilization of the resources of society. Here is where the mass communication enters the calculus—the required amount of information and learning is so vast that only by making effective use of the great information multipliers, the mass media, can the developing countries hope to provide information on the rates their timetables for development demand". Let us elaborate a little. Schramm very clearly mentioned that a lot of feedback is required when one uses communication for development. It should never be one-way traffic. The users should be able to give feedback to the implements. This would help the implementers to find out whether or not the communication is meeting their purpose or aim. Schramm has also said that each person could have the information required by the work that he would undertake. And there might be thousands and lakhs of workers requiring various information. The conventional channels of communication would never be able to meet this demand. Therefore, modem communication technologies would be of great use to meet this demand by multiplying the messages and reaching each and every worker.

## COMMUNICATION NEEDS AND RESOURCES

So far, we have discussed the positive role of communication, and have seen how the communication inputs work to make a developmental programme. But how does one go about formulating the communication strategy or the inputs a programme? In planning communication strategy for development, the most important element is identification of communication needs and resources. Unless one is careful about this, or if one overlooks these elements, communication strategy and plan will not be effective, and all efforts will go in-vain. It is necessary to assess carefully the communication needs of the community and the country. To identify communication needs and resources of a country, the following process has been suggested by the UNESCO.

*UNESCO Guidelines:*

- The collection of basic data and systematic analysis of the country upon such bases as population densities, geographic limitations of communication, variety of social structures, ecology and agriculture transportation, physical communication, mobility, population, electrification, industrial capacity, manpower capacity, etc.
- The production of an inventory of the present communication

resources, including the modem and traditional media, and analysis of the variety of present communication structures. Such an inventory should also include the study of the audience, its communication consumption patterns, etc.

- Critical analysis of the present communication politics, including such considerations as ownership, structures, decision-making, etc.
- Critical analysis of the communication needs of each society, especially, in relation to the existing social and communication structures, and the uses to which communication is put.

Analysis of the communication components in all aspects of the national development plans and programmes in order to ascertain the communication requirements of the programmes, and the communication capacity which is essential to the execution of the plan. These needs must then be reconciled with the means and capacities that are available. A similar process may be followed to identify the communication needs and resources at the institutional or project level or wherever development activities are in progress.

## STRATEGIES IN DEVELOPMENT COMMUNICATION

A strategy is the careful formulation of plans towards achieving a goal. Since development communication is goal oriented, one has to be careful in planning communication strategies. There may be a number of communication strategies for the achievement of a particular communication goal. There is a need to analyse these very carefully. Since these strategies are formulated in the context of the developing countries, one should give keen consideration to cost-benefit factors before selecting the right strategy. In the modern world, there are a number of new technologies, media and techniques, which are available to a communication strategy planner. One has to evaluate these alternatives available to him, using cost-benefit analysis and administrative feasibility. Always, one has to keep in mind the target audience.

## INTERPRETATIVE ANALYSIS ON INTERNET

## FREQUENCY OF USING INTERNET

Through the chi-square test there is significant association between mode of study and frequency of using Internet. It is also similar to the association between area of institution and frequency of using internet. This could be understood in the context of unequal spread of internet in India. Frequency of using internet and medium of instruction were also found to be significantly associated. The predominant language medium of the vast majority of web sites would be English. Further, it was concluded that there is significant association between gender and frequency of using internet. There is significant relationship between course of study and frequency of using internet. It can be concluded that there is significant association between year of study and frequency of using Internet. As years go by, a student tends to be more independent and moves towards a wide range of experiences according to personality theorists like Chris Argyris.

**Approximate Time Spent on Internet**

There is significant association between mode of study and approximate time spent to use internet. Also there is significant association between area of institution and approximate time spent to use internet.

This result could be viewed in relation to the findings of another study described below in which educational media have been found to benefit the rural students than the urban students. Rural students, tested against rural control groups, benefited more than urban students tested against urban control groups as per the writings of Galda and Searle.

The project evaluators hypothesized that radio lessons were particularly effective in raising the level of knowledge of those who knew least, which in this case were the rural students. The findings of the present study could be understood in the light of the earlier finding.

Similarly there is significant association between medium of instruction and approximate time spent on Internet. Approximate time spent to use Internet and course of study were also significantly associated.

The analysis resulted in the conclusion that there is significant association between course of study and approximate time spent to use Internet.

A comparative analysis of all the suggestions provided by respondents through their answers to the open ended questions reveals noticeable commonality among the suggestions to the various media, they are the need felt for greater subject-orientation, enhanced exposure to scientific advancements, examination-centreed contents, need for user-interface and contribution and the like. As suggestions, the users have provided opinions that more visual, movable content should be available with the facility of interaction. Educational media, when used in classrooms are likely to produce maximum learning then using them elsewhere. This has been the theme of the variables analysed. While data on viewing time suggested that 65.36 per cent watch TV every day a week, 35.71 per cent of those who listen to radio do it everyday a week, only 19.36 per cent of those using internet, do it everyday a week. Majority of the respondents tend to be frequent listeners of radio and TV, while TV has more regular audience than radio.

A vast majority of respondents possess radio sets as well as TV sets. It was found that 37.06 per cent listen to radio for education, 35.08 per cent watch TV for education, while 40 per cent use internet always to gather information about study. Data indicate that home is the place where most of the respondents have been listening to radio, while vast majorities of 86.64 per cent of the students watch TV at home; only 22.56 per cent stated that they browse at home. 41.28 per cent stated that they browse the internet at institutions, whereas only a negligible segment of students use radio and TV at their institutions. Among the less interactive media, 61.62 per cent answered that they need interactive programmes in radio, while only 21.86 per cent have answered that interactive programmes are needed for educational purpose on TV programmes. Majority 66.90 per cent use Internet, which, in comparison to the fact that very few owned computers, is a significant achievement of media planners in higher education.

Media planners would benefit by basing their interventions based on the comparative standing of various educational media as understood through the viewing patterns presented with the help of the findings of the study.

It is suggested that measures be on to improve the viewership, listening frequency, the priority being on the latter, which is found to be the least frequently used educational media among the students in the area of study.

Since majority of the respondents have not used any of the media for educational purposes, the top priority is to be given to strengthen the educational usage of the powerful electronic media. Use of electronic media at educational institutions is found to be low. The usage needs to be enhanced in order to facilitate the increased usage of the media for educational purposes, as indicated by the previous suggestion. Creation of awareness among students about educational media should be taken up on a massive scale with a sense of urgency. Local inputs and interaction should be made a regular feature in the educational radio.

Programmes and contents in regional and locally understood languages should be featured for more duration and frequency than it is being done at present.

In order to achieve localization of educational contents of the electronic media, well-equipped media centres carrying out research and producing need based programmes should be created in each University. Campus based electronic media systems could be introduced to produce and present programmes of specific educational needs.

## TELECOMMUNICATIONS ACT HIGHLIGHTS

The Telecommunications Act of 1996 still requires broadcasters and cable companies to continue to observe the "public interest, convenience, and necessity" rule. As Krasnow, Longley, and Terry observe, the FCC' s powers to regulate are limited, at times, because of the fact that regulatory decisions must be based on the "public interest" standard. The public interest standard is mentioned and maintained throughout the Telecommunications Act. As specific regulations are presented, there is some discussion regarding how well it was embraced by all parties involved in the process of creating the legislation.

## BROADCAST OWNERSHIP

The primary issues that the House, Senate, and the president had trouble resolving included particulars relating to broadcast ownership. Both the Senate and the House wanted television national audience caps regarding broadcast ownership changed from 25 per cent to 35 per cent. Further, both the House and Senate wanted the ownership caps for radio to be eliminated completely. After negotiations, it was determined that station ownership could not exceed 35 per cent of the nation's TV homes. For radio, the national ownership limits were eliminated while the local ownership limits were relaxed. The 1996 Act repealed the duopoly rule for radio station ownership, stipulating that in a market with forty-five or more stations an owner may operate eight stations, in a market with thirty to forty-four stations an owner may operate seven stations, in a market with fifteen to twenty-nine stations an owner may operate six stations, and in a market with fourteen or fewer stations an owner may operate five stations.

The Republicans pushed for even fewer regulations in this area, but eventually accepted the suggestions of the Democrats. This caused some anger among those in the Republican party because of the perception that the Republicans allowed the Democrats to gain the upper hand with this issue and several others.

## OPEN VIDEO SYSTEMS

Before the Telecommunications Act, there existed a "cross-ownership" restriction that prevented telephone companies from offering cable service in the same areas where they were offering telephone service. The cross-ownership restriction provided cable companies protection from the large, established telephone companies. The 1996 Act lifted the cross-ownership restriction in an effort "to stimulate local competition in the multi-channel video market."

*The Act allows telephone companies to provide video services in one of four ways*:

- As an over-the-air provider;
- As a common carrier;
- As a cable television operator;
- As an open video service.

The open video service is a newly created hybrid service that allows telephone companies to offer video services and act as both a cable system and common carrier simultaneously. The 1996 Act requires that if demand is greater than existing available space, the telephone company cannot control more than one third of its system's capacity. These open video systems are not franchised locally. Local authorities, however, are allowed a portion of the open video system's revenues, which is similar to franchise fees that cable operators are required to pay to municipalities. Also, traditional cable systems may opt to offer video services via an open video system and thereby avoid many regulations that normally apply to cable systems and to avoid all of the regulations that apply to common carriers. Open video systems are required to provide channels to local non-commercial and commercial broadcasters.

*Healey states that open video system operators must abide by cable regulations that do the following*:

- Require the operator to pay for any commercially broadcast programmes that it carried voluntarily;
- Bar the duplication of certain network, sports, and syndicated programmes;
- Regulate contracts to transmit programmes known as carriage agreements;
- Bar the billing of programming that customers had not requested but had not canceled either;
- Bar programme distribution arrangements that prevent competition;
- Protect customer's privacy;
- Bar employment discrimination.

Unlike the regulatory issues discussed thus far, other issues required several months of negotiations. Before agreements were reached, the Senate and House of Represen-tatives agreed upon several things rather early in the process:

- Broadcast licensing;
- Advanced television and spectrum flexibility;
- Direct broadcast satellite;
- Must-carry rules;
- V-chip and TV programme ratings;
- Cable deregulation;
- Signal scrambling for indecent programming;
- Cable right of refusal of public and leased-access programming;
- Closed captioning; and
- FCC funding.

## BROADCAST LICENSING

The agreement reached regarding broadcast licensing extended the license terms for television and radio to eight years. The previously amended 1934 Act allowed for television licenses to be renewed every five years and radio every seven years. The 1996 Act streamlines the license renewal process by automatically renewing broadcasters' licenses if:

- The station has served the public interest standard;
- If there have been no serious violations by the licensee of the rules and regulations of FCC;

- If there have been no other violations by the licensee that might constitute a pattern of abuse.

Competing applications are reviewed only if a license is not renewed. The 1996 Act also requires broadcasters to maintain a "summary" in their public files of all complaints they receive from viewers pertaining to violent programming.

## ADVANCED TELEVISION SERVICES AND SPECTRUM FLEXIBILITY

The Telecommunications Act of 1996 allows the FCC to assign licenses for advanced television services, and the licenses are limited to existing television stations.

Advanced television service is defined as digital broadcasts. If the broadcaster receives a second channel, then one of the two eventually must be returned to the U.S. government. The public interest requirement continues to apply to the second channel if one is assigned to the broadcaster.

Critics suggest that broadcasters are getting a "sweet" deal by having the new digital frequencies automatically assigned to them rather than having to purchase the rights to use the new frequencies. Former senator Bob Dole believed the provision was a multibillion dollar give-away.

Andrews stated, "Government officials estimate the licenses would be worth anywhere from $11 billion to $70 billion, if the Government auctioned them in the way it is doing for licenses to operate new wireless phone services."

## DIRECT BROADCAST SATELLITE (DBS)

Complete control of "direct-to-home satellite services" is granted to the FCC under the Telecommunications Act of 1996. This prevents local communities, including homeowners associations, from prohibiting direct broadcast satellite dishes. The must-carry rule was established in April 1965 and requires all cable companies to carry the signal of local stations within a sixty-mile radius of the system. The must-carry rule is maintained in the new telecommunications bill. The Telecommunications Act requires the FCC to act upon must-carry complaints within a 120 days of the filing date.

Additionally, the Act stipulates that markets are to be defined by commercial publications that delineate television markets based on viewing patterns (or Nielsen's Designated Market Area map) when considering the must-carry issue.

## RESTRICTIONS ON OBSCENITY, INDECENCY, AND VIOLENCE

The 1996 Act established the fines for transmitting obscene, lewd, lascivious, filthy, or indecent material with intent to annoy, abuse, threaten, or harass another person at $250,000 for individuals and $500,000 for corporations. This includes broadcasting media, cable systems, and computer networks. Section 501 of the Telecommunications Act of 1996 is cited as the "Communications Decency Act of 1996."

Immediately after the Communications Decency Act was passed, there was a challenge as to whether it was constitutional. There were several lawsuits filed, and in mid-1996 at least two federal courts prevented its enforcement. In June of 1997, the Supreme Court, in a 7-to-2 decision, ruled that Internet communication indeed was protected by the First Amendment.In Reno v. American Civil Liberties Union, the court stated that the Internet deserved the same protection as, media such as books, magazines, or newspapers. Thus, the Supreme Court essentially invalidated Title V of the Telecommunications Act. The Supreme Court dismissed the government's argument that if children were not prevented from accessing indecent material over the Internet then the Internet would not grow to be an important and pervasive media outlet.

The government's rational was that the general public would not access the Internet because of the risk that children might be exposed to indecent material. The Supreme Court rejected this argument stating that it was unpersuasive.

## V-CHIP AND TV PROGRAMME RATINGS

The Telecommunications Act requires television sets to be sold with a V-chip, or violence chip, which allows for the "ability to block programming based on an electronically encoded rating." The entertainment industry was required to develop a ratings system for "violence, sex and other indecent materials and to agree voluntarily to broadcast signals containing such ratings."

The bill requires the FCC to develop a ratings system if the industry fails to meet that requirement. The FCC was charged with the duty of overseeing the development of standards for blocking technologies.As a result of such findings, the Act states that there is a "compelling governmental interest" in providing parents the means to block such influences.

## CABLE DEREGULATION

The 1996 Act deregulates cable rates for the expanded basic tier which usually includes such networks as MTV, Lifetime, ESPN, and Cable News Network. The cable companies are allowed to increase prices on the expanded basic tier within three years of the telecommunication bill's enactment (or on March 31, 1999). The bill requires that equipment rates continue to be regulated. Further, the Act allows for the complete deregulation of small cable companies, defined as including 50,000 or fewer subscribers. The Act allows for cable systems to be free from rate regulation if "a telephone company offers cable service by any means that is comparable to the competing cable system."

## SET-TOP BOXES

With the 1996 Telecommunications Act, consumers now are able to purchase their own set-top boxes in retail stores. Cable companies are allowed to continue providing set-top boxes, but they no longer may subsidize the boxes by subscription fees. Discussion over this issue caused the "first major impasse" on the telecommunications bill.

Cable companies opposed the sale of set-top boxes in retail stores, asserting that it would "freeze the current technology in place." The new rules regarding set-top boxes were designed to prevent theft of cable services.

*The rules expire in a market where*:

- There are competing multichannel video providers,
- There are competing sources of set-top boxes,
- Where the rules stifle competition and do not promote the public interest standard.

## SIGNAL SCRAMBLING FOR INDECENT PROGRAMMING

The bill requires cable operators to scramble any audio or video of programming that subscribers deem "unsuitable" for children. This service must be provided at no extra cost to the subscriber.

## CABLE RIGHT OF REFUSAL OF PUBLIC AND LEASED-ACCESS PROGRAMMING

Under the new bill, cable companies can refuse to broadcast programmes that contain "obscenity, nudity, or indecency."

## CLOSED CAPTIONING

The Federal Communications Commission was required to look into the possibility of making closed captioning a requirement for video programming. The Telecommunications Act of 1996 stipulated that the FCC can waive the requirement for certain classes of programmes if closed captioning is economically burdensome.

## FCC FUNDING

Finally, the bill authorizes appropriations needed by the FCC to carry out the provisions of the 1996 Act. Quello' s comment could not have been more foreshadowing. Others held similar opinions regarding the future of telecommuni-cations regulation.

Approximately a year after Quello's remark, both the Senate and the House of Representatives introduced different versions of a bill that essentially would do exactly what Quello suggested, that is, modernize the regulatory framework under which the entire telecommunications sector operates. Simply put, modernization was needed because when the Communications Act of 1934 was enacted, telephone, telegraph, and radio defined the field. Today, "television, cable, cellular, and satellite only scratch the surface of modern digital telecommunications." Hence, a new piece of legislation was needed to accommodate technological advances.

The Telecommunications Act of 1996 serves as that modernized regulatory framework for the telecommunications industry that Quello suggested is needed to help in the proliferation of new media. The 1996 legislation essentially creates "one marketplace for telecommunications services " Technological developments will transform the multimedia world as we know it today.

The Telecommunications Act of 1996 attempts to regulate media as a whole rather than as individual entities. Chong suggested this approach was needed for there to be a healthy and prosperous development of multimedia technology in the United States. To illustrate how just one aspect of the telecommunications bill attempts to converge the electronic media, examine the overlapping markets of the telephone and cable companies. The cable companies will be allowed to offer telephone services and the telephone companies will be allowed to offer cable services.

Fundamentally, the 1996 Act takes a deregulatory approach and relies on the marketplace as a control over electronic media policies and procedures. The telecommuni-cation legislation diminishes barriers that have prevented widespread competition and work towards the convergence of all media.

Because of the belief that competition is good, the Act allows for competition between and among different telecommunication outlets. As one could expect, new competition is not welcomed by the entire electronic media industry.

For example, the industry opposed the cable-telco cross-ownership rules. Only time will allow observers of the telecommunications industry to determine the new legislation's effectiveness. The Telecommunications Act has created an ironic juxtaposition. Technology and programming were specific areas that the new legislation attempts to deregulate, or regulate in certain circumstances (*e.g.*, violent programming).

The foundation of the legislation is built upon deregulatory theory. Head, *et al.* Suggest that there are many motives fueling efforts to deregulate, such as a need to discard outdated rules, simplify complex rules, ensure that rules actually can achieve their intended objective, and lighten administrative roles. Additionally, they suggest that deregulation also originates from ideological motives stemming from the belief that the government should play a limited role in the everyday lives of Americans. This approach relies on the marketplace to regulate industries.

Yet the marketplace approach of regulating industries does not always work effectively. On one hand, the Telecommunications Act of 1996 essentially promotes the convergence of technology by disassembling the cross-ownership restriction and by establishing specific regulations regarding the promotion of direct broadcast satellite, set-top boxes, closed captioning, and cable deregulation.On the other hand, it attempts to regulate programming through must-carry rules, v-chip technology, signal scrambling for indecent programming, and cable right of refusal of public and leased-access programming. Meyerson suggests that if "these new combinations do not compete with one another, then the Act may have only permitted the creation of large, deregulated monopolists (or oligopolists)." Monopolies were just what the Clinton administration wanted to prevent.

Finally, another juxtaposition includes the requirement that programme ratings be implemented. The industry was required to create a ratings system that would be content-based and would alert parents about programming they might want to prevent their children from viewing by way of the new v-chip. Initially, the industry created ratings that were age-based. Critics argued that the age-based system would not provide enough information to make a decision.

The industry argued that content-based ratings would be confusing and that advertisers might not want advertise during programming that had a perceived negative rating. Eventually, the industry adopted a content-based ratings system. Overall, it will require time to determine the effectiveness of the Telecommunications Act of 1996.

## CORPORATE COMMUNICATION ENCODES AND PROMOTES

- Strong corporate culture
- Coherent corporate identity
- Reasonable corporate philosophy
- Genuine sense of corporate citizenship
- An appropriate and professional relationship with the press, including quick, responsible ways of commun-icating in a crisis
- Understanding of communication tools and techno-logies
- Sophisticated approaches to global communications

How an organization communicates with its employees, its extended audiences, the press and its customers brings its values to life. Corporate communications is all about managing perceptions and ensuring:

- Effective and timely dissemination of information
- Positive corporate image
- Smooth and affirmative relationship with all stakeholders

Be it a corporate body, company, organization, institution, non-governmental organization, governmental body, all of them need to have a respectable image and reputation. In today's day and age of increasing competition, easy access to information and the media explosion, reputation management has gained even more importance. Therefore, corporate communications as a role has become significant and professional in nature.Gone are the days when corporate communication merely meant 'wining and dining the client' - it has now emerged as a science and art of perception management.

### Key Tasks of Corporate Communication

*The responsibilities of corporate communication are therefore:*

- To flesh out the profile of the "company behind the brand" (corporate branding)
- To develop initiatives that minimize discrepancies between the company's desired identity and brand features;
- To indicate who should perform which tasks in the field of communication;
- To formulate and execute effective procedures in order to facilitate decision making about matters concerning communication;
- To mobilize internal and external support behind corporate objectives.
- To co ordinate with international business firms

### Tools of Corporate Communication

Integrated communication can be achieved in various ways.

*The main four practices are*:

1. Application of visual identity systems (sometimes referred to as "house style")
2. Use of integrated marketing communications;
3. Reliance on coordinating teams;
4. Adoption of a centralized planning system.

### The communication Agenda: To Build Reputation

Corporate communication helps an organization to create distictive and appealing images with its stakeholder groups, build a strong corporate brand, and develop reputation capital.To achieve those ends, all forms of communication must be orchestrated into a coherent whole, and success criteria developed that enable measuring the effects of the organization's communication on its reputation and value.

### External Communication

This involves building and maintaining a positive relationship with the media (television, print, web,). This inclu-des, but is not limited to, drafting and dissemination of press releases, organizing press conferences and meeting with media professionals and organizing events for the media as a group.

### External Events

Could involve vendor/ supplier/ distributor meets, channel partner meetings, events related to product launches, important initiatives, et cetera.

**Company/Spokesperson Profiling**

Ensuring that the company/organization spokesperson is in the public limelight, is well-known and considered as an authority in the respective sector/ field.

- Managing content of corporate web sites and/or other external touch points
- Managing corporate publications - for the external world
- Managing print media

**Brand Management**

- Development and upkeep of the corporate identity to ensure adherence to corporate brand guidelines

To improve overall business communications so as to clearly and effectively communicate the essence of the company.

**Corporate Identity/Organizational Identity**

There are two approaches for Identity, respectively Corporate Identity and Organizational Identity.

- "Corporate identity is the reality and uniqueness of an organization, which is integrally related to its external and internal image and reputation through corporate communication"
- "Organizational Identity comprises those characteri-stics of an organization that its members believe are central, distinctive and enduring. That is, organiza-tional identity consists of those attributes that members feel are fundamental to (central) and uniquely descriptive of (distinctive) the organization and that persist within the organization over time (enduring)".

**Corporate reputation**

Reputations are overall assessments of organizations by their stakeholders. They are aggregate perceptions by stakeholders of an organizaitons's ability to fulfil their expectations, whether these stakeholders are interested in buying the company's products, working for the company, or investing in the company's shares.

In 2000, the US based Council of PR Firms identified seven programmes that were developed by either media organizations or market research firms, and that were being used by companies to assess or benchmark their corporate reputations. Of these only three are conducted regularly and have broad visibility:

- "America's Most Admired Companies" by Fortune Magazine;
- The "Brand Asset Valuator" by Young and Rubicam;
- "RepTrak" by Reputation Institute.

**Crisis communications**

Crisis has four defining characteristics. Seeger, Sellnow and Ulmer explain that a crises are "specific, unexpected, and non-routine events or series of events that [create] high levels of uncertainty and threat or perceived threat to an organization's high priority goals."

*Thus the first three characteristics are that the event is*:

1. Unexpected (*i.e.*, a surprise),
2. Creates uncertainty,
3. Is seen as a threat to important goals.

Venette argues that "crisis is a process of transformation where the old system can no longer be maintained." Therefore the fourth defining quality is the need for change. If change is not needed, the event could more accurately be described as a failure.

Crisis communication can be broadly defined as the exchange of information before, during, or after a crisis event. Crisis communication is sometimes considered a sub-specialty of the public relations profession that is designed to protect and defend an individual, company, or organization facing a public challenge to its reputation. These challenges may come in the form of an investigation from a government agency, a criminal allegation, a media enquiry, a shareholders lawsuit, a violation of environmental regulations, or any of a number of other scenarios involving the legal, ethical, or financial standing of the entity.

Crisis communication professionals preach that an organization's reputation is often its most valuable asset. When that reputation comes under attack, protecting and defending it becomes the highest priority. This is particularly true in today's 24 hour news cycle, fuelled by government investigations, Congressional or parliamentary hearings, lawsuits, and "gotcha journalism".

When events like these happen, the media firestorm can quickly overwhelm the ability of the entity to effectively respond to the demands of the crisis. To emerge with its reputation intact, an organization must anticipate every move and respond immediately and with confidence. Companies facing such a threat will often bring in experienced crisis communications specialists to help prepare and guide them through the process.

Effectively responding to the challenges of a crisis requires more than the typical skills of the public relations professional, requiring instead experience at the highest levels of the field, such as investigative reporting, politics, and the White House. Crisis communication can include crafting thorough and compelling statements, known as "messages," often tested by research and polling.

A rapid response capability—pioneered by the 1992 Clinton-Gore campaign operatives and refined during Bill Clinton's eight years under attack by his political adversaries while in the White House, has also become an essential element of crisis communication. Additional tactics may include proactive media outreach to get messages and context to the media, identifying and recruiting credible third-party allies who can attest to the company's side of the story, and striking first, not waiting to be hit. Crisis communication is a part of larger process referred to as crisis management though it may well be a major tool of handling a crisis situation in government, organization or business. Crisis Communication is also sometimes considered a sub-speciality of the Business Continuity area of modern business.

The aim of crisis communication in this context is to assist organisations to achieve continuity of critical business processes and information flows under crisis, disaster or event driven circumstances. Responding quickly, efficiently, effectively and in a premeditated way are the primary objectives of an effective crisis communication strategy and/or solution.

Harnassing technology and people to ensure a rapid and co-ordinated response to a range of potentially crippling scenarios distinguishes a well thought out and executed plan from a poorly or ill-considered one. The inherent lag time in marshalling responses to a crisis can result in considerable losses to company revenues, reputation as well as substantially impacting on costs.

Effective crisis communication strategies will typically consider achieving most, if not all, of the following objectives:

- Maintain connectivity
- Be readily accessible to the news media
- Show empathy for the people involved
- Allow distributed access
- Streamline communication processes
- Maintain information security
- Ensure uninterrupted audit trails
- Deliver high volume communications
- Support multi-channel communications
- Remove dependencies on paper based processes

By definition a crisis is an unexpected and detrimental situation or event. Crisis communication can play a significant role by transforming the unexpected into the anticipated and responding accordingly.

Some of the most effective recent examples of crisis communication include Richard Branson's (Virgin) and John Armitt's (Network Rail) dignified press conference after the Grayrigg rail disaster of 2007 and US Airways handling of the media after their crashlanding on the Hudson river.

*Employee communication*:

- Sharing information with employees, building employer pride, managing employee issues, et cetera.
- Manage the Intranet and other internal web portals

Organizational communication: Encourage and enable the employees to plan for new ideas and effectively implement them.

*Internal communication*:

- Managing corporate publications for employees and partners
- Organising internal events for staff

**Corporate Communication Officers**

Recent research on the corporate communication function reports that corporate communication officers (CCOs) in Global Fortune 500 companies tend to have average tenures of about 4.5 years and that nearly one-half (48 per cent) report to the Chief Executive Officer.

CCOs say that approximately 42 per cent of their job is strategic and 58 per cent is tactical. Over the next year, they will be focusing more on social responsibility, social media and reputation. The research done by Weber Shandwick and Spencer Stuart found distinct differences between CCOs in Most Admired companies versus Contender companies.

# Bibliography

Amitabh Singh: *International Mediation in the Inter Ethnic Conflict in Eastern Europe*, Academic Excellence, Delhi, 2004.

Anil K. Rai 'Ankit': *Communication Management : Listening Versus Hearing*, Shree Publication, Delhi, 2006.

Arun Bhatia: *Media and Communication Ethics*, Akansha Publication, Delhi, 2005.

Bhanu Pratap Singh: *Communication Management in Journalism*, Anmol Publication, Delhi, 2011.

D K S Rawat: *Digital Media and Communication Technology*, Swastik Publication, Delhi, 2007.

D S Verma: *Media and Communication Management*, Pearl Books, Delhi, 2007.

G.K. Parthasarathy: *Electronic Media and Communication Research Methods*, GNOSIS, 2006.

Girish Saxena: *Advanced Media and Communication Management*, Vista International Publication, Delhi, 2010.

Ian Richards: *Quagmires and Quandaries : Exploring Journalism Ethics*, Anmol Publication, Delhi, 2006.

J.P. Ahluwaliya: *International Media*, Adhyayan Publication, Delhi, 2007.

Kate Coyer, Tony Dowmunt and Alan Fountain: *The Alternative Media Handbook*, Routledge, 2009.

Klaus Bruhn Jensen: *A Handbook of Media and Communication Research*, T and F / Routledge, 2005.

M S N Murthy: *Encyclopaedia of Multimedia and Communication Technology (3 Vols-Set)*, Arise Publication, Delhi, 2007.

Manikant Singh: *Communication Management : A Global Perspective for Identification and Corporate Branding*, Global India Publication, Delhi, 2011.

Manoj Kumar Singh: *Communication Management in Journalism*, Mohit Publication, Delhi, 2007.

Marcel Danesi: *Dictionary of Media and Communications*, Pentagon Press, New York, 2009.

Meena Devi: *Fundamentals of Mass Media and Communication*, Alfa Publication, Delhi, 2006.

Namita Agrawal: *Mass Media and Communication : Career Opportunities*, Book Enclave, Delhi, 2012.

Narendra Ojha: *Mass Media and Communication*, ABD Publication, Delhi, 2006.

Narendra Tripathi: *Communication Management*, Reference Press, Delhi, 2005.

Naval Prabhakar and Narendra Basu: *Encyclopaedia of Mass Media and Communication in 21 Century (14 Vols-Set)*, Commonwealth Publication, Delhi, 2006.

Naval Prabhakar: *Development Dynamics of Media and Communication*, Commonwealth Publication, Delhi, 2003.

Om Gupa and Sudesh Sharma: *Media and Communication Research : Changing Paradigms*, Gyan Publication, Delhi, 2011.

Pawan Kumar Saxena: *Journalism Ethics*, Random Publications, Delhi, 2012.

R. Choudhary: *Journalism Ethics*, Centrum Press, Delhi, 2010.

Ramesh Chandra: *Analysis of Media and Communication Trends*, Isha Books, Delhi, 2004.

S P Phadke: *Media and Journalism Ethics*, ABD Publication, Delhi, 2008.

Sandhir Sharma, Pavitar Parkash Singh and Rajpal Kaur: *Communication Management*, Deep and Deep Publication, Delhi, 2005.

Sanjay Gaur: *Handbook of Media and Communication*, Book Enclave, Delhi, 2007.

Sanjay Gaur: *Mass Media and Communication : A Study With Public Relations, Print and Electronic Media*, Book Enclave, Delhi, 2006.

Sourabh Verma: *International Media Communication in a Global Age*, Prateeksha Publications, Delhi, 2011.

# Index